CGP

Radiate Science knowledge with CGP...

OK, so there's a lot to learn in GCSE Combined Science — it is worth two GCSEs, after all.

Not to worry. This chunky CGP book explains the facts, theory and practical skills you'll need, with essential exam practice questions to test your knowledge. It's a beautiful thing.

How to access your free Online Edition

This book includes a free Online Edition to read on your PC, Mac or tablet.
To access it, just go to **cgpbooks.co.uk/extras** and enter this code...

2338 3612 3809 1482

By the way, this code only works for one person. If somebody else has used this book before you, they might have already claimed the Online Edition.

CGP — still the best! ☺

Our sole aim here at CGP is to produce the highest quality books —
carefully written, immaculately presented and dangerously close to being funny.

Then we work our socks off to get them out to you
— at the cheapest possible prices.

Contents

Published by CGP.
From original material by Richard Parsons.

Editors: Katie Braid, Charlotte Burrows, Robin Flello, Emily Forsberg, Emily Garrett, Emily Howe, Sharon Keeley-Holden, Ciara McGlade, Paul Jordin, Chris Lindle, Duncan Lindsay, Sarah Pattison, Frances Rooney, Charlotte Whiteley and Sarah Williams.
Contributors: Paddy Gannon.

With thanks to Susan Alexander, Mary Falkner, Katherine Faudemer, Peter Rich, Glenn Rogers, Sophie Scott and Jamie Sinclair for the proofreading.

With thanks to Ana Pungartnik for the copyright research.

Stopping distances data on page 215 from the Highway Code. Contains public sector information licensed under the Open Government Licence v3.0. http://www.nationalarchives.gov.uk/doc/open-government-licence/version/3/

Printed by Elanders Ltd, Newcastle upon Tyne.
Clipart from Corel®

The Scientific Method

This section isn't about how to 'do' science — but it does show you the way most scientists work.

Science is All About Testing Hypotheses

Scientists make an observation.

1) Scientists OBSERVE (look at) something they don't understand, e.g. an illness.
2) They come up with a possible explanation for what they've observed.
3) This explanation is called a HYPOTHESIS.

Hundreds of years ago, we thought demons caused illness.

They test their hypothesis.

4) Next, they test whether the hypothesis is right or not.
5) They do this by making a PREDICTION — a statement based on the hypothesis that can be tested.
6) They then TEST this prediction by carrying out experiments.
7) If their prediction is right, this is EVIDENCE that their hypothesis might be right too.

Other scientists test the hypothesis too.

8) Other scientists check the evidence — for example, they check that the experiment was carried out in a sensible way. This is called PEER-REVIEW.
9) Scientists then share their results, e.g. in scientific papers.
10) Other scientists carry out more experiments to test the hypothesis.
11) Sometimes these scientists will find more evidence that the hypothesis is RIGHT.
12) Sometimes they'll find evidence that shows the hypothesis is WRONG.

Then we thought it was caused by 'bad blood' (and treated it with leeches).

The hypothesis is accepted or rejected.

13) If all the evidence that's been found supports the hypothesis, it becomes an ACCEPTED THEORY and goes into textbooks for people to learn.
14) If the evidence shows that the hypothesis is wrong, scientists must:
   • Change the hypothesis, OR
   • Come up with a new hypothesis.

Now we know that illnesses that can be spread between people are due to microorganisms.

Theories Can Involve Different Types of Models

1) A model is a simple way of describing or showing what's going on in real life.
2) Models can be used to explain ideas and make predictions. For example:

   • The Bohr model of an atom is a simple picture of what an atom looks like.
   • It can be used to explain trends in the periodic table. (See p.107 for more.)

3) All models have limits — a single model can't explain everything about an idea.

I'm off to the zoo to test my hippo-thesis...

You can see just how much testing has to be done before something gets accepted as a theory. If scientists aren't busy testing their own hypothesis, then they're busy testing someone else's. Or just playing with their models.

Communication & Issues Created by Science

Scientific developments can be great, but they can sometimes <u>raise more questions</u> than they answer...

It's Important to Tell People About Scientific Discoveries

1) Scientific discoveries can make a big difference to <u>people's lives</u>.
2) So scientists need to <u>tell the world</u> about their discoveries.
3) They might need to tell people to <u>change their habits</u>, e.g. stop smoking to protect against lung cancer.
4) They might also need to tell people about new <u>technologies</u>. For example:

> The discovery of molecules called <u>fullerenes</u> has led to a new technology that delivers medicine to <u>body cells</u>. <u>Doctors</u> and <u>patients</u> might need to be given <u>information</u> about this technology.

Scientific Evidence can be Presented in a Biased Way

1) <u>Reports</u> about scientific discoveries in the <u>media</u> (e.g. newspapers or television) can be <u>misleading</u>.
2) The data might be <u>presented</u> in a way that's <u>not quite right</u> — or it might be <u>oversimplified</u>.
3) This means that people may not <u>properly understand</u> what the scientists found out.
4) People who want to make a point can also sometimes <u>present data</u> in a <u>biased way</u> (in a way that's <u>unfair</u> or <u>ignores</u> one side of the argument). For example:

- A <u>scientist</u> may talk a lot about <u>one particular relationship</u> in the data (and not mention others).
- A <u>newspaper article</u> might describe data <u>supporting</u> an idea without giving any evidence <u>against</u> it.

Scientific Developments are Great, but they can Raise Issues

1) Scientific developments include <u>new technologies</u> and <u>new advice</u>.
2) These developments can create <u>issues</u>. For example:

<u>Economic (money) issues:</u> Society <u>can't</u> always <u>afford</u> to do things scientists recommend, like spend money on green energy sources.

<u>Social (people) issues:</u> Decisions based on scientific evidence affect <u>people</u> — e.g. should alcohol be banned (to prevent health problems)?

<u>Personal issues:</u> Some decisions will affect <u>individuals</u> — e.g. people may be upset if a <u>wind farm</u> is built next to their house.

<u>Environmental issues:</u> <u>Human activity</u> often affects the <u>environment</u> — e.g. some people think that <u>genetically modified crops</u> (see p.78) could cause <u>environmental problems</u>.

Science Can't Answer Every Question — Especially Ethical Ones

1) At the moment scientists <u>don't agree</u> on some things — like what the universe is made of.
2) This is because there <u>isn't</u> enough <u>data</u> to <u>support</u> the scientists' hypotheses.
3) But <u>eventually</u>, we probably <u>will</u> be able to answer these questions once and for all.
4) Experiments <u>can't tell us</u> whether something is <u>ethically right or wrong</u>. For example, whether it's right for people to use new drugs to help them do better in exams.
5) The best we can do is make a decision that <u>most people</u> are more or less happy to live by.

Tea to milk or milk to tea? — Totally unanswerable by science...

Science can't tell you whether or not you should do something. That's for you and society to decide. But there are tons of questions science might be able to answer, like where life came from and where my superhero socks are.

Risk

By reading this page you are agreeing to the risk of a paper cut...

Nothing is Completely Risk-Free

1) A hazard is something that could cause harm.
2) All hazards have a risk attached to them — this is the chance that the hazard will cause harm.
3) New technology can bring new risks. E.g. scientists are creating technology to capture and store carbon dioxide. But if the carbon dioxide leaked out it could damage soil or water supplies. These risks need to be considered alongside the benefits of the technology, e.g. lower greenhouse gas emissions.
4) To make a decision about activities that involve hazards, we need to think about:
   • the chance of the hazard causing harm,
   • how bad the outcome (consequences) would be if it did.

People Make Their Own Decisions About Risk

1) Not all risks have the same consequences. For example, if you chop veg with a sharp knife you risk cutting your finger, but if you go scuba-diving you risk death.
2) Most people are happier to accept a risk if the consequences don't last long and aren't serious.
3) People tend to think familiar activities are low-risk. They tend to think unfamiliar activities are high-risk. But this isn't always true. For example:

> • Cycling on roads is often high-risk. But it's a familiar activity, so many people are happy to do it.
> • Air travel is actually pretty safe, but a lot of people think it is high-risk.

4) The best way to estimate the size of a risk is to look at data. E.g. you could estimate the risk of a driver crashing by recording how many people in a group of 100 000 drivers crashed their cars over a year.

Investigations Can Have Hazards

1) Hazards from science experiments include things like:

microorganisms
(e.g. bacteria)

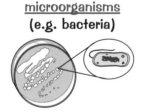

chemicals

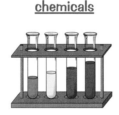

electricity

fire

2) When you plan an investigation you need to make sure that it's safe.
3) You should identify all the hazards that you might come across.
4) Then you should think of ways of reducing the risks. For example:

> • If you're working with sulfuric acid, always wear gloves and safety goggles. This will reduce the risk of the acid burning your skin and eyes.
> • If you're using a Bunsen burner, stand it on a heat proof mat. This will reduce the risk of starting a fire.

There's more on safety in experiments on page 235.

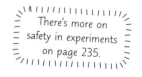

Not revising — an unacceptable exam hazard...

The world is a dangerous place. You need to look out for hazards and find ways to reduce their risks.

Working Scientifically

Designing Investigations

Dig out your lab coat and dust down your safety goggles... it's <u>investigation time</u>.
Investigations include <u>lab experiments</u> and <u>studies</u> done in the <u>real world</u>.

Investigations Produce Evidence to Support or Disprove a Hypothesis

1) Scientists <u>observe</u> things and come up with <u>hypotheses</u> to explain them (see p.1).
    You need to be able to do the same. For example:

    > <u>Observation</u>: People have big feet and spots. <u>Hypothesis</u>: Having big feet causes spots.

2) To <u>find out</u> if your hypothesis is <u>right</u>, you need to do an <u>investigation</u> to gather evidence.

3) To do this, you need to use your hypothesis to make a <u>prediction</u> — something you think <u>will happen</u>
    that you can <u>test</u>. E.g. people who have bigger feet will have more spots.

4) Investigations are used to see if there are <u>patterns</u> or <u>relationships</u> between <u>two variables</u> (see below).

To Make an Investigation a Fair Test You Have to Control the Variables

1) In a lab experiment you usually <u>change one thing</u> (a variable)
    and <u>measure</u> how it affects <u>another thing</u> (another variable).

    > <u>EXAMPLE:</u> you might <u>change</u> the <u>concentration</u> of a reactant
    > and <u>measure</u> how it affects the <u>temperature change</u> of the reaction.

2) <u>Everything else</u> that could affect the results needs to <u>stay the same</u>.
    Then you know that the thing you're <u>changing</u> is the <u>only</u> thing that's affecting the results.

    > <u>EXAMPLE continued:</u> you need to keep the volume of the reactants the same.
    > If you don't, you won't know if any change in the temperature is caused by the
    > change in concentration, or the change in volume.

3) The variable that you <u>CHANGE</u> is called the <u>INDEPENDENT</u> variable.

4) The variable you <u>MEASURE</u> is called the <u>DEPENDENT</u> variable.

5) The variables that you <u>KEEP THE SAME</u> are called <u>CONTROL</u> variables.

6) Because you can't always control all the variables,
    you often need to use a <u>CONTROL EXPERIMENT</u>.

> <u>EXAMPLE continued:</u>
> Independent = concentration
> Dependent = temperature
> Control = volume of reactants,
> pH, etc.

7) This is an experiment that's kept under the <u>same conditions</u> as the rest of the investigation, but <u>doesn't</u>
    have anything <u>done</u> to it. This is so that you can see what happens when you don't change <u>anything</u>.

Evidence Needs to be Repeatable, Reproducible and Valid

1) <u>REPEATABLE</u> means that if the <u>same person</u> does the experiment again, they'll get <u>similar results</u>.
    To check your results are repeatable, <u>repeat</u> the readings <u>at least three times</u>.
    Then check the repeat results are all similar.

2) <u>REPRODUCIBLE</u> means that if <u>someone else</u> does the experiment, the results will still be <u>similar</u>.
    To make sure your results are reproducible, get <u>another person</u> to do the experiment too.

3) <u>VALID results</u> come from experiments that were designed to be a <u>fair test</u>.
    They're also repeatable and reproducible.

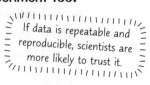

If data is repeatable and reproducible, scientists are more likely to trust it.

This is no high street survey — it's a designer investigation...

You need to be able to plan your own investigations. You should also be able to look at someone else's plan and
decide whether anything needs to be changed to make it better. Those examiners are pretty demanding.

Collecting Data

Ah ha — now it's time to get your hands mucky and <u>collect some data</u>.

The Bigger the Sample Size the Better

1) Sample size is <u>how many things you test</u> in an investigation, e.g. 500 people or 20 types of metal.

2) The <u>bigger</u> the sample size the <u>better</u> — to <u>reduce</u> the chance of any <u>weird results</u>.

3) But scientists have to be <u>realistic</u> when choosing how big their sample should be. E.g. if you were studying how lifestyle affects weight it'd be great to study everyone in the UK (a huge sample), but it'd take ages and cost loads.

4) When you choose a sample, you need to make sure you've got a <u>range</u> of different people.

5) For example, both <u>men</u> and <u>women</u> with a range of <u>different ages</u>.

Your Data Should be Accurate and Precise

Repeat	Data set 1	Data set 2
1	12	11
2	14	17
3	13	14
Mean	13	14

1) <u>ACCURATE</u> results are results that are <u>really close</u> to the <u>true answer</u>.

2) The accuracy of your results usually depends on your <u>method</u>. You need to make sure you're measuring the <u>right thing</u>.

3) You also need to make sure you <u>don't miss anything</u> that should be included in the measurements. For example:

Data set 1 is more precise than data set 2 — the results are all close to the mean (not spread out).

> If you're measuring the <u>volume of gas</u> released by a reaction, make sure you <u>collect all the gas</u>.

4) <u>PRECISE results</u> are ones where the data is <u>all really close</u> to the <u>mean</u> (average) of your repeated results.

Your Equipment has to be Right for the Job

1) The <u>measuring equipment</u> you use has to be able to <u>accurately</u> measure the chemicals you're using. E.g. if you need to measure out 11 cm³ of a liquid, use a <u>measuring cylinder</u> that can measure to 1 cm³ — not 5 or 10 cm³.

2) You also need to <u>set up the equipment properly</u>. For example, make sure your <u>mass balance</u> is set to <u>zero</u> before you start weighing things.

You Need to Look out for Errors and Anomalous Results

1) The results of your experiment will always <u>vary a bit</u> because of <u>RANDOM ERRORS</u> — for example, mistakes you might make while <u>measuring</u>.

2) You can <u>reduce</u> the effect of random errors by taking <u>repeat readings</u> and finding the <u>mean</u>. This will make your results <u>more precise</u>.

3) If a measurement is wrong by the <u>same amount every time</u>, it's called a <u>SYSTEMATIC ERROR</u>. For example:

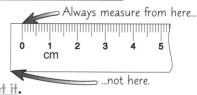

Always measure from here...

...not here.

> If you measure from the <u>very end</u> of your <u>ruler</u> instead of from the <u>0 cm mark</u> every time, <u>all</u> your measurements would be a bit <u>small</u>.

4) If you know you've made a systematic error, you might be able to <u>correct it</u>. For example, by adding a bit on to all your measurements.

5) Sometimes you get a result that <u>doesn't fit in</u> with the rest. This is called an <u>ANOMALOUS RESULT</u>.

6) You should try to <u>work out what happened</u>. If you do (e.g. you find out you measured something wrong) you can <u>ignore</u> it when processing your results (see next page).

The bigger the better — what's true for cakes is true for samples...

Make sure you take lots of care when collecting data — there's plenty to watch out for, as you can see.

Processing and Presenting Data

Processing your data means doing <u>calculations</u> with it so it's <u>more useful</u>. Then you get to draw pretty graphs...

Data Needs to be Organised

1) <u>Tables</u> are useful for <u>organising data</u>.
2) When you draw a table <u>use a ruler</u>.
3) Make sure <u>each column</u> has a <u>heading</u> (including the <u>units</u>).

Test tube	Repeat 1 (cm³)	Repeat 2 (cm³)
A	28	37
B	47	51

You Might Have to Find the Mean, the Range, the Median or the Mode

1) When you've done repeats of an experiment you should always calculate the <u>mean</u> (a type of average).
2) You might also need to calculate the <u>range</u> (how spread out the data is).

EXAMPLE: The results of an experiment to find the volume of gas produced in a reaction are shown in the table below. Calculate the mean volume and the range.

Volume of gas produced (cm³)		
Repeat 1	Repeat 2	Repeat 3
28	37	32

1) To calculate the <u>mean</u>, <u>add together</u> all the data values. Then <u>divide</u> by the <u>total number</u> of values in the sample. $(28 + 37 + 32) \div 3$ = 32 cm³

2) To calculate the <u>range</u>, <u>subtract</u> the <u>smallest</u> number from the <u>largest</u> number. $37 - 28 = 9$ cm³

3) To find the <u>median</u>, put all your data in <u>order</u> from smallest to largest. The median is the <u>middle value</u>.
4) The number that appears <u>most often</u> is the <u>mode</u>.

If you have an even number of values, the median is halfway between the middle two values.

E.g. if you have the data set: 1 2 1 1 3 4 2
The <u>median</u> is: 1 1 1 <u>2</u> 2 3 4.   The <u>mode</u> is <u>1</u> because 1 appears most often.

5) When calculating any of these values, always <u>ignore</u> any <u>anomalous results</u>.

Round to the Lowest Number of Significant Figures

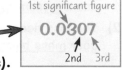
1st significant figure
0.0307
2nd   3rd

1) The <u>first significant figure</u> of a number is the first digit that's <u>not zero</u>.
2) The second and third significant figures come <u>straight after</u> (even if they're zeros).
3) In <u>any</u> calculation, you should round the answer to the <u>lowest number of significant figures</u> (s.f.) given.
4) If your calculation has more than one step, <u>only</u> round the <u>final</u> answer.

EXAMPLE: The mass of a solid is 0.24 g and its volume is 0.715 cm³. Calculate the density of the solid.
Density = 0.24 g ÷ 0.715 cm³ = 0.33566... = 0.34 g/cm³ (2 s.f.) — Final answer should be rounded to 2 s.f.
2 s.f.   3 s.f.

If Your Data Comes in Categories, Present It in a Bar Chart

If the independent variable comes in <u>clear categories</u> (e.g. blood group, types of metal) or can be <u>counted exactly</u> (e.g. number of protons) you should use a <u>bar chart</u> to display the data. Here's what to do:

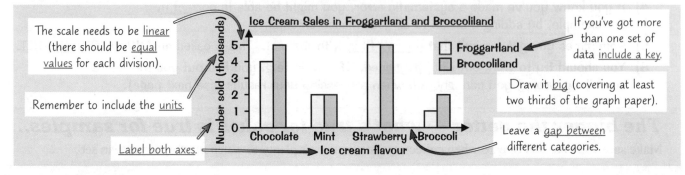

The scale needs to be <u>linear</u> (there should be <u>equal values</u> for each division).

Remember to include the <u>units</u>.

Label both axes.

If you've got more than one set of data <u>include a key</u>.

Draw it <u>big</u> (covering at least two thirds of the graph paper).

Leave a <u>gap between</u> different categories.

If Your Data is Continuous, Plot a Graph

If both variables can have any value <u>within a range</u> (e.g. length, volume) use a <u>graph</u> to display the data.

Here are the rules for plotting points on a graph:

Use the biggest data values you've got to draw a <u>sensible scale</u> on your axes.

The <u>dependent</u> variable goes on the <u>y-axis</u> (the <u>vertical</u> one).

The <u>independent</u> variable goes on the <u>x-axis</u> (the <u>horizontal</u> one).

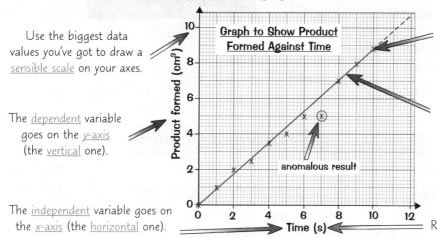

Graph to Show Product Formed Against Time

Product formed (cm³)

anomalous result

Time (s)

To plot points, use a sharp pencil and make <u>neat little crosses</u> (don't do blobs).

nice clear mark

smudged unclear marks

To draw a <u>line</u> (or <u>curve</u>) of <u>best fit</u>, draw a line <u>through</u>, or as <u>near</u> to, as <u>many points as possible</u>. Ignore any <u>anomalous results</u>. <u>Don't</u> join the crosses up.

Draw it <u>big</u> (covering at least two thirds of the graph paper).

Remember to include the <u>units</u>.

You Can Calculate the Rate of a Reaction from the Gradient of a Graph

1) This is the <u>formula</u> you need to calculate the <u>gradient</u> (slope) of a graph:
2) You can use it to work out the <u>rate of a reaction</u> (how <u>quickly</u> the reaction happens).

$$\text{gradient} = \frac{\text{change in } y}{\text{change in } x}$$

EXAMPLE: The graph shows the volume of gas produced in a reaction against time. Calculate the rate of reaction.

1) To calculate the <u>gradient</u>, pick <u>two points</u> on the line that are easy to read. They should also be a <u>good distance</u> apart.
2) Draw a line <u>down</u> from the higher point. Then draw a line <u>across</u> from the other, to make a <u>triangle</u>.
3) The line drawn <u>down the side</u> of the triangle is the <u>change in y</u>. The line <u>across the bottom</u> is the <u>change in x</u>.
4) Read the x and y values of the points <u>off the graph</u> and work out the change in y and the change in x:

Change in y = 6.8 − 2.0 = **4.8 cm³**   Change in x = 5.2 − 1.6 = **3.6 s**

5) Then put these numbers in the formula above to find the rate of the reaction:

$$\text{Rate} = \text{gradient} = \frac{\text{change in } y}{\text{change in } x} = \frac{4.8 \text{ cm}^3}{3.6 \text{ s}} = 1.3 \text{ cm}^3/\text{s}$$

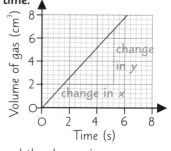

Volume of gas (cm³)

change in y

change in x

Time (s)

To calculate a rate, the graph must have time on the x-axis.

The units are (units of y)/(units of x). cm³/s can also be written as cm³ s⁻¹.

Graphs Show the Relationship Between Two Variables

1) You can get <u>three</u> types of <u>correlation</u> (relationship) between variables:
2) A correlation <u>doesn't mean</u> the change in one variable is <u>causing</u> the change in the other (see page 9).

<u>POSITIVE correlation:</u> as one variable <u>increases</u> the other <u>increases</u>.

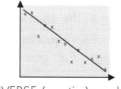

<u>INVERSE (negative) correlation:</u> as one variable <u>increases</u> the other <u>decreases</u>.

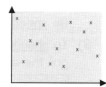

<u>NO correlation:</u> <u>no relationship</u> between the two variables.

I love eating apples — I call it core elation...

Science is all about finding relationships between things. And I don't mean that scientists gather together in corners to discuss whether or not Devini and Sebastian might be a couple... though they probably do that too.

Units

Graphs and maths skills are all very well, but the numbers don't mean much if you can't get the <u>units</u> right.

S.I. Units Are Used All Round the World

1) All scientists use the same <u>units</u> to measure their data.

2) These are <u>standard units</u>, called S.I. units.

3) Here are some S.I. units you might see:

Quantity	S.I. Base Unit
mass	kilogram, kg
length	metre, m
time	second, s
temperature	kelvin, K

Different Units Help you to Write Large and Small Quantities

1) Quantities come in a huge <u>range</u> of sizes.

2) To make the size of numbers <u>easier to handle</u>, larger or smaller units are used.

3) Larger and smaller units are written as the <u>S.I. base unit</u> with a <u>little word</u> in <u>front</u> (a prefix). Here are some <u>examples</u> of <u>prefixes</u> and what they mean:

Kilogram is an exception. It's an S.I. unit with the prefix already on it.

prefix	mega (M)	kilo (k)	deci (d)	centi (c)	milli (m)	micro (μ)
how it compares to the base unit	1 000 000 times bigger	1000 times bigger	10 times smaller	100 times smaller	1000 times smaller	1 000 000 times smaller

E.g. 1 <u>kilo</u>metre is <u>1000</u> metres.

E.g. there are <u>1000</u> <u>milli</u>metres in 1 metre.

You Need to be Able to Convert Between Units

You need to know how to <u>convert</u> (change) one unit into another. Here are some useful conversions:

DIVIDE to go from a <u>smaller unit</u> to a <u>bigger unit</u>.

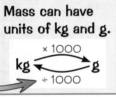

Mass can have units of kg and g.
$$kg \xrightarrow{\times 1000} g \qquad kg \xleftarrow{\div 1000} g$$

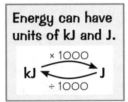

Energy can have units of kJ and J.
$$kJ \xrightarrow{\times 1000} J \qquad kJ \xleftarrow{\div 1000} J$$

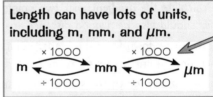

Length can have lots of units, including m, mm, and μm.
$$m \xrightarrow{\times 1000} mm \xrightarrow{\times 1000} \mu m$$
$$m \xleftarrow{\div 1000} mm \xleftarrow{\div 1000} \mu m$$

MULTIPLY to go from a <u>bigger unit</u> to a <u>smaller unit</u>.

EXAMPLE: A car has travelled 0.015 kilometres. How many metres has it travelled?

1 km = 1000 m. So to convert from km (a bigger unit) to m (a smaller unit) you need to <u>multiply</u> by 1000.

0.015 km × 1000 = 15 m

Always make sure the values you put into an equation or formula have the right units.

You Can Rearrange Equations

1) Equations show <u>relationships</u> between <u>variables</u>. For example, $speed = \dfrac{distance}{time}$.

2) The <u>subject</u> of an equation is the variable <u>by itself</u> on one side of the equals sign. So <u>speed</u> is the <u>subject</u> in the equation above.

3) To <u>change</u> the <u>subject</u> of an equation do the same thing to <u>both sides</u> of the equation until you've got the subject you <u>want</u>. E.g. you can make <u>distance</u> the subject of the equation above:

1) <u>Multiply</u> both sides by <u>time</u>: $speed = \dfrac{distance}{time} \longrightarrow speed \times time = \dfrac{distance \times time}{time}$

2) Time is now on the top <u>and</u> the bottom of the fraction, so it cancels out: $speed \times time = \dfrac{distance \times \cancel{time}}{\cancel{time}}$

3) This leaves <u>distance</u> by itself. So it's the <u>subject</u>: $speed \times time = distance$

I wasn't sure I liked units, but now I'm converted...

If you're moving from a smaller unit to a larger unit (e.g. g to kg) the number should get smaller, and vice versa.

Drawing Conclusions

Congratulations — you've made it to the final step of an investigation — drawing conclusions.

You Can Only Conclude What the Data Shows and NO MORE

1) To come to a conclusion, look at your data and say what pattern you see.

EXAMPLE: The table on the right shows the heights of pea plant seedlings grown for three weeks with different fertilisers.

Fertiliser	Mean growth / mm
A	13.5
B	19.5
No fertiliser	5.5

CONCLUSION: Pea plant seedlings grow taller over a three week period with fertiliser B than with fertiliser A.

2) It's important that the conclusion matches the data it's based on — it shouldn't go any further.

EXAMPLE continued: You can't conclude that any other type of plant grows taller with fertiliser B than with fertiliser A — the results could be totally different.

3) You also need to be able to use your results to justify your conclusion (i.e. back it up).

EXAMPLE continued: The pea plants grow 6 mm more on average with fertiliser B than with fertiliser A.

4) When writing a conclusion you need to say whether or not the data supports the original hypothesis:

EXAMPLE continued: The hypothesis might have been that adding different types of fertiliser would affect the growth of pea plants by different amounts. If so, the data supports the hypothesis.

Correlation DOES NOT Mean Cause

1) If two things are correlated, there's a relationship between them — see page 7.
2) But a correlation doesn't always mean that a change in one variable is causing the change in the other.
3) There are three possible reasons for a correlation:

1 CHANCE

The results happened by chance. Other scientists wouldn't get a correlation if they carried out the same investigation.

2 LINKED BY A 3rd VARIABLE

There's another factor involved.

E.g. there's a correlation between water temperature and shark attacks. They're linked by a third variable — the number of people swimming (more people swim when the water's hotter, which means you get more shark attacks).

3 CAUSE

Sometimes a change in one variable does cause a change in the other. You can only conclude this when you've controlled all the variables that could be affecting the result.

I conclude that this page is a bit dull...

In the exams you could be given a conclusion and asked whether some data supports it — so make sure you understand how far conclusions can go. And remember, correlation does not mean cause.

Uncertainties and Evaluations

Hurrah! The end of another investigation. Well, now you have to work out all the things you did <u>wrong</u>.

Uncertainty is the Amount of Error Your Measurements Might Have

1) Measurements you make will have some <u>uncertainty</u> in them (i.e. they won't be completely perfect).

2) This can be due to <u>random errors</u> (see page 5). It can also be due to <u>limits</u> in what your <u>measuring equipment</u> can measure.

3) This means that the <u>mean</u> of your results will have some uncertainty to it.

4) You can <u>calculate</u> the uncertainty of a <u>mean result</u> using this equation: ⟹

5) The <u>less precise</u> your results are, the <u>higher</u> the uncertainty will be.

6) Uncertainties are shown using the '±' symbol.

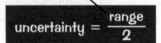 The range is the largest value minus the smallest value (p.6).

$$\text{uncertainty} = \frac{\text{range}}{2}$$

 **EXAMPLE:** The table below shows the results of an experiment to find the speed of a trolley. Calculate the uncertainty of the mean.

Repeat	1	2	3	mean
Speed (m/s)	2.02	1.98	2.00	2.00

1) First work out the range:
Range = 2.02 − 1.98
= 0.04 m/s

2) Use the range to find the uncertainty:
Uncertainty = range ÷ 2 = 0.04 ÷ 2 = 0.02 m/s   So, uncertainty of the mean = **2.00 ± 0.02 m/s**

Evaluations — Describe How it Could be Improved

I'd value this E somewhere in the region of 250-300k

In an evaluation you look back over the whole investigation.

1) You should comment on the <u>method</u> — was it <u>valid</u>? Did you control all the other variables to make it a <u>fair test</u>?

2) Comment on the <u>quality</u> of the <u>results</u> — was there <u>enough evidence</u> to reach a valid <u>conclusion</u>? Were the results <u>repeatable</u>, <u>reproducible</u>, <u>accurate</u> and <u>precise</u>?

3) Were there any <u>anomalous</u> results? If there were <u>none</u> then <u>say so</u>. If there were any, try to <u>explain</u> them — were they caused by <u>errors</u> in measurement?

4) You should comment on the level of <u>uncertainty</u> in your results too.

5) Thinking about these things lets you say how <u>confident</u> you are that your conclusion is <u>right</u>.

6) Then you can suggest any <u>changes</u> to the <u>method</u> that would <u>improve</u> the quality of the results, so you could have <u>more confidence</u> in your conclusion.

7) For example, taking measurements at <u>narrower intervals</u> could give you a <u>more accurate result</u>. **E.g.**

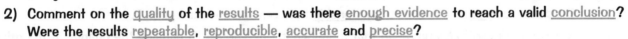

- Say you do an experiment to find the <u>temperature</u> at which an enzyme <u>works best</u>.
- You take measurements at <u>30 °C</u>, <u>40 °C</u> and <u>50 °C</u>. The results show that the enzyme works best at <u>40 °C</u>.
- To get a more accurate result, you could <u>repeat</u> the experiment and take <u>more measurements around 40 °C</u>. You might then find that the enzyme actually works best at <u>42 °C</u>.

8) You could also make more <u>predictions</u> based on your conclusion. You could then carry out <u>further experiments</u> to test the new predictions.

Evaluation — next time, I'll make sure I don't burn the lab down...

So there you have it — Working Scientifically. Make sure you know this stuff like the back of your hand. It's not just in the lab that you'll need to know how to work scientifically. You can be asked about it in the exams as well.

Cells

Cells are the <u>building blocks</u> of <u>every organism on the planet</u>.

Cells can be Prokaryotic or Eukaryotic

1) <u>All living things</u> are made of <u>cells</u>.
2) <u>Eukaryotic</u> cells are <u>complex</u>. All <u>animal</u> and <u>plant</u> cells are eukaryotic.
3) <u>Prokaryotic</u> cells are <u>smaller</u> and <u>simpler</u>. <u>Bacteria</u> are prokaryotic cells.

Plant and Animal Cells have Similarities and Differences

The different parts of a cell are called <u>subcellular structures</u>.
Most <u>animal</u> cells have these subcellular structures:

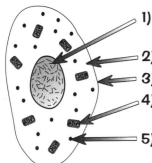

1) <u>Nucleus</u> — contains <u>genetic material</u> (see page 66).
   The genetic material controls what the cell <u>does</u>.
2) <u>Cytoplasm</u> — where most of the <u>chemical reactions</u> happen.
3) <u>Cell membrane</u> — controls what goes <u>in</u> and <u>out</u> of the cell.
4) <u>Mitochondria</u> — where most <u>aerobic respiration</u> happens (see page 54).
   Respiration transfers <u>energy</u> that the cell needs to work.
5) <u>Ribosomes</u> — these are where <u>proteins</u> are made in the cell.

Plant cells usually have <u>all the bits</u> that <u>animal</u> cells have.
They also have:

1) A <u>cell wall</u> — made of <u>cellulose</u>.
   It <u>supports</u> the cell and strengthens it.
2) A <u>permanent vacuole</u> — contains <u>cell sap</u>.
3) <u>Chloroplasts</u> — where <u>photosynthesis</u> happens.
   Photosynthesis makes food for the plant (see page 50).

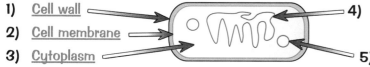

The cells of algae (e.g. seaweed) also have a rigid cell wall and chloroplasts.

nucleus   ribosome   cell membrane   mitochondria

Bacterial Cells Have These Subcellular Structures:

1) <u>Cell wall</u>
2) <u>Cell membrane</u>
3) <u>Cytoplasm</u>

4) A <u>single loop</u> of <u>DNA</u>.
   Bacteria <u>don't</u> have a 'true' <u>nucleus</u>.
5) <u>Plasmids</u> — small <u>rings</u> of <u>extra DNA</u>.

You Can Estimate the Area of a Subcellular Structure

If you want to <u>estimate</u> the <u>area</u> of a subcellular structure, you should treat it like a <u>regular shape</u>:

EXAMPLE: Estimate the area of this mitochondrion:

1) The shape of the mitochondrion is close to a <u>rectangle</u>.
2) The <u>area</u> of a rectangle is found by the formula: <u>length × width</u>
   So the area of the mitochondrion is roughly 10 μm × 1 μm = 10 μm^2

10 μm

1 μm

Cell structures — become an estate agent...

In the exam, you might see the sizes of cells written in standard form — see the next page for more about this.

Q1   Give two differences in structure between bacterial cells and animal cells.   [2 marks]

Microscopy

<u>Microscopes</u> are pretty important for biology. So here are a couple of pages all about them...

Microscopes Magnify Things (Make Them Look Bigger)

1) The ways we can <u>use</u> microscopes have <u>developed</u> over the years.
   This is because <u>technology</u> and <u>knowledge</u> have <u>improved</u>.

2) <u>Light microscopes</u> can be used to <u>look at cells</u>.
   They let us see <u>large subcellular structures</u> (like the <u>nucleus</u>).

3) <u>Electron microscopes</u> have a higher <u>resolution</u> than light microscopes — they show things in <u>more detail</u>.

4) Electron microscopes also have a higher <u>magnification</u> than light microscopes.
   They can let us see <u>really small</u> things like <u>ribosomes</u> and <u>plasmids</u>.

5) Electron microscopes were invented <u>after</u> light microscopes.
   They helped scientists <u>understand more</u> about <u>subcellular structures</u>.

See the next page for how to use a light microscope.

Magnification is How Many Times Bigger the Image is than the Real Thing

You can work out the magnification of an image using <u>this formula</u>:

$$\text{magnification} = \frac{\text{image size}}{\text{real size}}$$

Image size and real size should have the same units.

 **EXAMPLE:**
The width of a cell is 0.02 mm. The width of its image under a microscope is 8 mm. What magnification was used to view the cell?
magnification = 8 mm ÷ 0.02 mm = × 400

 What are you looking at?

You Can Write Numbers in Standard Form

Standard form is useful for writing <u>very big</u> or <u>very small</u> numbers in a <u>simpler</u> way.

EXAMPLE: Write 0.0025 mm in standard form.

1) The first number needs to be <u>between 1 and 10</u> so the decimal point needs to move after the '2'.

2) <u>Count</u> how many places the decimal point has <u>moved</u> — this is the power of 10.

3) The power of 10 is <u>positive</u> if the decimal point is moved to the <u>left</u>. It's <u>negative</u> if the decimal point has moved to the <u>right</u>.
   Here, the decimal point has moved <u>right</u>, so it needs a <u>minus sign</u>.

0.0025 → 2.5
1 2 3

The decimal point has moved 3 places = 10^3

2.5×10^{-3}

Mi-cros-copy — when my twin gets annoyed...

Keep an eye on the units for that equation — if they're not the same, you'll need to convert them (see page 8).

Q1 An onion cell is 0.075 mm wide. The image of the cell is 7.5 mm wide.
What magnification was used to view the cell?   [1 mark]

More on Microscopy

So you know what microscopes <u>do</u>... now you need to know how to <u>use</u> one.

You Need to Prepare Your Slide

Lots of different animal and plant cells can be looked at under a light microscope.

1) Add a <u>drop of water</u> to the middle of a clean slide.
2) Cut up an onion and take off one <u>layer</u>.
3) Use <u>tweezers</u> to peel off some <u>epidermal tissue</u> (the clear 'skin') from the <u>bottom</u> of the layer.
4) Using the tweezers, place the skin into the <u>water</u> on the slide.
5) Add a drop of <u>iodine solution</u>. Iodine solution is a <u>stain</u>. Stains can make different parts of a cell <u>easier to see</u>.
6) Place a <u>cover slip</u> on top. Try <u>not</u> to get any <u>air bubbles</u> under it.

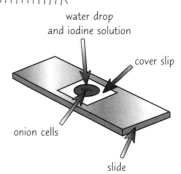

water drop and iodine solution

cover slip

onion cells

slide

Use a Light Microscope to Look at Your Slide

1) Clip the <u>slide</u> onto the <u>stage</u>.
2) Select the <u>objective lens</u> with the lowest magnification.
3) Use the <u>coarse adjustment knob</u> to move the stage up to <u>just below</u> the objective lens.
4) Look down the <u>eyepiece</u>. Move the stage downwards until the image is <u>roughly in focus</u>.
5) Move the <u>fine adjustment knob</u>, until you get a <u>clear image</u> of what's on the slide.
6) If you want a bigger image, use an <u>objective lens</u> with a <u>higher magnification</u> and refocus.

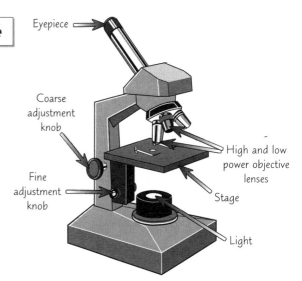

Eyepiece

Coarse adjustment knob

Fine adjustment knob

High and low power objective lenses

Stage

Light

Draw Your Observations Neatly with a Pencil

1) You should use a <u>pencil</u> with a <u>sharp point</u> to draw <u>what you see</u> under the microscope.
2) Use <u>smooth lines</u> to draw the <u>outlines</u> of the <u>main features</u> (e.g. nucleus, chloroplasts).
3) <u>Don't</u> do any <u>shading</u> or <u>colouring in</u>.
4) <u>Label</u> the features with <u>straight lines</u>. Make sure the lines <u>don't cross over</u> each other.
5) The drawing should take up <u>at least half</u> the space available.
6) Include a <u>title</u> and a <u>scale</u>.
7) Write down the <u>magnification</u> that it was observed under.

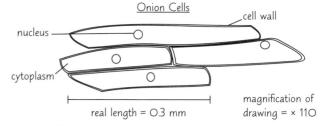

Onion Cells

cell wall

nucleus

cytoplasm

real length = 0.3 mm

magnification of drawing = × 110

You can measure the real size of the cells using a ruler that fits onto your microscope (see p.234).

A light microscope is better than a heavy one...

If you can use a microscope, you're halfway to ruling the world. That's what I like to think, anyway.

Q1   Why might you add stain to the sample on a microscope slide?   [1 mark]

Cell Differentiation and Specialisation

Cells <u>don't</u> all look the <u>same</u>. They have <u>different structures</u> to carry out their <u>different functions</u>.

Specialised Cells are Cells that Carry Out a Specific Function

1) The process by which cells <u>change</u> to become <u>specialised</u> is called <u>differentiation</u>.
2) As cells change, they develop <u>different subcellular structures</u>.
   They turn into <u>different types of cells</u>. This allows them to carry out <u>specific functions</u>.
3) Most differentiation occurs as an organism <u>develops</u>.
4) Most <u>animal</u> cells can only differentiate at an <u>early stage</u> of the animal's life.
5) But lots of <u>plant</u> cells can differentiate for the <u>whole</u> of the plant's life.
6) The cells that differentiate in <u>adult animals</u> are mainly used for <u>repairing</u> and <u>replacing cells</u>.
7) Some cells are <u>undifferentiated</u> — they are called <u>stem cells</u>.
   There's more about them on page 16.

undifferentiated cell

differentiated white blood cell

There Are Many Examples of Specialised Cells...

SPERM CELLS take the MALE DNA to the EGG

1) A sperm cell has a <u>tail</u> to help it <u>swim</u> to the egg.
2) It has a lot of <u>mitochondria</u> (see p.11). These provide <u>energy</u> for swimming.

NERVE CELLS carry ELECTRICAL SIGNALS around the BODY

1) Nerve cells are <u>long</u> to cover <u>more distance</u> in the body.
2) They have <u>branches</u> at the end to <u>connect</u> to other nerve cells.

MUSCLE CELLS CONTRACT (SHORTEN)

1) Muscle cells are <u>long</u> so they have space to <u>contract</u>.
2) They have <u>lots of mitochondria</u>. These provide <u>energy</u> for contracting.

ROOT HAIR CELLS absorb WATER and MINERALS

1) Root hair cells grow into long "<u>hairs</u>" that stick out into the soil.
2) This gives the plant a <u>big surface area</u> for absorbing <u>water</u> and <u>mineral ions</u> from the soil.

PHLOEM CELLS transport FOOD and XYLEM CELLS transport WATER

1) <u>Phloem</u> and <u>xylem cells</u> form phloem and xylem <u>tubes</u>.
2) To form the tubes, the cells are <u>long</u> and joined <u>end to end</u>.
3) Xylem cells are <u>hollow</u> and phloem cells have <u>very few</u> subcellular structures.
   So there's lots of space inside the cells for stuff to <u>flow through</u> them.

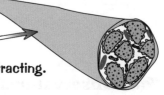
There's more about phloem and xylem on page 39.

xylem   phloem
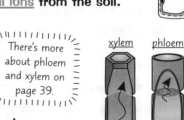

Tadpoles and tent pegs — cells are masters of disguise...

You need to know how the cells on this page are specialised to carry out their functions. Lucky you.

Q1   Describe how a root hair cell is specialised for its function.   [2 marks]

Chromosomes and Mitosis

In order to survive and grow, our cells have got to be able to <u>divide</u>. And that means our DNA as well...

Chromosomes Contain Genetic Information

1) The <u>nucleus</u> of a cell contains <u>chromosomes</u>.
2) Chromosomes are <u>coiled up</u> lengths of <u>DNA molecules</u>.
3) Each chromosome carries a <u>large number</u> of genes.
4) Different genes <u>control</u> the development of different <u>characteristics</u>, e.g. hair colour.
5) <u>Body cells</u> normally have <u>two copies</u> of each <u>chromosome</u>.
6) There are <u>23 pairs of chromosomes</u> in a human cell.

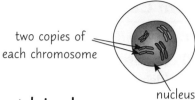

two copies of each chromosome

nucleus

The Cell Cycle Makes New Cells

1) <u>Body cells</u> in <u>multicellular organisms</u> (e.g. like you, me or a plant) <u>divide</u> to make new cells. This is part of a series of stages called the <u>cell cycle</u>.
2) The stage of the cell cycle when the cell <u>divides</u> is called <u>mitosis</u>.
3) Multicellular organisms use <u>mitosis</u> to <u>grow</u> and <u>develop</u>.
4) You need to know about these main stages of the <u>cell cycle</u>:

growth and DNA replication

The Cell Cycle

mitosis

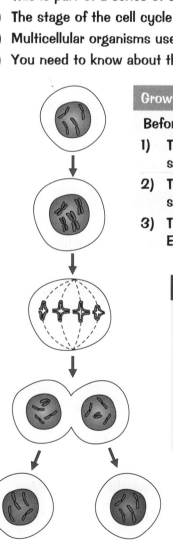

Growth & DNA Replication

Before it divides:

1) The cell <u>grows</u> and <u>increases</u> the amount of <u>subcellular structures</u> such as <u>ribosomes</u> and <u>mitochondria</u> (see page 11).
2) The DNA is <u>replicated</u> (copied) — so there's one copy for each new cell.
3) The DNA forms <u>X-shaped</u> chromosomes. Each 'arm' of the chromosome is an <u>exact copy</u> of the other.

The left arm has the same DNA as the right arm of the chromosome.

Mitosis

The cell is now ready for <u>dividing</u>...

4) The chromosomes <u>line up</u> at the centre of the cell.
5) The <u>two arms</u> of each chromosome are <u>pulled apart</u> to <u>opposite ends</u> of the cell.
6) This <u>divides</u> the <u>nucleus</u>.
7) Each set of chromosomes become the <u>nucleus</u> of a new cell.
8) The <u>cytoplasm</u> and <u>cell membrane</u> divide.

9) The cell has now produced <u>two new cells</u>.
   • They both contain the <u>same DNA</u> — they're <u>identical</u>.
   • They're also <u>identical</u> to the <u>original cell</u>.

A cell's favourite computer game — divide and conquer...

Mitosis can seem tricky at first. But don't worry — just go through it slowly, one step at a time.

Q1   Describe the events of the cell cycle that need to occur before mitosis can begin.   [2 marks]

Stem Cells

Stem cell research is pretty <u>exciting</u>... but not everyone agrees it should be done.

Stem Cells can Differentiate into Different Types of Cells

1) Cells <u>differentiate</u> (change) to become <u>specialised</u> for their job (see p.14).
2) <u>Undifferentiated</u> cells are called <u>stem cells</u>.
3) Stem cells can produce lots <u>more</u> undifferentiated cells and differentiate into <u>different types of cell</u>.
4) Stem cells found in early <u>human embryos</u> are called <u>embryonic stem cells</u>.
5) Embryonic stem cells can turn into <u>any</u> kind of cell at all.
6) <u>Adults</u> also have stem cells. They're only in <u>certain places</u> in the body, like <u>bone marrow</u> (a tissue inside bones).
7) Adult stem cells can <u>only</u> produce <u>certain types</u> of specialised cell, e.g. blood cells.
8) Stem cells from embryos and bone marrow can be <u>cloned</u> (copied) in a lab. The cloned cells can be used in <u>medicine</u> or <u>research</u>.

> An embryo is an unborn baby at an early stage of growth.

Stem Cells May Be Able to Cure Many Diseases

1) <u>Embryonic stem cells</u> could be used to <u>replace faulty cells</u> in sick people.

> E.g. you could make <u>nerve cells</u> for people with <u>paralysis</u> (where they can't move part of the body due to an injury to their spine) or <u>insulin-producing cells</u> for people with <u>diabetes</u> (see page 62).

2) It's possible to <u>make an embryo</u> that has the <u>same genes</u> as a <u>patient</u>. This is called <u>therapeutic cloning</u>.
3) This means that the <u>stem cells</u> from the embryo <u>wouldn't</u> be <u>rejected</u> by the patient's body.
4) However, there are <u>risks</u> involved in using stem cells in medicine. For example, the stem cells could be <u>infected</u> with a <u>virus</u>. The virus could be <u>passed on</u> to a patient and make them <u>sicker</u>.

Some People Are Against Stem Cell Research

1) Some people feel embryos <u>shouldn't</u> be used for research because each one could be a <u>human life</u>.
2) Others think that <u>curing patients</u> who are <u>suffering</u> is <u>more important</u> than the rights of embryos.
3) They argue that the embryos used in the research are usually <u>unwanted ones</u> from <u>fertility clinics</u>. If they weren't used for research, would probably just be <u>destroyed</u>.
4) Some people feel that scientists should be finding <u>other sources</u> of stem cells.

Stem Cells Can Produce Identical Plants

1) Plants have tissues called <u>meristems</u>. Meristems are where <u>growth</u> occurs — in the tips of <u>roots</u> and <u>shoots</u>.
2) The meristems contain <u>stem cells</u> that can differentiate into <u>any type</u> of plant cell. They can do this all through the plant's <u>entire life</u>.
3) These stem cells can be used to make <u>clones</u> (identical copies) of plants <u>quickly</u> and <u>cheaply</u>. Clones can be made of:

   • <u>rare species</u> (to prevent them being wiped out).
   • <u>crop plants</u> that have <u>features</u> that are useful for farmers, e.g. plants <u>aren't killed</u> by a <u>disease</u>.

meristems

But florists cell stems, and nobody complains about that...

Stem cells are pretty clever. Make sure you know the uses of stem cells and the arguments about using them.

Q1   How can stem cells be used to preserve rare plant species?   [2 marks]

Diffusion

Particles <u>move about</u>, and after a bit they end up <u>evenly spaced</u>. It's not rocket science...

Don't Be Put Off by the Fancy Word

1) "<u>Diffusion</u>" is the <u>movement</u> of particles from where there are <u>lots</u> of them to where there are <u>fewer</u> of them.

2) You have to learn this fancy way of saying it:

> DIFFUSION is the SPREADING OUT of particles from an area of HIGHER CONCENTRATION to an area of LOWER CONCENTRATION.

3) Diffusion happens in <u>solutions</u> and <u>gases</u>. For example, the smell of perfume <u>diffuses</u> through the <u>air</u> in a room:

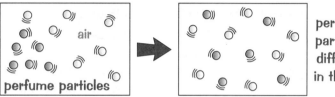

air

perfume particles

perfume particles diffused in the air

4) The <u>difference</u> in concentration is called the <u>concentration gradient</u>. The <u>bigger</u> the <u>difference</u> in concentration, the <u>faster</u> the diffusion rate.

5) A <u>higher temperature</u> will also give a <u>faster</u> diffusion rate. This is because the particles have <u>more energy</u>, so move around faster.

Cell Membranes Are Kind of Clever...

Oxygen is needed for aerobic respiration — see page 54.

1) Cell membranes let stuff diffuse <u>in and out</u> of the cell.

2) Only very <u>small</u> molecules can <u>fit</u> through cell membranes, e.g. <u>oxygen</u>, <u>glucose</u>, <u>amino acids</u> and <u>water</u>.

3) <u>Big</u> molecules like <u>starch</u> and <u>proteins</u> can't fit through the membrane:

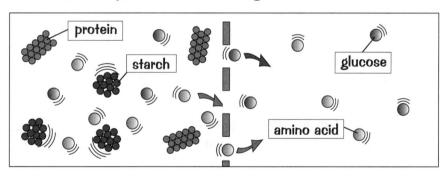

protein

starch

glucose

amino acid

4) Molecules flow through the membrane from where there's a <u>higher concentration</u> (a lot of them) to where there's a <u>lower concentration</u> (not such a lot of them).

5) They actually move <u>both</u> ways — but if there are a lot <u>more</u> particles on one side of the membrane, there's a <u>net</u> (overall) movement <u>from</u> that side.

6) The <u>larger</u> the <u>surface area</u> of the membrane, the <u>faster</u> the diffusion rate. This is because <u>more</u> particles can pass through <u>at the same time</u>.

Revision by diffusion — you wish...

Wouldn't it be great if all the ideas in this book would just slowly drift across into your mind...

Q1   Explain how the surface area of a membrane affects the rate of diffusion.   [2 marks]

Osmosis

If you've got your head round diffusion, osmosis will be a breeze. If not, have another read of the previous page.

Osmosis is the Movement of Water Molecules

OSMOSIS is the movement of water molecules across a partially permeable membrane from a less concentrated solution to a more concentrated solution.

1) A partially permeable membrane is just one with very small holes in it.
2) Tiny molecules (like water) can pass through it, but bigger molecules (e.g. sucrose) can't.
3) Water molecules actually pass both ways through the membrane during osmosis.
4) But overall, the water molecules move from the less concentrated solution (where there are lots of water molecules) to the more concentrated solution (where there are fewer water molecules).
5) This means the more concentrated solution gets more dilute.
6) The water acts like it's trying to "even up" the concentration either side of the membrane.

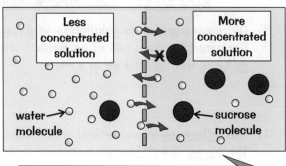

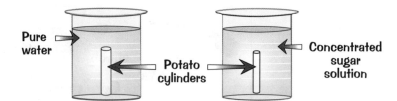
Overall movement of water molecules

You can Observe the Effect of Sugar Solutions on Plant Tissue   PRACTICAL

1) First, cut up a potato into cylinders with the same length and width.
2) Then get two beakers — one with pure water and another with a very concentrated sugar solution (e.g. 1 mol/dm³).
3) You can also have a few other beakers with less concentrated sugar solutions (e.g. 0.2 mol/dm³, 0.4 mol/dm³, etc.)
4) Measure the mass of each potato cylinder, then put one in each beaker.
5) Leave the potato cylinders for twenty four hours.
6) Then take them out and dry them with a paper towel.
7) Measure their masses again.
8) If the mass has increased, water has moved into the potato cells. If the mass has decreased, water has moved out of the potato cells.
9) You can calculate the percentage change in mass for each potato cylinder — see p.241. This means you can compare the effects of each sugar solution.
10) The only thing you should change in this experiment is the concentration of the sugar solution. Everything else (e.g. volume of solution, temperature, time, type of sugar used) should stay the same.

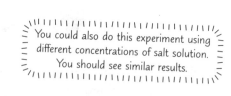

You could also do this experiment using different concentrations of salt solution. You should see similar results.

And to all you cold-hearted potato murderers...

Osmosis works a lot like diffusion really — water molecules will move from where there's more of them (a less concentrated solution) to where there's fewer of them (a more concentrated solution).

Q1   Explain what will happen to the mass of a piece of potato added to a concentrated salt solution.   [2 marks]

Topic B1 — Cell Biology

Active Transport

Sometimes substances need to be absorbed from a <u>lower concentration</u> to a <u>higher concentration</u> — <u>against</u> the <u>concentration gradient</u>. This process is called <u>ACTIVE TRANSPORT</u>.

Root Hairs Take In Minerals and Water

1) Plant roots are covered in <u>millions</u> of <u>root hair cells</u>.

2) These cells <u>stick out</u> into the soil.

3) The "hairs" give the roots a <u>large surface area</u>.

4) This is useful for absorbing <u>water</u> and <u>mineral ions</u> from the soil.

5) Plants <u>need</u> mineral ions for <u>healthy growth</u>.

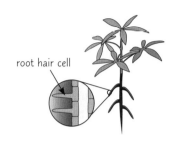

root hair cell

Root Hairs Take in Minerals Using Active Transport

1) The concentration of minerals is usually <u>higher</u> in the <u>root hair cells</u> than in the <u>soil</u> around them.

2) So the root hair cells <u>can't</u> use <u>diffusion</u> to take up minerals from the soil.

3) They use <u>active transport</u> instead.

4) Active transport allows the plant to absorb minerals from a very <u>dilute</u> solution in the soil — it moves the minerals <u>against</u> the <u>concentration gradient</u>.

5) But active transport needs <u>ENERGY</u> from <u>respiration</u> to make it work.

Water is taken into root hair cells by osmosis (see page 18).

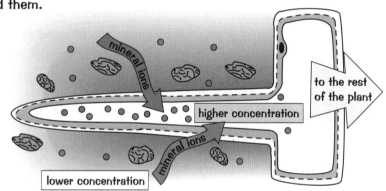

mineral ions

to the rest of the plant

higher concentration

mineral ions

lower concentration

We Need Active Transport to Stop Us Starving

1) The body needs to <u>absorb nutrients</u> (e.g. glucose and amino acids) from <u>food</u> to <u>survive</u>.

2) The nutrients have to move from the <u>gut</u> into the <u>blood</u>.

3) When there's a <u>higher concentration</u> of nutrients in the gut, they <u>diffuse</u> into the blood.

4) Sometimes there's a <u>lower concentration</u> of nutrients in the gut than there is in the blood.

5) The body uses <u>active transport</u> to move the nutrients (like glucose) from a <u>lower concentration</u> in the <u>gut</u> to a <u>higher concentration</u> in the <u>blood</u>.

6) This means <u>glucose</u> can be taken into the blood <u>against</u> the concentration gradient. The glucose is then transported to <u>cells</u>, where it's used for <u>respiration</u> (see p.53).

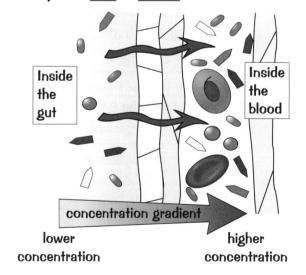

Inside the gut

Inside the blood

concentration gradient

lower concentration

higher concentration

Active transport — get on yer bike...

An important difference between active transport and diffusion is that active transport uses energy.

Q1   What is the purpose of active transport in the gut?   [1 mark]

Exchanging Substances

How easily stuff <u>moves</u> between an <u>organism</u> and its <u>environment</u> depends on its <u>surface area to volume ratio</u>.

Organisms Exchange Substances with their Environment

1) Cells can use <u>diffusion</u> to <u>take in</u> substances from the <u>environment</u>, such as <u>oxygen</u>.

2) They also use diffusion to <u>get rid</u> of <u>waste products</u>, such as:

   • <u>Carbon dioxide</u> (from <u>respiration</u>).

   • <u>Urea</u> (from the <u>breakdown</u> of <u>proteins</u>) — urea diffuses from <u>cells</u> into the <u>blood plasma</u> (see p.32). It is then removed from the body by the <u>kidneys</u>.

3) How <u>easy</u> it is for an organism to <u>exchange</u> (swap) substances with its environment depends on the organism's <u>surface area to volume ratio</u>.

You Can Calculate an Organism's Surface Area to Volume Ratio

1) A <u>ratio</u> shows <u>how big</u> one value is <u>compared</u> to another.

2) So a <u>surface area to volume ratio</u> shows how big a shape's <u>surface</u> is compared to its <u>volume</u>.

3) E.g. a <u>2 cm × 4 cm × 4 cm block</u> can be used to <u>estimate</u> the surface area to volume ratio of this <u>hippo</u>:

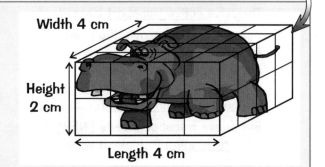

Width 4 cm

Height 2 cm

Length 4 cm

SURFACE AREA

   • The <u>area</u> of a square or rectangle is found by the equation: LENGTH × WIDTH.

   • So the hippo's <u>total surface area</u> is:
   $(4 \times 4) \times 2$ (top and bottom surfaces)
   $+ (4 \times 2) \times 4$ (four sides)
   $= \underline{64 \text{ cm}^2}$.

VOLUME

   • The <u>volume</u> of a block is found by the equation: LENGTH × WIDTH × HEIGHT.

   • So the hippo's <u>volume</u> is $4 \times 4 \times 2 = \underline{32 \text{ cm}^3}$.

SURFACE AREA TO VOLUME RATIO

   • The surface area to volume ratio (<u>SA : V</u>) of the hippo can be written as <u>64 : 32</u>.

   • To get the ratio so that volume is equal to <u>one</u>, <u>divide both sides</u> of the ratio by the <u>volume</u>.
   $64 \div 32 = 2$ $32 \div 32 = 1$ So the SA : V of the hippo is <u>2 : 1</u>.

4) A <u>1 cm × 1 cm × 1 cm block</u> can be used to estimate the surface area to volume ratio of a <u>mouse</u>. It's found that the SA : V of the mouse is <u>6 : 1</u>.

5) The <u>larger</u> the organism, the <u>smaller</u> its surface area is compared to its volume.

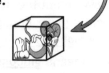

   Example: The <u>surface area</u> of the <u>mouse</u> is <u>six times</u> its <u>volume</u>.
   The <u>surface area</u> of the <u>hippo</u> is only <u>two times</u> its <u>volume</u>.
   So the <u>hippo</u> has a <u>smaller</u> surface area compared to its volume.

6) The <u>smaller</u> its <u>surface area</u> compared to its <u>volume</u>, the <u>harder</u> it is for an organism to <u>exchange substances</u> with its environment.

Not that I think you should put animals in boxes...

And now here's some practice for calculating surface area to volume ratios.

Q1   A bacterial cell can be represented by a 1 μm × 2 μm × 2 μm block. Calculate the cell's surface area to volume ratio.

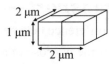

2 μm
1 μm
2 μm

[3 marks]

More on Exchanging Substances

The human body has special surfaces for diffusion to make sure that we can take in enough substances.

Multicellular Organisms Need Exchange Surfaces

1) Single-celled organisms have a large surface area compared to their volume.
2) So, they can exchange all the substances they need across their surface (the cell membrane).
3) Multicellular organisms (such as animals) have a smaller surface area compared to their volume.
4) They can't normally exchange enough substances across their outside surface alone.
5) Instead, multicellular organisms have specialised exchange surfaces — (see below and the next page for some examples).
6) They also have transport systems that carry substances to and from their exchange surfaces.
7) The exchange surfaces are ADAPTED to allow enough of different substances to pass through:
   • They have a thin membrane (so substances only have a short distance to diffuse).
   • They have a large surface area (so lots of a substance can diffuse at once).
   • Exchange surfaces in animals have lots of blood vessels (so stuff can get into and out of the blood quickly).
   • Gas exchange surfaces in animals (e.g. alveoli) are ventilated too — air moves in and out.

Gas Exchange Happens in the Lungs

1) Oxygen (O_2) and carbon dioxide (CO_2) are exchanged in the lungs.
2) The lungs contain millions of little air sacs called alveoli. This is where gas exchange happens.
3) The alveoli are specialised for the diffusion of oxygen and carbon dioxide. They have:

   • A large surface area.
   • Very thin walls (so gases don't have far to diffuse).
   • A good blood supply.

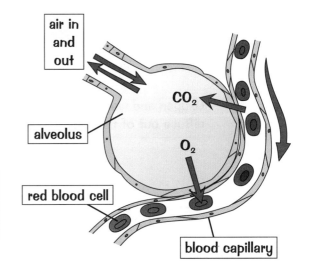

The Villi Provide a Really Big Surface Area

1) The inside of the small intestine is covered in millions of villi.
2) They increase the surface area so that digested food is absorbed more quickly into the blood.
3) They have:
   • a single layer of surface cells,
   • a very good blood supply.

The digested food moves into the blood by diffusion and by active transport (see page 19).

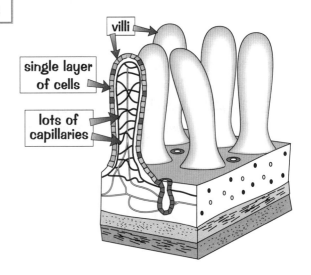

More on Exchanging Substances

More stuff on exchange surfaces for diffusion now — only this time they're in <u>plants</u> and <u>fish</u>. Whoopee...

The Structure of Leaves Lets Gases Diffuse In and Out of Cells

1) Plant leaves need to <u>take in carbon dioxide</u> for photosynthesis, and <u>get rid</u> of <u>oxygen</u> and <u>water vapour</u>.
2) The underneath of the leaf is an <u>exchange surface</u>. It's covered in small <u>holes</u> called <u>stomata</u>.
3) <u>Carbon dioxide diffuses</u> through the stomata <u>into</u> the leaf.
4) <u>Oxygen</u> and <u>water vapour</u> diffuse <u>out</u> through the stomata.
5) The size of the stomata are controlled by <u>guard cells</u> — see page 40.
6) The <u>flattened shape</u> of the leaf increases the <u>area</u> of its exchange surface.
7) The <u>walls of the cells</u> inside the leaf are another exchange surface. Gases diffuse <u>into</u> and <u>out of</u> the cells through these walls.
8) There are <u>air spaces</u> inside the leaf to <u>increase</u> the <u>area</u> of these surfaces.

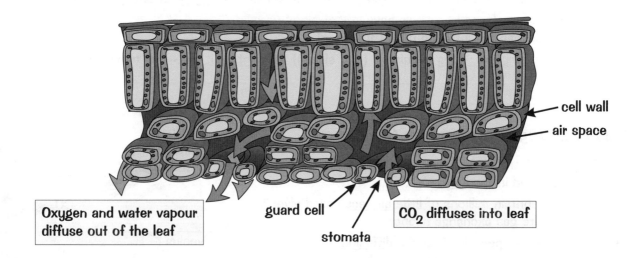

cell wall
air space

Oxygen and water vapour diffuse out of the leaf

guard cell

stomata

CO$_2$ diffuses into leaf

Gills Have a Large Surface Area for Gas Exchange

1) The <u>gills</u> are the <u>gas exchange surface</u> in <u>fish</u>.
2) Water (containing <u>oxygen</u>) flows into the fish's <u>mouth</u> and passes out through the <u>gills</u>.
3) In the gills, <u>oxygen</u> diffuses from the <u>water</u> into the <u>blood</u>. Carbon dioxide diffuses from the <u>blood</u> into the <u>water</u>.
4) The gills are made up of lots of <u>thin plates</u>. This gives them a <u>large surface area</u> for <u>gases</u> to be <u>exchanged</u>.
5) The plates have lots of <u>blood capillaries</u>. So they have a <u>good blood supply</u> to <u>speed up diffusion</u>.
6) They also have a <u>thin layer</u> of surface cells. So the gases only have to diffuse a <u>short distance</u>.

mouth

water

gill

In, out, in, out, shake that oxygen about...

Multicellular organisms are well adapted for getting the substances they need to their cells. Make sure you learn the adaptations for all the examples on these pages — you need to know them for your exam.

Q1   Give two ways in which a gill is adapted for gas exchange.   [2 marks]

Revision Questions for Topic B1

Well, that's <u>Topic B1</u> done and dusted. Now there's only one way to find out whether you've learnt anything from it. And you know what that is, I'll bet. It's obvious... I mean, there's a whole load of questions staring you in the face — chances are, it's got to involve those in some way. And sure enough, it does.

- Try these questions and <u>tick off each one</u> when you <u>get it right</u>.
- When you've done <u>all the questions</u> under a heading and are <u>completely happy</u> with it, tick it off.

Cells and Microscopy (p.11-13) ☑

1) What type of cell are bacteria — prokaryotic or eukaryotic?
2) Name five subcellular structures that both plant and animal cells have.
3) What three things do plant cells have that animal cells don't?
4) Where is the genetic material found in:
   a) animal cells,
   b) bacterial cells?
5) Which has a higher resolution — a light microscope or an electron microscope?

Differentiation and Division (p.14-15) ☐

6) What is cell differentiation?
7) Give two ways that a sperm cell is adapted for swimming to an egg.
8) Draw a diagram of a nerve cell. Why is it this shape?
9) What are chromosomes?
10) What is the cell cycle?
11) What do multicellular organisms use mitosis for?

Stem Cells (p.16) ☐

12) Give one way that embryonic stem cells could be used to cure diseases.
13) Why might some people be against using human embryos in stem cell research?

Exchanging Substances (p.17-22) ☐

14) What is diffusion?
15) How does temperature affect the rate of diffusion?
16) What type of molecules move by osmosis?
17) Name the process that plants use to take up mineral ions from the soil.
18) Give three ways that exchange surfaces can be adapted for diffusion.
19) Give one way in which alveoli are adapted for gas exchange.
20) Give two ways that the villi in the small intestine are adapted for absorbing digested food.
21) Name the holes in the surface of a leaf that gases diffuse through.

Cell Organisation

Some organisms are made of <u>lots</u> of cells. To get a <u>working</u> organism, these cells need to be <u>organised</u>.

Large Multicellular Organisms are Made Up of Organ Systems

1) <u>Cells</u> are the <u>basic building blocks</u> that make up <u>all living organisms</u>.
2) <u>Specialised cells</u> carry out a <u>particular function</u> (see p.14).
3) These specialised cells form <u>tissues</u>, which form <u>organs</u>, which form <u>organ systems</u> (see below).
4) <u>Large multicellular organisms</u> (e.g. humans) have different <u>systems</u> inside them for <u>exchanging</u> and <u>transporting</u> materials.

Epithelial cell

Similar Cells Make Up Tissues

1) A <u>tissue</u> is a <u>group</u> of <u>similar cells</u> that work together to carry out a <u>function</u>.
2) E.g. <u>epithelial tissue</u> is a type of tissue made of <u>epithelial cells</u>.
    It <u>covers</u> some parts of the human body, e.g. the <u>inside</u> of the <u>gut</u>.

Epithelial tissue

Tissues Make Up Organs

1) An <u>organ</u> is a group of <u>different tissues</u> that work together to perform a certain <u>function</u>.
2) For example, the <u>stomach</u> is an organ.
    <u>Epithelial tissue</u> lines the inside and outside of the stomach.

Stomach

Organs Make Up Organ Systems

1) An <u>organ system</u> is a <u>group of organs</u> working together to perform a <u>function</u>.
2) The <u>digestive system</u> is an organ system found in humans and other mammals.
3) It <u>breaks down</u> and <u>absorbs</u> food.
4) It's made up of these organs:

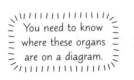
You need to know where these organs are on a diagram.

Salivary glands
Produce digestive juices.

Liver
Produces bile.

Large intestine
Absorbs water from undigested food, leaving faeces (poo).

Digestive system

Stomach
Digests food.

Pancreas
Produces digestive juices.

Small intestine
Digests food and absorbs soluble food molecules, e.g. glucose.

5) Organ systems work together to make entire <u>organisms</u>.

Soft and quilted — the best kind of tissues...

So, an organism is made of organ systems, which are groups of organs working together. And organs are made of tissues, which are groups of cells working together. Right. Now just for the thrill of it, here's a practice question.

Q1   The bladder is an organ. Explain what this means.   [2 marks]

Enzymes

Chemical reactions are what make you work. And enzymes are what make them work.

Enzymes Are Catalysts

1) Living things have tons of reactions going on inside their cells.
2) These reactions are controlled by enzymes.
3) Enzymes are large proteins.
4) They speed up reactions inside living things by acting as catalysts:

> Enzymes are important in metabolism — see page 53.

> A CATALYST is a substance which INCREASES the speed of a reaction, without being CHANGED or USED UP in the reaction.

Enzymes Have Special Shapes

1) Chemical reactions usually involve things either being split apart or joined together.
2) Every enzyme has an active site with a unique shape.
3) The substance involved in the reaction has to fit into the active site for the enzyme to work.
4) So enzymes are really picky — they usually only catalyse one specific reaction.
5) This diagram shows the 'lock and key' model of enzyme action:

> The substance that an enzyme acts on is called the substrate.

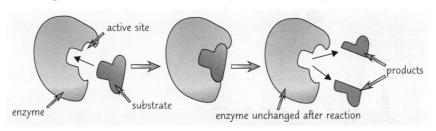

active site

products

enzyme   substrate   enzyme unchanged after reaction

> This is a useful model but it's a bit simpler than how enzymes actually work.

Enzymes Need the Right Temperature and pH

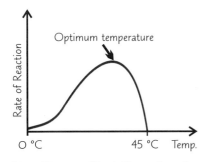

Optimum temperature

Rate of Reaction

0 °C   45 °C   Temp.

1) Temperature affects the rate of a reaction involving an enzyme.
2) A higher temperature increases the rate at first.
3) But if it gets too hot, some of the bonds holding the enzyme together break.
4) This changes the shape of the enzyme's active site, so the substrate won't fit any more — the enzyme is denatured.
5) All enzymes have a temperature that they work best at — their optimum temperature.
6) pH can affect the rate of a reaction involving an enzyme.
7) If the pH is too high or too low, it affects the bonds holding the enzyme together.
8) This changes the shape of the active site, and denatures the enzyme.
9) All enzymes have a pH that they work best at — their optimum pH.

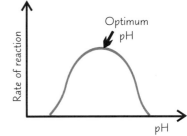

Optimum pH

Rate of reaction

pH

If only enzymes could speed up revision...

Make sure you use the special terms like 'active site' and 'denatured' — the examiners will love it.

Q1   Explain why an enzyme is denatured if the pH is too high.   [2 marks]

Investigating Enzymatic Reactions

You'll soon know how to investigate the effect of <u>pH</u> on the rate of <u>enzyme activity</u>... I bet you're thrilled.

You Can Investigate the Effect of pH on Enzyme Activity | PRACTICAL

> 1) The enzyme <u>amylase</u> catalyses the breakdown of <u>starch</u> to <u>sugar</u>.
>
> 2) You can <u>detect starch</u> using <u>iodine solution</u> — if starch is present, the iodine solution will change from <u>browny-orange</u> to <u>blue-black</u>.

1) Put a <u>drop</u> of <u>iodine solution</u> into every <u>well</u> of a <u>spotting tile</u>.

2) Set up a <u>water bath</u> at **35 °C**.
   (You could use a Bunsen burner and a beaker of water, or an electric water bath.)

3) Add some <u>amylase solution</u> and a <u>buffer solution</u> with a <u>pH</u> of <u>5</u> to a boiling tube.

4) Put the boiling tube in the water bath and wait for five minutes.

5) Add some <u>starch solution</u> to the boiling tube, <u>mix</u>, and start a <u>stop clock</u>.

6) <u>Every 30 seconds</u>, take a <u>sample</u> from the boiling tube using a dropping pipette.

7) Put a <u>drop</u> of the sample into a <u>well</u> on the spotting tile.

8) When the iodine solution <u>stays browny-orange</u>, all the starch in the sample has been broken down. <u>Record how long</u> this takes.

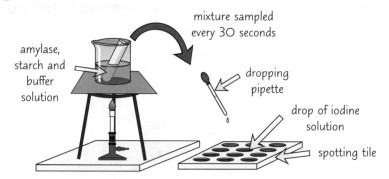

9) <u>Repeat</u> the experiment with buffer solutions of different <u>pH values</u>.

10) As the <u>pH changes</u>, the <u>time</u> it takes for the starch to be broken down should also <u>change</u>.

11) Remember to <u>control any variables</u> each time you repeat the experiment. This will make it a <u>fair test</u>. For example, the <u>concentration</u> and <u>volume</u> of the <u>amylase solution</u> should always be the <u>same</u>.

Here's How to Calculate the Rate of Reaction

1) <u>Rate</u> is a measure of <u>how much</u> something <u>changes</u> over <u>time</u>.

2) For the <u>experiment above</u>, you can calculate the rate of reaction using <u>this formula</u>:

$$Rate = \frac{1000}{time}$$

EXAMPLE: The time taken for amylase to break down all of the starch in a solution was 90 seconds. Calculate the rate of the reaction. Write your answer in s^{-1}.

Rate of reaction = 1000 ÷ time = 1000 ÷ 90 s
    = 11 s^{-1}

s^{-1} just means 'per second'.

Mad scientists — they're experi-mental...

Repeating the experiment at each pH is a great idea — this lets you find a mean value of your results for each pH.

Q1   Calculate the rate of a reaction that finished in 50 seconds. Give your answer in s^{-1}.   [1 mark]

Topic B2 — Organisation

Enzymes and Digestion

The enzymes used in digestion are produced by cells. They're released into the gut to mix with food.

Digestive Enzymes Break Down Big Molecules

1) Starch, proteins and fats are BIG molecules.
2) They're too big to pass through the walls of the digestive system.
3) So digestive enzymes break these BIG molecules down into smaller ones.
4) These smaller, soluble molecules can easily be absorbed into the bloodstream.

CARBOHYDRASES
- Amylase is an example of a carbohydrase.
- Amylase is made in the salivary glands, pancreas and small intestine.
- It works in the mouth and small intestine.

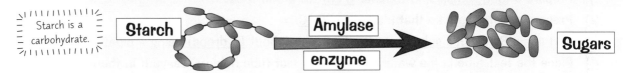

Starch is a carbohydrate.

Starch → Amylase enzyme → Sugars

PROTEASES
- Proteases are made in the stomach, pancreas and small intestine.
- They work in the stomach and small intestine.

Proteins → Protease enzymes → Amino acids

LIPASES
- Lipases are made in the pancreas and small intestine.
- They work in the small intestine.

Lipids are fats and oils.

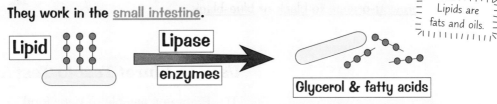

Lipid → Lipase enzymes → Glycerol & fatty acids

5) The products of digestion can be used to make new carbohydrates, proteins and lipids.
6) Glucose is a sugar produced by digestion. Some of it is used in respiration (see p.53).

Bile Neutralises the Stomach Acid and Emulsifies Fats

1) Bile is produced in the liver. It's stored in the gall bladder before it's released into the small intestine.
2) Bile is alkaline. It neutralises hydrochloric acid (from the stomach) and makes conditions alkaline.
3) The enzymes in the small intestine work best in these alkaline conditions.
4) Bile also emulsifies fats. Emulsify means that it breaks the fats down into tiny droplets.
   This gives a bigger surface area of fat for lipase to work on. This makes its digestion faster.

What do you call an acid that's eaten all the pies... *(A fatty acid)*

Make sure you know what amylase, protease and lipase enzymes do, where they're made and where they work.

Q1   Describe and explain how bile helps the digestion of fats.   [4 marks]

Food Tests

Here are some tests you can use to find out what kind of molecules are present in a sample of <u>food</u>.
For each test, you need to prepare a <u>food sample</u>. It's the same each time though — here's what you'd do:

1) Get a piece of food and <u>break it up</u> using a <u>pestle and mortar</u>.
2) Transfer the ground up food to a <u>beaker</u> and add some <u>distilled water</u>.
3) Give the mixture a good <u>stir</u> with a glass rod to <u>dissolve</u> some of the food.
4) <u>Filter</u> the solution using a <u>funnel</u> lined with <u>filter paper</u>. This will <u>get rid</u> of the <u>solid</u> bits of food.

pestle

mortar

Use the Benedict's Test to Test for Sugars

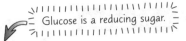
Glucose is a reducing sugar.

The <u>Benedict's test</u> is used to test for a type of sugar called a <u>reducing sugar</u>. Here's how you do it:

1) Prepare a <u>food sample</u> and transfer <u>5 cm³</u> to a test tube.
2) Prepare a <u>water bath</u> so that it's set to <u>75 °C</u>.
3) Add some <u>Benedict's solution</u> to the test tube (about <u>10 drops</u>) using a pipette.
4) Place the test tube in the water bath using a test tube holder. Leave it in there for <u>5 minutes</u>.
5) If the food sample contains a reducing sugar, the solution in the test tube will change from the normal <u>blue</u> colour to <u>green</u>, <u>yellow</u> or <u>brick-red</u>. The colour change depends on <u>how much</u> sugar is in the food.

Use Iodine Solution to Test for Starch

1) Make a <u>food sample</u> and transfer <u>5 cm³</u> to a test tube.
2) Add a few drops of <u>iodine solution</u>. <u>Gently shake</u> the tube to mix the contents.
3) If the sample contains <u>starch</u>, the colour of the solution will change from <u>browny-orange</u> to <u>black</u> or <u>blue-black</u>.

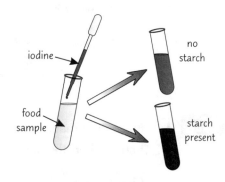

iodine

food sample

no starch

starch present

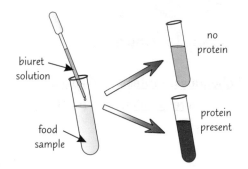

biuret solution

food sample

no protein

protein present

Use the Biuret Test to Test for Proteins

1) Prepare a <u>sample</u> of your food and transfer <u>2 cm³</u> to a test tube.
2) Add 2 cm³ of <u>biuret solution</u> to the sample. Mix the contents of the tube by <u>gently shaking</u> it.
3) If the food sample contains <u>protein</u>, the solution will change from <u>blue</u> to <u>purple</u>.

Use the Sudan III Test to Test for Lipids

1) Prepare a <u>food sample</u> using the method above but <u>don't</u> filter it. Transfer <u>5 cm³</u> to a test tube.
2) Add <u>3 drops</u> of <u>Sudan III stain solution</u> to the test tube. <u>Gently shake</u> the tube.
3) If the sample contains <u>lipids</u>, the mixture will separate out into <u>two layers</u>. The top layer will be <u>bright red</u>.

All this talk of food is making me hungry...

Make sure you do a risk assessment before starting these tests — there are lots of chemicals to use here.

Q1   Name the solution that you would use to test for starch.   [1 mark]

The Lungs

You need oxygen to supply your cells for respiration (see p.54). You also need to get rid of carbon dioxide.
This all happens in your lungs when you breathe air in and out.

Air Moves In and Out of the Lungs

1) This diagram shows the structure of the lungs:

2) The air that you breathe in
    goes through the trachea.

3) Then it passes through the bronchi,
    then the bronchioles and ends up
    in the alveoli (small air sacs).

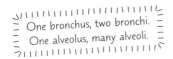
One bronchus, two bronchi.
One alveolus, many alveoli.

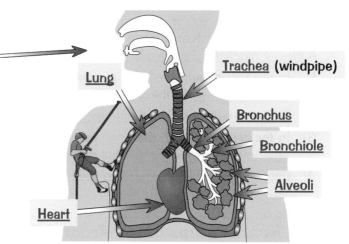
Lung
Trachea (windpipe)
Bronchus
Bronchiole
Alveoli
Heart

Alveoli Carry Out Gas Exchange

1) Alveoli in the lungs are surrounded by blood capillaries.

2) Blood comes into the lungs through the capillaries.
    It contains lots of carbon dioxide and very little oxygen.

3) Oxygen diffuses (see p.17) out of the air in the
    alveolus (where there's a higher concentration)
    into the blood (where there's a lower concentration).

4) Carbon dioxide diffuses out of the blood (higher concentration)
    into the air in the alveolus (lower concentration).

5) The blood then leaves the lungs and travels around the body.

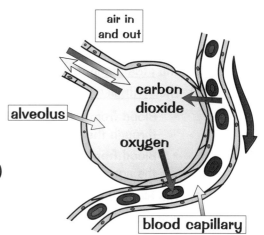
air in and out
carbon dioxide
alveolus
oxygen
blood capillary

You Can Calculate the Breathing Rate

Breathing rate is how fast a person moves air in and out of their lungs. Here's how to calculate it:

EXAMPLE:

Bob takes 91 breaths in 7 minutes. Calculate his average breathing rate in breaths per minute.

breaths per minute = number of breaths ÷ number of minutes

= 91 ÷ 7

= 13 breaths per minute

Stop huffing and puffing and just learn it...

Alveoli are really well adapted for carrying out gas exchange — if you need a reminder of how, flick back to p.21.

Q1 During a 12 minute run, Aaqib took 492 breaths.
Calculate his average breathing rate in breaths per minute.
[1 mark]

Circulatory System — The Heart

The circulatory system carries <u>food</u> and <u>oxygen</u> to every cell in the body, and <u>waste</u> to where it can be removed.

Humans Have a DOUBLE Circulatory System

The circulatory system is made up of the <u>heart</u>, <u>blood vessels</u> and <u>blood</u>. A <u>double circulatory system</u> is <u>two circuits</u> joined together:

1) In the first circuit, the <u>heart</u> pumps <u>deoxygenated</u> blood (blood <u>without oxygen</u>) to the <u>lungs</u>. The blood picks up oxygen in the lungs.
2) <u>Oxygenated</u> blood (blood <u>with oxygen</u>) then <u>returns</u> to the heart.
3) In the second circuit, the <u>heart</u> pumps <u>oxygenated</u> blood around all the <u>other organs</u> of the <u>body</u>. This delivers oxygen to the body cells.
4) <u>Deoxygenated</u> blood <u>returns</u> to the heart to be pumped out to the <u>lungs</u> again.

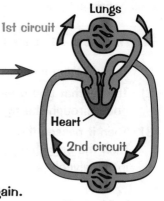

Blue = deoxygenated blood.
Red = oxygenated blood.

The Heart Pumps Blood Around The Body

1) The <u>heart</u> is an organ with <u>four chambers</u>. The walls of the chambers are mostly made of <u>muscle tissue</u>.
2) This muscle tissue is used to <u>pump blood</u> around the body. Here's how:

   1) <u>Blood flows into</u> the two <u>atria</u> from the <u>vena cava</u> and the <u>pulmonary vein</u>.
   2) The <u>atria pump</u> the blood into the <u>ventricles</u>.
   3) The <u>ventricles</u> pump the blood <u>out</u> of the heart:
     • Blood from the <u>right ventricle</u> goes through the <u>pulmonary artery</u> to the <u>lungs</u>.
     • Blood from the <u>left ventricle</u> goes through the <u>aorta</u> to the rest of the <u>body</u>.
   4) The blood then flows to the <u>organs</u> through <u>arteries</u>, and <u>returns</u> through <u>veins</u> (see next page).
   5) The atria fill again — the whole cycle <u>starts over</u>.

Atrium is when there is just one. Atria is plural.

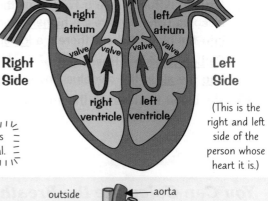

Right Side

Left Side

(This is the right and left side of the person whose heart it is.)

3) The <u>valves</u> in the heart stop the blood flowing <u>backwards</u>.
4) The heart also needs its <u>own</u> supply of <u>oxygenated</u> blood.
5) It gets oxygenated blood from arteries called <u>coronary arteries</u>. These branch off the <u>aorta</u> and <u>surround</u> the heart.

The Heart Has a Pacemaker

1) Your resting heart rate is <u>controlled</u> by a group of cells in the <u>right atrium</u> wall.
2) These cells act as a <u>pacemaker</u> — they tell the heart <u>when</u> to <u>pump blood</u>.
3) A pacemaker that doesn't work properly causes an <u>irregular heartbeat</u>. An <u>artificial pacemaker</u> (a small electrical device) can be used to keep the heart beating <u>regularly</u>.

Okay — let's get to the heart of the matter...

Interesting fact — when doctors use a stethoscope to listen to your heart, it's the valves closing that they hear.

Q1   Which chamber of the heart pumps deoxygenated blood to the lungs?   [1 mark]

Circulatory System — Blood Vessels

Blood flows around the body in blood vessels. There are three different types — arteries, capillaries and veins.

Arteries Carry Blood Under Pressure

1) Arteries carry blood away from the heart.
2) The heart pumps the blood out at high pressure.
3) So artery walls are strong and elastic.
4) They have thick layers of muscle to make them strong.
5) They also have elastic fibres to allow them to stretch and spring back.
6) The walls are thick compared to the size of the hole down the middle (the "lumen" — silly name!).

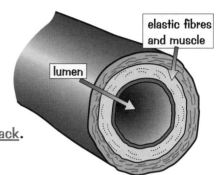

Capillaries are Really Small

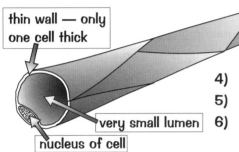

1) Arteries branch into capillaries.
2) Capillaries are really tiny — too small to see.
3) They carry the blood really close to every cell in the body to exchange substances with them.
4) They have gaps in their walls, so substances can diffuse in and out.
5) They supply food and oxygen, and take away waste like CO_2.
6) Their walls are usually only one cell thick. This means that diffusion is very fast because there is only a short distance for molecules to travel.

Veins Take Blood Back to the Heart

1) Capillaries join up to form veins.
2) The blood is at lower pressure in the veins. This means the walls don't need to be as thick as artery walls.
3) Veins have a bigger lumen than arteries. This helps the blood flow despite the lower pressure.
4) They also have valves. These help keep the blood flowing in the right direction.

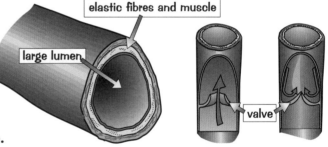

You Can Calculate the Rate of Blood Flow

The rate of blood flow is the amount of blood that passes through a blood vessel in a given time. Here's how to calculate it:

EXAMPLE: 1300 ml of blood passed through an artery in 4 minutes. Calculate the rate of blood flow through the artery in ml per minute.

rate of blood flow = volume of blood ÷ number of minutes
= 1300 ÷ 4
= 325 ml per minute

Learn this page — don't struggle in vein...

Another interesting fact for you — your body contains about 60 000 miles of blood vessels.

Q1   Describe how the features of veins help them to carry blood back to the heart.   [2 marks]

Circulatory System — Blood

Blood is a tissue (see p.24). One of its jobs is to act as a huge transport system. It has four main parts...

Red Blood Cells Carry Oxygen

1) The job of red blood cells is to carry oxygen from the lungs to all the cells in the body.
2) Their shape gives them a large surface area for absorbing oxygen.
3) They contain a red substance called haemoglobin.
4) Haemoglobin is the stuff that allows red blood cells to carry oxygen.
5) Red blood cells don't have a nucleus — this leaves more space for carrying oxygen.

White Blood Cells Defend Against Infection

1) White blood cells are part of your immune system — see page 46.
2) Some can change shape to gobble up unwelcome microorganisms.
3) Others produce molecules called antibodies and antitoxins to defend against microorganisms.
4) Unlike red blood cells, they do have a nucleus.

Platelets Help Blood Clot

1) These are small fragments of cells. They have no nucleus.
2) They help the blood to clot (clump together) at a wound.
3) This stops all your blood pouring out.
4) It also stops any microorganisms getting in.

Plasma is the Liquid That Carries Everything in Blood

This is a pale straw-coloured liquid. It carries:
1) Red and white blood cells and platelets.
2) Food molecules (like glucose and amino acids).
3) Waste products (like carbon dioxide and urea).
4) Hormones.
5) Proteins.

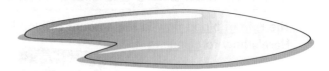

Platelets — ideal for small dinners...

Right now, tons of blood cells are carrying oxygen to your brain, so you can get on with learning this page.

Q1   Describe the job of platelets in blood.   [1 mark]

Q2   Describe three ways in which red blood cells are adapted to carry oxygen.   [3 marks]

Topic B2 — Organisation

Cardiovascular Disease

Cardiovascular diseases are diseases of the heart or blood vessels. One example is coronary heart disease.

Coronary Heart Disease is a Disease of the Coronary Arteries

1) The coronary arteries supply the heart muscle with blood.
2) Coronary heart disease is when layers of fatty material (called fatty deposits) build up in the coronary arteries. This causes the arteries to become narrow.
3) This reduces the blood flow to the heart muscle.
4) This means less oxygen can get to the heart muscle. This can result in a heart attack.

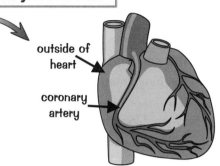
outside of heart

coronary artery

Stents Keep Coronary Arteries Open

1) Stents are tubes that are put inside coronary arteries by surgery. They keep the arteries open.
2) This allows blood to reach the heart muscles and reduces the risk of a heart attack.

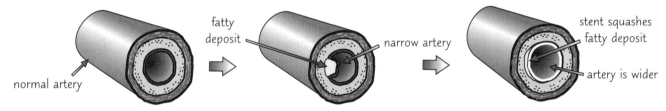

normal artery

fatty deposit

narrow artery

stent squashes fatty deposit

artery is wider

3) Stents are effective for a long time. Recovery time from the surgery is also quite quick.
4) But there are risks. These include having a heart attack during the operation, or getting an infection after surgery. Patients may also develop a blood clot near the stent.

Statins Reduce Cholesterol in the Blood

1) Cholesterol is a lipid that your body needs.
2) However, too much cholesterol can cause fatty deposits to form inside arteries.
3) Statins are drugs that can reduce the amount of cholesterol in the blood.
4) This slows down the rate of fatty deposits forming.

Advantages

1) Statins reduce the risk of strokes, coronary heart disease and heart attacks.
2) Some studies suggest that statins may also help prevent some other diseases.

Disadvantages

1) Statins must be taken regularly over a long time. A person could forget to take them.
2) Statins can cause unwanted side effects, for example, headaches.
3) The effect of statins isn't instant. It takes time for their effect to work.

Unlike stents and statins, using CGP books only has advantages...

Make sure you're aware of the problems as well as the advantages of both stents and statins.

Q1   Suggest two disadvantages of treating patients using stents.   [2 marks]

More on Cardiovascular Disease

Here are a few more ways of dealing with problems when things go wrong in the circulatory system.

An Artificial Heart Can Pump Blood Round the Body

1) A heart transplant is when a person's heart is replaced by a donor heart (a heart from someone who has recently died).

2) This can happen if someone has heart failure. Heart failure is when the heart can't pump enough blood.

3) The lungs may also be replaced if they are diseased.

4) If a donor heart isn't available, doctors may fit an artificial heart (a machine that pumps blood around the body).

5) Artificial hearts can be used to keep a person alive until a donor heart is available. Or they can help a person recover by allowing the heart to rest and heal.

6) Sometimes artificial hearts are permanent, so a donor heart isn't needed anymore.

7) Here are some of the advantages and disadvantages of artificial hearts:

Advantage: Artificial hearts are made from metals or plastics. This makes them less likely to be attacked by the body's immune system (see page 46) than a donor heart.

Disadvantages:

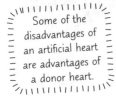
Some of the disadvantages of an artificial heart are advantages of a donor heart.

- Surgery to fit an artificial heart can lead to bleeding and infection. (This can also happen with transplant surgery.)
- Artificial hearts don't work as well as healthy natural ones.
- Blood doesn't flow through artificial hearts as smoothly as through a natural heart. This can cause blood clots and lead to strokes.
- The patient has to take drugs to thin their blood. This means they can bleed a lot more than is usual if they have an accident.

Faulty Heart Valves Can Be Replaced

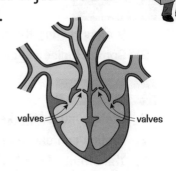

1) The valves (see p.30) in the heart can be damaged by heart attacks, infection or old age.

2) This may cause the valve to stiffen, so it won't open properly.

3) A valve may also become leaky — blood flows in both directions instead of just forward.

4) This means that blood doesn't flow around the body as well as normal.

5) Damaged valves may be replaced by biological valves — valves from humans or other mammals (e.g. cows or pigs). Or they can be replaced by mechanical valves — these are man-made valves.

6) Replacing a valve is less risky than a heart transplant but there can still be problems with blood clots.

valves ← → valves

Pity they can't fit me with an artificial brain before the exam...

You should know the advantages and disadvantages of the treatments here.

Q1   Suggest one disadvantage of treating coronary heart disease with an artificial heart.   [1 mark]

Health and Disease

First learn the <u>definition</u> of health. Then you can find out the many things that can cause <u>ill health</u>.

Diseases are a Major Cause of Ill Health

1) <u>Health</u> is the <u>state</u> of <u>physical</u> and <u>mental wellbeing</u>.
2) This means that both the <u>body</u> and <u>mind</u> are <u>well</u>.
3) Diseases are often responsible for causing <u>ill health</u>.
4) Diseases can be <u>communicable</u> or <u>non-communicable</u>:

Communicable diseases are sometimes called infectious diseases.

Communicable diseases

1) These are diseases that can <u>spread</u> from <u>person to person</u> or between <u>animals</u> and <u>people</u>.
2) Communicable diseases can be caused by <u>bacteria</u>, <u>viruses</u>, <u>parasites</u> or <u>fungi</u>.
3) <u>Measles</u> and <u>malaria</u> are examples of communicable diseases. See pages 43-45 for more.

Non-communicable diseases

1) These are diseases that <u>cannot spread</u> between people or between animals and people.
2) <u>Coronary heart disease</u> (see page 33) is an example of a non-communicable disease.

Different Types of Disease Can Interact

Sometimes a disease can cause <u>other</u> physical and mental health issues. Here are a few examples:

1) The <u>immune system</u> helps to fight off <u>pathogens</u> (see page 46). Some people have <u>problems</u> with their immune system. This makes them <u>more likely</u> to <u>suffer</u> from communicable diseases.

Pathogen is just the fancy term for a microorganism that can cause disease.

2) An <u>immune system reaction</u> (caused by a pathogen) may lead to an <u>allergic</u> reaction, such as a <u>skin rash</u>. Or it may worsen the symptoms of <u>asthma</u> for asthma sufferers.
3) <u>Viruses</u> infect <u>cells</u> in the body. This can lead to some types of <u>cancer</u>.
4) <u>Physical</u> health problems may also lead to <u>mental</u> health problems. For example, a person may become <u>depressed</u> if they can't carry out <u>everyday activities</u> because of <u>ill health</u>.

Other Factors Can Also Affect Your Health

1) A <u>poor diet</u> can affect your physical and mental health. A good diet is <u>balanced</u> and provides your body with <u>everything</u> it needs, in the <u>right amounts</u>.
2) Being constantly under <u>lots of stress</u> can lead to <u>poor health</u>.
3) Your <u>life situation</u> can affect your health. This is because it affects how easily you can <u>access medicine</u> or things that prevent you from <u>getting ill</u>. E.g. being able to buy <u>condoms</u> to prevent the <u>spread</u> of some sexually transmitted diseases.

If stress can affect your health, why do we have exams...

You really need to get the terms communicable and non-communicable disease into your head. They could come up in the exam and you'd be really sad if you didn't understand the question.

Q1　What is meant by 'health'?　　　　　　　　　　　　　　　　　　　　　[1 mark]

Risk Factors for Non-Communicable Diseases

Non-communicable diseases are linked to <u>risk factors</u>. There are lots of <u>examples</u> of risk factors on this page.

Risk Factors Increase Your Chance of Getting a Disease

1) Risk factors are things that are linked to an <u>increased chance</u> of getting a certain disease.

2) However, risk factors <u>don't mean</u> that someone <u>will</u> definitely get the disease.

3) They can be:
   - part of a person's <u>lifestyle</u> (for example, how much exercise they do),
   - substances in a person's <u>environment</u> (e.g. air pollution),
   - substances in a person's <u>body</u> (e.g. asbestos fibres in the lungs can cause cancer).

4) Many <u>non-communicable</u> diseases are caused by <u>several</u> risk factors that <u>interact</u> with each other.

5) Lifestyle factors can have different effects <u>locally</u>, <u>nationally</u> and <u>globally</u>.

> - <u>Globally</u>, non-communicable diseases are <u>more common</u> in developed countries.
>   This is because people in developed countries generally <u>earn more</u> and can buy <u>high-fat</u> food.
> - <u>Nationally</u>, cardiovascular disease, obesity and Type 2 diabetes are more common in <u>poorer</u> areas.
>   This is because people in <u>poorer areas</u> are <u>more likely</u> to smoke, have a poor diet and not exercise.
> - Your <u>individual choices</u> affect how common a disease is <u>locally</u>.

Some Risk Factors Can Cause a Disease Directly

1) Some risk factors are able to <u>directly cause</u> a disease. For example:

> - <u>Smoking</u> can cause <u>cardiovascular disease</u>, <u>lung disease</u> and <u>lung cancer</u>.
>   It damages the <u>walls</u> of <u>arteries</u> and the <u>lining</u> of the <u>lungs</u>.
> - <u>Obesity</u> may cause <u>Type 2 diabetes</u> by making the body
>   <u>less sensitive</u> or <u>resistant to</u> (not affected by) insulin (see p.62).
> - Drinking <u>too much alcohol</u> can damage the <u>brain</u> and the <u>liver</u>.
> - <u>Smoking</u> and drinking <u>alcohol</u> when <u>pregnant</u> can cause <u>health problems</u> for the <u>unborn baby</u>.
> - Cancer can be caused by <u>exposure</u> to certain <u>substances</u> or <u>radiation</u>. Things that cause cancer
>   are known as <u>carcinogens</u>. <u>Ionising radiation</u> (e.g. from X-rays) is an example of a <u>carcinogen</u>.

2) Some risk factors don't <u>directly cause</u> a disease.
   BUT there is a <u>correlation</u> (see p.9) between the risk factor and the disease.

3) For example, a <u>lack of exercise</u> and a <u>high fat diet</u> are risk factors for <u>cardiovascular disease</u>, but they can't cause the disease. It's the resulting <u>high cholesterol levels</u> (see p.33) that can <u>cause</u> it.

Non-Communicable Diseases Can Be Costly

1) <u>Tens of millions</u> of people around the world die from non-communicable diseases every year.
   People with these diseases may have a <u>lower quality of life</u> or a <u>shorter lifespan</u> — this is the <u>human cost</u>.

2) The <u>financial</u> cost of <u>researching</u> and <u>treating</u> these diseases is huge.

3) It can also be expensive for individuals if they have to <u>move</u> or <u>adapt their home</u> because of a disease.
   If a person has to give up work or if they die, then their family's <u>income</u> will be reduced.

4) A <u>reduction</u> in the number of people <u>able to work</u> can also affect a <u>country's economy</u>.

Best put down that cake and go for a run...

You might be asked to interpret data about risk factors. See p.9 for a few tips on what you can and can't say.

Q1   Give one type of risk factor that isn't part of a person's lifestyle.   [1 mark]

Cancer

The more we understand <u>cancer</u>, the better our chances of <u>avoiding</u> and <u>beating</u> it. Read on to find out more.

Cancer is Caused by Uncontrolled Cell Growth and Division

1) Changes in cells can lead to <u>uncontrolled</u> growth and division. This results in a <u>tumour</u> (a mass of cells).

2) Tumours can be <u>benign</u> or <u>malignant</u>:

> 1) <u>Benign</u> tumours are masses of <u>abnormal cells</u>.
> 2) They stay in <u>one place</u> (usually within a membrane).
> 3) They don't <u>invade</u> other parts of the body.
> 4) This type <u>isn't</u> normally dangerous, and the tumour <u>isn't</u> cancerous.

> 1) <u>Malignant</u> tumours spread to other parts of the body.
> 2) The cells can <u>break off</u> and travel in the <u>bloodstream</u>.
> 3) The cells <u>get into</u> healthy tissues and form <u>secondary tumours</u>.
> 4) Malignant tumours are <u>dangerous</u> and can be fatal — <u>they are cancers</u>.

Risk Factors Can Increase the Chance of Some Cancers

1) Scientists have identified <u>lots</u> of risk factors for cancers. For example:

LIFESTYLE FACTORS

- <u>Smoking</u> — Smoking is linked to <u>many types</u> of cancer.
- <u>Obesity</u> — Obesity has also been linked to <u>many different cancers</u>.
- <u>Viral infection</u> — Infection with some viruses can <u>increase</u> the chances of developing <u>certain types</u> of cancer.
- <u>UV exposure</u> — The Sun produces <u>UV radiation</u>. This radiation has been linked to an increased chance of developing skin cancer.

GENETIC FACTORS

- Genes are passed on (<u>inherited</u>) from <u>parent</u> to <u>offspring</u> — see page 67.
- Sometimes you can <u>inherit faulty genes</u> that make you <u>more likely</u> to get cancer.

2) People are now <u>more likely</u> to <u>survive</u> cancer. This is because:
- <u>Treatments</u> have improved.
- Doctors can diagnose cancer <u>earlier</u>.
- More people are being <u>screened</u> (tested) for cancer.
- People know more about the <u>risk factors</u> for cancer.

At least our rubbish summers reduce our UV exposure...

UV radiation can still reach us through the clouds, but we can reduce the risk, e.g. by wearing sun block.

Q1   What are tumours the result of?   [1 mark]

Q2   Give three lifestyle factors that can increase the risk of developing cancer.   [3 marks]

Plant Cell Organisation

Just like in animals, plant cells are also organised. Here are a few examples of plant <u>tissues</u> and <u>organs</u>.

Plant Cells Are Organised Into Tissues And Organs

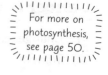

For more on photosynthesis, see page 50.

1) Plants are made of <u>organs</u>. These organs <u>work together</u> to make <u>organ systems</u>.

2) For example, <u>stems</u>, <u>roots</u> and <u>leaves</u> are all plant organs. They work together to <u>transport</u> (carry) substances around the plant.

3) Plant <u>organs</u> are made of <u>tissues</u>. Examples of plant tissues are:

- <u>Epidermal tissue</u> — this <u>covers</u> the whole plant.
- <u>Palisade mesophyll tissue</u> — this is the part of the leaf where most <u>photosynthesis</u> happens.
- <u>Spongy mesophyll tissue</u> — this is the part of the leaf that has big <u>air spaces</u>. This allows <u>gases</u> to <u>diffuse</u> in and out of cells.
- <u>Xylem</u> and <u>phloem</u> — these transport things like <u>water</u>, <u>mineral ions</u> and <u>food</u> around the roots, stems and leaves (see next page).
- <u>Meristem tissue</u> — this is found at the <u>growing tips</u> of <u>shoots</u> and <u>roots</u>.

A merry stem.

Leaves Contain Epidermal, Mesophyll, Xylem and Phloem Tissue

1) The leaf is where <u>photosynthesis</u> and <u>gas exchange</u> happens in a plant.

2) The <u>structures</u> of the tissues in a leaf are <u>related</u> to their <u>function</u>:

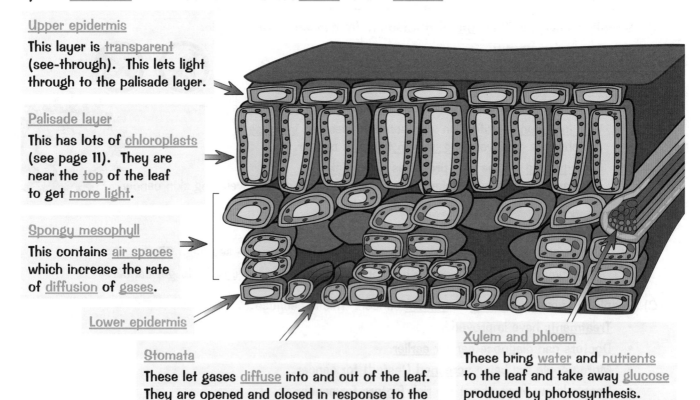

Upper epidermis

This layer is <u>transparent</u> (see-through). This lets light through to the palisade layer.

Palisade layer

This has lots of <u>chloroplasts</u> (see page 11). They are near the <u>top</u> of the leaf to get <u>more light</u>.

Spongy mesophyll

This contains <u>air spaces</u> which increase the rate of <u>diffusion</u> of <u>gases</u>.

Lower epidermis

Stomata

These let gases <u>diffuse</u> into and out of the leaf. They are opened and closed in response to the <u>environment</u>. This is controlled by <u>guard cells</u>.

Xylem and phloem

These bring <u>water</u> and <u>nutrients</u> to the leaf and take away <u>glucose</u> produced by photosynthesis. They also <u>support</u> the leaf.

Plant cell organisation — millions of members worldwide...

There are a lot of weird names here, so make sure you spend plenty of time on this page.
Try drawing your own leaf diagram. Label it with the different tissues and describe each type of tissue.

Q1   Where is meristem tissue found in a plant?   [1 mark]

Transpiration and Translocation

This page is about how things get <u>moved</u> around a plant so that all the right stuff ends up in the <u>right place</u>.

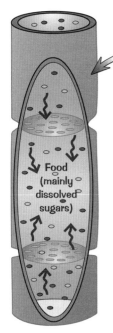

Phloem Tubes Transport Food

1) Phloem tubes are made of <u>elongated</u> (stretched out) <u>living cells</u>.

2) There are <u>end walls</u> between the cells.
   These have <u>pores</u> (small holes) to allow <u>cell sap</u> to flow through.

3) Plants make <u>food substances</u> (e.g. dissolved <u>sugars</u>) in their <u>leaves</u>.

4) Phloem tubes transport these <u>food substances</u> around the plant for <u>immediate use</u> or for <u>storage</u>.

5) The transport goes in <u>both directions</u>.

6) This process is called <u>translocation</u>.

Cell sap is a liquid that's made up of the substances being transported and water.

Xylem Tubes Take Water Up

1) Xylem tubes are made of <u>dead cells</u>.

2) The cells are joined together with a <u>hole</u> down the <u>middle</u>.

3) There are no <u>end walls</u> between the cells.

4) The cells are <u>strengthened</u> with a material called <u>lignin</u>.

5) Xylem tubes carry <u>water</u> and <u>mineral ions</u> from the <u>roots</u> to the <u>stem</u> and <u>leaves</u>.

6) The movement of water from the <u>roots</u>, through the <u>xylem</u> and out of the <u>leaves</u> is called the <u>transpiration stream</u> (see below).

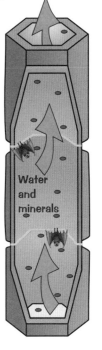

Water and minerals

Transpiration is the Loss of Water from the Plant

1) Transpiration is caused by <u>evaporation</u> and <u>diffusion</u> of water from a plant's surface (mainly the leaves).

2) Here's how it happens:

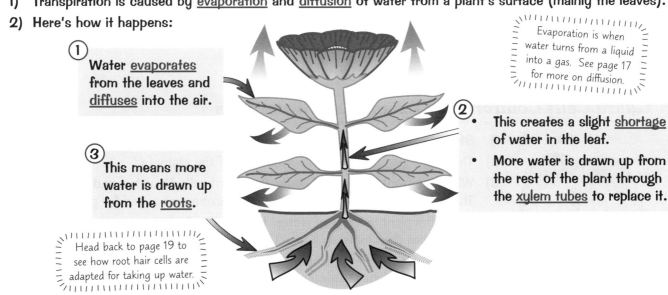

① Water <u>evaporates</u> from the leaves and <u>diffuses</u> into the air.

Evaporation is when water turns from a liquid into a gas. See page 17 for more on diffusion.

② • This creates a slight <u>shortage</u> of water in the leaf.
   • More water is drawn up from the rest of the plant through the <u>xylem tubes</u> to replace it.

③ This means more water is drawn up from the <u>roots</u>.

Head back to page 19 to see how root hair cells are adapted for taking up water.

3) There's a constant <u>stream of water</u> through the plant. This is called the <u>transpiration stream</u>.

Don't let revision stress you out — just go with the phloem...

Phl<u>oe</u>m transports substances in b<u>o</u>th directions, but xylem only transports things upwards — x<u>y</u> to the sk<u>y</u>.

Q1   Describe the structure of xylem.   [3 marks]

Transpiration and Stomata

Sorry, more on transpiration. But then it's quickly through stomata and out of the other end of the topic.

Transpiration Rate is Affected by Four Main Things:

1) Air Flow

- The more windy it is, the faster transpiration happens.
- Fast moving air means that water vapour around the leaf is swept away.
- This means there's a higher concentration of water vapour inside the leaf compared to outside. So water will diffuse out of the leaf more quickly.

2) Temperature

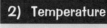

- The warmer it is, the faster transpiration happens.
- This is because the water particles have more energy. So they evaporate and diffuse out of the stomata faster.

Many factors affect transpiration rate by affecting the rate of diffusion of water. There's more about diffusion on page 17.

3) Humidity

- If the air is humid there's a lot of water in it already.
- This means there isn't much of a difference between the inside and the outside of the leaf.
- This means that diffusion will not happen very fast.
- The drier the air around a leaf, the faster transpiration happens.

4) Light Intensity

- The brighter the light, the greater the transpiration rate.
- Photosynthesis can't happen in the dark, so stomata begin to close as it gets darker.
- When the stomata are closed, very little water can escape.

Guard Cells Control Gas Exchange and Water Loss

guard cell

stoma
(plural — stomata)

1) Stomata are surrounded by guard cells.
2) These change shape to control the size of the stomata.
3) When the plant has lots of water the guard cells fill with it and get fat. This makes the stomata open so gases can be exchanged for photosynthesis.
4) When the plant is short of water, the guard cells lose water and become floppy. This makes the stomata close. This helps stop too much water vapour escaping.
5) There are usually more stomata on the bottoms of leaves than on the tops. This is because the lower surface is cooler — so less water gets lost.

I say stomaaarta, you say stomaaayta...

You can peel off the epidermis of a leaf and count the stomata using a microscope (see p.13). It's thrilling stuff.

Q1   Explain how low light intensity affects the rate of transpiration.   [3 marks]

Revision Questions for Topic B2

Well, that's Topic B2 finished. Now it's time for *the* greatest quiz on Earth. Please hold your excitement in.

* Try these questions and tick off each one when you get it right.
* When you've done all the questions under a heading and are completely happy with it, tick it off.

Cell Organisation (p.24) ☑

1) What is a tissue? ☐
2) Explain what is meant by the term 'organ system'. ☐

The Role of Enzymes and Food Tests (p.25-28) ☑

3) Why can enzymes be described as catalysts? ☐
4) Why do enzymes only usually catalyse one reaction? ☐
5) What does it mean when an enzyme has been 'denatured'? ☐
6) Describe how you could investigate the effect of pH on the rate of amylase activity. ☐
7) List the three places where amylase is made in the human body. ☐
8) What is the role of lipases? ☐
9) Where is bile stored? ☐
10) Name the solution that you would use to test for the presence of proteins in a food sample. ☐

The Lungs and Circulatory System (p.29-32) ☐

11) Where does gas exchange happen in the lungs? ☐
12) Name the four chambers of the heart. ☐
13) Why does the heart have valves? ☐
14) How is the resting heart rate controlled in a healthy heart? ☐
15) How are arteries adapted to carry blood away from the heart? ☐
16) Why do red blood cells not have a nucleus? ☐

Diseases and Risk Factors (p.33-37) ☐

17) Give two advantages and two disadvantages of statins. ☐
18) What is the difference between biological and mechanical replacement heart valves? ☐
19) What is a non-communicable disease? ☐
20) Give an example of different types of disease interacting in the body. ☐
21) What is meant by a risk factor for a disease? ☐
22) Which type of tumour is cancerous — benign or malignant? ☐

Plant Cell Organisation and Transport (p.38-40) ☐

23) List the tissues that make up a leaf. ☐
24) Explain how the structure of the palisade layer in a leaf is related to its function. ☐
25) What is the function of phloem tubes? ☐
26) What is transpiration? ☐
27) List the four main things that affect transpiration. ☐
28) Name the type of cell that helps open and close stomata. ☐

Communicable Disease

If you're hoping I'll ease you gently into this new topic... no such luck. Straight on to the baddies of biology.

There Are Several Types of Pathogen

1) Pathogens are <u>microorganisms</u> that enter the body and cause <u>disease</u>.
2) They cause <u>communicable</u> (infectious) diseases.
3) Communicable diseases are diseases that can <u>spread</u> (see p.35).
4) Both <u>plants</u> and <u>animals</u> can be infected by pathogens.
5) There are <u>four main types</u> of pathogens:

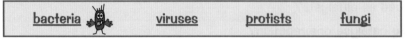

<u>bacteria</u>   <u>viruses</u>   <u>protists</u>   <u>fungi</u>

Pathogens Can Be Spread in Different Ways

Here are a few ways that pathogens can be <u>spread</u>:

1) <u>WATER</u> — Some pathogens can be picked up by <u>drinking</u> or <u>bathing</u> in <u>dirty water</u>.
2) <u>AIR</u> — Pathogens can be carried in the <u>air</u> and can then be <u>breathed in</u>.
    Some pathogens are carried in the air in <u>droplets</u> made when you <u>cough</u> or <u>sneeze</u>.
3) <u>DIRECT CONTACT</u> — Some pathogens can be picked up by <u>touching</u> surfaces they're on (e.g. the skin).

The Spread of Disease Can Be Reduced or Prevented

There are things that we can do to <u>reduce</u> or <u>prevent</u> the spread of disease, such as...

① <u>Being hygienic</u> (clean) — For example, <u>washing your hands</u> before making food
can stop you <u>spreading pathogens</u> onto the food and infecting a person who <u>eats</u> it.

② <u>Destroying vectors</u> — Vectors are <u>organisms</u> that <u>spread disease</u>.
Killing them helps to <u>stop</u> the disease from being passed on.
Vectors that are <u>insects</u> can be killed using <u>insecticides</u>.
Their <u>habitats</u> can also be destroyed so that they can't <u>breed</u>.

③ <u>Isolating infected individuals</u> — If you keep someone who has a communicable
disease away from other people, it <u>prevents</u> them from <u>passing it on</u> to anyone else.

④ <u>Vaccination</u> (see page 47) — Vaccinations can <u>stop</u> people and animals from
<u>getting</u> a communicable disease. This also stops them <u>passing it on</u> to others.

Coughs and sneezes spread diseases...

Yuck, lots of nasties out there that can cause disease. Plants need to be worried too, as you'll find out.

Q1   Name two types of pathogen.   [2 marks]

Q2   Suggest why it is important for chefs to wash their hands before cooking.   [1 mark]

Bacterial Diseases

First up from the <u>pathogen</u> hall of fame are... <u>bacteria</u>.

Bacteria are Very Small Living Cells

1) Bacteria <u>reproduce rapidly</u> inside your body.
2) They can make you <u>feel ill</u> by <u>producing toxins</u> (poisons).
3) Toxins <u>damage</u> your <u>cells and tissues</u>.

Salmonella and Gonorrhoea are Bacterial Diseases

SALMONELLA

1) <u>Salmonella</u> is a type of <u>bacteria</u>. It causes <u>food poisoning</u>.
2) Infected people can suffer from <u>fever</u>, <u>stomach cramps</u>, <u>vomiting</u> and <u>diarrhoea</u>. Nice.
3) These symptoms are caused by <u>toxins</u> from the bacteria.
4) You can get *Salmonella* food poisoning by:
   - Eating <u>food</u> that's got *Salmonella* bacteria in it already, e.g. eating chicken that caught the disease whilst it was alive.
   - Eating food that has been <u>made</u> where the bacteria is present, e.g. in an <u>unclean kitchen</u> or on the <u>hands</u> of the person making the food.
5) In the UK, most <u>poultry</u> (e.g. chickens and turkeys) are given a <u>vaccination</u> against *Salmonella*. This is to control the <u>spread</u> of the disease.

GONORRHOEA

1) Gonorrhoea is caused by <u>bacteria</u>.
2) <u>Gonorrhoea</u> is a <u>sexually transmitted disease</u> (STD).
3) STDs are passed on by <u>sexual contact</u>, e.g. having unprotected sex.
4) A person with gonorrhoea will get <u>pain</u> when they <u>urinate</u> (wee). Another symptom is a thick yellow or green <u>discharge</u> (fluid) from the <u>vagina</u> or the <u>penis</u>.
5) Gonorrhoea <u>used to be treated</u> with an <u>antibiotic</u> called <u>penicillin</u>. There are now <u>new strains</u> (types) of gonorrhoea that are <u>resistant</u> to (not killed by) penicillin. So this antibiotic <u>doesn't work</u> anymore.
6) To prevent the <u>spread</u> of gonorrhoea:
   - people can be treated with <u>other antibiotics</u>,
   - people should use <u>barrier methods</u> of contraception (see page 65), such as <u>condoms</u>.

I knew that old sandwich was 💀...

Once bacteria start reproducing inside your body, they cause lots of problems and make you feel ill.

Q1   Give two symptoms of *Salmonella*. [2 marks]

Q2   What has made it harder to treat gonorrhoea? [1 mark]

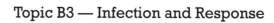

Viral Diseases

Viruses may be teeny tiny but there are lots of diseases caused by them.

Viruses Are Not Cells — They're Much Smaller

1) Viruses reproduce rapidly inside your body.
2) They live inside your cells.
3) Inside your cells, they make lots of copies of themselves.
4) The cells will usually then burst, releasing all the new viruses.
5) This cell damage is what makes you feel ill.

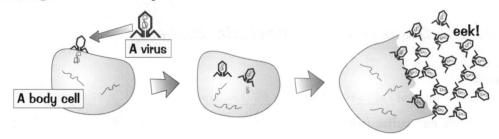

Different Viruses Cause Different Diseases, Such as...

Measles

1) Measles is a viral disease. It is spread by droplets from an infected person's sneeze or cough.
2) People with measles develop a red skin rash. They'll also show signs of a fever (a high temperature).
3) Measles can be very serious. People can die from measles if there are complications (problems).
4) Because of this, most people are vaccinated against measles when they're young.

HIV

1) HIV is a virus spread by sexual contact or by exchanging bodily fluids (e.g. blood). This can happen when people share needles when taking drugs.
2) To start with, HIV causes flu-like symptoms for a few weeks.
3) After that the person doesn't usually have any symptoms for several years.
4) HIV can be controlled with antiretroviral drugs. These stop the virus copying itself in the body.
5) If it's not controlled, the virus attacks the immune cells (see page 46).
6) If the body's immune system is badly damaged, it can't cope with other infections or cancers. At this stage, the virus is known as late stage HIV infection or AIDS.

Tobacco mosaic virus

1) Tobacco mosaic virus (TMV) is a virus that affects many species of plants, e.g. tomatoes.
2) It causes parts of the leaves to become discoloured. This gives them a mosaic pattern.
3) The discoloured leaves have less chlorophyll to absorb light (see p.50).
4) This means less photosynthesis happens in the leaves, so the plant can't make enough food to grow.

I've heard this page has gone viral...

The examiner could grill you on any one of these viral diseases, so make sure you know them all inside out.

Q1   Give one way that HIV can be spread.   [1 mark]

Fungal and Protist Diseases

Sorry — I'm afraid there are some more diseases to learn about here...

Rose Black Spot is a Fungal Disease

1) Rose black spot is a disease caused by a fungus.
2) The fungus causes purple or black spots on the leaves of rose plants.
3) The leaves can then turn yellow and drop off.
4) This means that less photosynthesis can happen, so the plant doesn't grow very well.
5) It is spread in water or by the wind.
6) Gardeners can treat the disease using fungicides (chemicals that kill fungi).
7) They can also strip the affected leaves off the plant.
8) These leaves then need to be destroyed so that the fungus can't spread to other rose plants.

Malaria is a Disease Caused by a Protist

1) Malaria is caused by a protist.
2) Part of the protist's life cycle takes place inside the mosquito.
3) The mosquitoes are vectors. They help spread malaria like this...

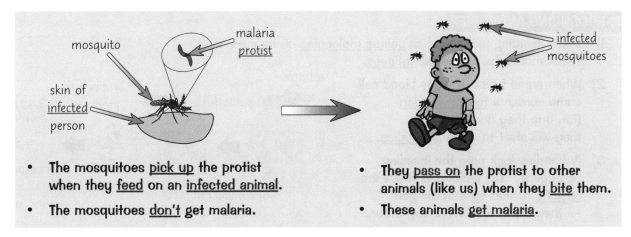

mosquito

malaria protist

skin of infected person

infected mosquitoes

- The mosquitoes pick up the protist when they feed on an infected animal.
- The mosquitoes don't get malaria.

- They pass on the protist to other animals (like us) when they bite them.
- These animals get malaria.

4) Malaria causes repeating episodes of fever. People can die from malaria.
5) The spread of malaria can be reduced by stopping the mosquitoes from breeding.
6) People can be protected from mosquito bites using mosquito nets.

Rose black spot — coming to a plant near you...

OK, I promise, that's it. No more diseases to learn about in this topic. You may be sick of them already (joke), but here are some questions to do before you go onto the next page.

Q1 Give two ways rose black spot can be treated so it doesn't spread to other plants. [2 marks]

Q2 What type of pathogen causes malaria? [1 mark]

Fighting Disease

The human body has some pretty neat features when it comes to <u>fighting disease</u>.

Your Body Has a Pretty Good Defence System

The human body has got features that stop a lot of nasties getting inside. For example:

1) The <u>skin</u> — It <u>stops pathogens</u> getting <u>inside</u> you. It also <u>releases substances</u> that <u>kill pathogens</u>.
2) <u>Nose hairs</u> — They <u>trap</u> particles that could contain pathogens.
3) <u>Mucus</u> (<u>snot</u>) — The <u>trachea</u> and <u>bronchi</u> (airways — see page 29) release <u>mucus</u> to <u>trap</u> pathogens.
4) <u>Cilia</u> (hair-like structures) — The <u>trachea</u> and <u>bronchi</u> are lined with <u>cilia</u>.
   They <u>move</u> the <u>mucus</u> up to the back of the throat where it can be <u>swallowed</u>.
5) <u>Stomach acid</u> — The stomach makes <u>hydrochloric acid</u>. This <u>kills pathogens</u> in the stomach.

Your Immune System Can Attack Pathogens

1) If pathogens do make it into your body, your <u>immune system</u> kicks in to <u>destroy</u> them.
2) The most important part of your immune system is the <u>white blood cells</u>.
3) When they come across an invading pathogen they have <u>three lines of attack</u>:

1) PHAGOCYTOSIS

White blood cells can <u>engulf</u> (surround) pathogens and <u>digest</u> them. This is called <u>phagocytosis</u>.

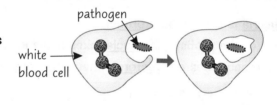

2) PRODUCING ANTIBODIES

1) Every invading pathogen has <u>unique molecules</u> on its surface. These molecules are called <u>antigens</u>.

2) When some types of white blood cell come across a <u>foreign antigen</u> (i.e. one they don't know), they will start to make <u>antibodies</u>.

3) Antibodies <u>lock onto</u> the invading pathogens. The antibodies made are <u>specific</u> to that type of antigen — they won't lock on to any others.

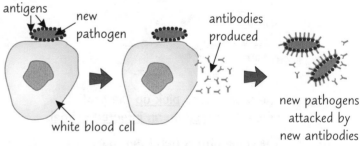

4) The antibodies make sure the pathogens can be <u>found</u> and <u>destroyed</u> by other white blood cells.

5) If the person is infected with the <u>same pathogen</u> again, the white blood cells will <u>rapidly</u> make the antibodies to kill it. This means the person is <u>naturally immune</u> to that pathogen and <u>won't get ill</u>.

3) PRODUCING ANTITOXINS These <u>stop toxins</u> produced by the <u>invading bacteria</u> from working.

Fight disease — blow your nose with boxing gloves...

So there are three ways that white blood cells kill those pesky pathogens. Make sure you know them all.

Q1   Explain one way that the bronchi are adapted to defend against the entry of pathogens.   [2 marks]

Fighting Disease — Vaccination

Vaccinations mean we don't always have to treat a disease — we can stop the disease in the first place.

Vaccination — Protects from Future Infections

1) Vaccinations involve injecting small amounts of dead or inactive pathogens into the body.

2) These pathogens have antigens on their surface.

3) The antigens cause your white blood cells to produce antibodies to attack the pathogens.

4) If you're infected with the same pathogen later, your white blood cells quickly produce lots of antibodies.

5) These antibodies kill the pathogen so you don't become ill. Cool.

6) For example, children are vaccinated to protect them against the measles virus...

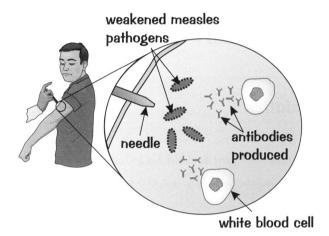

weakened measles pathogens

needle

antibodies produced

white blood cell

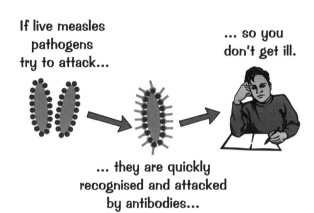

If live measles pathogens try to attack...

... so you don't get ill.

... they are quickly recognised and attacked by antibodies...

There are Pros and Cons of Vaccination

PROS

① Vaccines have helped to control lots of communicable diseases that used to be common in the UK, e.g. polio.

② 1) A big outbreak of a disease is called an epidemic.
2) Epidemics can be prevented if lots of people are vaccinated.
3) That way, even the people who aren't vaccinated are unlikely to catch the disease because there are fewer people able to pass it on.

CONS

① Vaccines don't always work — sometimes they don't give you immunity.

② You can sometimes have a bad reaction to a vaccine (e.g. swelling or a fever).

Prevention is better than cure...

Although vaccinations aren't perfect, it's better to have a vaccine than risk catching a nasty disease.

Q1   What do vaccinations cause white blood cells to produce?   [1 mark]

Fighting Disease — Drugs

Well knock me down with a feather — it looks like there are even more ways of fighting disease.

Some Drugs Get Rid of Symptoms — Others Cure the Problem

1) Some drugs help to get rid of the symptoms of a disease, e.g. painkillers reduce pain.
2) But these drugs don't kill the pathogens that cause the disease.
3) Antibiotics (e.g. penicillin) kill bacteria.
4) Different antibiotics kill different types of bacteria, so it's important to be treated with the right one.
5) The use of antibiotics has greatly reduced the number of deaths from communicable diseases caused by bacteria.
6) Antibiotics don't destroy viruses (e.g. flu viruses).
7) Viruses reproduce using your own body cells.
   This makes it very difficult to develop drugs that destroy the virus without killing the body's cells.

Bacteria Can Become Resistant to Antibiotics

1) Bacteria can mutate (change).
2) Some of these mutations cause the bacteria to become resistant to (not be killed by) an antibiotic.
3) Resistant strains (types) of bacteria, e.g. MRSA, have increased as a result of natural selection (see page 75).

Many Drugs First Came From Plants

1) Plants produce chemicals to defend themselves against pests and pathogens.
2) Some of these chemicals can be used as drugs to treat human diseases or relieve symptoms.
3) A lot of our medicines were found by studying plants used in old-fashioned cures. For example:

ASPIRIN   It's used as a painkiller. It was made from a chemical found in willow.

DIGITALIS   It's used to treat heart conditions. It was made from a chemical found in foxgloves.

4) Some drugs have come from microorganisms. For example:

PENICILLIN
- Alexander Fleming found that a type of mould (called *Penicillium*) makes a substance that kills bacteria.
- This substance is called penicillin.
- Penicillin is used as an antibiotic.

5) These days, new drugs are made by the pharmaceutical industry (companies that make and sell drugs).
6) The drugs are made by chemists in labs.
7) The process of making the drugs still might start with a chemical taken from a plant.

Ahh...Ahh... Ahhhhh Chooooooooo — urghh, this page is catching...

Once a drug is made it has to be tested. And guess what — you're about to find out more about it...

Q1   Which type of pathogen do antibiotics kill?   [1 mark]

Topic B3 — Infection and Response

Developing Drugs

Before drugs can be given to people like you and me, they have to go through a lot of tests.
This is what usually happens...

There Are Different Stages in the Development of New Drugs

1) Once a possible drug has been discovered, it needs to be developed.
2) This involves preclinical and clinical testing.

Preclinical testing:

1) Drugs are first tested on human cells and tissues in the lab.
2) Next the drug is tested on live animals. This is to find out:
   - its efficacy (whether the drug works and has the effect you're looking for),
   - its toxicity (how harmful it is and whether it has any side effects),
   - its dosage (the concentration of the drug that works best and how often it should be taken).

Clinical testing:

1) If the drug passes the tests on animals then it's tested on human volunteers in a clinical trial.
2) First, the drug is tested on healthy volunteers.
3) This is to make sure it doesn't have any harmful side effects when the body is working normally.
4) At the start of the trial, a very low dose of the drug is given. This dose is increased little by little.
5) If these results are good, the drugs can be tested on patients (people with the illness).
6) The optimum dose is found — this is the dose of drug that is the most effective and has few side effects.
7) To test how well the drug works, patients are put into two groups...

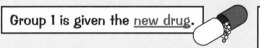

| Group 1 is given the new drug. | Group 2 is given a placebo (a substance that's like the drug being tested but doesn't do anything). |

8) The doctor compares the two groups of patients to see if the drug makes a real difference.
9) Clinical trials are blind — the patient doesn't know whether they're getting the drug or the placebo.
10) In fact, they're often double-blind — neither the patient nor the doctor knows who's taken the drug and who's taken the placebo until all the results have been gathered.
11) The results of these tests aren't published until they've been through peer review. This helps to prevent false claims.

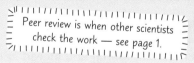

Peer review is when other scientists check the work — see page 1.

Drugs are tested — just like a GCSE student...

There's a lot of information to take in on this page, but just read it through slowly. You might have to go over it a few times to get it stuck in your head. Then you can *test* yourself by having a go at these questions...

Q1   What is meant by the efficacy of a drug?   [1 mark]

Q2   Why do clinical trials of a new drug begin with healthy volunteers?   [1 mark]

Photosynthesis

First, the photosynthesis equation. Then there are some more bits 'n' bobs you should know...

Photosynthesis Produces Glucose Using Light

1) Photosynthesis uses energy to change carbon dioxide and water into glucose and oxygen.
2) It takes place in chloroplasts in plant cells.
3) Chloroplasts contain chlorophyll that absorbs light.
4) Energy is transferred to the chloroplasts from the environment by light.
5) Photosynthesis is an endothermic reaction.
   This means that energy is transferred from the environment during the reaction.
6) You need to learn the word equation for photosynthesis:

$$\text{carbon dioxide} + \text{water} \xrightarrow{\text{light}} \text{glucose} + \text{oxygen}$$

7) You also need to know the chemical symbols for the substances involved in photosynthesis:

carbon dioxide: CO_2 water: H_2O glucose: $C_6H_{12}O_6$ oxygen: O_2

Plants Use Glucose in Five Main Ways...

1)   For respiration
- This transfers energy from glucose (see p.53).
- This allows the plants to change the rest of the glucose into other useful substances.

2)   For making cell walls
Glucose is changed into cellulose for making strong plant cell walls (see p.11).

3)   For making amino acids
- Glucose is combined with nitrate ions to make amino acids. Nitrate ions are absorbed from the soil.
- Amino acids are used to make proteins.

4)   Stored as oils or fats
Glucose is turned into lipids (fats and oils) for storing in seeds.

5)   Stored as starch
- Glucose is turned into starch and stored in roots, stems and leaves.
- Plants can use this starch when photosynthesis isn't happening.
- Starch is insoluble (it can't be dissolved).
- Being insoluble makes starch much better for storing than glucose.
  This is because a cell with lots of glucose in would draw in loads of water and swell up.

I'm working on sunshine — woah oh...

You've just got to learn the whole of this page I'm afraid. It'll help the rest of the topic make sense.

Q1   Name the products of photosynthesis.   [2 marks]

The Rate of Photosynthesis

The rate of photosynthesis can be affected by a few different things. Read on for excitement...

The Rate of Photosynthesis is Affected by Light, Temperature and CO_2

1) The rate of photosynthesis is affected by intensity of light (how bright the light is), concentration of CO_2 and temperature.
2) Any of these things can become the limiting factor of photosynthesis.
3) A limiting factor is something that stops photosynthesis from happening any faster.
4) Chlorophyll can also be a limiting factor of photosynthesis.

- The amount of chlorophyll in a plant can be affected by disease.
- It can also be affected by changes in the environment, such as a lack of nutrients.
- These factors can cause chloroplasts to become damaged or to not make enough chlorophyll.
- This means they can't absorb as much light. The rate of photosynthesis is reduced.

Three Important Graphs for Rate of Photosynthesis

1) Not Enough Light Slows Down the Rate of Photosynthesis

1) At first, the more light there is, the faster photosynthesis happens.
2) This means the rate of photosynthesis depends on the amount of light. Light is the limiting factor.
3) After a certain point the graph flattens out. Here photosynthesis won't go any faster — even if you increase the light intensity.
4) This is because light is no longer the limiting factor. Now it's either the temperature or the amount of carbon dioxide that's the limiting factor.

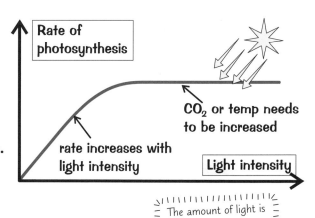

Rate of photosynthesis

CO_2 or temp needs to be increased

rate increases with light intensity

Light intensity

The amount of light is called light intensity.

2) Too Little Carbon Dioxide Also Slows it Down

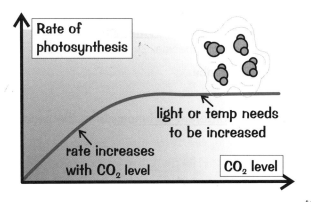

Rate of photosynthesis

light or temp needs to be increased

rate increases with CO_2 level

CO_2 level

1) The more carbon dioxide (CO_2) there is, the faster photosynthesis happens.
2) This means the amount of CO_2 is the limiting factor.
3) After a certain point, photosynthesis won't go any faster because CO_2 is no longer the limiting factor.
4) If there's plenty of light and carbon dioxide then it must be the temperature that's the limiting factor.

The Rate of Photosynthesis

3) The Temperature has to be Just Right

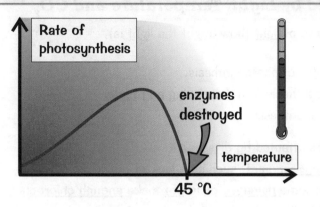

1) Usually, if the temperature is the limiting factor it's because it's too low.
2) This is because the enzymes (see page 25) needed for photosynthesis work more slowly at low temperatures.
3) But if the plant gets too hot, photosynthesis won't happen at all.
4) This is because the enzymes are damaged if the temperature's too high (over about 45 °C).

Oxygen Production Shows the Rate of Photosynthesis

PRACTICAL

Pondweed can be used to measure the effect of light intensity on the rate of photosynthesis.

Here's how the experiment works:

1) A ruler is used to measure a set distance from the pondweed.
2) A light is placed at that distance.
3) The pondweed is left to photosynthesise for a set amount of time.
4) As it photosynthesises, the oxygen released will collect in the capillary tube.
5) At the end of the experiment, the syringe is used to draw the gas bubble in the tube up alongside a ruler.

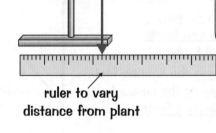
ruler to vary distance from plant

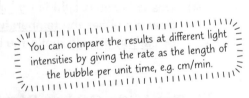

6) The length of the gas bubble is measured.

You can compare the results at different light intensities by giving the rate as the length of the bubble per unit time, e.g. cm/min.

7) The length of the gas bubble tells you how much oxygen has been produced during that amount of time. This means that the longer the gas bubble, the faster the rate of photosynthesis.
8) For this experiment, any variables that could affect the results should be controlled. E.g. the temperature and the time the pondweed is left to photosynthesise.
9) The experiment is repeated twice with the lamp at the same distance.
10) The mean length of the gas bubble is calculated.
11) Then the whole experiment is repeated with the light source at different distances from the pondweed.

Don't blame it on the sunshine, don't blame it on the CO_2...

...don't blame it on the temperature, blame it on the plant. Nothing like another song to help you revise.

Q1   Give four factors that affect the rate of photosynthesis.   [4 marks]

Topic B4 — Bioenergetics

Respiration and Metabolism

You need <u>energy</u> to keep your body going. Energy comes from <u>food</u>, and it's <u>transferred</u> by <u>respiration</u>.

Respiration is NOT "Breathing In and Out"

1) <u>All living things respire</u>.
2) <u>Respiration</u> is the process of <u>transferring energy</u> from the <u>breakdown of glucose</u> (a sugar).
3) Respiration goes on in <u>every cell</u> in your body <u>all the time</u>.
4) The energy transferred from respiration is used for <u>all living processes</u> (everything a cell needs to do).

> **RESPIRATION** is the process of <u>TRANSFERRING ENERGY</u>
> <u>FROM GLUCOSE</u>, which goes on <u>IN EVERY CELL</u>.

5) Respiration is <u>exothermic</u>. This means it <u>transfers energy</u> to the <u>environment</u>.

Respiration Transfers Energy for All Kinds of Things

Here are <u>three examples</u> of how organisms <u>use</u> the <u>energy</u> transferred by respiration:

1) To build up <u>larger molecules</u> from <u>smaller</u> ones (see below).
2) In animals, to <u>move</u> about.
3) In <u>mammals</u> and <u>birds</u>, to keep warm.

Metabolism is ALL the Chemical Reactions in an Organism

1) In a <u>cell</u> there are <u>lots</u> of <u>chemical reactions</u> happening <u>all the time</u>.
2) These reactions are controlled by <u>enzymes</u>.

There's more about enzymes on page 25.

3) In some of these reactions, <u>larger molecules</u> are <u>made</u> from smaller ones. For example:

> • Lots of small <u>glucose</u> (sugar) molecules are <u>joined together</u> in reactions to form:
>   • <u>starch</u> (a storage molecule in plant cells),
>   • <u>glycogen</u> (a storage molecule in animal cells),
>   • <u>cellulose</u> (a component of plant cell walls).
> • <u>Lipid</u> molecules are each made from <u>one molecule</u> of <u>glycerol</u> and <u>three fatty acids</u>.
> • <u>Glucose</u> is combined with <u>nitrate ions</u> to make <u>amino acids</u>. These are then made into <u>proteins</u>.

4) In other reactions, larger molecules are <u>broken down</u> into smaller ones. For example:

> • <u>Glucose</u> is broken down in <u>respiration</u>.
>   Respiration transfers energy to power <u>all</u> the reactions in the body that <u>make molecules</u>.
> • <u>Excess protein</u> is <u>broken down</u> in a <u>reaction</u> to produce <u>urea</u>. Urea is then <u>excreted</u> in <u>urine</u>.

5) The <u>sum</u> (total) of <u>all</u> of the <u>reactions</u> that happen in a <u>cell</u> or the <u>body</u> is called its <u>metabolism</u>.

Excreted is just a fancy word for 'released from the body'.

Don't stop respirin' — hold onto that feelin'...

Isn't it strange to think that each individual living cell in your body is respiring every second of every day.

Q1   Give two examples of how animals use the energy transferred by respiration.   [2 marks]

Q2   What is metabolism?   [1 mark]

Aerobic and Anaerobic Respiration

There are two types of respiration, don't you know...

Aerobic Respiration Needs Plenty of Oxygen

1) Aerobic respiration is respiration using oxygen.
2) Aerobic respiration goes on all the time in plants and animals.
3) Most of the reactions in aerobic respiration happen inside mitochondria (see page 11).
4) You need to learn the overall word equation for respiration:

$$\text{glucose} + \text{oxygen} \longrightarrow \text{carbon dioxide} + \text{water}$$

5) You also need to know the chemical symbols for the substances involved:

glucose: $C_6H_{12}O_6$ oxygen: O_2 carbon dioxide: CO_2 water: H_2O

Anaerobic Respiration is Used if There's Not Enough Oxygen

1) When you do hard exercise, your body sometimes can't supply enough oxygen to your muscles.
2) When this happens, they start doing anaerobic respiration as well as aerobic respiration.
3) Anaerobic respiration is the incomplete breakdown of glucose (the glucose isn't broken down properly).
4) Here's the word equation for anaerobic respiration in muscle cells:

$$\text{glucose} \longrightarrow \text{lactic acid}$$

5) Anaerobic respiration does not transfer anywhere near as much energy as aerobic respiration.
6) This is because the glucose has not combined with oxygen like it does in aerobic respiration.
7) The posh way of saying this is that the oxidation of glucose is not complete.

Anaerobic Respiration in Plants and Yeast is Slightly Different

1) Plants and yeast cells can respire without oxygen too.
2) Here is the word equation for anaerobic respiration in plants and yeast cells:

$$\text{glucose} \longrightarrow \text{ethanol} + \text{carbon dioxide}$$

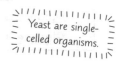

Yeast are single-celled organisms.

3) Anaerobic respiration in yeast cells is called fermentation.
4) In the food and drinks industry, fermentation by yeast is of great value.
5) It's used to make bread. It's the carbon dioxide from fermentation that makes bread rise.
6) It's used to make alcoholic drinks (beer and wine).
   It's the fermentation process that produces alcohol.

I'd like a ham and fermentation sandwich please... yum

Fermentation is a really important process because of its use in making wine and beer, and bread.

Q1   Give the word equation for aerobic respiration.   [2 marks]

Q2   What is the process of anaerobic respiration in yeast called?   [1 mark]

Exercise

When you exercise, your body responds in different ways to get enough energy to your cells.

When You Exercise You Respire More

1) Muscles need energy from respiration to contract (shorten).

2) When you exercise, some of your muscles contract more often.
    This means you need more energy.

3) This energy comes from increased respiration.

4) The increase in respiration in your cells means you need to get more oxygen into them.
    To do this:

    1) Your breathing rate (how fast you breathe) increases.

    2) Your breath volume (how deep the breaths you take are) increases.

    3) Your heart rate (how fast your heart beats) increases.

An unfit person's heart rate goes up a lot more during exercise than a fit person, and they take longer to recover.

5) Increasing your breathing rate and breath volume gets
    oxygen into your blood quicker. Blood containing oxygen
    is called oxygenated blood.

6) Your heart rate increases to get this oxygenated blood around the body faster.

Hard Exercise Can Lead to Anaerobic Respiration

1) When you do really hard exercise, your body can't supply oxygen to your muscles quickly enough.

2) This means your muscles start doing anaerobic respiration (see the previous page).

3) This is NOT the best way to transfer energy from glucose.
    This is because lactic acid builds up in the muscles, which gets painful.

4) Long periods of exercise also cause muscle fatigue.
    This is when the muscles get tired and stop contracting efficiently.

Anaerobic Respiration Leads to an Oxygen Debt

1) After anaerobic respiration stops, you'll have an "oxygen debt".

2) An oxygen debt is the amount of extra oxygen your body needs after exercise.

3) Your lungs, heart and blood couldn't keep up with the demand for oxygen earlier on.
    So you have to "repay" the oxygen that you didn't get to your muscles in time.

4) This means you have to keep breathing hard for a while after you stop.

5) This gets more oxygen into your blood, which is transported to the muscle cells.

Oxygen debt — cheap to pay back...

Phew... bet you're exhausted after reading this. Still, it needs learning before you have a pit stop.

Q1   What causes muscle fatigue?   [1 mark]

Revision Questions for Topics B3 & B4

It's all over for Topics B3 and B4 folks. I know how much you'll miss them, so here are some questions...
- Try these questions and tick off each one when you get it right.
- When you've done all the questions under a heading and are completely happy with it, tick it off.

Types of Disease (p.42-45) ☑

1) Give one way that pathogens can be spread. ☑
2) How can bacteria make us feel ill? ☑
3) What are the symptoms of gonorrhoea? ☑
4) What type of disease is measles? ☑
5) Why does tobacco mosaic virus affect photosynthesis? ☑
6) What are the vectors for malaria? ☑

Fighting Disease (p.46-49) ☑

7) What does the stomach produce that can kill pathogens? ☑
8) Give three ways that white blood cells can defend against pathogens. ☑
9) Give one pro and one con of vaccination. ☑
10) Why is it difficult to develop drugs that kill viruses? ☑
11) Which plant does the painkiller aspirin come from? ☑
12) Give two things that drugs are tested on in preclinical testing. ☑

Photosynthesis (p.50-52) ☑

13) Where in a plant cell does photosynthesis take place? ☑
14) What is an endothermic reaction? ☑
15) What is the word equation for photosynthesis? ☑
16) Why do plants store glucose as starch? ☑
17) What is meant by a 'limiting factor' of photosynthesis? ☑
18) What effect would a low carbon dioxide concentration have on the rate of photosynthesis? ☑
19) Describe how you could measure the effect of light intensity on the rate of photosynthesis. ☑

Respiration and Metabolism (p.53-55) ☑

20) What is respiration? ☑
21) What is an exothermic reaction? ☑
22) Give two molecules that can be made when lots of glucose molecules join together. ☑
23) What is glucose combined with to make amino acids? ☑
24) Give the chemical symbols for carbon dioxide and water. ☑
25) What is produced by anaerobic respiration in muscle cells? ☑
26) What is the word equation for anaerobic respiration in yeast cells? ☑
27) Name two products of the food and drink industry that fermentation is needed for. ☑
28) Give three things that increase to supply the muscles with more oxygenated blood during exercise. ☑

Homeostasis

Homeostasis — a word that strikes fear into the hearts of many GCSE students. But it's really not that bad.

Homeostasis — Keeping Conditions Inside Your Body Steady

1) Homeostasis is the fancy word for keeping the conditions in your body and cells
    at the right level. This happens in response to changes inside and outside of the body.

2) This is really important because your cells need the right conditions to work properly.

3) This includes having the right conditions for enzymes to work (see p.25).

Clive wishes he'd responded
to the changes outside.

Your Body Uses Control Systems for Homeostasis

1) You have loads of control systems that keep the conditions in your body steady.
    For example, they keep your body temperature, blood glucose level and water level steady.

2) These control systems are automatic — you don't have to think about them.

3) They can control conditions in the body using the nervous system or hormones.

4) Control systems are made up of three main parts:

    • receptors,

    • coordination centres (including the brain, spinal cord and pancreas),

    • effectors.

5) When the level of something (e.g. blood glucose) gets too high or too low,
    its control system brings it back to normal.

    If the level is too HIGH, the control system DECREASES the level.
    If the level is too LOW, the control system INCREASES the level.

6) Here's how a control system works:

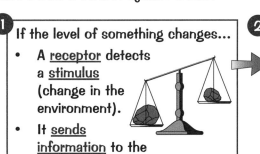

1 If the level of something changes...
    • A receptor detects
      a stimulus
      (change in the
      environment).
    • It sends
      information to the
      coordination centre.

2 • The coordination centre
      receives and processes
      the information.
    • It then organises
      a response.

3 • An effector produces
      a response.
    • This returns the
      level to its
      optimum
      (ideal) level.

My sister's not coming out today — she's got homeo-stay-sis...

Homeostasis is really important for keeping processes in your body working. It does this by keeping everything
in your body at the right level. Make sure you know what receptors, coordination centres and effectors do.

Q1   Why do the internal conditions of your body need to be kept steady?   [1 mark]

Q2   Name the part of a control system that detects stimuli.   [1 mark]

The Nervous System

Organisms need to <u>respond to stimuli</u> (changes in the environment). That's where the <u>nervous system</u> comes in.

The Nervous System Detects and Reacts to Stimuli

1) The <u>nervous system</u> means that humans can <u>react to their surroundings</u> and <u>coordinate their behaviour</u>.

2) The nervous system is made up of <u>different parts</u>:

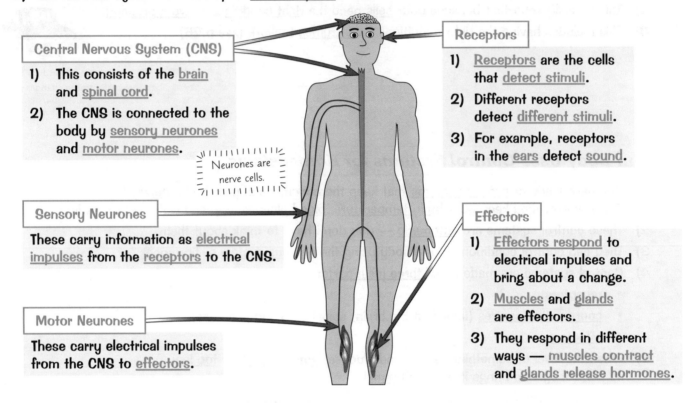

Central Nervous System (CNS)

1) This consists of the <u>brain</u> and <u>spinal cord</u>.

2) The CNS is connected to the body by <u>sensory neurones</u> and <u>motor neurones</u>.

Neurones are nerve cells.

Receptors

1) <u>Receptors</u> are the cells that <u>detect stimuli</u>.

2) Different receptors detect <u>different stimuli</u>.

3) For example, receptors in the <u>ears</u> detect <u>sound</u>.

Sensory Neurones

These carry information as <u>electrical impulses</u> from the <u>receptors</u> to the CNS.

Effectors

1) <u>Effectors respond</u> to electrical impulses and bring about a change.

2) <u>Muscles</u> and <u>glands</u> are effectors.

3) They respond in different ways — <u>muscles contract</u> and <u>glands release hormones</u>.

Motor Neurones

These carry electrical impulses from the CNS to <u>effectors</u>.

The Central Nervous System (CNS) Coordinates the Response

1) The CNS is a <u>coordination centre</u>.

2) It receives <u>information</u> from the <u>receptors</u> and then <u>coordinates a response</u> (decides what to do about it).

3) The response is carried out by <u>effectors</u>.

For example, a small bird is eating some seed...

1) ...when it spots a cat coming towards it (this is the <u>stimulus</u>).

2) The <u>receptors</u> in the bird's eye are <u>stimulated</u> (activated).

3) <u>Sensory neurones</u> carry the information <u>from</u> the <u>receptors</u> to the <u>CNS</u>.

4) The CNS <u>decides</u> what to do about it.

5) The CNS sends information to the muscles in the bird's wings (the <u>effectors</u>) along <u>motor neurones</u>.

6) The <u>muscles contract</u> and the bird flies away to safety.

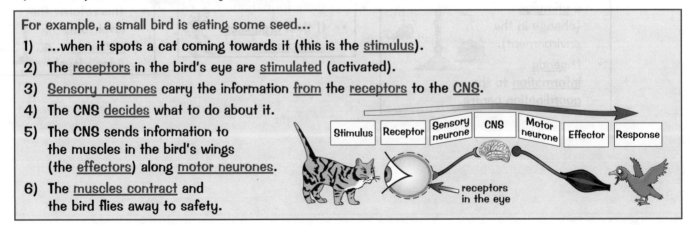

| Stimulus | Receptor | Sensory neurone | CNS | Motor neurone | Effector | Response |

receptors in the eye

Don't let the thought of exams play on your nerves...

Make sure you understand how the different parts of the nervous system work together to coordinate a response.

Q1   Name two types of effector.   [2 marks]

Synapses and Reflexes

Information is passed between neurones really quickly, especially when there's a reflex involved...

Synapses *Connect Neurones*

1) A synapse is where two neurones join together.
2) The electrical impulse is passed from one neurone to the next by chemicals.
3) These chemicals move across the gap.
4) The chemicals set off a new electrical impulse in the next neurone.

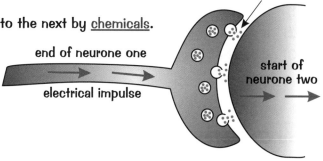

chemicals released

end of neurone one

electrical impulse

start of neurone two

Reflexes *Help Prevent Injury*

1) Reflexes are automatic responses — you don't have to think about them.
2) This makes them really quick.
3) They can help stop you getting injured.
4) The passage of information in a reflex (from receptor to effector) is called a reflex arc.
5) The neurones in reflex arcs go through the spinal cord or through an unconscious part of the brain (part of the brain not involved in thinking).
6) Here's an example of how a reflex arc would work if you were stung by a bee:

Reflexes are also called reflex reactions.

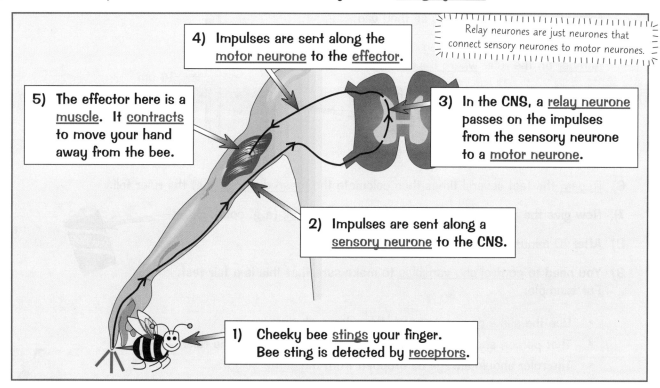

Relay neurones are just neurones that connect sensory neurones to motor neurones.

4) Impulses are sent along the motor neurone to the effector.

5) The effector here is a muscle. It contracts to move your hand away from the bee.

3) In the CNS, a relay neurone passes on the impulses from the sensory neurone to a motor neurone.

2) Impulses are sent along a sensory neurone to the CNS.

1) Cheeky bee stings your finger. Bee sting is detected by receptors.

Don't get all twitchy — just learn it...

Remember, you don't think about reflexes at all. They're useful for when you need to respond really quickly.

Q1 A chef touches a hot tray. A reflex causes him to immediately move his hand away.
    a) State the effector in this reflex.   [1 mark]
    b) Describe the pathway of the reflex from stimulus to effector.   [4 marks]

Topic B5 — Homeostasis and Response

PRACTICAL | Investigating Reaction Time

On your marks... get set... read this page.

Reaction Time is How Quickly You Respond

1) Reaction time is the time it takes to respond to a stimulus.
2) It's often less than a second. This means it may be measured in milliseconds (ms).
3) It can be affected by factors such as age, gender or drugs.

You Can Measure Reaction Time

Caffeine is a drug. It can speed up a person's reaction time.
The effect of caffeine on reaction time can be measured like this...

1) The person being tested should sit with their arm resting on the edge of a table.

2) Hold a ruler upright between their thumb and forefinger. Make sure that the zero end of the ruler is level with their thumb and finger. Don't let them grip the ruler.

3) Then let go without giving any warning.

4) The person being tested should try to catch the ruler as quickly as they can.

5) Reaction time is measured by the number on the ruler where it's caught.

   • The number should be read from the top of the person's thumb.
   • The higher the number, the slower their reaction time.

6) Repeat the test several times then calculate the mean distance that the ruler fell.

7) Now give the person being tested a caffeinated drink (e.g. cola).

8) After 10 minutes, repeat steps 1 to 6.

9) You need to control any variables to make sure that this is a fair test. For example:

   • Use the same person to catch the ruler each time.
   • That person should always use the same hand to catch the ruler.
   • The ruler should always be dropped from the same height.

Ready... Steady...

... Ah, too slow.

Q1   A student was measuring her reaction time using a computer test.
     She had to click the mouse when the screen changed from red to green. She repeated the test five times.
     Her results were as follows: 242 ms, 256 ms, 253 ms, 249 ms, 235 ms.
     Calculate the mean reaction time of the student.   [2 marks]

Topic B5 — Homeostasis and Response

The Endocrine System

As well as along nerves, information is sent around the body using hormones.

Hormones Are Chemical Messengers Sent in the Blood

1) Hormones are chemicals released by glands. They're released directly into the blood.
2) These glands are called endocrine glands. They make up your endocrine system.
3) Hormones are carried in the blood to other parts of the body.
4) They only affect particular cells in particular organs (called target organs).
5) Here are some examples of glands:

THE PITUITARY GLAND
1) Sometimes called the 'master gland'.
2) This is because it produces many hormones that regulate body conditions.
3) These hormones act on other glands. They make the glands release hormones that bring about change.

OVARIES — females only
1) Produce oestrogen.
2) This is involved in the menstrual cycle (see page 63).

TESTES — males only
1) Produce testosterone.
2) This controls puberty and sperm production in males (see page 63).

THYROID
1) Produces thyroxine.
2) This is involved in regulating things like the rate of metabolism, heart rate and temperature.

ADRENAL GLAND
1) Produces adrenaline.
2) This is used to prepare the body for a 'fight or flight' response.

THE PANCREAS
1) Produces insulin.
2) This is used to regulate the blood glucose level (see next page).

Hormones and Nerves Have Differences

NERVES:
Very FAST action.
Act for a very SHORT TIME.
Act on a very PRECISE AREA.

HORMONES:
SLOWER action.
Act for a LONG TIME.
Act in a more GENERAL way.

Nerves, hormones — no wonder revision makes me tense...

Hormones control many different organs and cells in the body. They tend to control things that aren't immediately life-threatening (so things like sexual development, blood sugar level, water content, etc.).

Q1   How do hormones travel from their glands to their target organs?   [1 mark]

Controlling Blood Glucose

The amount of glucose in your blood is controlled as part of homeostasis.

Insulin Reduces the Blood Glucose Level

1) Eating carbohydrates puts glucose (a type of sugar) into the blood.

2) Glucose is removed from the blood by cells (which use it for energy).

3) When you exercise, a lot more glucose is removed from the blood.

4) Changes in the blood glucose concentration are monitored and controlled by the pancreas.

5) If blood glucose concentration gets too high, the pancreas releases the hormone insulin.

6) Insulin causes glucose to move into cells (so it removes glucose from the blood).

7) Glucose can be stored as glycogen.

8) Glucose is converted to glycogen in liver and muscle cells.

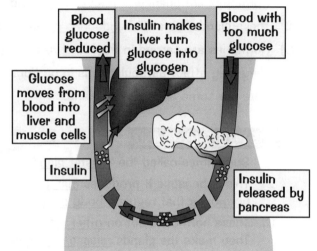

Blood glucose reduced

Insulin makes liver turn glucose into glycogen

Blood with too much glucose

Glucose moves from blood into liver and muscle cells

Insulin

Insulin released by pancreas

With Diabetes, You Can't Control Your Blood Sugar Level

There are two types of diabetes:

Type 1 Diabetes

1) Type 1 diabetes is where the pancreas produces little or no insulin.

2) This means a person's blood glucose level can rise to a level that can kill them.

3) People with Type 1 diabetes need injections of insulin throughout the day.

4) This makes sure that glucose is removed from the blood quickly after the food is digested.

Large amounts of glucose in the blood can damage organs like the heart.

Type 2 Diabetes

1) Type 2 diabetes is where a person becomes resistant to their own insulin.

2) This means they still produce insulin, but their body's cells don't respond properly to it.

3) This can cause a person's blood sugar level to rise to a dangerous level.

4) Being obese (very overweight) can increase your chance of developing Type 2 diabetes.

5) Type 2 diabetes can be controlled by eating a carbohydrate-controlled diet.

6) This is a diet where the amount of carbohydrates eaten is carefully measured.

7) Type 2 diabetes can also be controlled by taking regular exercise.

And people used to think the pancreas was just a cushion... (true)

In the exam, you might be given a graph showing the effect of insulin on blood glucose level.
Don't freak out — just use what you know about graphs to make sense of the data.

Q1   Describe how insulin returns the blood glucose level to normal when it is too high.   [2 marks]

Topic B5 — Homeostasis and Response

Puberty and the Menstrual Cycle

The monthly release of an egg from a woman's ovaries is part of the menstrual cycle.

Hormones Cause Sexual Characteristics To Develop at Puberty

1) At puberty, your body starts releasing sex hormones.
2) These sex hormones trigger secondary sexual characteristics.
   For example, the development of facial hair in men and breasts in women.
3) Female sex hormones also cause eggs to mature (develop) in women.
4) In men, the main reproductive hormone is testosterone.
   It's produced by the testes. It stimulates sperm production.
5) In women, the main reproductive hormone is oestrogen. It's produced by the ovaries.
   Oestrogen is involved in the menstrual cycle.

The Menstrual Cycle Has Four Stages

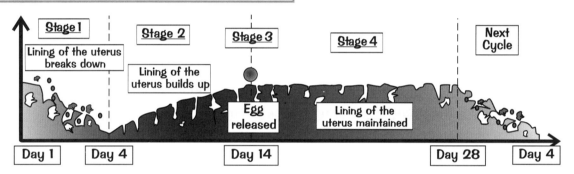

Stage 1 — Day 1 is when menstruation (bleeding) starts. The uterus lining breaks down for about four days.

Stage 2 — The uterus lining builds up again from day 4 to day 14.
It builds into a thick spongy layer full of blood vessels. It's now ready to receive a fertilised egg.

Stage 3 — An egg develops and is released from the ovary at day 14. This is called ovulation.

Stage 4 — The wall is then maintained (kept the same) for about 14 days until day 28.
If no fertilised egg has landed on the uterus wall by day 28,
the spongy lining starts to break down. The whole cycle starts again.

An egg is released once every 28 days.

The Menstrual Cycle is Controlled by Four Hormones...

HORMONE	WHAT THE HORMONE DOES
FSH (Follicle-Stimulating Hormone)	Causes an egg to mature in one of the ovaries.
LH (Luteinising Hormone)	Causes the release of an egg (ovulation).
Oestrogen	These hormones are involved in the growth
Progesterone	and maintenance of the uterus lining.

Which came first — the chicken or the luteinising hormone...

Female or not, learn this page... till you know which hormone does what.

Q1   Name the hormone that causes an egg to mature in the ovary.   [1 mark]

Q2   Where is testosterone produced in the male body?   [1 mark]

Controlling Fertility

Pregnancy can happen if sperm reaches the egg. Contraception tries to stop this happening.

Hormones Can Be Used to Reduce Fertility

1) Fertility is how easy it is for a woman to get pregnant.
2) Contraceptives are things that prevent pregnancy.
3) Hormones can be used in contraceptives — these are called hormonal contraceptives.

Oral Contraceptives Contain Hormones

1) Oral contraceptives are taken through the mouth as pills.
2) They stop the hormone FSH from being released.
3) This stops eggs maturing.
4) Oral contraceptives are over 99% effective at preventing pregnancy.
5) But they can have bad side effects.
   For example, they can cause headaches and make you feel sick.

Some Hormonal Contraceptives Release Progesterone

1) Some hormonal contraceptives work by slowly releasing progesterone.
2) This stops eggs from maturing or being released from the ovaries.
3) Examples of contraceptives that work this way are:

Contraceptive patch
1) This is a small patch that is stuck to the skin.
2) It lasts one week.

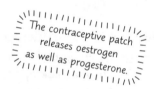

The contraceptive patch releases oestrogen as well as progesterone.

Contraceptive implant
1) This is inserted under the skin of the arm.
2) An implant can last for three years.

Contraceptive injection
Each dose lasts two to three months.

Some Intrauterine Devices Contain Hormones

1) An intrauterine device (IUD) is a T-shaped device that's inserted into the uterus (womb).
2) It can stop fertilised eggs from implanting in the uterus wall.
3) Some types of IUD release a hormone.

I've got 99 problems, but a baby ain't one...

Hormones are needed for a woman to get pregnant, but they can also be used to help stop her getting pregnant.

Q1   Name two types of contraception that use hormones.   [2 marks]

Topic B5 — Homeostasis and Response

More on Controlling Fertility

There are even more methods of contraception...

Barriers Stop Egg and Sperm Meeting

1) Non-hormonal contraceptives (types that don't use hormones) stop the sperm from getting to the egg.
2) Barrier methods are one type of non-hormonal contraceptive. For example:

Condom

1) Condoms are worn over the penis during sexual intercourse.
2) Female condoms are worn inside the vagina.
3) Condoms are the only form of contraception that will protect against sexually transmitted diseases.

Diaphragm

1) A diaphragm is a shallow plastic cup that fits over the entrance to the uterus.
2) It has to be used with spermicide (a chemical that disables or kills the sperm).
3) Spermicide can be used alone as a form of contraception. But when used alone, it is not as effective (it's only about 70-80% effective at preventing pregnancy).

I've got this barrier thing sorted...

There are More Drastic Ways to Avoid Pregnancy

Sterilisation

1) In females, sterilisation involves cutting or tying the fallopian tubes (tubes that connect the ovaries to the uterus).
2) In males, it involves cutting or tying the sperm ducts (tubes between the testes and the penis).
3) Sterilisation is permanent (lasts for life).

Natural Methods

1) Pregnancy may be avoided by not having sexual intercourse when a woman is at the stage of the menstrual cycle when she is most likely to get pregnant.
2) It's popular with people who think that hormonal and barrier methods are unnatural.
3) But it's not very effective.

Abstinence

1) The only way to be sure that sperm and egg don't meet is to not have intercourse.
2) This is called abstinence.

The winner of best contraceptive ever — just not doing it...

You might be asked to evaluate the different hormonal and non-hormonal methods of contraception in your exam. This means you need to write about both the pros and the cons of each method. Exciting stuff.

Q1   Explain how barrier methods of contraception work.   [1 mark]

DNA

Your DNA is what makes you you. Time to find out what DNA actually is...

Chromosomes Are Really Long Molecules of DNA

1) DNA is the chemical that all of the genetic material in a cell is made up from.

2) It contains all the instructions to put an organism together and make it work.

3) A DNA molecule is made up of two strands of DNA coiled together.
They make a double helix (a double-stranded spiral).

4) A DNA strand is a polymer. A polymer is something made up of lots of smaller pieces joined together.

5) DNA is found in the nucleus of animal and plant cells.

6) It's found in really long structures called chromosomes.

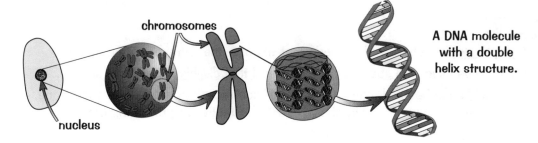

chromosomes

nucleus

A DNA molecule
with a double
helix structure.

A Gene Codes for a Specific Protein

1) A gene is a small section of DNA found on a chromosome.

2) Each gene codes for a particular sequence of amino acids.

3) These amino acids are joined together to make a protein.

Every Organism Has a Genome

1) Genome is just the fancy term for all of the genetic material in an organism.

2) Scientists have worked out the whole human genome.

3) Understanding the human genome is really important for medicine.
This is because:

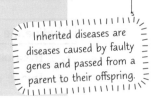

1) Scientists can find genes in the genome that are linked to different types of disease.

2) If scientists know which genes are linked to inherited diseases, they can understand them better. This could help us to develop treatments.

3) Scientists can look at tiny differences in the genomes of different people. This can help them find out about the migration (movement) of certain populations of people around the world over history.

Inherited diseases are diseases caused by faulty genes and passed from a parent to their offspring.

Insert joke about genes and jeans here...

Make sure you've got that info about genes, DNA and chromosomes stuck in your head. It can be tricky stuff.

Q1   What is a gene?   [1 mark]

Q2   What is an organism's genome?   [1 mark]

Reproduction

Ooo err, <u>reproduction</u>... It can happen in <u>two</u> different ways...

Sexual Reproduction Produces Genetically Different Cells

1) <u>Sexual reproduction</u> is where genes from <u>two</u> organisms (a <u>father</u> and a <u>mother</u>) are mixed.

2) The mother and father produce <u>gametes</u> (sex cells). E.g. <u>egg</u> and <u>sperm</u> cells in animals.

3) The gametes are produced by <u>meiosis</u> (see next page).
   Each gamete contains <u>half</u> the number of <u>chromosomes</u> of a normal cell.

4) The <u>egg</u> (from the mother) and the <u>sperm</u> cell (from the father) <u>fuse</u> (<u>join</u>) <u>together</u>.
   This forms a cell with the <u>full</u> number of chromosomes (<u>half from the father</u>, <u>half from the mother</u>).

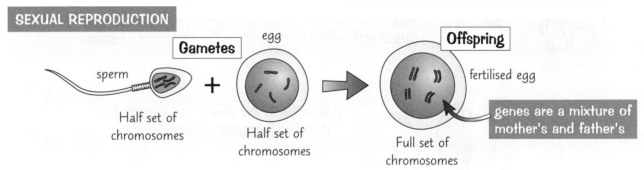

5) The offspring receives a <u>mixture</u> of genes, so <u>inherits features</u> from <u>both parents</u>.

6) This <u>mixture of genes</u> produces <u>variation</u> in the offspring. Pretty cool, eh.

7) <u>Flowering plants</u> can reproduce in this way <u>too</u>. Their gametes are <u>egg cells</u> and <u>pollen</u>.

Asexual Reproduction Produces Genetically Identical Cells

1) <u>Asexual reproduction</u> happens by <u>mitosis</u>.

2) <u>One parent cell</u> makes a new cell by <u>dividing in two</u> (see page 15).

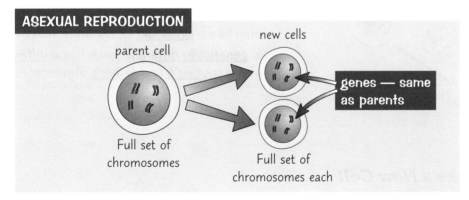

3) There's <u>no fusion of gametes</u>.

4) So there's <u>no mixing of genes</u>.

5) This means there's <u>no genetic variation</u> in the new cells.

6) Each <u>new cell</u> is <u>genetically identical</u> to the parent cell — it has <u>exactly the same genes</u>.
   The new cell is a <u>clone</u>.

You need to reproduce these facts in the exam...

They might have similar names, but you need to know how sexual and asexual reproduction are different.

Q1   What type of cell division is involved in asexual reproduction?   [1 mark]

Q2   Suggest why there is variation in the offspring of sexual reproduction.   [2 marks]

Topic B6 — Inheritance, Variation and Evolution

Meiosis

Ever wondered how sperm and egg cells are made? Well today's your lucky day.

Gametes Are Produced by Meiosis

1) Gametes only have <u>half the number</u> of chromosomes of normal cells.
2) To make gametes, cells divide by <u>meiosis</u>.
3) In humans, meiosis <u>only</u> happens in the <u>reproductive organs</u> (the <u>ovaries</u> in females and <u>testes</u> in males).
4) Here's how meiosis happens:

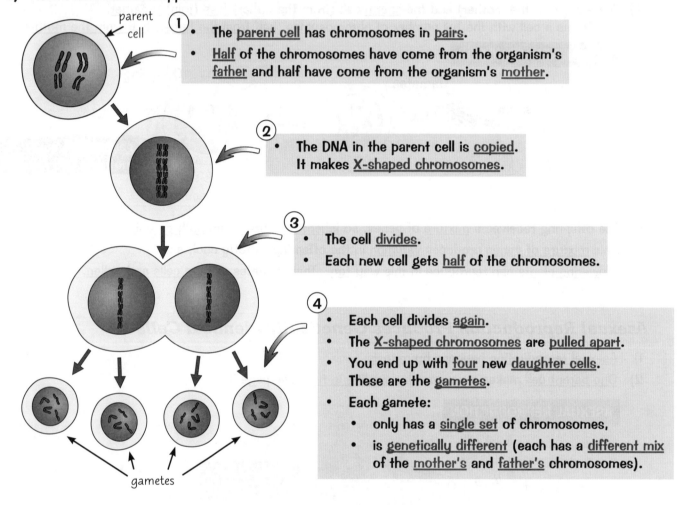

parent cell

1.
   • The <u>parent cell</u> has chromosomes in <u>pairs</u>.
   • <u>Half</u> of the chromosomes have come from the organism's <u>father</u> and half have come from the organism's <u>mother</u>.

2.
   • The DNA in the parent cell is <u>copied</u>. It makes <u>X-shaped chromosomes</u>.

3.
   • The cell <u>divides</u>.
   • Each new cell gets <u>half</u> of the chromosomes.

4.
   • Each cell divides <u>again</u>.
   • The <u>X-shaped chromosomes</u> are <u>pulled apart</u>.
   • You end up with <u>four</u> new <u>daughter cells</u>. These are the <u>gametes</u>.
   • Each gamete:
      • only has a <u>single set</u> of chromosomes,
      • is <u>genetically different</u> (each has a <u>different mix</u> of the <u>mother's</u> and <u>father's</u> chromosomes).

gametes

Gametes Fuse to Make a New Cell

1) During fertilisation, two gametes <u>fuse together</u> (see p.67). This makes a <u>new cell</u>.
2) This new cell has the <u>normal number</u> of chromosomes.
3) The new cell <u>divides</u> by <u>mitosis</u> many times to produce <u>lots</u> of new cells. This forms an <u>embryo</u>.
4) As the embryo develops, these cells <u>differentiate</u> (see page 14). The cells become <u>different types</u> of <u>specialised cell</u> that make up a <u>whole organism</u>.

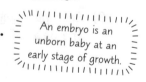

An embryo is an unborn baby at an early stage of growth.

Now that I have your undivided attention...

Remember, gametes are sex cells. They have only half the number of chromosomes of normal body cells.

Q1   How many cell divisions take place in meiosis?   [1 mark]

X and Y Chromosomes

Now for a couple of <u>very</u> important little chromosomes...

Your Chromosomes Control Whether You're Male or Female

1) There are <u>23 pairs</u> of chromosomes in every human body cell.
2) <u>22</u> are <u>matched pairs</u> of chromosomes that just control your <u>characteristics</u>.
3) The <u>23rd pair</u> are labelled <u>XY</u> or <u>XX</u>.
4) They're the two chromosomes that <u>decide</u> your sex (whether you turn out <u>male</u> or <u>female</u>).

> All <u>males</u> have an <u>X</u> and a <u>Y</u> chromosome: XY
> The <u>Y chromosome</u> causes <u>male characteristics</u>.

> All <u>females</u> have <u>two X chromosomes</u>: XX
> The <u>XX combination</u> allows <u>female characteristics</u> to develop.

5) Each sperm has <u>either</u> an **X** or a **Y** chromosome.
6) <u>All</u> egg cells have a **X** chromosome.

Genetic Diagrams Show the Possible Gamete Combinations

1) To find the <u>probability</u> (chance) of getting a boy or a girl, you can draw a <u>genetic diagram</u>.
2) This type of genetic diagram is called a <u>Punnett square</u>.
3) Put the <u>possible gametes</u> (eggs or sperm) from <u>one</u> parent down the side. Put those from the <u>other</u> parent along the top.
4) Then in each middle square you <u>fill in</u> the letters from the top and side that line up with that square.
5) The <u>pairs of letters</u> in the middle show the possible combinations of the gametes.
6) There are <u>two XX results</u> and <u>two XY results</u>.
7) This means that there's the <u>same probability</u> of getting a boy or a girl — each one has a <u>1 in 2 chance</u> (which is the same as <u>50%</u>).

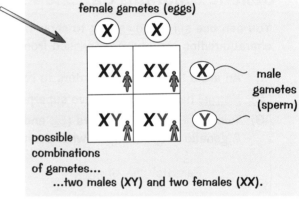

The <u>other type</u> of genetic diagram looks a bit more complicated, but it shows <u>exactly the same</u> thing.

1) At the top are the <u>parents</u>.
2) The middle circles show the <u>possible gametes</u> that are formed. One gamete from the female combines with one gamete from the male (during fertilisation).
3) The criss-cross lines show <u>all</u> the <u>possible</u> ways the X and Y chromosomes <u>could</u> combine.
4) The <u>possible offspring</u> you could get are shown in the bottom circles.

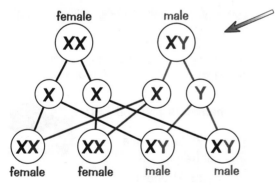

Have you got the Y-factor...

Genetic diagrams only show probabilities. They don't say what will definitely happen. So for each pregnancy, a women has a 50% chance of having a boy or a girl. It doesn't matter how many boys or girls she's had before.

Q1 What combination of sex chromosomes do human females have? [1 mark]

Genetic Diagrams

Genetic diagrams don't always show chromosomes. They might show just a <u>single gene</u> instead.

Different Genes Control Different Characteristics

1) <u>Some</u> characteristics are controlled by a <u>single</u> gene.
   For example, <u>mouse fur colour</u> and <u>red-green colour blindness</u> in humans.

2) However, <u>most</u> characteristics are controlled by <u>several genes</u>.

All Genes Exist in Different Versions Called Alleles

1) You have <u>two</u> alleles of <u>every gene</u> in your body — <u>one</u> on <u>each chromosome</u> in a pair.

2) If the two alleles are <u>the same</u>, then the organism is <u>homozygous</u> for that characteristic.

3) If the two alleles are <u>different</u>, then the organism is <u>heterozygous</u> for that characteristic.

4) Some alleles are <u>dominant</u> (these are shown with a <u>capital letter</u> on genetic diagrams, e.g. '<u>C</u>').
   Some alleles are <u>recessive</u> (these are shown by a <u>small letter</u> on genetic diagrams, e.g. '<u>c</u>').

5) For an organism to show a <u>recessive characteristic</u>, <u>both</u> its alleles must be <u>recessive</u> (e.g. cc).
   But to show a <u>dominant</u> characteristic, only <u>one</u> allele needs to be dominant (e.g. <u>either CC or Cc</u>).

6) The mix of <u>alleles</u> you have is called your <u>genotype</u>.

7) Your alleles determine your <u>characteristics</u>. The characteristics you have is called your <u>phenotype</u>.

Genetic Diagrams Can Show How Characteristics are Inherited

You can use <u>genetic diagrams</u> to show how <u>single genes</u> for characteristics are <u>inherited</u> (passed from parents to offspring). For example:

1) An allele that causes hamsters to have superpowers is <u>recessive</u> ("b").

2) <u>Normal</u> hamsters don't have superpowers due to a <u>dominant</u> allele ("B").

3) Two <u>homozygous</u> hamsters (<u>BB</u> and <u>bb</u>) are crossed (bred together).
   A genetic diagram shows what could happen:

> A hamster with the genotype BB or Bb will be normal.
> A hamster with the genotype bb will have superpowers.

	Normal	Superpowered	
Parents' <u>phenotypes</u>:	Normal	Superpowered	
Parents' <u>genotypes</u>:	BB	bb	

Gametes' <u>genotypes</u>:
(each gamete just has one allele)
B   B   b   b

The lines show all the possible ways the parents' alleles could combine.

Offspring's <u>genotypes</u>: Bb   Bb   Bb   Bb

Each offspring must have one allele from each of its parents.

Offspring's <u>phenotypes</u>: All the offspring are <u>normal</u> (boring).

4) This Punnett square shows a cross between <u>two heterozygous</u> hamsters (<u>Bb</u> and <u>Bb</u>):

gametes' genotypes are written at the top and side

	B	b
B	BB	Bb
b	Bb	bb

offspring's genotypes are shown in the squares

- There's a <u>3 in 4</u> (75%) chance that offspring will be <u>normal</u>.
- There's a <u>1 in 4</u> (25%) chance that offspring will have <u>superpowers</u>.
- This gives a 3 normal : 1 superpowers <u>ratio</u> (<u>3:1</u>).

Your meanotype determines how nice you are to your sibling...

Make sure you understand all the scientific terms on this page. It will help you understand diagrams too.

Q1   What is meant by the term genotype?   [1 mark]

Inherited Disorders

Inherited disorders are <u>health conditions</u>. They are caused by <u>inheriting</u> faulty <u>alleles</u>.

Cystic Fibrosis is Caused by a Recessive Allele

1) <u>Cystic fibrosis</u> is an <u>inherited disorder</u> of <u>cell membranes</u>.
2) The allele which causes cystic fibrosis is a <u>recessive allele</u>, 'f'.
3) Because it's recessive, people with only <u>one copy</u> of the allele <u>won't</u> have the disorder
   — they're known as <u>carriers</u>.
4) For a child to have the disorder, <u>both parents</u> must be either <u>carriers</u> or have the disorder <u>themselves</u>.
5) As the diagram shows, there's a <u>1 in 4 chance</u> of a child having the disorder if <u>both</u> parents are <u>carriers</u>.

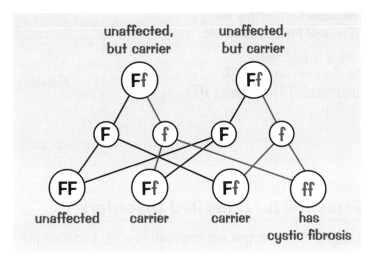

Polydactyly is Caused by a Dominant Allele

1) <u>Polydactyly</u> is an <u>inherited disorder</u> where a baby's born with <u>extra fingers or toes</u>.
2) The disorder is caused by a <u>dominant allele</u>, 'D'.
3) This means that it can be inherited if just <u>one parent</u> carries the faulty allele.
4) The <u>parent</u> that <u>has</u> the faulty allele <u>will have</u> the disorder too since the allele is dominant.
5) As the diagram shows, there's a <u>50% chance</u> of a child having the disorder if <u>one</u> parent has <u>one</u> D allele.

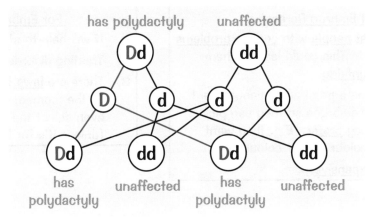

Unintentional mooning — caused by faulty genes...

The important bits from this page are that the allele for cystic fibrosis is recessive and for polydactyly it's dominant.

Q1   A person has cystic fibrosis. How many copies of the cystic fibrosis allele do they have?   [1 mark]

Family Trees and Embryo Screening

Just when you thought you'd finished with genetic diagrams, these family trees show up...

Family Trees Show the Inheritance of Alleles

1) The diagram on the right is a family tree for cystic fibrosis (p.71).

2) From the family tree, you can tell that the allele for cystic fibrosis isn't dominant. This is because plenty of the family carry the allele but don't have the disorder.

3) There is a 25% chance that the new baby will have the disorder and a 50% chance that it will be a carrier. This is because both of the baby's parents are carriers (Eve and Phil are both Ff).

4) The case of the new baby is just the same as in the genetic diagram on page 71. The baby could be unaffected (FF), a carrier (Ff) or have cystic fibrosis (ff).

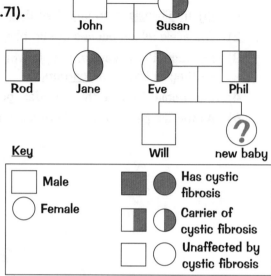

Key

☐ Male	◼ Has cystic fibrosis
○ Female	◐ Carrier of cystic fibrosis
	☐ ○ Unaffected by cystic fibrosis

Embryos Can Be Screened for Inherited Disorders

1) During in vitro fertilisation (IVF), embryos are fertilised in a lab and then put in the mother's womb.

2) Before they are put into the mother, scientists can remove a cell from each embryo and look at its genes. This is called embryo screening.

3) Many inherited disorders can be picked up in this way.

4) It's also possible to get DNA from an embryo in the womb and test that for disorders.

5) There are lots of concerns about embryo screening.

6) Some people don't agree with embryonic screening because of the decisions it can lead to.

7) For embryos produced by IVF — after screening, embryos with 'bad' alleles would be destroyed.

8) For embryos in the womb — screening could lead to the decision to stop the pregnancy.

9) Here are some more arguments for and against embryo screening:

Against Embryo Screening

1) It suggests that people with genetic problems are not wanted. This could lead to them being treated unfairly.

2) There may come a point when people want to screen their embryos so they can pick the features they prefer. E.g. they want a certain eye colour or hair colour.

3) Screening is expensive.

For Embryo Screening

1) It will help to stop people suffering.

2) Treating disorders costs a lot of money.

3) There are laws to stop it going too far. At the moment parents cannot even select the sex of their baby (unless it's for health reasons).

Embryo screening — it's a tricky one...

Arguments about things like embryo screening don't have a simple answer — there are pros and cons to think about.

Q1   Why is embryonic screening carried out?   [1 mark]

Topic B6 — Inheritance, Variation and Evolution

Variation

You'll probably have noticed that not all people are identical. There are reasons for this.

Organisms of the Same Species Have Differences

1) Different species look... well... different — my dog definitely doesn't look like a daisy.

2) But even organisms of the <u>same species</u> will usually look at least <u>slightly</u> different.

3) These <u>differences</u> are called the <u>variation</u> within a <u>species</u>.

4) Variation can be <u>huge</u> within a <u>population</u>.

5) Variation can be <u>genetic</u>. This means it's caused by differences in <u>genes</u> that are <u>inherited</u>.

6) Variation can also be <u>environmental</u>. This means it's caused by the <u>conditions</u> in which an organism <u>lives</u>.

• For example, a plant grown on a nice sunny windowsill could grow <u>healthy</u> and <u>green</u>.
• The same plant grown in darkness would grow <u>tall</u> and <u>spindly</u> and its leaves would turn <u>yellow</u>.

7) Most variation in phenotype is caused by a <u>mixture</u> of <u>genes</u> and the <u>environment</u>.

• For example, the <u>maximum height</u> that an animal or plant could grow to is determined by its <u>genes</u>.
• But whether it actually grows that tall depends on its <u>environment</u> (e.g. how much food it gets).

Mutations are Changes to the Genome

1) Sometimes, a gene can <u>mutate</u>.

2) A mutation is a <u>random change</u> in an organism's <u>DNA</u> that can be <u>inherited</u>.

3) Mutations occur <u>continuously</u>.

4) Mutations mean that the gene is <u>changed</u>.
This produces a <u>genetic variant</u> (a different form of the gene).

5) Most <u>genetic variants</u> have <u>very little</u> or <u>no effect</u> on an organism's <u>phenotype</u> (its characteristics).

Well, I suppose it's time for some new jeans.

6) <u>Some</u> variants have a <u>small effect</u> on the organism's <u>phenotype</u>. They alter the individual's characteristics but only slightly. For example:

• Some characteristics (e.g. eye colour) are controlled by <u>more than one gene</u>.
• A mutation in <u>one</u> of the genes may <u>change</u> the <u>eye colour</u> a bit, but the difference might not be huge.

7) Very <u>rarely</u>, variants can have such a <u>big effect</u> that they lead to a <u>new phenotype</u>, e.g. cystic fibrosis.

8) A new phenotype may be <u>useful</u> if the <u>environment</u> that an organism lives in <u>changes</u>.

9) This is because sometimes a new phenotype makes an individual <u>more suited</u> to a new environment.

10) If this happens, the mutation can become common <u>throughout</u> the species <u>relatively quickly</u>. This happens by <u>natural selection</u> — see the next page.

My mum's got no trousers — cos I've got her jeans...

So you can't blame all of your faults on your parents — the environment usually plays a role too.

Q1   Explain what is meant by environmental variation.   [2 marks]

74

Evolution

THEORY OF EVOLUTION: All of today's species have evolved from simple life forms that first started to develop over three billion years ago.

Only the Fittest Survive

1) Charles Darwin came up with a really important theory about evolution — it's called evolution by natural selection. It works like this:

   - Organisms in a species show wide variation in their characteristics.
   - Organisms have to compete for resources in an ecosystem.
   - This means organisms with characteristics that make them better adapted to their environment will be better at competing with other organisms.
   - These organisms are more likely to survive and reproduce.
   - So the genes for the useful characteristics are more likely to be passed on to their offspring.
   - Over time, useful characteristics become more common in the population and the species changes. This is evolution.

2) Darwin's theory wasn't perfect. At the time he couldn't explain how new characteristics appeared or were passed on. Nowadays we have evidence to back up Darwin's theory, such as:

   - The discovery of genetics — it showed that characteristics are passed on in an organism's genes. It also showed that genetic variants (see page 73) produce the characteristics (phenotypes) that are better adapted to the environment.
   - Fossils — by looking at fossils of different ages (the fossil record), scientists could see how changes in organisms developed slowly over time.
   - Antibiotic resistance — how bacteria are able to evolve to become resistant to antibiotics also further supports evolution by natural selection (see the next page).

3) This means Darwin's theory of evolution by natural selection is now widely accepted.

Evolution Can Lead to New Species Developing

1) Over a long period of time, the phenotype of organisms can change a lot because of natural selection.
2) Sometimes, the phenotype can change so much that a completely new species is formed.
3) New species develop when populations of the same species change so much that they can't breed with each other to produce fertile offspring.

Extinction is When No Individuals of a Species Are Left

Species become extinct for these reasons:

1) The environment changes too quickly (e.g. their habitat is destroyed).
2) A new predator kills them all (e.g. humans hunting them).
3) A new disease kills them all.
4) They can't compete with another (new) species for food.
5) A catastrophic event happens that kills them all (e.g. a volcanic eruption).

"Natural selection" — sounds like vegan chocolates...

Natural selection's all about the organisms with the best characteristics surviving to pass on their genes.

Q1   Give three reasons why a species may become extinct.   [3 marks]

Topic B6 — Inheritance, Variation and Evolution

Antibiotic-Resistant Bacteria

Antibiotic-resistant bacteria are the super villains of the medical world. Trust me on this.

Bacteria can Evolve and Become Antibiotic-Resistant

Antibiotics are drugs that kill bacteria.
Bacteria can become resistant to antibiotics by natural selection.
Here's what happens:

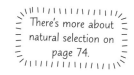
There's more about natural selection on page 74.

1) Bacteria can develop random mutations (changes) in their DNA.

2) These can lead to the bacteria being resistant to (not killed by) a particular antibiotic.

3) These new strains (types) of bacteria are called antibiotic-resistant bacteria.

4) The ability to resist antibiotics is a big advantage for the bacteria.

5) It means that the bacteria are able to survive in a host who's being treated to get rid of an infection.

6) So the antibiotic-resistant bacteria can reproduce many more times.

7) They pass on their gene for antibiotic resistance to their offspring.

8) The gene for antibiotic resistance becomes more common in the population over time — the bacteria have evolved.

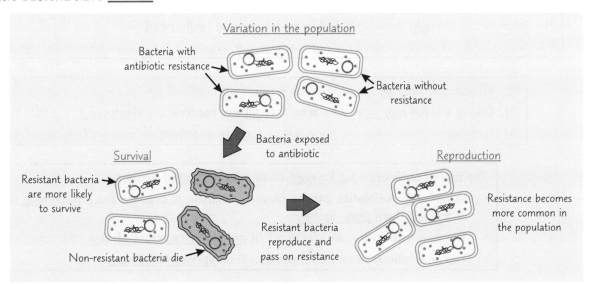

9) Because bacteria are so rapid at reproducing, they can evolve quite quickly.

10) The antibiotic-resistant bacteria keep reproducing.
This increases the population size of the antibiotic-resistant strain.

Antibiotic Resistant Bacteria Spread Easily

1) Antibiotic-resistant bacteria are a problem because:
   • There is no effective treatment for the infection.
   • People are not immune to the new strain.

2) This means that the antibiotic-resistant strain is able to easily spread between people.

The spread of resistance — not what I want on my toast...

Understanding natural selection is key to this page really. If you're not sure about it, have a flick back to page 74.

Q1   Give one reason why antibiotic resistant bacteria can be easily spread between people.   [1 mark]

More on Antibiotic-Resistant Bacteria

Antibiotic-resistance is getting <u>worse</u>. But there are ways to <u>fight it</u>...

Antibiotic Resistance is Becoming More Common

1) The problem of <u>antibiotic resistance</u> is getting <u>worse</u> because:

> - Antibiotics are being <u>overused</u>.
> - People <u>aren't</u> using antibiotics <u>correctly</u>.

2) 'Superbugs' (bacteria that are resistant to most known antibiotics) are becoming more common.

> E.g. <u>MRSA</u> is a relatively common 'superbug' that's really hard to get rid of.

Antibiotics Need to Be Used Sensibly

There are a few things that can be done to <u>avoid</u> antibiotic-resistant bacteria forming:

> 1) Doctors should <u>only</u> prescribe antibiotics when they <u>really need</u> to.
> 2) They <u>shouldn't be</u> prescribed for <u>non-serious conditions</u> or infections caused by <u>viruses</u>.

Antibiotics don't kill viruses.

> 1) You should take <u>all</u> the antibiotics a doctor prescribes for you.
> 2) Taking the <u>full course</u> makes sure that <u>all</u> the bacteria are <u>destroyed</u>.
> 3) This means that there are <u>none left</u> to <u>mutate</u> and develop into <u>antibiotic-resistant strains</u>.

> The use of antibiotics by <u>farmers</u> should be <u>restricted</u> because:
> - In farming, antibiotics can be given to animals to prevent them <u>becoming ill</u> and make them <u>grow faster</u>.
> - This can lead to the development of <u>antibiotic-resistant strains</u> of bacteria in the animals.
> - The antibiotic-resistant bacteria can then <u>spread to humans</u>.

We Can't Make New Antibiotics Fast Enough

1) Drug companies are working on developing <u>new antibiotics</u> that kill the resistant strains.

2) But there are problems:
> - The rate of development is <u>slow</u>.
> - The process is really <u>expensive</u>.

3) This means that we're unlikely to be able to <u>keep up</u> with the demand for <u>new drugs</u> to fight new antibiotic-resistant strains.

Aaargh, a giant earwig! Run from the attack of the superbug...

The reality of 'superbugs' is even scarier than giant earwigs. Bacteria that are resistant to all our drugs are a worrying thought. It'll be like going back in time to before antibiotics were invented.

Q1   Explain why it's important that people take the full course of antibiotics they are prescribed.   [2 marks]

Topic B6 — Inheritance, Variation and Evolution

Selective Breeding

'Selective breeding' sounds like it could be a tricky topic, but it's actually quite simple.

Selective Breeding is Very Simple

1) Selective breeding is when humans choose which plants or animals are going to breed.
2) Organisms are selectively bred to develop features that are useful or attractive.
   For example:

   - Animals that produce more meat or milk.
   - Crops with disease resistance (that are not killed by disease).
   - Dogs with a good, gentle personality.
   - Decorative plants with big or unusual flowers.

3) This is the basic process involved in selective breeding:

   - From your existing plants or animals select the ones which have the feature you're after.
   - Breed them with each other.
   - Select the best of the offspring, and breed them together.
   - Continue this process over several generations. Eventually, all offspring will have the feature you want.

Selective breeding is also known as 'artificial selection'.

4) Selective breeding is nothing new — people have been doing it for thousands of years.
5) This is how we ended up with edible crops from wild plants and domesticated animals like cows and dogs.

Here's an Example:

A farmer might want his cattle to produce more meat.

- Genetic variation means some cattle will have better characteristics for producing meat than others, e.g. a larger size.
- The farmer could select the largest cows and bulls and breed them together.
- He could then select the largest offspring and breed them together.
- After several generations, he would get cows with a very high meat yield.

Selective Breeding Has Disadvantages

There's more on alleles on page 70.

1) The main problem with selective breeding is that it reduces the number of different alleles in a population.
2) This is because the "best" animals or plants are always used for breeding, and they are all closely related — this is known as inbreeding.
3) This means there's more chance of selectively bred organisms having health problems caused by their genes, e.g. they may inherit harmful genetic defects.
4) There can also be serious problems if a new disease appears.
5) This is because it's less likely that individuals in the population will have alleles that make them resistant to the disease.
6) So, if one individual is affected by the disease, the rest are also likely to be affected.

Oh Eck!

I use the same genes all the time too — they flatter my hips...

Different breeds of dog came from selective breeding. For example, somebody thought 'I really like this small, yappy wolf — I'll breed it with this other one'. After thousands of generations, we got poodles.

Q1   Give one use of selective breeding in agriculture.   [1 mark]

Topic B6 — Inheritance, Variation and Evolution

Genetic Engineering

As well as selective breeding, humans can also use genetic engineering to control an organism's features.

Genetic Engineering Involves Changing an Organism's DNA

1) Genetic engineering is used to give organisms new and useful characteristics.

2) It involves cutting a gene out of one organism and putting it into another organism's cells.

3) Organisms that have had a new gene inserted are called genetically modified (GM) organisms.

Genetic Engineering is Useful in Agriculture and Medicine

For example, in agriculture:

1) Crops can be genetically engineered — this makes genetically modified (GM) crops.

2) They may be genetically engineered to be resistant to herbicides (chemicals that kill plants). This means that farmers can spray their crops to kill weeds, without affecting the crop itself.

3) Crops can also be genetically engineered to be resistant to insects or disease. Or they can be made to grow bigger and better fruit.

4) These things can increase crop yield (the amount of food produced).

In medicine:

- Bacteria can be genetically engineered to produce human insulin. This can be used to treat diabetes (see p.62).

- Treatments using genetic modification for inherited diseases are being researched.

But There are Some Concerns About Genetic Engineering

There are concerns about using genetic engineering in animals:

1) It can be hard to predict how changing an animal's DNA will affect the animal.

2) Many genetically modified embryos don't survive.

3) Some genetically modified animals also suffer from health problems later in life.

I say it's great.

There are also concerns about growing GM crops:

1) Some people say that growing GM crops will affect the number of wild flowers. This could also affect the population of insects.

2) Some people are worried that we might not understand the effects of GM crops on human health.

If only there was a gene to make revision easier...

Genetically modified (GM) organisms could be very useful. But we don't yet know what all the consequences of using them might be — so make sure you know what they can be used for and the arguments against them.

Q1   Give one beneficial feature that GM crops can be engineered to have.   [1 mark]

Topic B6 — Inheritance, Variation and Evolution

Fossils

Fossils are great. If they're <u>well-preserved</u>, you can see what really old creatures <u>looked</u> like.

Fossils are the Remains of Plants and Animals

1) Fossils are the <u>remains</u> of organisms from <u>many thousands of years ago</u>. They're found in <u>rocks</u>.
2) They provide the <u>evidence</u> that organisms lived ages ago.
3) Fossils can tell us a lot about <u>how much</u> or <u>how little</u> organisms have <u>changed</u> (<u>evolved</u>) over time.
4) Fossils form in rocks in one of <u>three</u> ways:

1) FROM <u>GRADUAL REPLACEMENT</u> BY MINERALS   (Most fossils happen this way.)

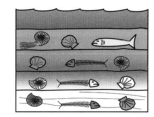

1) Things like <u>teeth</u>, <u>shells</u> and <u>bones</u> don't easily decay.
2) This means they can last a <u>long time</u> when <u>buried</u>.
3) When they do decay, they get <u>replaced by minerals</u>.
4) The minerals form a <u>rock-like substance</u> shaped like the original hard part.

2) FROM <u>CASTS</u> AND <u>IMPRESSIONS</u>

1) Fossils can be formed when an organism is <u>buried</u> in a <u>soft</u> material like <u>clay</u>. The clay <u>hardens</u> around it and the organism <u>decays</u>. The organism leaves a <u>cast</u> of itself. An animal's <u>burrow</u> or a plant's <u>roots</u> can also be preserved as casts.
2) Things like <u>footprints</u> are <u>pressed</u> into soft materials. This leaves an <u>impression</u> when they harden.

3) FROM <u>PRESERVATION</u> IN PLACES WHERE NO DECAY HAPPENS

1) <u>Decay microbes</u> only work if there's <u>oxygen</u>, <u>moisture</u>, <u>warmth</u> and the right <u>pH</u>.
2) In <u>some substances</u> these conditions <u>aren't</u> all <u>present</u>, so decay doesn't happen. For example, there's <u>no oxygen</u> or <u>moisture</u> in <u>amber</u> so decay organisms can't survive.

A preserved organism in amber.

But No One Knows How Life Began

1) Fossils show <u>how much</u> or <u>how little</u> different organisms have changed (<u>evolved</u>) as life has developed on Earth over millions of years.
2) There are lots of <u>hypotheses</u> (see p.1) suggesting how life first came into being. For example:
   • Maybe the <u>first life forms</u> appeared in a <u>swamp</u> (or under the <u>sea</u>) here on <u>Earth</u>.
   • Or maybe simple carbon molecules were brought here on <u>comets</u> and developed into simple life forms.
   But no one really knows.
3) These hypotheses can't be supported or disproved because there's a <u>lack</u> of <u>valid</u> evidence.
4) There's a lack of evidence because many early organisms were <u>soft-bodied</u>. Soft tissue tends to decay away <u>completely</u>. So the fossil record is <u>incomplete</u> (unfinished).
5) Plus, fossils that did form millions of years ago may have been <u>destroyed</u> by <u>geological activity</u>. E.g. the movement of tectonic plates may have <u>crushed</u> fossils already formed in the rock.

Fossils rock my world...

It's a bit mind-boggling really how fossils can still exist even millions of years after the organism died. They really are amazing things, and scientists have learned a whole lot from studying them in detail.

Q1   What are fossils?   [2 marks]

Classification

People really seem to like <u>putting things</u> into <u>groups</u> — biologists certainly do anyway...

Classification is Organising Living Organisms into Groups

1) In the past, organisms were <u>classified</u> according to <u>characteristics</u> you can see (like number of legs). They were also classified by the <u>structures</u> that make them up (like mitochondria in cells).

2) The more similar two organisms <u>appeared</u>, the more <u>closely related</u> they were thought to be.

3) These characteristics were used to classify organisms in the <u>five kingdom classification system</u>.

4) In this system, living things are divided into <u>five groups</u> called <u>kingdoms</u>. These are:

- <u>Animals</u> — fish, mammals, reptiles, etc.
- <u>Plants</u> — grasses, trees, etc.
- <u>Fungi</u> — mushrooms and toadstools, yeasts, all that mouldy stuff on your loaf of bread (yuck).
- <u>Prokaryotes</u> — all <u>single-celled</u> organisms <u>without</u> a nucleus.
- <u>Protists</u> — <u>eukaryotic single-celled</u> organisms.

There's more on prokaryotes and eukaryotes on p.11.

5) The <u>kingdoms</u> are then split into smaller and smaller groups.

6) These groups are <u>phylum</u>, <u>class</u>, <u>order</u>, <u>family</u>, <u>genus</u> and <u>species</u>. ➞

7) The five kingdom classification system was made up by <u>Carl Linnaeus</u>.

Kingdom
Phylum
Class
Order
Family
Genus
Species

Classification Systems Change Over Time

1) Over time, our knowledge of the <u>processes</u> taking place inside organisms has developed.

2) <u>Microscopes</u> have also <u>improved</u> over time. This has allowed us to find out more about the <u>internal structures</u> of organisms.

3) Using this new knowledge, scientists made <u>new</u> models of classification.

4) One of these new models was the <u>three-domain system</u>. It was made up by <u>Carl Woese</u>.

5) He used evidence from <u>analysing chemicals</u> to come up with the system.

6) It showed him that some species were <u>less closely related</u> than first thought.

7) Here's how the three-domain system works:

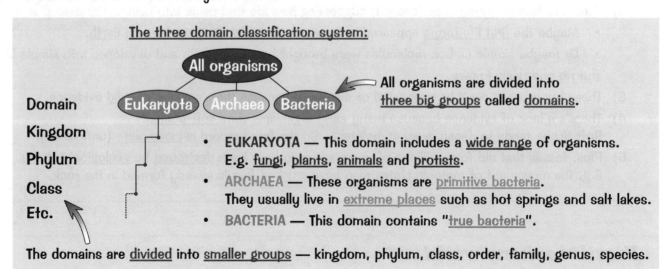

The three domain classification system:

All organisms

Domain — Eukaryota   Archaea   Bacteria

All organisms are divided into <u>three big groups</u> called <u>domains</u>.

Kingdom
Phylum
Class
Etc.

- EUKARYOTA — This domain includes a <u>wide range</u> of organisms. E.g. <u>fungi</u>, <u>plants</u>, <u>animals</u> and <u>protists</u>.
- ARCHAEA — These organisms are <u>primitive bacteria</u>. They usually live in <u>extreme places</u> such as hot springs and salt lakes.
- BACTERIA — This domain contains "<u>true bacteria</u>".

The domains are <u>divided</u> into <u>smaller groups</u> — kingdom, phylum, class, order, family, genus, species.

Classification

Organisms Are Named According to the Binomial System

1) In the binomial system, every organism is given its own <u>two-part</u> Latin name.

2) The <u>first</u> part refers to the <u>genus</u> that the organism belongs to.
   This gives you information on the organism's <u>ancestry</u> (the organisms it's related to).

3) The <u>second</u> part refers to the <u>species</u>.

E.g. humans are known as *Homo sapiens*.

'*Homo*' is the <u>genus</u>...   ...and '*sapiens*' is the <u>species</u>.

Evolutionary Trees Show Relationships

1) Evolutionary trees show how scientists think <u>different species</u> are <u>related</u>.

2) They show <u>common ancestors</u> and relationships between species.

3) The more <u>recent</u> the common ancestor, the more <u>closely related</u> the two species.
   Also, the <u>more characteristics</u> they are likely to <u>share</u>.

4) Scientists look at lots of different types of data to <u>work out</u> these relationships.
   For example:

   • For <u>living</u> organisms, they use <u>current classification data</u>.
   • For <u>extinct</u> species, they use information from the <u>fossil record</u> (see page 74).

Extinct species are species that don't exist any more.

5) Here's an example of an evolutionary tree:

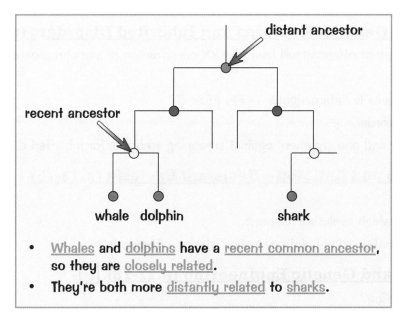

   • <u>Whales</u> and <u>dolphins</u> have a <u>recent common ancestor</u>, so they are <u>closely related</u>.
   • They're both more <u>distantly related</u> to <u>sharks</u>.

Why did the Bacterium break up with the Archaean?

...they didn't have much in common. Biologists have the best jokes. Archaea and Bacteria actually look really similar, but they are more different than we are to a mushroom. It's a strange, strange world we live in...

Q1   What genus does the Eurasian beaver, *Castor fiber*, belong to?   [1 mark]

Revision Questions for Topics B5 & B6

So you've finished Topics B5 and B6 — Hoorah. Now here's a page full of questions to test your knowledge.
*   Try these questions and tick off each one when you get it right.
*   When you've done all the questions under a heading and are completely happy with it, tick it off.

Homeostasis and the Nervous System (p.57-60) ☑

1) What is homeostasis?
2) What makes up the central nervous system?
3) What is a synapse?
4) What is the purpose of a reflex action?
5) Name one factor that can affect reaction time.

Hormones in Humans (p.61-65) ☑

6) Give two differences between nervous and hormonal responses.
7) Name the hormone that reduces the blood glucose concentration.
8) What does luteinising hormone (LH) do?
9) What hormone does the contraceptive injection contain?
10) Which of the following is a hormonal contraceptive — condom, implant or diaphragm?

DNA, Genes, Reproduction and Meiosis (p.66-68) ☑

11) What is meant by 'double helix'?
12) What do genes code for?
13) What is the name for all of the genetic material in an organism?
14) Name the male and female gametes of animals.
15) State the type of cell division used to make gametes in humans.

Sex Chromosomes, Genetic Diagrams and Inherited Disorders (p.69-72) ☑

16) What is the probability that offspring will have the XX combination of sex chromosomes?
17) What are alleles?
18) Which of these genotypes is heterozygous — FF, Ff or ff?
19) Name one inherited disorder.
20) Give one argument for and one argument against screening embryos for inherited disorders.

Variation, Evolution and Antibiotic-Resistant Bacteria (p.73-76) ☑

21) What is variation?
22) Name the process by which evolution happens.
23) What leads to the formation of antibiotic-resistant strains of bacteria?

Selective Breeding and Genetic Engineering (p.77-78) ☑

24) What is selective breeding?
25) What is genetic engineering?

Fossils and Classification (p.79-81) ☑

26) Give one way that fossils can be formed.
27) What is the smallest group in the Linnaean system of classification?
28) Who proposed the 'three-domain system' of classification?

Topic B6 — Inheritance, Variation and Evolution

Competition

Organisms <u>interact</u> with <u>each other</u> and their <u>environment</u>. This is what <u>ecology</u> is all about.

Learn These Words Before You Start

1) <u>Habitat</u> — the place where an organism <u>lives</u>.
2) <u>Population</u> — <u>all</u> the organisms of <u>one species</u> in a <u>habitat</u>.
3) <u>Community</u> — all the <u>populations</u> of <u>different species</u> in a habitat.
4) <u>Ecosystem</u> — the <u>interaction</u> of a <u>community</u> of organisms with the <u>non-living</u> parts of their environment.

Organisms Compete for Resources to Survive

1) <u>Resources</u> are things that organisms need from their <u>environment</u> and <u>other organisms</u> to <u>survive</u> and <u>reproduce</u>:

 - <u>Animals</u> need food, territory (space) and mates.
 - <u>Plants</u> need light, water, space and mineral ions.

2) Organisms <u>compete with other species</u> (and members of their <u>own species</u>) for the <u>same resources</u>.

Organisms in a Community are Interdependent

1) In a community, different species <u>depend</u> on each other for things like <u>food</u>, <u>shelter</u>, <u>pollination</u> and <u>seed dispersal</u>. This is called <u>interdependence</u>.

2) This means that a big change in <u>one part</u> of an ecosystem (e.g. a <u>species</u> being <u>removed</u>) can affect the <u>whole community</u>.

3) The diagram on the right shows part of a <u>food web</u> (a diagram of what eats what) from a <u>stream</u>.

4) If all the stonefly larvae die, then for example:

 - there would be <u>less food</u> for <u>waterboatmen</u>, so their population might <u>decrease</u>.
 - the <u>blackfly larvae</u> would not have to <u>compete</u> with the <u>stonefly larvae</u> for <u>food</u> (algae) so their population might <u>increase</u>.

5) In <u>stable communities</u>, all the species and environmental factors are in <u>balance</u>. This means that the <u>population sizes</u> stay about the <u>same</u>.

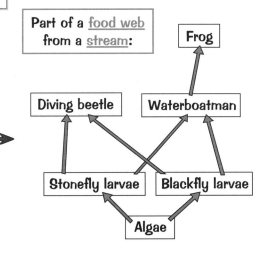

Part of a <u>food web</u> from a <u>stream</u>:

Frog

Diving beetle   Waterboatman

Stonefly larvae   Blackfly larvae

Algae

Everybody needs good neighbours...

Lots of words to learn on this page — but if you do learn them, it'll make your life much easier in the exam.

Q1   What is an ecosystem?   [1 mark]

Q2   Give three resources that plants compete for.   [3 marks]

Abiotic and Biotic Factors

The environment in which organisms live changes all the time. The things that change are either abiotic (non-living) or biotic (living) factors. These changes can have a big effect on a community...

Abiotic Factors Can Change in an Ecosystem...

1) Abiotic factors are the non-living factors in an environment. For example:

2) An increase or decrease in an abiotic factor is a change in the environment.

3) This can affect the size of populations in a community.

4) A change in an abiotic factor that affects one species could also affect the population sizes of other species that depend on them (see previous page). For example:

- Moisture level
- Light intensity
- Temperature
- Carbon dioxide level (for plants)
- Wind intensity and direction
- Oxygen level (for animals that live in water)
- Soil pH and mineral content

- A decrease in the mineral content of the soil could affect the growth of a plant species.
- This could cause a decrease in the population size of the plant species.
- A decrease in the plant population could affect any animal species that depend on it for food.

...and So Can Biotic Factors

1) Biotic factors are the living factors in an environment.

2) A change in a biotic factor could affect the population size of some species. This could then affect species that depend on them (see previous page).

3) Biotic factors include:

1 Competition — one species may outcompete another so that numbers are too low to breed.

- Red and grey squirrels live in the same habitat and eat the same food.
- Grey squirrels outcompete the red squirrels for food and shelter.
- So the population of red squirrels is decreasing.

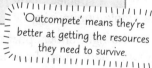
'Outcompete' means they're better at getting the resources they need to survive.

2 New predators (animals that kill other animals)

A new predator could cause a decrease in the prey population. There's more about predator-prey populations on p.86.

3 Availability of food

If there is less food available, the population size will decrease.

4 New pathogens (microorganisms that cause disease)

A new pathogen could quickly decrease the population of an affected species.

Exams — an abiotic factor affecting my environment...

It would be a good idea to learn these two lists of factors. I reckon this is a good time for you to shut the book, scribble them all down and then check how you did. It's the only way they'll get stuck in your brain.

Q1   Give four examples of abiotic factors that could affect a plant species.   [4 marks]

Adaptations

Life exists in so many different environments. It's all because of the adaptations that organisms have...

Adaptations Allow Organisms to Survive

1) Organisms, including microorganisms, are adapted to survive in the conditions of their environment.

2) This means they have special features that suit their environment.

3) These features are called adaptations. Adaptations can be:

- Structural — these are features of an organism's body structure — such as shape or colour. For example:

> Arctic animals (like the Arctic fox) have white fur so they can't be seen against the snow. This helps them avoid predators and sneak up on prey.

> Animals that live in hot places (like camels) have a thin layer of fat and a large surface area compared to their volume. This helps them lose heat.

- Behavioural — these are ways that organisms behave.

> E.g. many species (e.g. swallows) migrate (move away) to warmer climates during the winter. So they avoid the problems of living in cold conditions.

- Functional — these are things that go on inside an organism's body. They can be related to processes like metabolism (all the chemical reactions happening in the body).

> E.g. desert animals make sure they don't lose too much water. They produce very little sweat and small amounts of concentrated urine (wee without much water in it).

Extremophiles Live in Extreme Places

Some microorganisms (e.g. bacteria) are extremophiles — they're adapted to live in extreme conditions. For example:

- at high temperatures (e.g. in super hot volcanic vents),
- in places with a high salt concentration (e.g. very salty lakes),
- at high pressure (e.g. in deep sea vents).

Now I know why my dad refuses to put the heating on...

It's not his fault he's so hairy. If you want to figure out how an organism is adapted to its environment, first think about the conditions it lives in (e.g. temperature). Then look at its features and think how they could be useful.

Q1 The diagram on the right shows a penguin. Some of its adaptations are labelled. Penguins live in the cold, icy environment of the Antarctic. They swim in the sea to hunt for fish to eat. Some penguins huddle together in groups to keep warm.

thick layer of fat
flippers
webbed feet

    a) What type of adaptation is being described when penguins 'huddle together'? [1 mark]

    b) Use the labels on the diagram to explain one way that the penguin is adapted to its environment. [2 marks]

Food Chains

If you like <u>food</u>, and you like <u>chains</u>, then <u>food chains</u> might just blow your mind. Steady now, here we go...

Food Chains Show What's Eaten by What

1) <u>Food chains</u> always start with a <u>producer</u>.
    Producers <u>make</u> (produce) <u>their own food</u> using energy from the Sun.

2) Producers are usually <u>green plants</u> or <u>algae</u> — they make <u>glucose</u> by <u>photosynthesis</u> (see page 50).

3) Some of this glucose is used to make the plant's <u>biomass</u> — its <u>mass</u> of <u>living material</u>.

4) Biomass is <u>passed along</u> a food chain when an organism <u>eats</u> another organism.

5) <u>Consumers</u> are organisms that <u>eat other organisms</u>:
    *   <u>Primary</u> consumers eat <u>producers</u>.
    *   <u>Secondary</u> consumers eat <u>primary</u> consumers.
    *   <u>Tertiary</u> consumers eat <u>secondary</u> consumers.

6) Here's an example of a food chain:

Producers	Primary consumers	Secondary consumer

Populations of Prey and Predators Go in Cycles

1) Consumers that <u>hunt and kill</u> other animals are called <u>predators</u>. The animals they eat are called <u>prey</u>.

2) In a <u>stable community</u>, the <u>population size</u> of a species is <u>limited</u> by the amount of <u>food</u> it has.
    So the population size of <u>predators</u> is <u>affected</u> by the number of their <u>prey</u>.

For more about a stable community see page 83.

1) Foxes are <u>predators</u>. Rabbits are their <u>prey</u>.

2) If the <u>number of rabbits increases</u>, then the number of <u>foxes</u> will <u>increase</u>.

3) This is because there is <u>more food</u> for the foxes.

4) But as the number of foxes <u>increases</u>, then the number of rabbits will <u>decrease</u>.

5) This is because <u>more</u> rabbits will be <u>eaten</u> by the foxes.

Population

Rabbits

Foxes

Time

A peak in rabbit numbers is followed by a peak in foxes

3) It <u>takes a while</u> for one population to <u>respond</u> to changes in the other one.

4) E.g. the number of foxes goes up <u>after</u> the number of rabbits goes up.
    This is because it <u>takes time</u> for the foxes to <u>reproduce</u>.

When the TV volume goes up... my revision goes down...

'Primary' means 'first', so primary consumers are the first consumers in a food chain. Secondary consumers are second and tertiary consumers are third. Producers don't have to be plants, they just have to make their own food.

Q1   Look at the following food chain: grass → grasshopper → rat → snake
      a) Name the producer in the food chain.   [1 mark]
      b) Name the primary consumer in the food chain.   [1 mark]

Using Quadrats PRACTICAL

Studying <u>ecology</u> gives you the chance to <u>rummage around</u> in bushes and get your hands <u>dirty</u>. It's proper fun.

Organisms Live in Different Places Because The Environment Varies

1) The <u>distribution</u> of an organism is <u>where</u> an organism is <u>found</u>.
2) Where an organism is found is affected by <u>biotic and abiotic factors</u> (see page 84).
3) An organism might be <u>more common</u> in <u>one area</u> than another due to <u>differences</u> in <u>factors</u> between the two areas. For example, in a field, you might find daisies are more common in the <u>open</u> than <u>under trees</u>, because there's <u>more light</u>.
4) To <u>study</u> the distribution of an organism you can use <u>quadrats</u> or <u>transects</u> (p.88).

Use Quadrats to Study The Distribution of Small Organisms

Here's how to compare <u>how common</u> an organism is in <u>two different areas</u> — these are called <u>sample areas</u>.

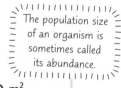
A quadrat (square frame)

1) Place a <u>quadrat</u> on the ground in the <u>first</u> sample area. It needs to be placed at <u>random</u> (see p.240).
2) <u>Count</u> all the organisms you're interested in <u>within</u> the quadrat.
3) <u>Repeat</u> steps 1 and 2 as many times as you can.
4) <u>Work out</u> the <u>mean</u> number of organisms per quadrat within the first sample area.

> **EXAMPLE:** Anna counted the number of daisies in 7 quadrats within her first sample area. She recorded the following results: 18, 20, 22, 23, 23, 23, 25
>
> Here the MEAN is: $\frac{\text{TOTAL number of organisms}}{\text{NUMBER of quadrats}} = \frac{154}{7} = 22$ daisies per quadrat

5) <u>Repeat</u> steps 1 to 4 in the <u>second</u> sample area.
6) Finally <u>compare</u> the two means. E.g. you might find 2 daisies per quadrat in a shady area, and 22 daisies per quadrat (lots more) in a sunny area.

You Can Work Out the Population Size of an Organism

The population size of an organism is sometimes called its abundance.

> **EXAMPLE:** Students used 0.25 m² quadrats to randomly sample daisies in a field. They found a mean of 10 daisies per quadrat. The field's area was 800 m². Estimate the population of daisies in the field.
>
> 1) Divide the area of the habitat by the quadrat size.   800 ÷ 0.25 = 3200
> 2) Multiply this by the mean number of organisms per quadrat.   3200 × 10 = 32 000 daisies in the field

Drat, drat, and double drat — my favourite use of quadrats...

It's key that you make sure you put your quadrat down in a random place before you start counting.

Q1 A field was randomly sampled for buttercups using 0.25 m² quadrats. The field had an area of 1200 m². A mean of 0.75 buttercups was found per quadrat. Estimate the total population of buttercups. [2 marks]

Using Transects

So, now you think you've learnt all about distribution. Well hold on — there's more ecology fun to be had.

Use Transects to Study The Distribution of Organisms Along a Line

You can use lines called transects to help find out how organisms are distributed across an area.
E.g. if an organism becomes more or less common as you move from a hedge towards the middle of a field.
Here's what to do:

1) Mark out a line in the area you want to study using a tape measure.

2) Collect data along the line by either:

- Counting all the organisms you're interested in that touch the line.

- Or by using quadrats (see previous page) placed along the line.

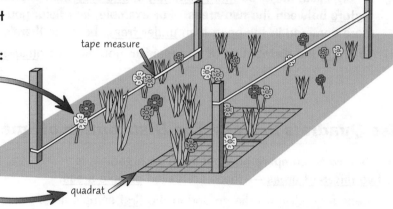

tape measure

quadrat

You Can Estimate the Percentage Cover of a Quadrat

1) Sometimes it can be difficult to count all of the organisms in a quadrat (e.g. if they're grass).

2) In this case, you can find the percentage cover instead.

3) This means estimating the percentage area of the quadrat that the organisms cover.

4) You can do this by counting the number of little squares they cover.

EXAMPLE: Some students were measuring the distribution of an organism across a school playing field. They placed quadrats at regular intervals along a transect. Below is a picture of one of the quadrats. Calculate the percentage cover of the organism in this quadrat.

One quadrat

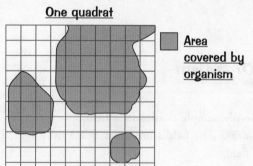

☐ Area covered by organism

1) Count the number of squares covered by the organism. You count a square if it's more than half covered.

47 squares are covered by the organism.

2) Make this into a percentage:
- Divide the number of squares covered by the organism by the total number of squares in the quadrat (100).
- Multiply the result by 100.

$(47/100) \times 100$

$= 0.47 \times 100 = 47\%$

A slug that's been run over — definitely a widely-spread organism

So if you want to measure the distribution of an organism across an area, you could use a transect. You can use it alone or you can use it with quadrats. Now who's for a game of tennis... I've got my transect up.

Q1 Some students want to measure how the distribution of dandelions changes across a field. Describe a method they could use to do this.

[2 marks]

The Water Cycle

Without the water cycle, we wouldn't get enough water to survive.
And I don't just mean there'd be no paddling pools, ice lollies or bubble baths...

The Water Cycle Means Water is Constantly Recycled

1) Energy from the Sun makes water evaporate from the land and sea.
   This turns the water into water vapour.

2) Water also evaporates from plants — this is called transpiration (see p.39).

3) The warm water vapour is carried upwards.
   When it gets higher up, the water vapour cools. It condenses to form clouds.

4) Water falls from the clouds as precipitation (usually rain, but sometimes snow or hail).
   Precipitation provides fresh water for plants and animals:

Plants

- Some water is absorbed by the soil. Plants take up the water through their roots.
- Plants need water for things like photosynthesis (p.50).
- Some water becomes part of the plants' tissues. It's passed to animals when plants are eaten.

Animals

- Animals need water for the chemical reactions in their bodies.
- They return water to the soil and atmosphere in their waste (e.g. sweat and urine).

5) Water that doesn't get absorbed by the soil will run off into streams and rivers.

6) The water drains back into the sea. Then it evaporates all over again.

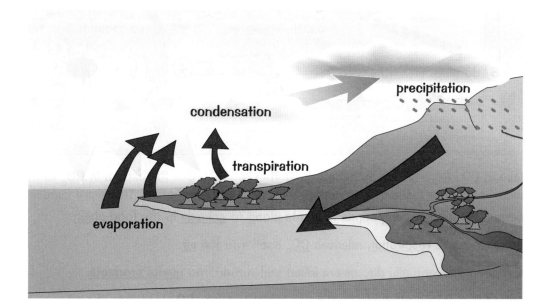

Come on out, it's only a little water cycle, it won't hurt you...

The most important thing to remember is that it's a cycle — there's no beginning or end. Water that falls
to the ground as rain will end up back as clouds again. Then fall again... then rise again... and so on.

Q1   a) In the water cycle, how does water move from the land into the air?   [1 mark]
     b) How does the water cycle benefit plants and animals?   [1 mark]

The Carbon Cycle

All the <u>nutrients</u> in our environment get <u>recycled</u> — there's a balance between what <u>goes in</u> and what <u>goes out</u>.

Materials are Recycled by Decay

1) <u>Living things</u> are made of <u>materials</u> they <u>take</u> from the world around them.

> E.g. plants take up <u>mineral ions</u> from the soil.
> These are used to make <u>molecules</u> that make up the plant.
> The molecules are <u>passed up the food chain</u> when the plant is <u>eaten</u>.

2) These materials are <u>returned</u> to the environment in <u>waste products</u>, or when <u>dead</u> organisms <u>decay</u>.

3) Materials decay because they're <u>broken down</u> by <u>microorganisms</u>.

4) <u>Decay</u> puts stuff that plants need to <u>grow</u> (e.g. mineral ions) <u>back</u> into the <u>soil</u> — they are <u>recycled</u>.

The Constant Cycling of Carbon is called the Carbon Cycle

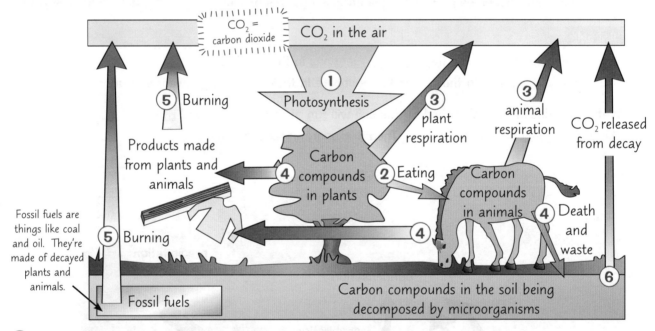

① <u>Plants</u> take in CO_2 from the air during <u>photosynthesis</u>. They use the carbon in CO_2 to make <u>glucose</u>. This glucose is used to make carbon compounds, e.g. <u>carbohydrates</u>. These are used for <u>growth</u>.

② <u>Eating</u> passes the carbon compounds in plants along to <u>animals</u> in the <u>food chain</u>.

③ Both plant and animal <u>respiration</u> releases CO_2 back into the <u>air</u>.

④ Plants and animals eventually <u>die</u>, or are killed and turned into <u>useful products</u>.

⑤ <u>Burning</u> plant and animal products (and fossil fuels) releases CO_2 back into the air.

⑥ <u>Microorganisms</u> break down <u>animal waste</u> and <u>dead organisms</u>. As they break down the material, they <u>release CO_2</u> back into the air through <u>respiration</u>.

See p.53-54 for more on respiration.

What goes around comes around...

Carbon is very important for living things — it's the basis for loads of the molecules in our bodies.

Q1   What causes materials to decay?   [1 mark]

Q2   Describe how carbon is removed from the atmosphere in the carbon cycle.   [1 mark]

Biodiversity and Waste Management

Unfortunately, human activity can <u>negatively affect</u> the <u>planet</u> and its <u>variety of life</u>. Read on for bad news...

Earth's Biodiversity is Important

Biodiversity is the variety of different species of organisms on Earth, or within an ecosystem.

1) Different species <u>depend</u> on each other for different things in an ecosystem (see page 83).
2) Different species can also help keep the <u>conditions</u> in their <u>environment</u> right for each other, e.g. they can help keep the soil at the right pH.
3) So having a <u>high biodiversity</u> can mean that an ecosystem is more <u>stable</u>.
4) For the human species to <u>survive</u>, it's important that a good level of biodiversity is maintained.
5) Lots of human actions are <u>reducing</u> biodiversity (see below and pages 92-93).
6) It's only <u>recently</u> that we've started <u>taking measures</u> to <u>stop</u> biodiversity decreasing.

More People Means Greater Demands on the Environment

1) The <u>population</u> of the world is <u>increasing</u> very quickly.
2) <u>More people</u> need <u>more resources</u> to survive.
3) People are also demanding a <u>higher standard of living</u>. This means that more people want <u>luxuries</u> that make life more comfortable, e.g. cars, computers, etc.
4) This means that we use <u>more raw materials</u> and <u>more energy</u> to make things.
5) So resources are being <u>used</u> more quickly than they are being <u>replaced</u>.

We're Also Producing More Waste

1) As we make more things, we produce more <u>waste</u>. This includes <u>waste chemicals</u>.
2) This waste can cause <u>harmful pollution</u> if it's not <u>handled properly</u>.
3) Pollution <u>kills</u> plants and animals. This <u>reduces biodiversity</u>.
4) <u>Pollution</u> can affect:

> **1) Water**
> - <u>Sewage</u> and <u>toxic chemicals</u> from industry can pollute lakes, rivers and oceans.
> - <u>Fertilisers</u> (and other chemicals) used on land can be washed into water.
> - This will affect the plants and animals that rely on these sources of water for survival.

> **2) Land**
> - We use <u>toxic chemicals</u> for farming (e.g. pesticides and herbicides).
> - We dump a lot of <u>household waste</u> in landfill sites.

> **3) Air** <u>Smoke</u> and <u>acidic gases</u> can pollute the air if they are released into the atmosphere.

More people = more mess...

Biodiversity's a useful thing, but some of the things that humans do means that it's being reduced every day.

Q1   What is meant by the term 'biodiversity'?   [1 mark]

Global Warming

The Earth is getting <u>warmer</u>. Scientists are now trying to work out what the <u>effects</u> of this might be.

Carbon Dioxide and Methane Trap Energy from the Sun

1) Gases in the Earth's <u>atmosphere</u> trap energy from the Sun.

2) These gases mean that <u>not all</u> of the <u>energy</u> is <u>lost</u> into space. This helps to keep the Earth <u>warm</u>.

3) These gases are called <u>greenhouse gases</u>. Without them the Earth would be <u>very cold</u>.

4) But the levels of two greenhouse gases are <u>increasing</u> — <u>carbon dioxide</u> (CO_2) and <u>methane</u>.

5) The increasing <u>levels</u> of greenhouse gases are causing the Earth to <u>heat up</u> — this is <u>global warming</u>.

The Results of Global Warming Could be Pretty Serious

There are several reasons to be <u>worried</u> about global warming. Here are a few:

Flooding

1) Higher temperatures cause <u>seawater</u> to <u>expand</u> and <u>ice</u> to <u>melt</u>. This causes the sea level to <u>rise</u>.

2) If it keeps rising it'll lead to <u>flooding</u> of low-lying land.

3) This will result in the loss of <u>habitats</u> (where organisms live).

Changes in the distribution of species

1) Global warming may lead to changes in <u>rainfall</u> and <u>temperature</u> in many areas.

2) This could cause the <u>distribution</u> (spread) of many <u>animal</u> and <u>plant species</u> to change.

3) E.g. if some areas become <u>warmer</u>:
- Species that <u>do well</u> in <u>warm</u> conditions may spread <u>further</u>.
- Species that need <u>cooler temperatures</u> may have a <u>smaller</u> area to live in.

Less biodiversity

1) Some species may not be able to <u>survive</u> a <u>change</u> in the climate.

2) These species might become <u>extinct</u>.

3) This could <u>reduce biodiversity</u> (see p.91).

Changes in migration patterns

1) There could be <u>changes in migration patterns</u> (where animals move to during different seasons).

2) E.g. some birds may migrate <u>further north</u>, as more northern areas are getting <u>warmer</u>.

The greenhouse effect — when you start growing into a tomato...

Global warming is rarely out of the news. Most scientists accept that it's happening and that human activity has caused most of the recent warming. However, they don't know exactly what the effects will be.

Q1   Explain how global warming could lead to the loss of low-lying habitats.   [3 marks]

Deforestation and Land Use

Trees and peat bogs trap carbon dioxide and lock it up. The problems start when it escapes...

Humans Use Lots of Land for Lots of Purposes

1) We use land for things like building, quarrying, farming and dumping waste.
2) This means that there's less land available for other organisms.
3) Sometimes, the way we use land has a bad effect on the environment.

Deforestation Can Cause Many Problems

1) Deforestation is the cutting down of forests. It is done for many reasons, like:
   - To clear land for farming (e.g. cattle or rice crops) to provide more food.
   - To grow crops to make biofuels.
2) This causes big problems when it's done on a large-scale, e.g. cutting down rainforests in tropical areas. These are:

LESS CARBON DIOXIDE TAKEN IN

1) Trees take in carbon dioxide (CO_2) from the atmosphere during photosynthesis (page 50).
2) So cutting down trees means that less carbon dioxide is removed from the atmosphere.
3) Trees 'lock up' some of the carbon in their wood. Removing trees means that less is locked up.

More CO_2 in the atmosphere causes global warming (see previous page).

MORE CARBON DIOXIDE RELEASED

1) Carbon dioxide is released when trees are burnt to clear land.
2) Microorganisms feeding on dead wood release carbon dioxide through respiration (p.54).

LESS BIODIVERSITY

1) Habitats like forests can contain many species of plants and animals — they have high biodiversity.
2) When forests are destroyed, many species may become extinct (p.74). This reduces biodiversity.

Destroying Peat Bogs Adds More CO_2 to the Atmosphere

1) Bogs are areas of land that are acidic and waterlogged.
2) Plants that live in bogs don't fully decay when they die. The partly-rotted plants build up to form peat.
3) So the carbon in the plants is stored in the peat.
4) Peat bogs can be drained, so the peat can be sold to gardeners as compost.
5) When the peat is drained, microorganisms can break it down. They release CO_2 when they respire.
6) Peat can also be sold as a fuel. CO_2 is released when the peat is burned.
7) Destroying the bogs reduces the area of the habitat.
8) This reduces the number of animals, plants and microorganisms that live there. So it reduces biodiversity.

Don't get bogged down with all these problems...

Removing trees and peat bogs means more carbon dioxide, which means more global warming. Bad times.

Q1   Give two reasons for carrying out deforestation.   [2 marks]

Maintaining Ecosystems and Biodiversity

It's really important that biodiversity is <u>maintained</u>...

Programmes Can be Set Up to Protect Ecosystems and Biodiversity

1) Human activities can <u>reduce biodiversity</u> and <u>damage ecosystems</u>.

2) In some areas, <u>programmes</u> to <u>minimise the damage</u> have been set up by <u>concerned citizens</u> and <u>scientists</u>.

3) Here are a few examples:

Breeding programmes

1) Animal species that are at <u>risk</u> of dying out are called <u>endangered species</u>.
2) They can be bred in <u>captivity</u>.
3) This makes sure some individuals will <u>survive</u> if the species <u>dies out</u> in the wild.
4) Individuals can sometimes be <u>released</u> into the <u>wild</u>. This can be to <u>boost</u> a population or <u>replace</u> one that's been wiped out.

Habitat protection

<u>Protecting</u> and <u>regenerating</u> (rebuilding) <u>rare habitats</u> helps to protect the <u>species</u> that live there.

Reintroducing hedgerows and field margins

1) Field margins are areas of land around the <u>edges</u> of fields where wild flowers and grasses are left to <u>grow</u>.
2) <u>Hedges</u> can be planted around fields to form <u>hedgerows</u>.
3) Hedgerows and field margins provide a <u>habitat</u> for <u>lots of types</u> of organisms.
4) This is very useful for fields that only have <u>one type of crop</u>. This is because these fields have <u>very low biodiversity</u>.

Recycling

1) This <u>reduces</u> the amount of <u>waste</u> that gets dumped in <u>landfill</u> sites.
2) This could <u>reduce</u> the amount of <u>land</u> taken over for landfill. So <u>ecosystems</u> can be left alone.

Government programmes

1) Deforestation <u>increases</u> the amount of <u>carbon dioxide</u> in the atmosphere (see previous page).
2) Some governments have made <u>rules</u> to <u>reduce deforestation</u>.
3) They have also made rules to reduce the amount of <u>carbon dioxide</u> released by <u>businesses</u>.
4) This could help to <u>stop global warming increasing</u> (see page 92).

If you go down to the woods today... there might be more bears than before.

Some people might not be keen on some of these programmes (e.g. people who are paid to cut down trees). You've got to learn all the examples above though, even if you don't like them. Sorry.

Q1   Explain how biodiversity can be increased in areas that farm single crops.   [2 marks]

Q2   Describe how breeding programmes preserve endangered species.   [2 marks]

Revision Questions for Topic B7

That's Topic B7 done with. I bet you're right in the mood for a long list of revision question now.
You're in luck.

- Try these questions and tick off each one when you get it right.
- When you've done all the questions under a heading and are completely happy with it, tick it off.

Competition, Abiotic and Biotic Factors, and Adaptations (p.83-85) ☑

1) Define 'habitat'. ☑
2) What things do animals compete for in an ecosystem? ☑
3) What is meant by a 'stable community'? ☑
4) What are biotic factors? ☑
5) What are functional adaptations? ☑

Food Chains (p.86) ☐

6) What do food chains always start with? ☑
7) Explain what happens to the population size of a predator
if the amount of its prey increases. ☑

Quadrats and Transects (p.87-88) ☐

8) Explain how a quadrat can be used to investigate the distribution of clover plants in two areas. ☑
9) Suggest why you might use a transect when investigating the distribution of organisms. ☑

The Water and Carbon Cycles (p.89-90) ☑

10) When water vapour cools and condenses in the atmosphere, what does it change into? ☑
11) How do microorganisms return carbon to the atmosphere? ☑

Human Impacts on the Planet (p.91-94) ☐

12) Suggest why it's important to have high biodiversity in an ecosystem. ☑
13) Name two gases linked to global warming. ☑
14) Give one way global warming could reduce biodiversity. ☑
15) Give two reasons why deforestation increases the amount of carbon dioxide in the atmosphere. ☑
16) Explain why the destruction of peat bogs adds more carbon dioxide to the atmosphere. ☑
17) How can recycling programmes help to protect ecosystems? ☑

Atoms

All substances are made of <u>atoms</u>. They're really <u>tiny</u> — too small to see. Atoms are so tiny
that a <u>50p piece</u> contains about 77 400 000 000 000 000 000 000 of them. Quite a lot then...

Atoms Contain Protons, Neutrons and Electrons

1) Atoms have a radius of about <u>0.1 nanometers</u> (that's 1×10^{-10} m).
There are a few different modern models of the atom —
but chemists tend to like the model below best.

A nanometer (nm) is
0.000000001 m. Shown in
standard form, that's 1×10^{-9} m.
Standard form is used for showing
really large or really small numbers.

<u>Nucleus</u>:

- It's in the <u>middle</u> of the atom.
- It contains <u>protons</u> and <u>neutrons</u>.
- The nucleus has a <u>radius</u> of around 1×10^{-14} m
  (that's around 1/10 000 of the atomic radius).
- It has a <u>positive charge</u> because of the protons.
- Almost the <u>whole</u> mass of the atom is in the nucleus.

atomic
radius

<u>Electrons</u>:

- Move <u>around</u> the nucleus
  in electron <u>shells</u> (levels).
- They're <u>negatively charged</u>.
- Electrons have almost <u>no</u> mass.

2) You need to know the <u>charges</u> of protons, neutrons and electrons. You also need to know how
<u>heavy</u> they are compared to each other (their <u>relative masses</u>).

3) <u>Protons</u> are <u>heavy</u> (compared to electrons) and <u>positively</u> charged.

4) <u>Neutrons</u> are <u>heavy</u> (compared to electrons) and <u>neutral</u>.

5) <u>Electrons</u> are <u>tiny</u> and <u>negatively</u> charged.

Particle	Relative Mass	Relative Charge
Proton	1	+1
Neutron	1	0
Electron	Very small	−1

Atomic Number and Mass Number Describe an Atom

1) The <u>nuclear symbol</u> of an atom tells you its
<u>atomic (proton) number</u> and <u>mass number</u>.

<u>atomic number</u> = number of protons

<u>mass number</u> = number of protons + number of neutrons

<u>number of neutrons</u> = mass number – atomic number

Nuclear symbol for sodium.

Mass number → 23
Atomic number → 11 **Na**

Element symbol
(see next page
for more on
symbols).

Number of <u>protons</u> = 11
Number of <u>neutrons</u> = 23 – 11 = 12
Number of <u>electrons</u> = 11

2) Atoms have <u>no charge</u> overall. They're neutral.

3) This is because they have the <u>same number</u> of <u>protons</u> as <u>electrons</u>. So, in an atom...

<u>number of electrons</u> = atomic number

4) The <u>charge</u> on the electrons is the <u>same size</u> as the charge
on the <u>protons</u>, but <u>opposite</u> — so they <u>cancel out</u>.

5) In an <u>ion</u>, the number of protons <u>doesn't equal</u>
the number of <u>electrons</u>. This means it has an
<u>overall charge</u>. For example, an ion with a
<u>2– charge</u>, has <u>two more</u> electrons than protons.

An ion is an atom or
group of atoms that has
lost or gained electrons.

In a <u>positive ion</u>:
<u>number of electrons</u> = atomic number – charge

In a <u>negative</u> ion:
<u>number of electrons</u> = atomic number + charge

Let's be positive about this — unless you're an electron of course...

Atoms may be tiny, and the things inside them even smaller, but this stuff is still super important.

Q1   An atom of nitrogen has an atomic number of 7 and a mass number of 14.
Give the number of electrons, protons and neutrons in the atom.

[3 marks]

Elements

An <u>element</u> is a substance made up of atoms that all have the <u>same</u> number of <u>protons</u> in their nucleus.

Elements are Made Up of Atoms With the Same Atomic Number

1) The <u>smallest part</u> of an element that you can have is a <u>single atom</u> of that element.

2) The number of <u>protons</u> in the nucleus decides what <u>type</u> of atom it is.

There are about 100 different elements

3) For example, an atom with <u>one proton</u> in its nucleus is <u>hydrogen</u>. An atom with <u>two protons</u> is <u>helium</u>.

4) If a substance only contains atoms with the <u>same number</u> of <u>protons</u> it's called an <u>element</u>.

5) So <u>all the atoms</u> of a particular <u>element</u> have the <u>same number</u> of protons.
And <u>different elements</u> have atoms with <u>different numbers</u> of protons.

Atoms Can be Represented by Symbols

1) Atoms of each element can be represented by a <u>one or two letter symbol</u>.

2) You'll see these symbols on the periodic table (see page 107).

3) For example: | **C** = carbon **O** = oxygen **Na** = sodium **Mg** = magnesium **Fe** = iron

Isotopes are the Same Except for Extra Neutrons

1) <u>Isotopes</u> are atoms with the <u>same</u> number of <u>protons</u> but a <u>different</u> number of <u>neutrons</u>.

2) So they have the <u>same atomic number</u> but <u>different mass numbers</u>.

Carbon-12 and carbon-13 are isotopes of <u>carbon</u>.

<u>Carbon-12</u> $^{12}_{6}\text{C}$ 6 Protons
6 Electrons
6 Neutrons

<u>Carbon-13</u> $^{13}_{6}\text{C}$ 6 Protons
6 Electrons
7 Neutrons

The number of neutrons is the mass number minus the atomic number.

3) If an element has a number of isotopes, you can describe it using <u>relative atomic mass</u> (A_r) instead of mass number. This is an <u>average</u> mass.

4) A_r is worked out from the <u>different masses</u> and <u>abundances</u> (amounts) of each isotope.

5) You can use this <u>formula</u> to work out the <u>relative atomic mass</u> of an element:

$$\text{relative atomic mass } (A_r) = \frac{\text{sum of (isotope abundance} \times \text{isotope mass number)}}{\text{sum of abundances of all the isotopes}}$$

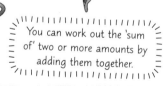

You can work out the 'sum' of two or more amounts by adding them together.

EXAMPLE: Copper has two stable isotopes. Cu-63 has an abundance of 69.2% and Cu-65 has an abundance of 30.8%. Calculate the relative atomic mass of copper to 1 decimal place.

abundance × mass number of Cu-63   abundance × mass number of Cu-65

$$\text{Relative atomic mass} = \frac{(69.2 \times 63) + (30.8 \times 65)}{69.2 + 30.8} = \frac{4359.6 + 2002}{100} = \frac{6361.6}{100} = 63.616 = \mathbf{63.6}$$

abundance of Cu-63 + abundance of Cu-65

Ah — the symbol for the element of surprise...

Atoms, elements and isotopes — make sure you know what they are and the differences between them.

Q1   What are isotopes?   [1 mark]

Compounds

It would be great if we only had to deal with elements. But unluckily for you, elements can mix and match to make lots of new substances called compounds. And this makes things a little bit more complicated...

Atoms Join Together to Make Compounds

1) During a chemical reaction, at least one new substance is made.
   You can usually measure a change in energy such as a temperature change, as well.

2) When two or more elements react, they form compounds.
   Compounds are substances that contain atoms of different elements.

3) The atoms of each element are in fixed proportions (amounts) in the compound.

4) The atoms are held together by chemical bonds.

5) The only way to separate a compound into its elements is by using a chemical reaction.

> There are different types of compound. For example, ionic compounds (see p.115) and covalent compounds (see p.117).

A Formula Shows What Atoms are in a Compound

1) Compounds can be represented by formulas.

2) The formulas are made up of element symbols in the same proportions as the elements in the compound.

3) The number of different element symbols tells you how many elements are in the compound.

4) For example, carbon dioxide, CO_2, is a compound made from a reaction between carbon and oxygen.

5) It contains 1 carbon atom and 2 oxygen atoms.

carbon + oxygen ⟶ carbon dioxide

As an element, oxygen goes around in pairs of atoms (so it's O_2).

6) Here's another example: the formula of sulfuric acid is H_2SO_4.
   So, each molecule contains 2 hydrogen atoms, 1 sulfur atom and 4 oxygen atoms.

7) There might be brackets in a formula, e.g. calcium hydroxide is $Ca(OH)_2$.

8) The little number 2 outside the bracket means there's two of everything inside the brackets.

9) So in $Ca(OH)_2$ there's 1 calcium atom, 2 oxygen atoms and 2 hydrogen atoms.

10) Here are some examples of formulas which might come in handy:

Carbon dioxide — CO_2	Sodium chloride — NaCl	Calcium chloride — $CaCl_2$
Ammonia — NH_3	Carbon monoxide — CO	Sodium carbonate — Na_2CO_3
Water — H_2O	Hydrochloric acid — HCl	Sulfuric acid — H_2SO_4

The formula for success — revision, more revision and cake...

Formulas are super important for showing chemical reactions. Make sure you understand how they work — you'll be coming across them quite a bit in the rest of this book.

Q1   How many atoms are in one particle of Na_2CO_3?   [1 mark]

Q2   What is a compound?   [3 marks]

Topic C1 — Atomic Structure and the Periodic Table

Chemical Equations

Chemical equations are really important to chemistry. Pretty much like tomato ketchup is to a bacon butty. Mmm... bacon butties... Sorry, I got distracted. Let's do this.

Chemical Reactions are Shown Using Chemical Equations

1) One way to show a chemical reaction is to write a word equation.

2) Word equations show the names of the chemicals that are reacting and being produced.

> **Here's an example** — methane reacts with oxygen to make carbon dioxide and water:
>
> The chemicals on the left-hand side of the equation are called the reactants (because they react with each other).
>
> methane + oxygen → carbon dioxide + water
>
> The chemicals on the right-hand side are called the products (because they've been produced from the reactants).

Symbol Equations Show the Atoms on Both Sides

1) Chemical reactions can be shown using symbol equations.

2) Symbol equations just show the symbols or formulas of the reactants and products.

magnesium + oxygen		magnesium oxide
$2Mg + O_2$	→	$2MgO$

You'll have spotted that there's a '2' in front of the Mg and the MgO. The reason for this is explained below...

Symbol Equations Need to be Balanced

1) There must always be the same number of atoms on both sides — they can't just disappear.

2) You balance the equation by putting numbers in front of the formulas.
Take this equation for reacting sulfuric acid with sodium hydroxide:

$$H_2SO_4 + NaOH \rightarrow Na_2SO_4 + H_2O$$

Left-hand side	Right-hand side
H = 3	H = 2
S = 1	S = 1
O = 5	O = 5
Na = 1	Na = 2

3) The formulas are all correct but the numbers of some atoms don't match up on both sides.

4) The more you practise, the quicker you get, but all you do is this:

> 1) Find an element that doesn't balance and pencil in a number in front of one of the substances to try and sort it out.
>
> 2) See where it gets you. The equation may still not be balanced. Don't worry, just pencil in another number and see where that gets you.
>
> 3) Keep doing this until the equation is completely balanced.

You can't change formulas like H_2SO_4 to H_2SO_5. You can only put numbers in front of them.

EXAMPLE: In the equation above you'll notice we're short of Na atoms on the LHS (Left-Hand Side).

1) The only thing you can do about that is make it 2NaOH instead of just NaOH:

$$H_2SO_4 + 2NaOH \rightarrow Na_2SO_4 + H_2O$$

2) But that now gives too many H atoms and O atoms on the LHS. So to balance that up you could try putting 2H₂O on the RHS (Right-Hand Side):

$$H_2SO_4 + 2NaOH \rightarrow Na_2SO_4 + 2H_2O$$

LHS	RHS
H = 4	H = 2
S = 1	S = 1
O = 6	O = 5
Na = 2	Na = 2

3) And suddenly there it is — everything balances. Woohoo.

Revision is all about getting the balance right...

Balancing equations is all about practice. Once you have a few goes you'll see it's much less scary than it seemed.

Q1   Balance the equation: $Fe + Cl_2 \rightarrow FeCl_3$ [1 mark]

Mixtures

Mixtures in <u>chemistry</u> are just like mixtures in baking, lots of <u>separate</u> things all mixed together. But most of the time they're considerably less delicious. And you probably shouldn't eat them. Or put them in an oven.

Mixtures are Easily Separated — Not Like Compounds

1) Mixtures contain <u>at least two</u> different <u>elements</u> or <u>compounds</u>.

2) There <u>aren't</u> any <u>chemical bonds</u> between the different parts of a mixture.

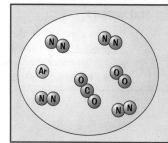

<u>Air</u> is a <u>mixture</u> of gases, mainly nitrogen, oxygen, carbon dioxide and argon.
The gases can all be <u>separated out</u> fairly easily.

<u>Crude oil</u> is a <u>mixture</u> of different length hydrocarbon molecules (see p.147).

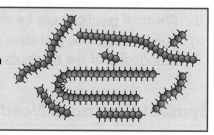

3) The different parts of a mixture can be <u>separated</u> out by <u>methods</u> such as:

- filtration (p.102)
- crystallisation (p.102)
- simple distillation (p.103)
- fractional distillation (p.103)
- chromatography (p.101)

Mikey, I said, "at least two elements..."

4) The methods are all <u>physical methods</u>.
This means they <u>don't</u> involve any chemical reactions, and don't form any new substances.

Each Part of a Mixture Keeps Its Own Properties

1) Properties describe what a substance is <u>like</u> and how it <u>behaves</u>, such as hardness or boiling point.

2) The <u>properties</u> of a mixture are just a <u>mixture</u> of the properties of the <u>separate parts</u>. The chemical properties of a substance <u>aren't</u> changed by it being part of a mixture.

For example, a <u>mixture</u> of <u>iron powder</u> and <u>sulfur powder</u> will show the <u>properties</u> of <u>both</u> iron and sulfur. It will contain grey magnetic bits of iron and bright yellow bits of sulfur.

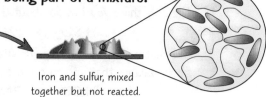

Iron and sulfur, mixed together but not reacted.

Revision and fun are a mixture — easily separated...

Think of mixtures like Pick 'n' Mix sweets. If you add a fizzy cola bottle to your bag of jelly snakes, fried eggs and chocolate mice, it stays as a fizzy cola bottle. You don't get a fizzy, fried jelly mouse or a chocolate cola snake egg.

Q1   Give two methods that can be used to separate mixtures.   [2 marks]

Chromatography

Ahh, chromatography. Chemistry mixed with pretty patterns of spots — what more could you want in a page...

You Need to Know How to Do Paper Chromatography

One method of separating substances in a mixture is chromatography.
Chromatography can be used to separate different dyes in an ink. Here's how you can do it:

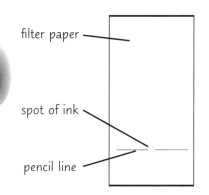

filter paper

spot of ink

pencil line

1) Draw a line near the bottom of a sheet of filter paper. (Use a pencil to do this — pencil marks won't dissolve in the solvent.)

2) Add a spot of the ink to the line.

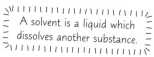
A solvent is a liquid which dissolves another substance.

3) Pour a small amount of solvent into a beaker so it forms a shallow layer.

4) The solvent used depends on what's being tested. Some compounds dissolve well in water, but sometimes other solvents, like ethanol, are needed.

5) Place the sheet in the beaker of solvent. Make sure the ink isn't touching the solvent — you don't want it to dissolve into it.

6) Place a lid on top of the container to stop the solvent evaporating.

7) The solvent seeps up the paper, carrying the ink with it.

8) When the solvent has nearly reached the top of the paper, take the paper out of the beaker and leave it to dry.

9) The end result is a pattern of spots called a chromatogram.

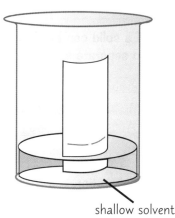

shallow solvent

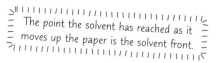
The point the solvent has reached as it moves up the paper is the solvent front.

Chromatography Separates the Parts of a Mixture Into Different Spots

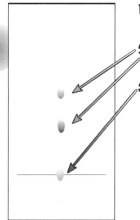

1) During chromatography, each different dye in the ink moves up the paper at a different speed. This separates the dyes.

2) Each dye will form a spot in a different place. So there should be 1 spot for each dye in the ink.

3) If any of the dyes in the ink don't dissolve in the solvent, they'll stay on the pencil line.

All hairdressers have to master Combatography...

Chromatography is actually mighty useful in real life. It's used to test whether athletes have taken drugs. It can also be used to test things from crime scenes. Eeek...

Q1   Give one reason why a dye might stay on the pencil line during chromatography.   [1 mark]

More Separation Techniques

Filtration and crystallisation are <u>methods</u> of <u>separating mixtures</u>. Chemists use these methods all the time to separate <u>solids</u> from <u>liquids</u>, so it's worth making sure you know how to do them.

Filtration Separates Insoluble Solids from Liquids

<u>Filtration</u> can be used to <u>separate</u> an <u>insoluble solid</u> from a <u>liquid reaction mixture</u> (insoluble solids <u>can't</u> be dissolved in the liquid). This can help make substances <u>pure</u>.

1) Put some <u>filter paper</u> in a <u>funnel</u>.

2) <u>Pour</u> the mixture into the filter paper.

3) Make sure the mixture <u>doesn't</u> go above the filter paper.

4) The <u>liquid passes through</u> the paper into the beaker. The <u>solid is left</u> behind in the filter paper.

Filter paper folded into a cone shape — the solid is left in the filter paper.

Two Ways to Separate Soluble Solids from Solutions

If a solid can be <u>dissolved</u> we say it's <u>soluble</u>. There are <u>two</u> methods you can use to separate a soluble salt from a solution — <u>evaporation</u> and <u>crystallisation</u>.

You could also use a water bath, or an electric heater.

Evaporation

1) Slowly <u>heat</u> the solution in an <u>evaporating dish</u>. The <u>solvent</u> will evaporate.

2) Eventually, <u>crystals</u> will start to form.

3) Keep heating until all you have left are <u>dry crystals</u>.

evaporating dish
Bunsen burner

Evaporation is a really <u>quick</u> way of separating a soluble salt from a solution. But, you can only use it if the salt <u>doesn't</u> break down when it's heated. Otherwise, you'll have to use <u>crystallisation</u>.

You should also use crystallisation if you want to make nice big crystals of your salt.

Crystallisation

1) Gently <u>heat</u> the solution in an <u>evaporating dish</u>. Some of the <u>solvent</u> will evaporate.

2) Once some of the solvent has evaporated, <u>or</u> when you see crystals start to form, stop heating. Leave the solution to <u>cool</u>.

3) The salt should start to form <u>crystals</u>.

4) <u>Filter</u> the crystals out of the solution. Leave them in a warm place to <u>dry</u>.

Salt crystallising out of solution.

Filtration and Crystallisation can be Used to Separate Rock Salt

1) <u>Rock salt</u> is a <u>mixture</u> of <u>salt</u> and <u>sand</u>. <u>Salt dissolves</u> in water and <u>sand doesn't</u>.

2) This <u>difference</u> in <u>physical properties</u> means we can <u>separate</u> them. Here's what to do...

1) <u>Grind</u> the mixture to make sure the salt crystals are small, so will dissolve easily.

You can heat the mixture to help dissolve the salt.

2) Put the mixture in water and stir. The <u>salt</u> will <u>dissolve</u>, but the <u>sand won't</u>.

3) <u>Filter</u> the mixture. The grains of <u>sand</u> won't fit through the tiny holes in the filter paper, so they collect on the <u>paper</u> instead. The <u>salt</u> passes <u>through</u> the filter paper as it's part of the solution.

4) Use <u>evaporation</u> or <u>crystallisation</u> so that you end up with <u>dry crystals</u> of the salt.

Revise mixtures — just filter out the important bits...

That's almost all the pages on separating mixtures done, phew... But before you dash on to the next page (I know, it's just so exciting), make sure you know this page to a T. Talking about Tea, I need a cuppa...

Q1   Describe how you could use crystallisation to separate a soluble salt from a solution.   [4 marks]

Topic C1 — Atomic Structure and the Periodic Table

Distillation

Distillation is used to separate mixtures which contain liquids.
There are two types that you should know about — simple and fractional.

Simple Distillation is Used to Separate Solutions

1) Simple distillation is used to separate a liquid from a solution.
2) First, the solution is heated.
3) The part of the solution that has the lowest boiling point evaporates first and turns into a gas.
4) The gas travels into the condenser.
5) In the condenser, the gas is cooled and condenses (turns back into a liquid).
6) The liquid drips out of the condenser and can be collected.
7) The rest of the solution is left behind in the flask.

   You can use simple distillation to get pure water from seawater. The water evaporates. It is then condensed and collected. This leaves the salt behind in the flask.

8) Simple distillation can't be used to separate mixtures of liquids with similar boiling points. So, you need to use another method instead — like fractional distillation...

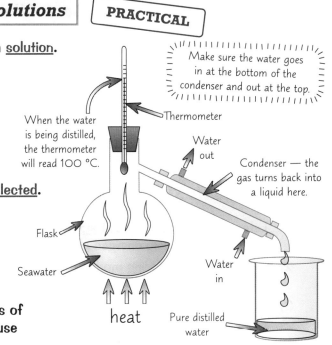

Make sure the water goes in at the bottom of the condenser and out at the top.

Thermometer

Water out

Condenser — the gas turns back into a liquid here.

When the water is being distilled, the thermometer will read 100 °C.

Flask

Seawater

heat

Water in

Pure distilled water

Fractional Distillation is Used to Separate a Mixture of Liquids

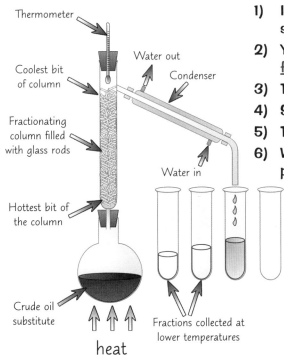

Thermometer

Water out

Coolest bit of column

Condenser

Fractionating column filled with glass rods

Water in

Hottest bit of the column

Crude oil substitute

heat

Fractions collected at lower temperatures

1) If you've got a mixture of liquids you can separate it using fractional distillation.
2) You put your mixture in a flask and stick a fractionating column on top. Then you heat it.
3) The different liquids will have different boiling points.
4) So, they will evaporate at different temperatures.
5) The substance with the lowest boiling point evaporates first.
6) When the temperature on the thermometer matches the boiling point of this substance, it will reach the top of the column.
7) The substance will then enter the condenser, where it cools and condenses.
8) You can collect the liquid as it drips out of the condenser.
9) When the first liquid has been collected, you raise the temperature until the next one reaches the top.

This experiment can be used to show how fractional distillation of crude oil at a refinery works (see p.148).

Fractionating — sounds a bit too much like maths to me...

You made it to the end of separation techniques. Congratulations. Now all you need to do is learn them all.

Q1 A mixture contains three liquids. Liquid A boils at 97 °C, liquid B boils at 65 °C and liquid C boils at 78 °C. A student uses fractional distillation to separate a mixture of these liquids. Explain which liquid will be collected in the first fraction. [2 marks]

The History of the Atom

You might have thought you were done with the <u>atom</u> after page 96. Unfortunately pal, you don't get away that easily — there's more you need to learn. Hold on to your hat, you're going on a journey through <u>time</u>...

Ideas About What Atoms Look Like Have Changed Over Time

1) Scientists used to think that atoms were <u>solid spheres</u>.

2) They then found atoms contain even smaller, negatively charged particles — <u>electrons</u>.

3) This led to a model called the '<u>plum pudding model</u>' being created.

4) The plum pudding model showed the atom as a <u>ball</u> of <u>positive charge</u> with <u>electrons scattered</u> in this ball.

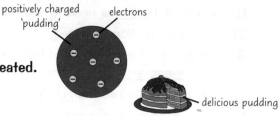

Experiments Showed that the Plum Pudding Model Was Wrong

1) Later, scientists carried out <u>alpha particle scattering experiments</u>. They fired positively charged <u>alpha particles</u> at a very thin sheet of gold.

2) From the plum pudding model, they <u>expected</u> most of the particles to <u>go straight through</u> the sheet. They predicted that a few particles would <u>change direction</u> by a <u>small</u> amount.

3) But instead, some particles changed direction <u>more than expected</u>. A small number even went <u>backwards</u>.

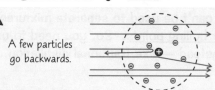

A few particles go backwards.

Most of the particles pass through empty space, but a few change direction.

4) This meant the plum pudding model <u>couldn't</u> be right.

5) So, scientists came up with the <u>nuclear model</u> of the atom:

- There's a tiny, positively charged <u>nucleus</u> at the centre of the atom.
- Most of the <u>mass</u> is in the nucleus.
- The nucleus is surrounded by a 'cloud' of negative <u>electrons</u>.
- Most of the atom is <u>empty space</u>.

Bohr's Nuclear Model Explains a Lot

1) <u>Niels Bohr</u> changed the nuclear model of the atom.

2) He suggested that the electrons <u>orbit</u> (go around) the nucleus in <u>shells</u> (levels).

3) Each shell is a <u>fixed distance</u> from the nucleus.

4) Bohr's theory was supported by many <u>experiments</u>. Experiments later showed that Bohr's theory was correct.

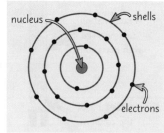

Later Experiments Found Protons and Neutrons

1) More experiments by scientists showed that the nucleus can be <u>divided</u> into smaller particles. Each particle has the <u>same positive charge</u>. These particles were named <u>protons</u>.

2) Experiments by <u>James Chadwick</u> showed that the nucleus also contained <u>neutral particles</u> — <u>neutrons</u>. This happened about 20 years after scientists agreed that atoms have nuclei.

3) This led to a model of the atom which was <u>pretty close</u> to the one we have today (see page 96).

I wanted to be a model — but I ate too much plum pudding...

In science, other people's work is always being built upon. So we keep learning more about a topic.

Q1 Describe the 'plum pudding' model of the atom.

[1 mark]

Topic C1 — Atomic Structure and the Periodic Table

Electronic Structure

Electrons don't just float around the nucleus randomly. They move in areas called shells.
Just don't confuse these with the shells of snails and turtles...

Electron Shell Rules:

1) Electrons always move in shells (sometimes called energy levels).

2) The inner shells are always filled up first. These are the ones closest to the nucleus.

3) Only a certain number of electrons are allowed in each shell:
   1st shell: **2**   2nd shell: **8**   3rd shell: **8**

4) Atoms are a lot more stable when they have full electron shells.

5) In most atoms, the outer shell is not full. These atoms will react to fill it.

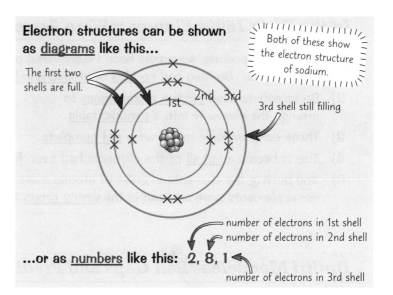

Electron structures can be shown as diagrams like this...

Both of these show the electron structure of sodium.

The first two shells are full.

1st 2nd 3rd

3rd shell still filling

number of electrons in 1st shell
number of electrons in 2nd shell

...or as numbers like this: 2, 8, 1

number of electrons in 3rd shell

Follow the Rules to Work Out Electronic Structures

You can easily work out the electronic structures for the first 20 elements of the periodic table (things get a bit more complicated after that).

EXAMPLE: What is the electronic structure of magnesium?

1) From the periodic table, you can see that magnesium's atomic number is 12. This means it has 12 protons. So it must have 12 electrons.

2) Follow the 'Electron Shell Rules' above. The first shell can only take 2 electrons.   2...

3) The second shell can take up to 8 electrons.   2, 8...

4) So far we have a total of 10 electrons (2 + 8). So the third shell must also be partly filled with 2 electrons. This makes 12 electrons in total (2 + 8 + 2).

Aren't you full?   Nope.

So the electronic structure for magnesium must be **2, 8, 2**.

Here are some more examples of electronic structures:

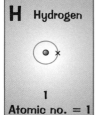

H Hydrogen

1
Atomic no. = 1

He Helium

2
Atomic no. = 2

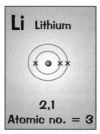

Li Lithium

2,1
Atomic no. = 3

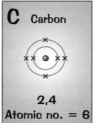

C Carbon

2,4
Atomic no. = 6

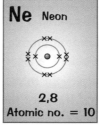

Ne Neon

2,8
Atomic no. = 10

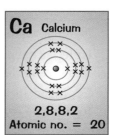

Ca Calcium

2,8,8,2
Atomic no. = 20

The electronic structure of the fifth element — it's a bit boron...

Electronic structures may seem a bit complicated at first but once you learn the rules, it's a piece of cake. And just like cake, you'll never regret going back for some more. Better get practising.

Q1   How many electrons are allowed in the first electron shell of an atom?   [1 mark]

Q2   Give the electronic structure of argon (atomic number = 18).   [1 mark]

Development of the Periodic Table

We haven't always known as much about chemistry as we do now. Oh no.
Early chemists looked at <u>patterns</u> in the elements' properties to help them understand chemistry better.

In the Early 1800s Elements Were Arranged By Atomic Mass

1) Until quite recently, scientists hadn't discovered protons, neutrons or electrons. So they had <u>no idea</u> of <u>atomic number</u>.

2) So scientists used <u>relative atomic mass</u> to arrange the elements into a <u>periodic table</u>.

3) These early periodic tables were <u>not complete</u>.

4) This is because <u>not all</u> of the elements had been <u>found</u> yet.

5) And putting the elements in order of atomic mass meant that some elements were also put in the <u>wrong group</u> (column).

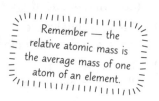

Remember — the relative atomic mass is the average mass of one atom of an element.

Dmitri Mendeleev Left Gaps and Predicted New Elements

1) In <u>1869</u>, a scientist called <u>Mendeleev</u> took all of the known elements and arranged them into a table.

<u>Mendeleev's Table of the Elements</u>

```
H
Li  Be                                    B  C  N  O  F
Na Mg                                     Al Si P  S  Cl
K  Ca *  Ti V  Cr Mn Fe Co Ni Cu Zn *  *  As Se Br
Rb Sr Y  Zr Nb Mo *  Ru Rh Pd Ag Cd In Sn Sb Te I
Cs Ba *  *  Ta W  *  Os Ir Pt Au Hg Tl Pb Bi
```

Mendeleev Table
~~£349.99~~
£199.99

2) He ordered them <u>mainly</u> by their <u>atomic mass</u>.

3) Sometimes he <u>switched</u> their positions or left <u>gaps</u> in the table.

4) This was so he could make sure that elements with <u>similar properties</u> stayed in the <u>same groups</u>.

5) Some of the <u>gaps</u> left space for elements that hadn't been found yet. Mendeleev used the position of the gaps to <u>predict the properties</u> of these elements.

6) <u>New elements</u> have been found since which <u>fit</u> into these gaps. This shows that Mendeleev's ideas were right.

- <u>Isotopes</u> were discovered a while after Mendeleev made his Table of Elements.
- Isotopes have different atomic masses but share the same properties. This means they have the <u>same position</u> on the periodic table.
- So, Mendeleev was <u>right</u> to swap some elements around to keep properties together — even if it meant they weren't in order of atomic mass.

The only elements I want on my table are Ba, Co, N...

Ahh more history... This is science at its best, discoveries building upon discoveries — all leading to the point where you have to learn it. Mendeleev would be proud... of himself and you of course.

Q1   How were elements ordered in the early 1800s?   [1 mark]

Q2   State two changes that Mendeleev made to early periodic tables.   [2 marks]

The Modern Periodic Table

So, as you've seen, it took a while to get to the periodic table that you will soon know and love.
I present to you a chemist's best friend...

The Periodic Table Helps you to See Patterns in Properties

1) There are about 100 elements.

2) In the periodic table the elements are laid out in order of increasing atomic number.

3) There are repeating (periodic) patterns in the properties of the elements.
   These periodic properties give the periodic table its name.

4) Metals are found to the left of the periodic table and non-metals are found to the right.

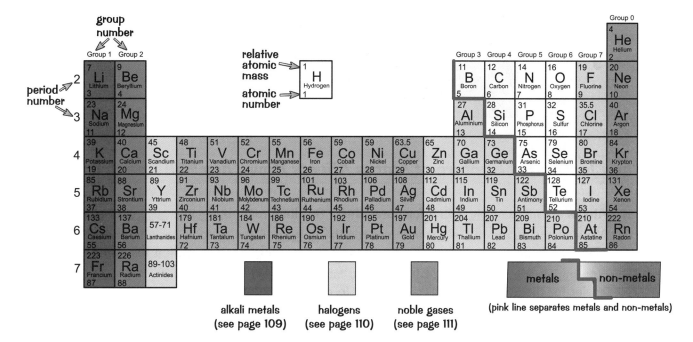

alkali metals (see page 109)   halogens (see page 110)   noble gases (see page 111)   (pink line separates metals and non-metals)

5) Elements with similar properties are arranged to form columns. These columns are called groups.

6) The group number of an element is the same as the number of outer shell electrons it has.
   (Except for Group 0 — helium has two electrons in its outer shell and the rest have eight.)

7) So, all the elements in a group have the same number of electrons in their outer shell.
   This means that elements in a group react in similar ways.

> **Example:** The Group 1 elements are Li, Na, K, Rb, Cs and Fr.
> They all have one electron in their outer shells.
> They're all metals and they react in a similar way.

See page 109 for more on Group 1 elements.

8) If you know the properties of one element, you can predict properties of other elements in that group.

9) You can also make predictions about trends in reactivity.
   E.g. in Group 1, the elements react more violently as you go down the group.

10) The rows in the periodic table are called periods. Each new period represents another shell of electrons.

I'm in a chemistry band — I play the symbols...

The periodic table is organised into groups and periods. This lets you see patterns in reactivity and properties.
And this means we can make predictions on how reactions will occur. How neat is that?

Q1   How many electrons does beryllium, Be, have in its outer shell? Use a periodic table to help you. [1 mark]

Q2   Chlorine reacts in a similar way to bromine. Suggest a reason why.   [1 mark]

Topic C1 — Atomic Structure and the Periodic Table

Metals and Non-Metals

I am almost dead certain you'll touch something <u>metallic</u> today, that's how important metals are to modern life.

Most Elements are Metals

1) Metals are elements which can <u>form positive ions</u> when they react.
2) They're towards the <u>bottom</u> and to the <u>left</u> of the periodic table.
3) <u>Most elements</u> in the periodic table are metals.
4) <u>Non-metals</u> are at the far <u>right</u> and <u>top</u> of the periodic table.
5) Non-metals <u>don't</u> usually <u>form positive ions</u> when they react.

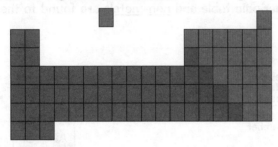

The red elements are metals.
The blue elements are non-metals.

The Electronic Structure of Atoms Affects How They Will React

1) Atoms are more <u>stable</u> with a full outer shell. So, they react by <u>losing</u>, <u>gaining</u> or <u>sharing</u> electrons.
2) Metal elements are to the <u>left</u> and towards the <u>bottom</u> of the periodic table so they lose electrons quite easily. When this happens, they <u>form positive ions</u>, with a full outer shell.
3) <u>Non-metals</u> are to the right of the periodic table or towards the top, so it's easier for them to <u>share</u> or <u>gain</u> electrons to get a full outer shell.

Metals and Non-Metals Have Different Physical Properties

1) All metals have <u>similar</u> physical properties.

- They're <u>strong</u> (hard to break), but can be <u>bent</u> or <u>hammered</u> into different shapes (malleable).
- They're great at <u>conducting heat</u> and <u>electricity</u>.
- They have high <u>boiling and melting points</u>.

2) Non-metals <u>don't</u> tend to show the same properties as metals.

- They tend to be <u>dull looking</u>.
- They're more <u>brittle</u>. This means they'll <u>break</u> more easily if you try to <u>bend</u> them.
- They're <u>not always solids</u> at room temperature.
- They <u>don't</u> usually <u>conduct electricity</u>.
- They often have a <u>lower density</u>.

You can 'rock out' to metal, you can sway gently to non-metal...

When it comes to properties, metals and non-metals couldn't be much more opposite. Much like me and my sister...

Q1   Iodine usually reacts by forming negative ions. Is iodine a metal or a non-metal?   [1 mark]

Q2   State two properties of metals.   [2 marks]

Group 1 Elements

Group 1 elements are known as the <u>alkali metals</u>. As metals go, they're pretty <u>reactive</u>.

The Group 1 Elements are Reactive, Soft Metals

1) The alkali metals are lithium, sodium, potassium, rubidium, caesium and francium.

2) They all have <u>one electron</u> in their outer shell. This makes them <u>very reactive</u>. It also gives them <u>similar properties</u>.

3) The alkali metals are all <u>soft</u>. They all have <u>low density</u> (they're quite <u>light</u>).

4) As you go <u>down</u> Group 1, the <u>properties</u> of the alkali metals <u>change</u>. For example:

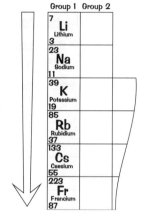

- <u>Reactivity increases</u> — the outer electron is <u>more easily lost</u> as it gets <u>further</u> from the nucleus. This is because it's <u>less attracted</u> to the nucleus.
- <u>Melting</u> and <u>boiling</u> points get lower.
- <u>Relative atomic mass</u> goes up.

5) These patterns in the properties are called <u>trends</u>.

Alkali Metals Form Ionic Compounds with Non-Metals

The Group 1 elements <u>easily</u> lose their one outer electron to form a full outer shell. So they form <u>1+ ions</u> easily.

Reaction with water

1) The reactions are <u>vigorous</u> and produce a <u>metal hydroxide</u> and <u>hydrogen gas</u>:

2) The <u>metal hydroxides</u> are salts that <u>dissolve</u> in the <u>water</u>.

alkali metal + water → metal hydroxide + hydrogen

sodium + water → sodium hydroxide + hydrogen

$$2Na_{(s)} + 2H_2O_{(l)} \rightarrow 2NaOH_{(aq)} + H_{2(g)}$$

The little letters in brackets after each substance in the reaction show what state the substance is in — see p.121.

3) The <u>more reactive</u> (lower down in the group) an alkali metal is, the more <u>violent</u> the reaction.

4) Lithium, sodium and potassium <u>float</u> and <u>move</u> around the surface, <u>fizzing</u> furiously.

5) The reaction with potassium gives out enough energy to <u>ignite</u> the hydrogen (set it on fire).

Reaction with chlorine

1) Group 1 metals react <u>vigorously</u> when heated in <u>chlorine gas</u> to form <u>white salts</u> called <u>metal chlorides</u>.

2) As you go down the group, the reaction gets <u>more vigorous</u>.

alkali metal + chlorine → metal chloride

sodium + chlorine → sodium chloride

$$2Na_{(s)} + Cl_{2(g)} \rightarrow 2NaCl_{(s)}$$

Reaction with oxygen

1) Group 1 metals can react with <u>oxygen</u> to form a <u>metal oxide</u>.

2) Different types of <u>oxide</u> will form depending on the Group 1 metal.

3) Group 1 metals are <u>shiny</u> but when they react with oxygen in the air they turn a <u>dull grey</u> (they <u>tarnish</u>). This is because a layer of <u>metal oxide</u> is formed on the surface.

Back to the drawing board with my lithium swim shorts design...

Reactions of alkali metals need safety precautions, but they fizz in water and might explode. Cool.

Q1   Why do Group 1 metals have similar properties?   [1 mark]

Q2   Write a word equation for the reaction between potassium and water.   [1 mark]

Topic C1 — Atomic Structure and the Periodic Table

Group 7 Elements

The Group 7 elements are known as the <u>halogens</u>. The whole 'trend thing' happens with the halogens as well.

The Halogens Show Patterns in their Properties

1) The <u>halogens</u> are fluorine, chlorine, bromine, iodine and astatine.

2) As <u>elements</u>, the halogens form molecules that contain <u>two atoms</u>. For example, <u>chlorine</u> (Cl_2) is a fairly reactive, poisonous <u>green gas</u>.

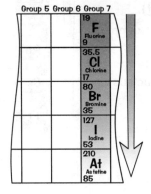

3) As you go <u>DOWN</u> Group 7, the <u>halogens</u>:

- become <u>less reactive</u> — it's <u>harder to gain</u> an extra electron as the outer shell is further from the nucleus.
- have <u>higher melting and boiling points</u>.
- have <u>higher relative atomic masses</u>.

You can use these trends to predict properties of halogens. E.g. iodine will have a higher boiling point than chlorine as it's further down the group.

4) All the Group 7 elements react in <u>similar ways</u>. This is because they all have <u>seven electrons</u> in their outer shell.

Halogens can Form Molecular Compounds

1) When halogen atoms react with other <u>non-metals</u>, they <u>share</u> electrons and form covalent bonds (see page 116). This is so they can get a <u>full outer shell</u>.

2) These reactions form compounds with <u>simple molecular structures</u> (see p.117).

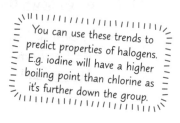

Bonding in hydrogen chloride, HCl.

Halogens Form Ionic Bonds with Metals

1) The halogens form <u>1– ions</u> called <u>halides</u>:

- <u>fluoride</u>, F^-
- <u>bromide</u>, Br^-
- <u>chloride</u>, Cl^-
- <u>iodide</u>, I^-

2) Halides form when halogens bond with <u>metals</u>. For example Na^+Cl^- or $Ca^{2+}Br^-_2$.

3) The compounds (halide salts) that form have <u>ionic structures</u>.

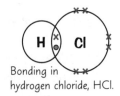

Bonding in sodium chloride, NaCl.

More Reactive Halogens React With Salts of Less Reactive Halogens

1) A reaction can take place between a <u>halogen</u> and the <u>halide salt</u> of a <u>less reactive</u> halogen.

2) These are called <u>displacement reactions</u>.

3) When this happens, the <u>less reactive</u> halogen changes from a halide (1– ion) to a <u>halogen</u>. The <u>more reactive</u> halogen changes from a halogen into a <u>halide ion</u> and becomes part of the <u>salt</u>.

4) E.g. chlorine is <u>more reactive</u> than bromine. So if you add <u>chlorine</u> to a solution containing a <u>bromide salt</u>, bromine will be <u>displaced</u>.

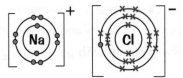

$$Cl_{2\,(g)} + 2KBr_{(aq)} \rightarrow Br_{2\,(aq)} + 2KCl_{(aq)}$$
Pale green $\quad\quad\quad\quad\quad\quad$ Orange

I can see your halo(gen), halo(gen) halo(gen)...

The halogens get less reactive as you go down the group. So a halogen will only be able to displace another halogen if it's higher up in Group 7. If it's lower down Group 7, no reaction will happen.

Q1   Why can bromine displace iodine from a solution of sodium iodide?   [1 mark]

Group 0 Elements

The Group 0 elements are known as <u>noble gases</u> — the most respectable gases you'll ever come across. They don't react with very much and you can't even see them. This makes them, well, a bit dull really.

Group 0 Elements are All Unreactive, Colourless Gases

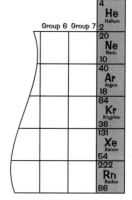

1) Group 0 elements are called the <u>noble gases</u>.
   They include the elements <u>helium</u>, <u>neon</u> and <u>argon</u> (plus a few others).

2) All elements in Group 0 are <u>colourless gases</u> at room temperature.

3) They all have <u>eight outer shell electrons</u>, apart from helium which has two. This means they have a <u>stable full outer shell</u>.

   Helium only has electrons in the first shell, which only needs 2 to be filled.

4) This stability makes them very <u>unreactive</u> (<u>inert</u>). This means they don't form molecules easily. So the elements are <u>single atoms</u>.

5) Because noble gases are unreactive, some reactions are carried out in an <u>atmosphere</u> that <u>only</u> contains a noble gas, instead of air.

6) This is done if the <u>reactants</u> could react with things in the <u>air</u> (e.g. oxygen or water) instead of taking part in the reaction you're trying to do. It's also done if the <u>products</u> react with things in the air.

There are Patterns in the Properties of the Noble Gases

1) As you go down Group 0, the <u>relative atomic masses</u> of the elements <u>increase</u>.

2) This means that as you go down the group, the elements have <u>more electrons</u>.

3) More electrons means <u>stronger forces</u> between atoms.

4) The stronger the forces, the <u>higher</u> the <u>boiling point</u>. So as you go down Group 0, the boiling points <u>increase</u>.

5) If you're given the boiling point of one noble gas you can <u>predict</u> the boiling point for <u>another one</u>. So make sure you know the <u>pattern</u>.

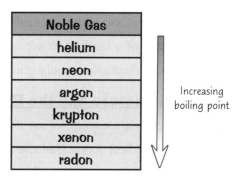

 **EXAMPLE:** Neon is a gas at 25 °C. Predict what state helium is at this temperature.

Helium has a lower boiling point than neon as it is further up the group.

So, helium must also be a gas at 25 °C.

 **EXAMPLE:** Radon has a boiling point of −62 °C and krypton has a boiling point of −153 °C. Predict the boiling point of xenon.

Xenon comes in between radon and krypton in the group.
So, you can predict that its boiling point would be between their boiling points.
E.g. xenon has a boiling point of −100 °C.

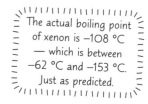

The actual boiling point of xenon is −108 °C — which is between −62 °C and −153 °C. Just as predicted.

Arrrgon — the pirate element...

As noble gases don't really react there isn't too much to learn about them. If you understand why they are unreactive and the trend in boiling points as you go down the group you're sorted.

Q1   Does xenon or neon have the higher boiling point?   [1 mark]

Revision Questions for Topic C1

Topic C1 — finished. But hold on there my friend, don't rush on to Topic C2 just yet.
There's one more thing for you to do...

- Try these questions and <u>tick off each one</u> when you <u>get it right</u>.
- When you've done <u>all the questions</u> under a heading and are <u>completely happy</u> with it, tick it off.

Atoms, Elements and Compounds (p.96-99) ☑

1) Draw an atom. Label the nucleus and the electrons.
2) What is the charge of a proton?
3) What is the smallest part of an element that you can have?
4) Give the formula for:
   a) Carbon dioxide   b) Water
5) Balance these equations:
   a) $Mg + O_2 \rightarrow MgO$ b) $H_2SO_4 + NaOH \rightarrow Na_2SO_4 + H_2O$

Mixtures and Separation (p.100-103) ☐

6) What is a mixture?
7) Are there any chemical bonds between the different parts of a mixture?
8) What method could you use to separate dyes in an ink?
9) What is the name of the pattern formed from carrying out paper chromatography?
10) Which method of separation is useful to separate an insoluble solid from a liquid?
11) Give the name of a method to separate a soluble solid from a solution.
12) Which type of distillation would you use to separate liquids with similar boiling points?

Electronic Structure and the History of the Periodic Table (p.104-106) ☑

13) What did scientists expect to see during the alpha particle scattering experiments?
14) Which scientist first found that the nucleus contains neutrons?
15) How many electrons are allowed in the second electron shell of an atom?
16) What is the electronic structure of sodium?
17) In the early 1800s, how were elements arranged in the periodic table?

Groups of the Periodic Table (p.107-111) ☑

18) What does the group number of an element tell you about its electrons?
19) Do metals form positive or negative ions?
20) Where are non-metals on the periodic table?
21) State two trends as you go down Group 1.
22) How do the boiling points of halogens change as you go down the group?
23) Halogens form ions when they react with metals. What is the charge of the ions?
24) Chlorine is added to a solution containing a bromide salt.
    Will the chlorine displace the bromine in the solution?
25) Why are the Group 0 elements single atoms?
26) How do the boiling points change as you go down Group 0?

Formation of Ions

Ions crop up all over the place in chemistry. You need to know <u>what</u> they are and <u>how</u> they form. Luckily for you, this page has got that covered. So crack on with it.

Ions are Made When Electrons are Transferred

1) <u>Ions</u> are <u>charged</u> particles — for example Cl^- or Mg^{2+}.

2) Ions are formed when atoms <u>gain</u> or <u>lose</u> electrons.

3) They do this to get a <u>full outer shell</u> — like a noble gas.

4) This is because a full outer shell is very <u>stable</u>.

5) <u>Metal</u> atoms <u>lose</u> electrons from their <u>outer shell</u> to form <u>positive ions</u>.

6) <u>Non-metal</u> atoms <u>gain</u> electrons into their <u>outer shell</u> to form <u>negative ions</u>.

7) The <u>number</u> of electrons lost or gained is the same as the <u>charge</u> on the ion.

8) If 2 electrons are <u>lost</u>, the particle now has two more protons than electrons. So the charge is <u>2+</u>.

9) If 3 electrons are <u>gained</u>, the particle now has three more electrons than protons. So the charge is <u>3–</u>.

Ions will always have a '+' or '–' sign after the formula. A '+' tells you the ion is positive. A '–' sign tells you the ion is negative.

The noble gases are in Group 0 of the periodic table.

You can Work Out What Ions are Formed by Groups 1 & 2 and 6 & 7

1) <u>Group 1 and 2 elements</u> are <u>metals</u>. They <u>lose</u> electrons to form <u>positive ions</u>.

2) <u>Group 6 and 7 elements</u> are <u>non-metals</u>. They <u>gain</u> electrons to form <u>negative ions</u>.

3) Elements in the same <u>group</u> all have the same number of <u>outer electrons</u>. So they have to <u>lose or gain</u> the same number to get a full outer shell. And this means that they form ions with the <u>same charges</u>.

4) You <u>don't</u> have to <u>remember</u> what ions <u>most elements</u> form. You can just look at the periodic table.

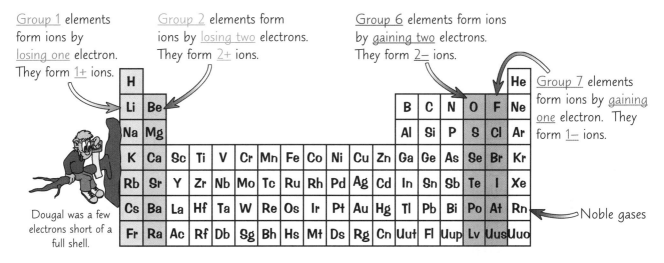

<u>Group 1</u> elements form ions by <u>losing one</u> electron. They form <u>1+</u> ions.

<u>Group 2</u> elements form ions by <u>losing two</u> electrons. They form <u>2+</u> ions.

<u>Group 6</u> elements form ions by <u>gaining two</u> electrons. They form <u>2–</u> ions.

<u>Group 7</u> elements form ions by <u>gaining one</u> electron. They form <u>1–</u> ions.

Dougal was a few electrons short of a full shell.

Noble gases

- A <u>sodium</u> atom (Na) is in <u>Group 1</u> so it <u>loses</u> 1 electron to form a sodium ion (Na^+).

- A magnesium atom (Mg) is in <u>Group 2</u> so it <u>loses</u> 2 electrons to form a magnesium ion (Mg^{2+}).

- A chlorine atom (Cl) is in <u>Group 7</u> so it <u>gains</u> 1 electron to form a chloride ion (Cl^-).

- An oxygen atom (O) is in <u>Group 6</u> so it <u>gains</u> 2 electrons to form an oxide ion (O^{2-}).

A '+' by itself means the ion has a 1+ charge. A '–' by itself means the ion has a 1– charge.

I've got my ion you...

You need to be able to predict the ions the atoms in Groups 1, 2, 6 and 7 will form. So have a look at the periodic table above to make sure you know what charged ion each group forms. Keep looking till you've got it sorted.

Q1   What is an ion?   [1 mark]

Q2   Predict the charges of the ions formed by these elements:
       a) Bromine (Br)   b) Calcium (Ca)   c) Potassium (K)   [3 marks]

Ionic Bonding

Time to find out how particles bond together to form compounds (bet you can't wait). There are <u>three</u> types of bonding you need to know about — <u>ionic</u>, <u>covalent</u> and <u>metallic</u>. First up, it's <u>ionic bonds</u>.

Ionic Bonding — Transfer of Electrons

1) <u>Metals</u> and <u>non-metals</u> can react together.

2) When this happens, the <u>metal</u> atoms <u>lose</u> electrons to form <u>positively charged ions</u>.

3) The <u>non-metal atoms gain</u> these <u>electrons</u> to form <u>negatively charged ions</u>.

4) These oppositely charged ions are <u>strongly attracted</u> to one another by <u>electrostatic forces</u>.

5) This attraction is called an <u>ionic bond</u>. It holds the ions togther to make an <u>ionic compound</u>.

Dot and Cross Diagrams Show How Ionic Compounds are Formed

1) <u>Dot and cross diagrams</u> show how electrons are <u>arranged</u> in an atom or ion.

2) Each electron is represented by a <u>dot</u> or a <u>cross</u>.

3) So these diagrams can show which <u>atom</u> the electrons in an <u>ion</u> originally came from.

The name's Bond. Ionic Bond.

Sodium Chloride (NaCl)

- The <u>sodium</u> (Na) atom loses its outer electron. It forms an <u>Na$^+$</u> ion.

- The <u>chlorine</u> (Cl) atom gains the electron. It forms a <u>Cl$^-$</u> (<u>chloride</u>) ion.

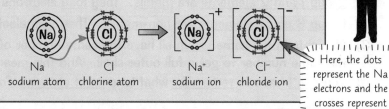

Here, the dots represent the Na electrons and the crosses represent the Cl electrons.

Magnesium Oxide (MgO)

- The <u>magnesium</u> (Mg) atom loses its <u>two</u> outer electrons. It forms an <u>Mg^{2+}</u> ion.

- The <u>oxygen</u> (O) atom gains the electrons. It forms an <u>O^{2-}</u> (<u>oxide</u>) ion.

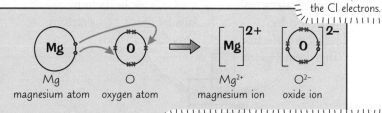

We've only shown the outer shells of electrons in these two dot and cross diagrams. It makes it easier to see what's going on.

Magnesium Chloride (MgCl$_2$)

- The <u>magnesium</u> (Mg) atom loses its <u>two</u> outer electrons. It forms an <u>Mg^{2+}</u> ion.

- The two <u>chlorine</u> (Cl) atoms gain <u>one electron each</u>. They form <u>two Cl$^-$</u> (chloride) ions.

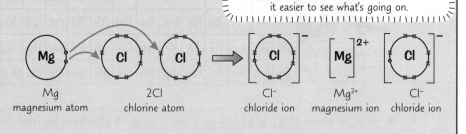

4) Dot and cross diagrams are useful for showing <u>how</u> ionic compounds are formed.

5) But they <u>don't</u> show the <u>structure</u> of the compound, the <u>size</u> of the ions or how they're <u>arranged</u>.

6) They also make it look like the electrons that are <u>crosses</u> might be <u>different</u> from the electrons that are <u>dots</u>. Really, they're all the same.

Any old ion, any old ion — any, any, any old ion...

Drawing dot and cross diagrams gets easier with practice. Here are some questions to get you started.

Q1   What type of forces hold the ions together in an ionic compound?   [1 mark]

Q2   Draw a dot and cross diagram to show how potassium (a Group 1 metal) and oxygen
       (a Group 6 non-metal) form potassium oxide (K$_2$O).*   [3 marks]

*Hint: the ions in K$_2$O need to have full outer shells.

Ionic Compounds

Ionic compounds may sound fancy, but don't be put off. One of the main ionic compounds you need to know about is sodium chloride. And that's just salt. Yep, like you put on your chips. Nothing fancy about that.

Ionic Compounds Have A Giant Ionic Lattice Structure

1) In ionic compounds, the ions are arranged in a pattern. This is called a giant ionic lattice.
2) There are strong electrostatic forces of attraction between oppositely charged ions.
3) These forces are called ionic bonds and they act in all directions.

Sodium chloride is a giant ionic lattice. It can be drawn in different ways:

- This is a 3D model. It shows how big the ions are compared to each other.
- It also shows that the ions are ordered in a pattern.
- But it only lets you see the outer layer of the compound.

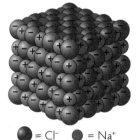

● = Cl⁻ ● = Na⁺

- This is a ball and stick model. It shows how the ions are arranged.
- But it doesn't show how big the ions are compared to each other.
- And it makes it look like there are gaps between the ions. But there aren't really.

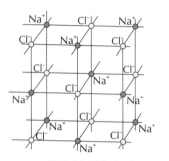

Ionic Compounds All Have Similar Properties

1) They all have high melting points and high boiling points. This is because lots of energy is needed to break all the strong ionic bonds.
2) When they're solid, the ions are held in place, so the solid compounds can't conduct electricity.
3) When ionic compounds melt, the ions are free to move and they can conduct electricity.
4) Some ionic compounds dissolve in water. The ions can move in the solution, so they can conduct electricity.

Look at Charges to Find the Empirical Formula of an Ionic Compound

1) For a dot and cross diagram, just count up and write down how many ions there are of each element.
2) For a 3D diagram, use the diagram to work out what ions are in the compound.
3) Then balance the charges of the ions so that the overall charge on the compound is zero.

EXAMPLE: What's the empirical formula of the ionic compound shown on the right?

1) Look at the diagram to work out what ions are in the compound.
2) Work out what charges the ions will form.
3) Balance the charges so the charge of the empirical formula is zero.

The empirical formula shows the smallest ratio of particles.

The compound contains potassium and oxide ions.

Potassium is in Group 1 so forms 1+ ions. Oxygen is in Group 6 so forms 2− ions.

A potassium ion has a 1+ charge, so two of them are needed to balance the 2− charge of an oxide ion. The empirical formula is K_2O.

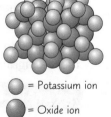

● = Potassium ion
● = Oxide ion

I'd take this page with a pinch of salt if I were you...

Here's where you can get a little practice explaining the properties of ionic compounds.

Q1 a) Explain whether an ionic compound will have a high or a low melting point. [2 marks]
    b) Explain why ionic compounds can conduct electricity when they've been melted [1 mark]

Topic C2 — Bonding, Structure and Properties of Matter

Covalent Bonding

Some elements bond ionically (see page 114) but others form strong <u>covalent</u> bonds.
This is where atoms <u>share</u> electrons with each other so that they've got full outer shells.

Covalent Bonds — Sharing Electrons

1) When <u>non-metal</u> atoms bond together, they <u>share</u> pairs of electrons to make <u>covalent bonds</u>.
2) Covalent bonds are <u>electrostatic forces</u> and are very <u>strong</u>.
3) Atoms only share electrons in their <u>outer shells</u>.
4) Atoms get one <u>extra</u> shared electron for each single <u>covalent bond</u> that they form.
5) Each atom usually makes <u>enough</u> covalent bonds to <u>fill up</u> its outer shell. This makes them very <u>stable</u>.

There are Different Ways of Drawing Covalent Bonds

Nitrogen has 5 outer electrons. To form <u>ammonia</u> (NH_3) it forms <u>3 covalent bonds</u> to get the extra
3 electrons it needs for a <u>full outer shell</u>. Here are different ways the bonding can be <u>shown</u>:

Dot and Cross Diagrams

1) Electrons shown in the <u>overlap</u> between two atoms are <u>shared electrons</u>.
2) Dot and cross diagrams show <u>which atoms</u> the electrons in a covalent bond come from
3) But they <u>don't</u> show how the atoms are <u>arranged</u>, or how <u>big</u> the atoms are compared to each other.

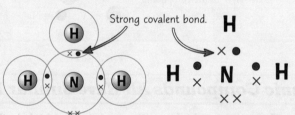

Strong covalent bond.

Two different ways of drawing dot and cross diagrams.

Displayed Formulas

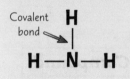

Covalent bond

1) <u>Displayed formulas</u> show the covalent bonds as single lines between atoms.
2) If it's a <u>single</u> covalent bond, there'll be <u>one</u> line.
   If it's a <u>double</u> covalent bond, there'll be <u>two</u> lines.
3) They're good for showing <u>how</u> atoms are connected in <u>large</u> molecules.
4) But they <u>don't</u> show the <u>3D structure</u> of the molecule. They also don't show <u>which atoms</u> the electrons in the covalent bond have come from.

3D Models

1) 3D models show the <u>atoms</u>, the <u>covalent bonds</u> and how they're <u>arranged</u>.
2) But 3D models can be <u>confusing</u> for large molecules.
3) And they don't show <u>where</u> the electrons in the bonds have <u>come from</u>.

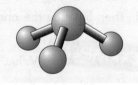

You can find the <u>molecular formula</u> of a simple molecular compound from these diagrams by <u>counting up</u> how many atoms of each element there are.

A molecular formula shows you how many atoms of each element are in a molecule.

EXAMPLE: Find the molecular formula of ethane from the diagram of ethane.

In the diagram, there are two carbon atoms and six hydrogen atoms. So the molecular formula is C_2H_6.

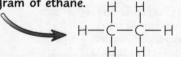

Sharing is caring...

Make sure you can draw the different diagrams that can be used to show the bonding in ammonia on this page.

Q1   Draw a dot and cross diagram to show the bonding in a molecule of ammonia (NH_3).   [2 marks]

Topic C2 — Bonding, Structure and Properties of Matter

Simple Molecular Substances

These molecules might be _simple_, but you've still gotta know about them. I know, the world is a cruel place.

Learn These Examples of Simple Molecular Substances

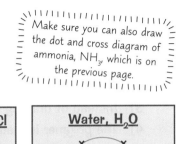
Make sure you can also draw the dot and cross diagram of ammonia, NH₃, which is on the previous page.

1) Simple molecular substances are made up of molecules that contain a few atoms joined together by covalent bonds.

2) Here are some common examples that you should know...

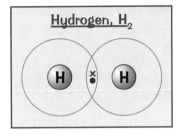
Hydrogen, H₂

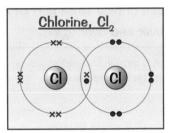
Chlorine, Cl₂

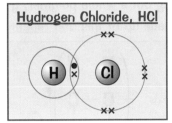
Hydrogen Chloride, HCl

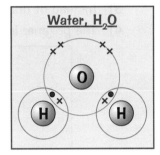
Water, H₂O

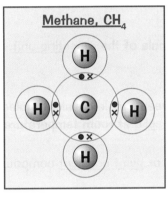
Methane, CH₄

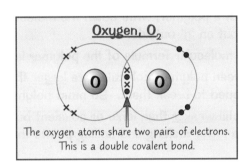
Oxygen, O₂
The oxygen atoms share two pairs of electrons. This is a double covalent bond.

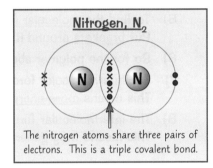
Nitrogen, N₂
The nitrogen atoms share three pairs of electrons. This is a triple covalent bond.

Properties of Simple Molecular Substances

1) Substances containing covalent bonds usually have simple molecular structures, like the examples above.

2) The atoms within the molecules are held together by very strong covalent bonds.

3) But the forces of attraction between these molecules are very weak.

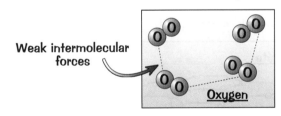
Weak intermolecular forces
Oxygen

4) To melt or boil a simple molecular compound, you only need to break the weak intermolecular forces and not the covalent bonds.

There's more about melting and boiling on page 122.

5) So the melting and boiling points are very low, because it's easy to break the intermolecular forces.

6) Most molecular substances are gases or liquids at room temperature.

7) As molecules get bigger, the intermolecular forces get stronger. More energy is needed to break the stronger forces, so the melting and boiling points increase.

8) Molecular compounds don't conduct electricity because they aren't charged.

May the intermolecular force be with you...

Never forget that it's the weak forces between molecules that are broken when a simple molecular substance melts.

Q1 Explain why oxygen, O₂, is a gas at room temperature.   [1 mark]

Q2 Explain why nitrogen, N₂, doesn't conduct electricity.   [1 mark]

Polymers and Giant Covalent Structures

Wouldn't it be great if the only covalent compounds you needed to know about were simple molecular substances? Well it's not like that. <u>Polymers</u> and <u>giant covalent substances</u> also have <u>covalent bonds</u>.

Polymers Have Very Large Molecules

1) In a polymer, lots of <u>small units</u> are joined together to form a <u>long molecule</u>.
2) All the atoms in a polymer are joined by strong <u>covalent bonds</u>.
3) Instead of drawing out a whole polymer, you can draw a small part of it, called the <u>repeating unit</u>.
4) The polymer is made up of this unit <u>repeated</u> over and over again.

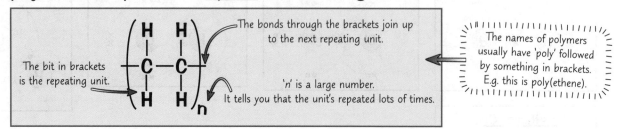

5) To find the <u>molecular formula</u> of a polymer, write down the molecular formula of the <u>repeating unit</u>. Put <u>brackets</u> around it. Then put an '<u>n</u>' outside.
6) So for the polymer above, the molecular formula of the polymer is $(C_2H_4)_n$.
7) The intermolecular forces between polymer molecules are <u>larger</u> than between simple covalent molecules. This means <u>more energy</u> is needed to break them. So most polymers are <u>solid</u> at room temperature.
8) The intermolecular forces are still <u>weaker</u> than ionic or covalent bonds. This means they generally have <u>lower</u> melting and boiling points than <u>ionic</u> or <u>giant covalent</u> compounds.

Giant Covalent Structures Include Diamond, Graphite and Silica

1) In <u>giant covalent</u> structures, <u>all</u> the atoms are <u>bonded</u> to <u>each other</u> by <u>strong</u> covalent bonds.
2) They have <u>very high</u> melting and boiling points. This is because lots of energy is needed to break the covalent bonds between the atoms.
3) They <u>don't</u> contain charged particles, so they <u>don't conduct electricity</u> (except for a few weird exceptions such as graphite, see next page).
4) Here are some examples you should know about:

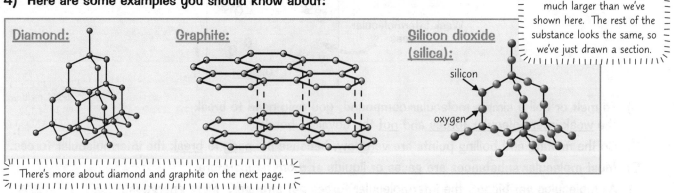

Polymers — the intermolecular force is strong in these ones...

Remember, to melt or boil a simple molecular substance or a polymer, only the weakish intermolecular forces need to be broken. To melt or boil a giant covalent substance, you have to break very strong covalent bonds.

Q1 The repeating unit of poly(chloroethene) is shown on the right. What's the molecular formula of poly(chloroethene)? [1 mark]

Q2 Explain whether diamond or the polymer poly(ethene) has a higher melting point. [3 marks]

Structures of Carbon

Carbon's a funny old element. Its atoms can arrange themselves into different <u>structures</u>. Here they are...

Diamond is Very Hard

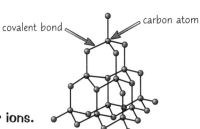

1) In diamond, each carbon atom forms <u>four covalent bonds</u>.
2) This makes diamond <u>really hard</u>.
3) It takes a lot of energy to <u>break</u> the covalent bonds. So diamond has a <u>very high melting point</u>.
4) Diamond <u>doesn't conduct electricity</u> because it has <u>no free electrons</u> or ions.

Graphite Contains Layers of Hexagons

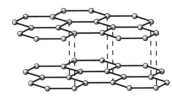

1) Graphite contains <u>layers</u> of <u>carbon atoms</u>. The carbon atoms are arranged in <u>hexagons</u> (rings of six carbon atoms).
2) Each carbon atom forms <u>three covalent bonds</u>.
3) There <u>aren't</u> any covalent bonds <u>between</u> the layers. So the layers can move over each other. This makes graphite <u>soft</u> and <u>slippery</u>.
4) <u>Lots of energy</u> is needed to break the covalent bonds in the layers. So graphite has a <u>high melting point</u>.
5) Each carbon atom has <u>one</u> electron that's <u>free to move</u> (delocalised). So graphite <u>conducts electricity</u> and <u>thermal energy</u> (heat) — a bit like a metal does (see p.120).

Graphene is One Layer of Graphite

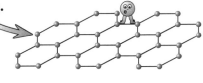

1) Graphene is a <u>sheet</u> of carbon atoms joined together in <u>hexagons</u>. You can think of it as <u>one layer</u> of graphite.
2) The covalent bonds make it very <u>strong</u>. It's also very <u>light</u>.
3) It can be added to <u>other materials</u> to make <u>composites</u>. The graphene makes the materials <u>stronger</u> but not much <u>heavier</u>.
4) Graphene contains <u>electrons</u> that are <u>free to move</u>. So it <u>conducts electricity</u>. This means it could be used in <u>electronics</u>.

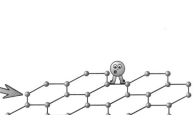

A free electron.

Fullerenes Form Spheres and Tubes

1) <u>Fullerenes</u> are molecules of <u>carbon</u>, shaped like <u>closed tubes</u> or <u>hollow balls</u>.
2) The carbon atoms are mainly arranged in <u>hexagons</u>. They can also form rings of <u>five</u> carbon atoms or rings of <u>seven</u> carbon atoms.
3) Fullerenes can be used to <u>deliver drugs</u> into the body. They also make great <u>catalysts</u> (see p.139).

<u>Buckminsterfullerene</u> (C_{60}) was the first fullerene to be found. It's shaped like a <u>hollow sphere</u> (ball).

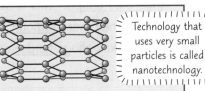

- Fullerenes can form <u>nanotubes</u> — tiny carbon <u>cylinders</u>.
- The ratio between the length and the diameter of nanotubes is very <u>high</u> (they're very <u>long</u> compared to their <u>width</u>).
- Nanotubes have properties that make them useful in <u>electronics</u>. They can also be used to <u>strengthen materials</u> without adding much <u>weight</u>.

Technology that uses very small particles is called nanotechnology.

CGP definitions: graphite — when a bar chart hits a line graph...

Before you go on, make sure you can explain the properties of all these forms of carbon. Not fun, but useful.

Q1 Describe the structure and bonding of graphite. [4 marks]

Metallic Bonding

Ever wondered what makes <u>metals</u> tick? Well, whether you have or you haven't, this is still the page for you.

Metallic Bonding Involves Delocalised Electrons

1) <u>Metals</u> are <u>giant structures</u> of atoms.
   This means they contain <u>lots and lots</u> of metal atoms bonded together.

2) The electrons in the <u>outer shell</u> of the metal atoms are <u>free to move around</u> (delocalised).

3) There are strong forces of <u>electrostatic attraction</u> between
   the <u>positive metal ions</u> and the shared <u>negative electrons</u>.

4) These forces of attraction are known as <u>metallic bonds</u>.
   They <u>hold</u> the <u>atoms</u> together in a <u>regular pattern</u>.

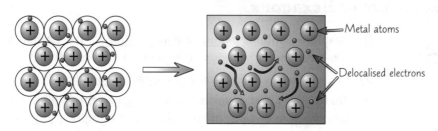

Metal atoms

Delocalised electrons

I don't think he's from round here.

The Bonding in Metals Affects their Properties

1) Metallic bonds are very <u>strong</u>, so <u>lots of energy</u> is needed to break them.

2) This means that most substances with metallic bonds have very <u>high</u> melting and boiling points.

3) They're usually <u>solids</u> at room temperature.

4) The <u>delocalised electrons</u> in the metal are <u>free to move</u>.

5) These electrons can carry <u>electrical current</u> and <u>thermal</u> (heat) energy through the whole structure.

6) This means metals are good <u>conductors</u> of <u>electricity</u> and <u>heat</u>.

7) The layers of atoms in a metal can <u>slide</u> over each other.

8) Because of this, metals can be <u>bent</u> or <u>formed</u> into different shapes.

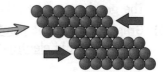

Metallic Bonding is Found in Alloys

1) <u>Pure metals</u> are often quite <u>soft</u>.

2) Most of the metals we use are <u>alloys</u>.
   An alloy is a <u>mixture</u> of <u>two or more metals</u> or a <u>metal and another element</u>.

3) Mixing another element with a pure metal causes the layers of metal atoms to
   <u>lose their shape</u>. This is because different elements have <u>different sized atoms</u>.

4) It becomes more <u>difficult</u> for the atoms to <u>slide</u> over each other.

5) This makes alloys <u>harder</u> and so <u>more useful</u> than pure metals.

I saw a metal on the bus once — he was the conductor...

If your knowledge of metals is still feeling a bit delocalised, the questions below will help...

Q1   What is a metallic bond?   [2 marks]

Q2   Copper is a metal. What property of copper means it can be used in electrical circuits?   [1 mark]

Q3   Suggest why an alloy of copper, rather than pure copper, is used to make hinges for doors.   [1 mark]

States of Matter

Better get your thinking hat on, as states of matter really... err.. matter. You'll need to imagine the particles in a substance as little snooker balls. Sounds strange, but it's useful for explaining lots of stuff in chemistry.

The Three States of Matter — Solid, Liquid and Gas

1) Materials come in three different forms — solid, liquid and gas. These are the three states of matter.

2) Particle theory is a model where each particle is seen as a small, solid sphere (ball).

3) You can use particle theory to show what solids, liquids and gases are like. It can be used to explain how the particles in solids, liquids and gases behave.

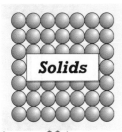

Solids

- In solids, there are strong forces of attraction between particles.
- The particles are held close together in fixed positions to form a pattern.
- Solids have a fixed shape and volume.

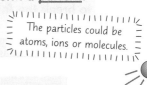
The particles could be atoms, ions or molecules.

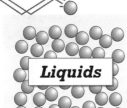

Liquids

- In liquids, there are weak forces of attraction between the particles.
- They're randomly arranged and free to move past each other, but they tend to stick closely together.
- Liquids have a fixed volume but don't keep a fixed shape. So they flow to fill the bottom of a container.

Gases

- In gases, the forces of attraction between the particles are very weak.
- The particles are free to move and are spaced far apart.
- The particles in gases travel in straight lines.
- Gases don't have a fixed shape or volume. They will always fill containers.

If you ever see something described as 'gaseous', it just means that it's a gas.

State Symbols Tell You the State of a Substance in an Equation

1) You saw on page 99 how a chemical reaction can be shown using a symbol equation.

2) Symbol equations can include state symbols next to each substance. They're always shown in brackets, and they're normally subscripts (slightly smaller and below the rest of the letters).

3) They tell you whether each substance is a solid, a liquid, a gas or dissolved in water:

| (s) — solid | (l) — liquid | (g) — gas | (aq) — aqueous |

'Aqueous' means 'dissolved in water'.

Example: $2HCl_{(aq)} + CaCO_{3(s)} \rightarrow CaCl_{2(aq)} + H_2O_{(l)} + CO_{2(g)}$

dissolved in water   solid   dissolved in water   liquid   gas

Phew, what a page — particle-ularly gripping stuff...

It's clever how you can explain the differences between solids, liquids and gases with a page of pink snooker balls.

Q1   Substance A does not have a definite shape or volume. What state is it in?   [1 mark]

Changing State

This page is like a game show. To start, everyone seems nice and solid, but turn up the <u>heat</u> and it all changes.

Substances Can Change from One State to Another

Solid → Liquid → Gas

- When a solid is <u>heated</u>, its particles gain <u>energy</u> and start to <u>move about</u>.
- Some of the forces between the particles <u>break</u>.
- At a <u>temperature</u> called the <u>melting point</u>, the particles have enough energy to <u>break free</u> from their positions. This is <u>MELTING</u>. The <u>solid</u> turns into a <u>liquid</u>.
- When a liquid is <u>heated</u>, the particles get even <u>more</u> energy.
- The forces holding the liquid together <u>weaken</u> and <u>break</u>.
- At a temperature called the <u>boiling point</u>, the particles have <u>enough</u> energy to <u>break</u> the forces. This is <u>BOILING</u>. The <u>liquid</u> becomes a <u>gas</u>.

Gas → Liquid → Solid

- As a gas <u>cools</u>, the particles have <u>less energy</u>.
- <u>Forces form</u> between the particles.
- At the <u>boiling point</u>, the forces between the particles are strong enough that the <u>gas</u> becomes a <u>liquid</u>. This is <u>CONDENSING</u>.
- When a <u>liquid cools</u>, the particles have <u>less energy</u>, so move around less.
- The <u>forces</u> between the particles become stronger.
- At the <u>melting point</u>, the forces between the particles are so strong that they're <u>held in place</u>. The <u>liquid</u> becomes a <u>solid</u>. This is <u>FREEZING</u>.

Solid

melting | freezing

Liquid

boiling | condensing

Gas

1) The <u>amount</u> of energy needed for a substance to <u>change state</u> depends on <u>how strong</u> the forces between particles are.

2) The <u>stronger</u> the forces, the <u>more energy</u> is needed to break them, and so the <u>higher</u> the melting and boiling points of the substance.

You Have to be Able to Predict the State of a Substance

1) You can predict <u>what state</u> a substance is in at a <u>certain temperature</u>.
2) If the temperature's <u>below</u> the <u>melting point</u> of substance, it'll be a <u>solid</u>.
3) If it's <u>above</u> the <u>boiling point</u>, it'll be a <u>gas</u>.
4) If it's <u>in between</u> the two points, then it's a <u>liquid</u>.

The bulk properties such as the melting point of a material depend on how lots of atoms interact together. An atom on its own doesn't have these properties.

EXAMPLE: Which of the substances in the table is a liquid at room temperature (25 °C)?

	melting point	boiling point
oxygen	−219 °C	−183 °C
nitrogen	−210 °C	−196 °C
bromine	−7 °C	59 °C

Oxygen and nitrogen have boiling points below 25 °C, so will both be gases at room temperature.

The answer's **bromine**. It melts at −7 °C and boils at 59 °C. So, it'll be a liquid at room temperature.

This page has put me in a terrible state...

Learn what all the terms like condensing, boiling, etc. mean. Then you'll sound like a states of matter pro.

Q1   Ethanol melts at −114 °C and boils at 78 °C. Predict the state that ethanol is in at:

   a) −150 °C   b) 0 °C   c) 25 °C   d) 100 °C   [4 marks]

Topic C2 — Bonding, Structure and Properties of Matter

Relative Formula Mass

Calculating relative formula mass is important for lots of calculations in chemistry.
It might sound a bit hard to begin with, but it gets easier with practice. We'd better get cracking...

Compounds Have a Relative Formula Mass, M_r

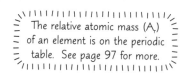
The relative atomic mass (A_r) of an element is on the periodic table. See page 97 for more.

To find the relative formula mass, M_r, of a compound, add together the relative atomic masses of all the atoms in the molecular formula.

EXAMPLES:

a) Find the relative formula mass of $MgCl_2$.

1) Look up the relative atomic masses of all the elements in the compound on the periodic table.

A_r of Mg = 24 A_r of Cl = 35.5

In the exams, you might be given the relative atomic masses you need in the question.

2) Add up all the relative atomic masses of the atoms in the compound.

$Mg + (2 \times Cl) = 24 + (2 \times 35.5)$
$= 24 + 71 = 95$

M_r of $MgCl_2$ = **95**

There are two chlorine atoms in $MgCl_2$, so the relative atomic mass of chlorine needs to be multiplied by 2.

b) Find the relative formula mass of $Ca(OH)_2$.

1) Look up the relative atomic masses of all the elements in the compound on the periodic table.

A_r of Ca = 40 A_r of O = 16 A_r of H = 1

2) Add up all the relative atomic masses of the atoms in the compound. The small number 2 after the bracket in the formula $Ca(OH)_2$ means that there's two of everything inside the brackets.

$Ca + [(O + H) \times 2] = 40 + [(16 + 1) \times 2]$
$= 40 + 34 = 74$

M_r of $Ca(OH)_2$ = **74**

You Can Calculate the Percentage Mass of an Element in a Compound

To work out the percentage mass of an element in a compound, you need to use this formula:

$$\text{Percentage mass of an element in a compound} = \frac{A_r \times \text{number of atoms of that element}}{M_r \text{ of the compound}} \times 100$$

EXAMPLE:

Find the percentage mass of sodium (Na) in sodium bromide (NaBr).

1) Look up the relative atomic masses of all the elements in the compound on the periodic table.

A_r of Na = 23 A_r of Br = 80

2) Add up the relative atomic masses of all the atoms in the compound to find the relative formula mass.

M_r of NaBr = 23 + 80
$= 103$

3) Use the formula to calculate the percentage mass.

$$\text{Percentage mass of sodium} = \frac{A_r \times \text{number of atoms of that element}}{M_r \text{ of the compound}} \times 100$$
$$= \frac{23 \times 1}{103} \times 100$$
$$= 22\%$$

Relative formula = sister + grandad + aunt + cousin...

The best way to get to grips with all this stuff is by practising. Start by having a go at these questions...

Q1   Calculate the relative formula mass (M_r) of: a) H_2O b) LiOH   c) H_2SO_4 [3 marks]

Q2   Calculate the percentage mass of potassium in potassium hydroxide (KOH).   [2 marks]

Conservation of Mass

You've probably realised by now that you can't magic stuff out of thin air. It can't magically disappear, either.

In a Chemical Reaction, Mass Always Stays the Same

1) During a chemical reaction <u>no atoms are lost</u> and <u>no atoms are made</u>.

2) This means there are the <u>same number and types of atoms</u> on each side of a reaction equation.

3) Because of this, no mass is lost or gained — we say that mass is <u>conserved</u> (stays the same) in a reaction.

E.g.

$$2Li + F_2 \rightarrow 2LiF$$

In this reaction, there are <u>2 lithium atoms</u> and <u>2 fluorine atoms</u> on <u>each side</u> of the equation.

4) You can see that mass stays the same if you <u>add up</u> the relative formula masses of the substances on each side of a <u>balanced symbol equation</u>.

5) The total M_r of all the reactants will be the <u>same</u> as the total M_r of the products.

If you're not sure what the big numbers and the little numbers in reaction equations mean, see p.98 and 99.

EXAMPLE:

Show that mass is conserved in this reaction: $2Li + F_2 \rightarrow 2LiF$.
Relative atomic masses (A_r): Li = 7, F = 19

1) Add up the relative formula masses on the <u>left-hand side</u> of the equation.

$2 \times A_r(Li) + 2 \times A_r(F) = (2 \times 7) + (2 \times 19)$
$= 14 + 38$
$= 52$

2) Add up the relative formula masses on the <u>right-hand side</u> of the equation.

$2 \times M_r(LiF) = 2 \times (7 + 19)$
$= 2 \times 26$
$= 52$

The total M_r on the left-hand side of the equation is the same as the total M_r on the right-hand side, so mass is conserved.

You can Calculate the Mass of a Reactant or Product

1) You can use the idea of conservation of mass to <u>work out</u> the mass of a reactant or product in a reaction.

2) You need to know the masses of <u>all</u> the reactants and products except for <u>one</u>.

3) You can work out the <u>total mass</u> of everything on one side of the equation.

4) You can also work out the total mass of everything on the other side of the equation, <u>except</u> for the thing you don't know the mass of.

5) The mass of the thing you <u>don't</u> know is the <u>difference</u> between these two totals.

EXAMPLE:

6 g of magnesium completely reacts with 4 g of oxygen in the following reaction:
$2Mg + O_2 \rightarrow 2MgO$
What mass of magnesium oxide is formed?

1) Find the total mass of reactants.

$4 + 6 = 10$ g

2) Magnesium oxide is the only product.
So the mass of products you do know is O g.

Mass of magnesium oxide = $10 - 0 = 10$ g

Leaving all the potatoes on your plate — that's mash conservation...

Never, ever forget that, in a reaction, the total mass of reactants is the same as the total mass of products.

Q1   When 6.00 g of calcium carbonate is heated, it breaks down to form carbon dioxide and 3.36 g of calcium oxide. Calculate the mass of carbon dioxide that forms.   [2 marks]

More on Conservation of Mass

Even though mass is always (always) conserved in a reaction, sometimes you can carry out an experiment where the mass of the reaction container changes. Time to find out why...

If the Mass Seems to Change, There's Usually a Gas Involved

In some experiments, the mass of an unsealed reaction container might change during a reaction. This usually happens for one of two reasons...

1) If One of the Reactants is a Gas, the Mass Could Go Up

If the mass goes up, it's probably because one of the things that reacts is a gas that's found in air (e.g. oxygen) and all the things that are made are solids, liquids or in solution.

1) Before the reaction, the gas is floating around in the air. It's there, but it's not trapped in the reaction container. This means you can't measure its mass.

2) When the gas reacts, its atoms become part of the product, which is held inside the reaction container.

3) So the total mass of the stuff inside the reaction container goes up.

- When a metal reacts with oxygen in an unsealed container, the mass of the container goes up.
- This is because the mass of the oxygen atoms isn't measured when they're part of the gas, but it is when they're in the metal oxide.

$$metal_{(s)} + oxygen_{(g)} \rightarrow metal\ oxide_{(s)}$$

Remember from the particle model on page 121 that a gas will spread out to fill any container it's in. So if the reaction container isn't sealed, the gas will escape into the air.

2) If One of the Products is a Gas, the Mass Could Go Down

If the mass goes down, it's probably because one of the products is a gas and all the things that react are solids, liquids or in solution.

1) Before the reaction, all the reactants are held in the reaction container.

2) If the container isn't sealed, then the gas can escape from the reaction container as it's formed.

3) It's no longer trapped in the reaction container, so you can't measure its mass.

4) This means the total mass of the stuff inside the reaction container goes down.

- When a metal carbonate is heated, it can break down to form a metal oxide and carbon dioxide gas.
- When this happens, the mass of the reaction container will go down if it isn't sealed.
- But really, the mass of the metal oxide and the carbon dioxide formed will be the same as the mass of the metal carbonate.

Reactions where substances are heated and break down are called thermal decomposition reactions.

$$metal\ carbonate_{(s)} \rightarrow metal\ oxide_{(s)} + carbon\ dioxide_{(g)}$$

My friend and I talked about grams — it was a mass conversation...

If all this information is escaping from your brain, have another read of the page and then try these questions...

Q1 During a reaction, the mass of a reaction container increases.
What does this tell you about the states of matter of the products and reactants? [2 marks]

Q2 A scientist carries out the reaction below. He does it in an unsealed reaction container:
$$2Na_{(s)} + 2HCl_{(aq)} \rightarrow 2NaCl_{(aq)} + H_{2(g)}$$
Predict how the mass of the reaction container will change as the reaction takes place. [1 mark]

Concentrations of Solutions

Lots of reactions take place between substances that are dissolved in a solution. And sometimes it's useful to find out the mass of a substance that's dissolved in a solution. Hold onto your hats and concentrate...

Concentration is a Measure of How Crowded Things Are

1) The amount of a substance (e.g. the mass) in a certain volume of a solution is called its concentration.

2) The more substance that's dissolved in a certain volume, the more concentrated the solution.

Concentration can be Measured in g/dm³

1) You can find the concentration of a solution if you know the mass of the substance dissolved and the volume of the solution.

The thing that dissolves the solid is called a 'solvent'. The solid that dissolves in the solvent is called a 'solute'.

2) The units will be units of mass/units of volume. For example, g/dm³.

3) Here's how to calculate the concentration of a solution in grams per decimetre cubed (g/dm³):

$$\text{in g/dm}^3 \longleftarrow \text{concentration} = \frac{\text{mass of dissolved substance}\; \longrightarrow \text{in g}}{\text{volume of solvent}\; \longrightarrow \text{in dm}^3}$$

EXAMPLES:

a) 30 g of sodium chloride is dissolved in 0.2 dm³ of water. What's the concentration of this solution in g/dm³?

Put the numbers into the formula to calculate the concentration.

$$\text{concentration} = \frac{30}{0.2} = 150 \text{ g/dm}^3$$

Gavin wasn't great at concentration.

b) 15 g of salt in 500 cm³ of water. What's the concentration of this solution in g/dm³?

1 dm³ = 1000 cm³

1) The units of the volume need to be dm³ so that the units of concentration are in g/dm³. So make the units of volume dm³ by dividing by 1000:

$$500 \div 1000 = 0.5 \text{ dm}^3$$

2) Now you've got the mass and the volume in the right units, just stick them in the formula:

$$\text{concentration} = \frac{15}{0.5} = 30 \text{ g/dm}^3$$

4) You can rearrange the equation above to find the mass of substance dissolved in a certain volume of solution if you know its concentration. Here's a formula triangle to help with rearranging the equation:

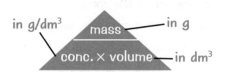

When you measure something like the mass of a substance or the volume of a solution, there's always some uncertainty to the measurement. You can calculate this uncertainty from a range — see pages 6 and 10 for more.

5) To use the formula triangle, just cover up the thing you want to find with your finger and write down what's left showing.

EXAMPLE:

A solution of magnesium chloride has a concentration of 24 g/dm³. What mass of magnesium chloride is there in 0.40 dm³ of this solution?

1) You want to find the mass. So cover up 'mass' in the formula triangle. This leaves 'concentration × volume'.

$$\text{mass} = \text{conc.} \times \text{volume}$$

2) Use this equation to calculate the mass:

$$\text{mass} = 24 \times 0.40 = 9.6 \text{ g}$$

CGP Revision Guides — not from concentrate...

Learning that formula could be a useful way to spend a few minutes. As could eating a biscuit. Why not try both?

Q1   A solution has a concentration of 32 g/dm³. What mass of salt is in 0.25 dm³ of this solution?   [1 mark]

Q2   0.015 dm³ of a solution contains 0.6 g of salt. Find the concentration, in g/dm³, of this solution.   [1 mark]

Revision Questions for Topics C2 & C3

Now you've finished Topics C2 and C3, I bet I can guess what you want next.
A lovely set of questions to test how much of these lovely topics you can remember. I knew it...

- Try these questions and tick off each one when you get it right.
- When you've done all the questions under a heading and are completely happy with it, tick it off.

Ions and Ionic Compounds (p.113-115) ☐

1) Do elements from Group 1 form positive or negative ions? ☐
2) What's the charge on the ions formed by Group 7 elements? ☐
3) What type of bond is formed when a metal reacts with a non-metal? ☐
4) Draw dot and cross diagrams to show the formation of:
   a) sodium chloride   b) magnesium oxide   c) magnesium chloride ☐
5) Give one advantage and one disadvantage of using a ball and stick model
   to show the structure of an ionic compound. ☐
6) List three properties of ionic compounds. ☐

Covalent Substances (p.116-119) ☐

7) How do covalent bonds form? ☐
8) Draw dot and cross diagrams showing the bonding in a molecule of:
   a) hydrogen (H_2)   b) water (H_2O)   c) hydrogen chloride (HCl) ☐
9) Explain why simple molecular compounds usually have low melting and boiling points. ☐
10) What type of bonds form between the atoms in a polymer? ☐
11) Give three examples of giant covalent substances. ☐
12) Explain why graphite can conduct electricity. ☐
13) What was the first fullerene to be discovered? ☐

Metallic Bonding (p.120) ☐

14) Explain why substances with metallic structures usually have high melting points. ☐
15) Explain why substances with metallic structures can conduct electricity. ☐
16) What is an alloy? ☐

States of Matter (p.121-122) ☐

17) Name the three states of matter. ☐
18) What is the state symbol of an aqueous substance? ☐
19) What is the name of the temperature at which a liquid becomes a gas? ☐
20) What state will a substance be in if the temperature is above its boiling point? ☐

Masses in Reactions (p.123-125) ☐

21) How do you calculate the relative formula mass, M_r of a substance? ☐
22) Why is mass conserved during a reaction? ☐
23) Suggest why the mass of a reaction container might decrease during a reaction. ☐

Concentrations of Solutions (p.126) ☐

24) What is concentration? ☐
25) Give the equation for working out the concentration of a solution in g/dm^3. ☐

Acids and Bases

Testing the pH of a solution means using an indicator — and that means pretty colours...

The pH Scale Goes From 0 to 14

1) The pH scale is a measure of how acidic or alkaline a solution is.
2) The lower the pH of a solution, the more acidic it is.
3) The higher the pH of a solution, the more alkaline it is.
4) A neutral substance (e.g. pure water) has pH 7.

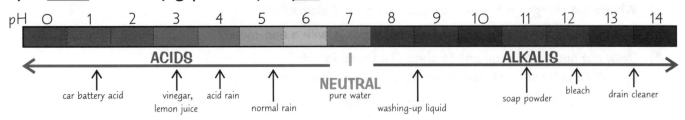

| pH | O | 1 | 2 | 3 | 4 | 5 | 6 | 7 | 8 | 9 | 10 | 11 | 12 | 13 | 14 |

ACIDS | ALKALIS

NEUTRAL

car battery acid   vinegar,   acid rain   washing-up liquid   soap powder   bleach   drain cleaner
                        lemon juice
                                    normal rain   pure water

You Can Measure the pH of a Solution

1) An indicator is a dye that changes colour depending on whether it's above or below a certain pH.
2) Wide range indicators are substances that gradually change colour as pH changes.
3) They're useful for estimating the pH of a solution.
4) For example, Universal indicator is a wide range indicator. It gives the colours shown above.
5) A pH probe attached to a pH meter can also be used to measure pH electronically.
6) The probe is put in the solution and the pH is shown as a number. This means it's more accurate than an indicator.

Acids and Bases Neutralise Each Other

1) When acids dissolve in water, they form solutions with a pH of less than 7. Acids form H^+ ions in water.
2) Bases have pHs greater than 7.
3) Alkalis are bases that dissolve in water to form solutions with a pH greater than 7. Alkalis form OH^- ions in water. For example, soluble metal hydroxides are alkalis.

I have no idea what I'm doing.

- The reaction between acids and bases is called neutralisation:

$$acid + base \rightarrow salt + water$$

- Neutralisation between acids and alkalis can be shown using $\underline{H^+}$ and $\underline{OH^-}$ ions like this:

$$H^+_{(aq)} + OH^-_{(aq)} \rightarrow H_2O_{(l)}$$

- The products of neutralisation reactions have a pH of 7. This means they're neutral.

Hydrogen (H^+) ions react with hydroxide (OH^-) ions to produce water.

4) You can add an indicator to the acid or alkali you're neutralising. Then gradually add the other substance. The indicator will change colour when the neutralisation reaction is over.
5) If you use Universal indicator, add the substance until the Universal indicator is green. This is when the pH of the solution is neutral.

This page should have all bases covered...

pHew, you finished the page... So here's an interesting(ish) fact about pH — your skin is slightly acidic (pH 5.5).

Q1   What colour would you expect Universal indicator to turn if you added it to lemon juice?   [1 mark]

Q2   The pH of a solution is 8. Is the solution acidic or alkaline?   [1 mark]

Reactions of Acids

Remember <u>neutralisation reactions</u> from the previous page? Well, there's more about them coming up...

Metal Oxides and Metal Hydroxides are Bases

1) <u>Metal oxides</u> and <u>metal hydroxides</u> react with <u>acids</u> in <u>neutralisation reactions</u> to form a <u>salt</u> and <u>water</u>.

2) The salt that forms depends upon the <u>acid</u> and the <u>metal ion</u> in the <u>oxide</u> or <u>hydroxide</u>.

3) HCl reacts to form <u>chlorides</u>, H_2SO_4 reacts to form <u>sulfates</u> and HNO_3 reacts to form <u>nitrates</u>.

hydrochloric acid	+	copper oxide	→	copper chloride	+	water
2HCl	+	CuO	→	$CuCl_2$	+	H_2O
sulfuric acid	+	potassium hydroxide	→	potassium sulfate	+	water
H_2SO_4	+	2KOH	→	K_2SO_4	+	$2H_2O$
nitric acid	+	sodium hydroxide	→	sodium nitrate	+	water
HNO_3	+	NaOH	→	$NaNO_3$	+	H_2O

Acids and Metal Carbonates Produce Carbon Dioxide

Metal carbonates are also <u>bases</u>. They react with acids to produce a salt, water and <u>carbon dioxide</u>.

hydrochloric acid	+	sodium carbonate	→	sodium chloride	+	water	+	carbon dioxide
2HCl	+	Na_2CO_3	→	2NaCl	+	H_2O	+	CO_2
sulfuric acid	+	calcium carbonate	→	calcium sulfate	+	water	+	carbon dioxide
H_2SO_4	+	$CaCO_3$	→	$CaSO_4$	+	H_2O	+	CO_2

You can Make Soluble Salts Using an Insoluble Base

1) If you react an <u>acid</u> with an <u>insoluble base</u> or a <u>metal</u>, you can make a <u>soluble salt</u>.

2) First, pick the <u>acid</u> that contains the same <u>negative ion</u> as the salt you want to make. For example, to make <u>copper chloride</u>, you'd choose <u>hydrochloric acid</u>.

PRACTICAL

3) Then pick an <u>insoluble base</u> with the same <u>positive ion</u> as the salt you want to make. You could use an <u>insoluble metal oxide</u>, <u>hydroxide</u>, or <u>carbonate</u>.

4) So to make <u>copper chloride</u>, you'd choose <u>copper oxide</u>, <u>copper hydroxide</u> or <u>copper carbonate</u>. Here's the equation for making copper chloride from <u>hydrochloric acid</u> and <u>copper oxide</u>:

$$CuO_{(s)} + 2HCl_{(aq)} → CuCl_{2\,(aq)} + H_2O_{(l)}$$

5) Gently <u>warm</u> the dilute acid using a <u>Bunsen burner</u>, then turn off the Bunsen burner.

6) Add the <u>insoluble base</u> to the <u>acid</u> until no more reacts (you'll see the solid at the bottom of the flask).

7) <u>Filter</u> out the solid that <u>hasn't reacted</u> to get the salt solution (see p.102).

8) To get <u>pure</u>, <u>solid</u> crystals of the <u>salt</u>, you need to <u>crystallise</u> it (see p.102).

9) To do this, gently heat the solution using a <u>water bath</u> or an <u>electric heater</u>. Some of the water will <u>evaporate</u>. Stop heating the solution and leave it to <u>cool</u>.

10) <u>Crystals</u> of the salt should form, which can be <u>filtered</u> out of the solution and then <u>dried</u>.

AHHHHH so many reactions...

There might be lots of reactions on this page, but I've treated you to a nice experiment as well. You're welcome.

Q1   Write a word equation for the reaction between calcium carbonate and hydrochloric acid.   [2 marks]

The Reactivity Series and Extracting Metals

You can place <u>metals</u> in order of reactivity. This can be a lot more useful than it sounds, promise.

The Reactivity Series — How Easily a Metal Reacts

1) The <u>reactivity series</u> lists metals in <u>order</u> of how <u>reactive</u> they are (their reactivity).

2) Metals react to form <u>positive ions</u>.

3) So for metals, their reactivity depends on how <u>easily</u> they lose electrons and form positive ions.

4) The <u>higher</u> up the reactivity series a metal is, the more easily it forms <u>positive ions</u>.

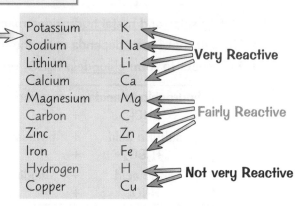

Carbon and hydrogen are non-metals but are often included in the reactivity series.

Potassium	K	Very Reactive
Sodium	Na	
Lithium	Li	
Calcium	Ca	
Magnesium	Mg	Fairly Reactive
Carbon	C	
Zinc	Zn	
Iron	Fe	
Hydrogen	H	Not very Reactive
Copper	Cu	

Metals Often Have to be Separated from their Oxides

1) Lots of common metals, like iron and aluminium, react with <u>oxygen</u> to form <u>oxides</u>.

2) This process is an example of <u>oxidation</u>.

3) These oxides are often the <u>ores</u> that the metals are removed (extracted) from.

4) A reaction that separates a metal from its oxide is called a <u>reduction reaction</u>.

An ore is a type of rock that contains metal compounds. Most metals are found in the earth as ores.

<u>Oxidation = Gain of Oxygen</u>

E.g. magnesium is <u>oxidised</u> to make magnesium oxide.

$$2Mg + O_2 \rightarrow 2MgO$$

<u>Reduction = Loss of Oxygen</u>

E.g. copper oxide is <u>reduced</u> to copper.

$$2CuO + C \rightarrow 2Cu + CO_2$$

Some Metals can be Extracted by Reduction with Carbon

1) Some metals can be <u>extracted</u> from their ores using a reaction with <u>carbon</u>.

2) In this reaction, the ore is <u>reduced</u> as oxygen is <u>removed</u> from it. Carbon <u>gains</u> oxygen, so it is <u>oxidised</u>.

3) For example:

iron(III) oxide + carbon → iron + carbon dioxide $2Fe_2O_3 + 3C \rightarrow 4Fe + 3CO_2$

Iron has lost oxygen.   Carbon has gained oxygen.

4) The <u>reactivity series</u> can tell you if a metal can be extracted with carbon.

- Metals <u>above carbon</u> in the reactivity series are extracted using <u>electrolysis</u> (p.132). This is expensive as it takes lots of <u>energy</u> to <u>melt</u> the ore and to produce the <u>electricity</u>.

- Electrolysis is also used to extract metals that <u>react</u> with carbon.

- Metals <u>below carbon</u> in the reactivity series can be extracted by <u>reduction</u> using <u>carbon</u>. For example, <u>iron oxide</u> is reduced in a <u>blast furnace</u> to make <u>iron</u>.

- This is because carbon <u>can only take the oxygen</u> away from metals which are <u>less reactive</u> than carbon <u>itself</u> is.

Make sure you can explain how and why different metals are extracted in different ways.

5) Some metals are <u>so unreactive</u> they are found in the earth as the metal <u>itself</u>. For example, <u>gold</u>.

Are you going to revise this page, ore what?

From the metals in the reactivity series above, only zinc, iron and copper can be extracted with carbon.

Q1   A mining company tried to extract calcium from calcium oxide by reduction with carbon. The process did not work. Explain why.

[1 mark]

Reactions of Metals

Metals react to form <u>salts</u>. And you, my friend, need to be able to <u>predict</u> the salt that'll form from a reaction.

Metals React With Acids

1) Some metals react with acids to produce a <u>salt</u> and <u>hydrogen gas</u>.

> Acid + Metal → Salt + Hydrogen

> HCl reacts to form chloride salts, H_2SO_4 reacts to form sulfate salts.

- hydrochloric acid + magnesium → magnesium chloride + hydrogen $2HCl + Mg \rightarrow MgCl_2 + H_2$
- sulfuric acid + zinc → zinc sulfate + hydrogen $H_2SO_4 + Zn \rightarrow ZnSO_4 + H_2$
- hydrochloric acid + iron → iron chloride + hydrogen $2HCl + Fe \rightarrow FeCl_2 + H_2$

2) <u>Very reactive</u> metals like potassium, sodium, lithium and calcium react <u>explosively</u> with acids.

3) <u>Less reactive</u> metals such as magnesium, zinc and iron react <u>less violently</u> with acids.

4) In general, copper <u>won't</u> react with cold, dilute acids.

Metals Also React with Water

1) Many metals will also react with <u>water</u>.

> Metal + Water → Metal Hydroxide + Hydrogen

2) For example, calcium: $Ca_{(s)} + 2H_2O_{(l)} \rightarrow Ca(OH)_{2(aq)} + H_{2(g)}$

3) The metals <u>potassium</u>, <u>sodium</u>, <u>lithium</u> and <u>calcium</u> will all react with water.

4) Less reactive metals like <u>zinc</u>, <u>iron</u> and <u>copper</u> won't react with water.

You Can Work Out a Reactivity Series from the Reactions of Metals

1) If you put metals in order from <u>most reactive</u> to <u>least reactive</u> based on their reactions with either an <u>acid</u> or <u>water</u>, the order you get is the <u>reactivity series</u> (see the previous page).

2) To compare the reactivities of metals, you could watch how quickly <u>bubbles</u> of hydrogen are formed in their reactions with water or acid. The more <u>reactive</u> the metal, the <u>faster</u> the bubbles will form.

> For these experiments to be fair, the mass and surface area of the metals should be the same each time.

3) You can also measure the <u>temperature change</u> of the reaction in a set time period. The <u>more reactive</u> the metal, the greater the temperature change should be.

More Reactive Metals can Displace Less Reactive Metals from Salts

1) <u>Displacement</u> reactions involve one metal <u>kicking another one out</u> of a compound. Here's the rule:

> A MORE REACTIVE metal will displace a LESS REACTIVE metal from its compound.

2) For example, <u>iron</u> is more reactive than <u>copper</u>. So if you add solid iron to copper sulfate solution, you get a <u>displacement reaction</u>.

3) The iron kicks the copper out of copper sulfate. You end up with <u>iron sulfate solution</u> and <u>copper solid</u>.

> iron + copper sulfate → iron sulfate + copper $Fe_{(s)} + CuSO_{4(aq)} \rightarrow FeSO_{4(aq)} + Cu_{(s)}$

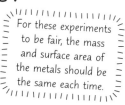

New information displaces old information from my brain...

See, experiments aren't just for fun — they can give you a thrilling insight into the relative reactivities of elements.

Q1   Complete the word equation for the reaction of sodium and water: sodium + water → ? + ?   [2 marks]

Electrolysis

Electrolysis uses <u>electricity</u> to cause a reaction. It's actually pretty cool. No, really...

Electrolysis Means 'Splitting Up with Electricity'

Elect Toad!

He's the best!
Froget the rest!

1) An <u>electrolyte</u> is just a <u>liquid or solution</u> that can <u>conduct electricity</u>.
   For example, an ionic compound that's either <u>dissolved</u> in water, or <u>melted</u> so it's a liquid.

2) An <u>electrode</u> is a <u>solid</u> that is put in the electrolyte and <u>conducts electricity</u>.

3) In <u>electrolysis</u>, an electric current is passed through an electrolyte.
   The ions move towards the electrodes, where they react. The compound then <u>breaks down</u>.

4) <u>Positive ions</u> in the electrolyte move towards the <u>cathode</u> (negative electrode). Here, they <u>gain</u> electrons.

5) <u>Negative ions</u> in the electrolyte move towards the <u>anode</u> (positive electrode). Here, they <u>lose</u> electrons.

6) The ions form the <u>uncharged element</u>. The ions are said to be <u>discharged</u> from the electrolyte.

7) A <u>flow of charge</u> is created through the <u>electrolyte</u> as the ions travel to the electrodes.

Electrolysis of Molten Ionic Solids Forms Elements

1) <u>Molten ionic compounds can</u> be electrolysed because
   the ions can <u>move freely</u> and conduct electricity.

2) Molten ionic liquids are always broken up into their <u>elements</u>.

3) The <u>metal</u> forms at the <u>cathode</u>. The <u>non-metal</u> is formed at the <u>anode</u>.

The electrodes should be inert (unreactive) so they don't react with the electrolyte.

When molten <u>lead bromide</u> is electrolysed, <u>lead</u> forms at the cathode and <u>bromine</u> forms at the anode.

Metals can be Extracted From Their Ores Using Electrolysis

1) Aluminium is extracted from an ore that contains <u>aluminium oxide</u>, Al_2O_3.

2) Aluminium oxide has a <u>very high</u> melting point so it's mixed
   with a substance called <u>cryolite</u>. This <u>lowers</u> the melting point.

3) The <u>positive Al^{3+} ions</u> are attracted to the <u>negative electrode</u> where they form <u>aluminium atoms</u>.

4) The <u>negative O^{2-} ions</u> are attracted to the <u>positive electrode</u> where they react to form O_2 molecules.

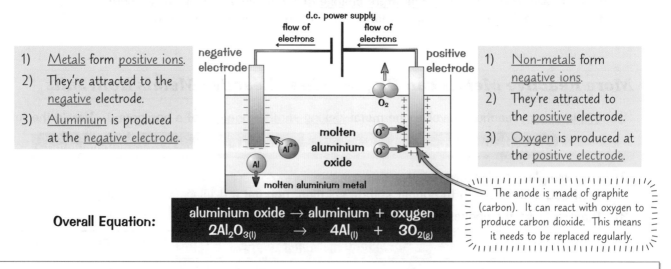

1) <u>Metals</u> form <u>positive ions</u>.
2) They're attracted to the <u>negative</u> electrode.
3) <u>Aluminium</u> is produced at the <u>negative electrode</u>.

1) <u>Non-metals</u> form <u>negative ions</u>.
2) They're attracted to the <u>positive</u> electrode.
3) <u>Oxygen</u> is produced at the <u>positive electrode</u>.

d.c. power supply
flow of electrons
flow of electrons
negative electrode
positive electrode
O_2
molten aluminium oxide
O^{2-}
Al^{3+}
Al
molten aluminium metal

The anode is made of graphite (carbon). It can react with oxygen to produce carbon dioxide. This means it needs to be replaced regularly.

Overall Equation:

aluminium oxide → aluminium + oxygen
$2Al_2O_{3(l)} \rightarrow 4Al_{(l)} + 3O_{2(g)}$

Faster shopping at the supermarket — use Electrolleys...

When you electrolyse a molten salt, the <u>non</u>-metal is formed at the <u>anode</u>. So the metal is formed at the cathode.

Q1   A student carries out electrolysis on molten sodium chloride. What is produced at:
      a) the anode?   b) the cathode?   [2 marks]

Topic C4 — Chemical Changes

Electrolysis of Aqueous Solutions

When you electrolyse a salt that's dissolved in water, you also have to think about the ions from the <u>water</u>.

You Can Predict what Forms when a Salt Solution is Electrolysed

1) <u>Water</u> can break down into H^+ and OH^- ions.

$$H_2O_{(l)} \rightleftharpoons H^+_{(aq)} + OH^-_{(aq)}$$

2) So in <u>solutions</u> that contain <u>water</u>, there will be the <u>ions</u> from the ionic compound as well as <u>hydrogen ions</u> (H^+) and <u>hydroxide ions</u> (OH^-) from the <u>water</u>.

The $\rightleftharpoons$ symbol in this reaction shows that it's reversible. For more about reversible reactions see p.144.

3) H^+ ions and <u>metal ions</u> will move to the <u>cathode</u>.

4) If the metal's more reactive than hydrogen, <u>hydrogen gas</u> will form.

5) If the metal is <u>less reactive</u> than hydrogen, a solid layer of the <u>pure metal</u> will form.

6) If the salt contains <u>halide ions</u> (Cl^-, Br^-, I^-), chlorine, bromine or iodine will form at the <u>anode</u>.

7) If <u>no halide ions</u> are present, then the OH^- ions lose electrons and <u>oxygen</u> will form at the anode.

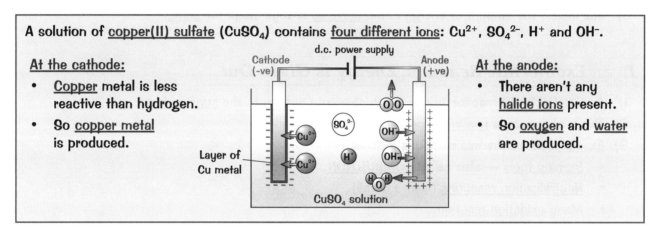

A solution of <u>copper(II) sulfate</u> ($CuSO_4$) contains <u>four different ions</u>: Cu^{2+}, SO_4^{2-}, H^+ and OH^-.

<u>At the cathode:</u>
- <u>Copper</u> metal is less reactive than hydrogen.
- So <u>copper metal</u> is produced.

d.c. power supply
Cathode (-ve)   Anode (+ve)
Layer of Cu metal
$CuSO_4$ solution

<u>At the anode:</u>
- There aren't any <u>halide ions</u> present.
- So <u>oxygen</u> and <u>water</u> are produced.

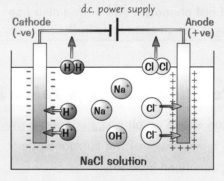

A solution of <u>sodium chloride</u> (NaCl) contains <u>four different ions</u>: Na^+, Cl^-, OH^- and H^+.

<u>At the cathode:</u>
- <u>Sodium</u> metal is more reactive hydrogen.
- So <u>hydrogen gas</u> is produced.

d.c. power supply
Cathode (-ve)   Anode (+ve)
NaCl solution

<u>At the anode:</u>
- <u>Chloride ions</u> are in the solution.
- So <u>chlorine gas</u> is produced.

8) You can set up an electrolysis <u>experiment</u> in the <u>lab</u> like the set-up on page 236.
9) This will let you <u>collect</u> any gases that form in the reaction.
10) Once the experiment is finished you can <u>test</u> the <u>gases</u> to work out what they are.
- Chlorine <u>bleaches</u> damp <u>litmus paper</u>, turning it white.
- Hydrogen makes a "<u>squeaky pop</u>" with a <u>lighted splint</u>.
- Oxygen will <u>relight</u> a <u>glowing splint</u>.

PRACTICAL

For more on tests for gases, turn to page 153.

I wrote a poem about my tabby — it was a cat ode...

So it's kinda confusing this electrolysis business — you need to take it slow and make sure you get it.

Q1 An aqueous solution of copper chloride, $CuCl_2$, is electrolysed using inert electrodes.
State what is produced at: a) the anode, b) the cathode. [2 marks]

Exothermic and Endothermic Reactions

In all chemical reactions, there's a change in <u>energy</u>. This means that when chemicals get together, things either heat up or cool right off. I'll give you a heads up — this page is a good 'un.

Energy is Moved Around in Chemical Reactions

1) Chemicals <u>store</u> a certain amount of energy — and <u>different chemicals</u> store <u>different amounts</u>.

2) Sometimes, the <u>products</u> of a reaction store <u>more</u> energy than the <u>reactants</u>. This means that the products have <u>taken in</u> energy from the <u>surroundings</u> during the reaction.

3) But if the products store <u>less</u> energy, then the <u>extra</u> energy was transferred (given out) <u>to the surroundings</u> during the reaction.

4) The amount of energy transferred is the <u>difference</u> between the energy of the products and the energy of the reactants.

5) The <u>overall</u> amount of energy doesn't change. This is because energy stays the <u>same</u> (is <u>conserved</u>) in reactions — it can't be made or destroyed, only <u>moved around</u>.

6) This means the amount of energy in the <u>universe</u> always stays the <u>same</u>.

In an Exothermic Reaction, Energy is Given Out

1) An <u>EXOTHERMIC</u> reaction is one which <u>gives out</u> energy to the <u>surroundings</u>.

2) This is shown by a <u>rise in temperature</u> of the surroundings.

3) <u>Examples</u> of exothermic reactions include:
   - <u>Burning fuels</u> — also called <u>COMBUSTION</u>.
   - <u>Neutralisation reactions</u> (acid + alkali).
   - Many <u>oxidation reactions</u>.

4) Exothermic reactions have lots of everyday <u>uses</u>. For example:

   - Some <u>hand warmers</u> use an exothermic reaction to <u>release energy</u>.
   - <u>Self heating cans</u> of hot chocolate and coffee also use <u>exothermic reactions</u> between chemicals in their bases.

In an Endothermic Reaction, Energy is Taken In

1) An <u>ENDOTHERMIC</u> reaction is one which <u>takes in</u> energy <u>from</u> the surroundings.

2) This is shown by a <u>fall in temperature</u> of the surroundings.

3) <u>Examples</u> of endothermic reactions include:
   - The reaction between <u>citric acid</u> and <u>sodium hydrogencarbonate</u>.
   - <u>Thermal decomposition</u> (when a substance breaks down when it's heated).

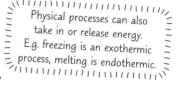
Physical processes can also take in or release energy. E.g. freezing is an exothermic process, melting is endothermic.

4) Endothermic reactions also have everyday uses. For example:

   Endothermic reactions are used in some <u>sports injury packs</u>. The chemical reaction allows the pack to become <u>instantly cooler</u> without having to put it in the <u>freezer</u>.

Right, so burning gives out heat — really...

Remember, "exo-" = exit, "-thermic" = heat, so an exothermic reaction is one that gives out heat — and endothermic means just the opposite. To make sure you really understand these terms, try this question.

Q1   A student has two solutions at the same temperature. He mixes the solutions together and they react. The temperature of the reaction mixture goes up. Is the reaction exothermic or endothermic?   [1 mark]

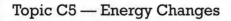

Measuring Energy Changes [PRACTICAL]

Sometimes it's not enough to just know if a reaction is endothermic or exothermic.
You may also need to measure <u>how much</u> the <u>temperature</u> changes during a reaction. Fun, fun, fun...

Energy Transfer can be Measured

1) You can use an experiment to investigate the <u>temperature change</u> of a chemical reaction.

2) You can do this by taking the <u>temperature of the reactants</u> and <u>mixing</u> them in a <u>polystyrene cup</u>.

3) If the temperature of the solution <u>rises</u> during the reaction, record the <u>highest temperature</u> that it reaches.
   If the temperature of the solution <u>falls</u> during the reaction, record the <u>lowest temperature</u> that it reaches.

4) To find the temperature change, <u>take away</u> this temperature from the temperature of the <u>reactants</u>.

5) If the temperature goes <u>up</u>, the reaction's <u>exothermic</u>.
   If the temperature goes <u>down</u>, the reaction's <u>endothermic</u>.

6) The biggest <u>problem</u> with temperature measurements is the amount of energy <u>lost to the surroundings</u>.

7) You can reduce this by putting a <u>lid</u> on the polystyrene cup
   and putting the cup into a <u>beaker of cotton wool</u>.

8) This method works for a number of <u>different</u> reactions.
   For example:
   - <u>neutralisation</u> reactions.
   - reactions between <u>metals</u> and <u>acids</u>.
   - reactions between <u>acids</u> and <u>carbonates</u>.
   - <u>displacement</u> reactions of metals.

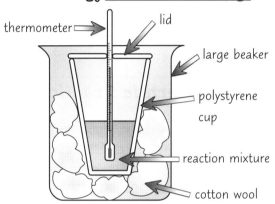

The Temperature Change of a Reaction Depends on Different Variables

1) You can also use this method to investigate what effect different <u>variables</u> have on the
   <u>temperature change</u> — e.g. the <u>mass</u> or <u>concentration</u> of the reactants used.

2) Here's how you could test the effect of <u>acid concentration</u> on the temperature change of
   a <u>neutralisation</u> reaction between hydrochloric acid (HCl) and sodium hydroxide (NaOH):

   - Put 25 cm³ each of 10 g/dm³ hydrochloric acid and sodium hydroxide in <u>separate beakers</u>.
   - Place the beakers in a water bath set to 25 °C until they are both at the <u>same temperature</u> (25 °C).
   - Add the HCl followed by the NaOH to a polystyrene cup with a lid — as in the diagram above.
   - Take the temperature of the mixture <u>every 30 seconds</u>, and record the highest temperature.
   - Use your <u>results</u> to work out the <u>temperature change</u> of the reaction.
   - <u>Repeat</u> these steps using 20 g/dm³ and then 30 g/dm³ of hydrochloric acid.
     Then <u>compare</u> your results to see how acid concentration <u>affects</u> the temperature change of the reaction.

Energy transfer — make sure you take it all in...

Fluffy cotton wool doesn't sound very sciencey but it's pretty important. Best check to make sure you know why...

Q1   When measuring the temperature change of a reaction, why is it important to
      put the polystyrene cup in a beaker of cotton wool and to keep a lid on the cup?   [1 mark]

Reaction Profiles

Reaction profiles are handy little diagrams which show you the changes in energy during a reaction.

Activation Energy is Needed to Start a Reaction

1) The activation energy is the minimum amount of energy the reactants need to have to react when they collide with each other.

2) The greater the activation energy, the more energy needed to start the reaction. This energy has to be given, e.g. by heating the reaction mixture.

There's more on activation energy and collision theory on pages 138-139.

Reaction Profiles Show Energy Changes

Reaction profiles are diagrams that show the difference between the energies of the reactants and products in a reaction, and how the energy changes over the course of the reaction.

Reaction profiles are sometimes called energy level diagrams.

Exothermic Reactions

1) The reaction profile on the right shows an exothermic reaction.

2) You can tell because the products are at a lower energy than the reactants.

3) The difference in height between the reactants and the products shows the overall energy change in the reaction (the energy given out).

4) The rise in energy at the start shows the energy needed to start the reaction. This is the activation energy.

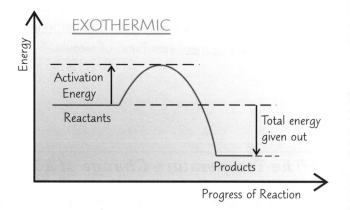

Endothermic Reactions

1) In this reaction profile, the products are at a higher energy than the reactants. So the reaction is endothermic.

2) The difference in height shows the overall energy change during the reaction (the energy taken in).

3) The rise in energy at the start is the activation energy.

You can also write the formulas for the reactants and products on the reaction profile instead of 'reactants' and 'products'.

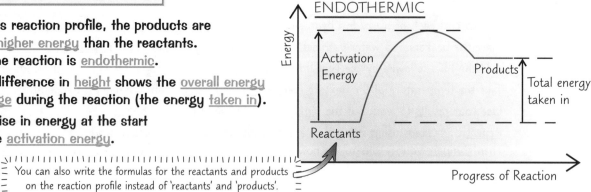

The activation energy needed for me to get out of bed is huuuge...

Don't get confused by these diagrams. In an exothermic reaction the particles release energy to their surroundings. So even though the reaction mixture gets warmer, the particles themselves have lost energy.

Q1 Here is the equation for the exothermic reaction between methane and oxygen:
$CH_{4(g)} + 2O_{2(g)} \rightarrow CO_{2(g)} + 2H_2O_{(g)}$. Draw a reaction profile for this reaction. [3 marks]

Revision Questions for Topics C4 & C5

Well, that wraps up Topic C5. Time to find out how much you really know from Topics C4 and C5.

- Try these questions and tick off each one when you get it right.
- When you've done all the questions under a heading and are completely happy with it, tick it off.

Acids and their Reactions (p.128-129) ☐

1) State whether the following pH values are acidic, alkaline or neutral.
   a) 9   b) 2   c) 7   d) 6

2) Give the general word equation for the reaction between an acid and a base.

3) Name the products that will form when hydrochloric acid reacts with sodium carbonate.

Reactions of Metals (p.130-131) ☐

4) Is zinc more or less reactive than iron?

5) What product forms when magnesium is oxidised by oxygen?

6) State where a metal will be in the reactivity series
   if it can be extracted from its oxide by reduction with carbon.

7) What is the general word equation for the reaction of a metal with an acid?

8) Complete the equation for the reaction of calcium with water: $Ca + ?H_2O \rightarrow ? + H_2$

Electrolysis (p.132-133) ☐

9) What is an electrolyte?

10) During electrolysis, what are the names for the positive electrode and the negative electrode?

11) Aluminium can be formed by electrolysing aluminium oxide. Which electrode is aluminium formed at?

12) A salt solution contains the ions of a metal that is more reactive than hydrogen.
    Will hydrogen gas be released if this solution is electrolysed?

13) A salt solution contains halide ions. Will oxygen gas be released if this solution is electrolysed?

Exothermic and Endothermic Reactions (p.134-136) ☐

14) In an exothermic reaction is energy transferred to or from the surroundings?

15) Name two different types of reaction which are exothermic.

16) Define what is meant by an endothermic reaction.

17) Draw a diagram of the equipment you would use to measure the temperature change of a reaction.

18) What is the activation energy of a reaction?

19) Sketch an energy level diagram for an endothermic reaction.

20) Is the following statement true or false?
    In an endothermic reaction, the products of the reaction have more energy than the reactants.

Rates of Reaction

Rates of reaction are pretty <u>important</u>. In the <u>chemical industry</u>, the <u>faster</u> you make <u>chemicals</u>, the <u>faster</u> you make <u>money</u> (and the faster everyone gets to go home for tea).

The Speed of a Reaction is Called its Rate

1) The <u>rate</u> of a chemical reaction is how <u>fast</u> the <u>reactants</u> are changed into <u>products</u>.
2) Some reactions are very <u>slow</u>, for example, rusting. Others, like burning, are <u>fast</u>.
3) <u>Graphs</u> can show you how the rate (speed) of a reaction changes.
4) The <u>steeper</u> the line on the graph, the <u>faster</u> the rate of reaction.
5) <u>Over time</u> the line becomes <u>less steep</u> as the reactants are <u>used up</u>.

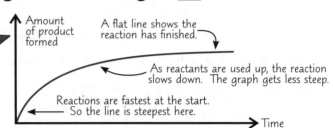

Amount of product formed

A flat line shows the reaction has finished.

As reactants are used up, the reaction slows down. The graph gets less steep.

Reactions are fastest at the start. So the line is steepest here.

Time

Reaction Rates Can Change when the Reaction Conditions Change

1) Faster <u>reactions</u> have <u>steeper</u> lines to begin with and become <u>flat</u> more quickly.
2) This graph shows how the <u>speed</u> of a particular reaction changes under <u>different conditions</u>.

- Line 1 shows the <u>original reaction</u>.
- Line 2 shows the same reaction taking place <u>faster</u>. It starts more <u>steeply</u> than line 1. It also goes <u>flat sooner</u>.
- Line 3 shows the same reaction taking place more <u>slowly</u>. It <u>isn't</u> as <u>steep</u> at the start as line 1 and goes <u>flat later</u>.
- Lines 1, 2 and 3 all meet at the <u>same level</u>. This shows that they all produce the <u>same amount</u> of product. They just take <u>different times</u> to produce it.
- Line 4 shows <u>more product</u> is formed. This can only happen if there were <u>more reactants</u> at the start.

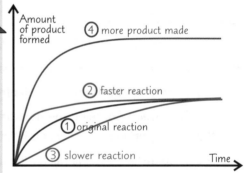

Amount of product formed

④ more product made

② faster reaction

① original reaction

③ slower reaction

Time

Particles Must Collide with Enough Energy in Order to React

1) Reaction rates can be explained by an idea called <u>collision theory</u>.
2) Collision theory says that a <u>reaction</u> will <u>only</u> take place when particles <u>collide</u> (crash into each other).
3) The particles also have to have a certain amount of <u>energy</u> when they collide, otherwise they won't <u>react</u>.
4) The <u>minimum</u> (smallest) amount of energy they need is called the <u>activation energy</u>.
5) Collision theory can explain rates of reactions in a bit more detail too...

- The more <u>often</u> the particles collide, the <u>faster</u> the reaction will happen.
- For example, if the reactant particles in a certain reaction collide with enough energy <u>twice as often</u>, the reaction will happen <u>twice as fast</u>.
- The <u>more energy</u> the particles have, the <u>faster</u> the reaction will be.
- This is because there's more chance that they'll have <u>at least</u> the <u>activation energy</u>.

How often the particles collide is sometimes called the 'collision frequency'.

Want a fast reaction? Tickle your teacher. That should do it...

Lots of important stuff to learn here. Make sure you understand the basics of collision theory before you move on. It's simple really — for particles to react they have to collide with each other, with enough energy.

Q1   What is meant by the term activation energy?   [1 mark]

Factors Affecting Rates of Reaction

I'd ask you to guess what this page is about, but the title pretty much says it all really. Read on...

The Rate of Reaction Depends on Four Things

1) Temperature.
2) Concentration of a solution (or pressure of a gas).
3) Surface area of a solid.
4) Whether a catalyst is used.

Increasing the Temperature Increases the Rate

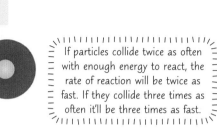

If particles collide twice as often with enough energy to react, the rate of reaction will be twice as fast. If they collide three times as often it'll be three times as fast.

1) When temperature increases, the particles move faster.
2) If they move faster, they collide more frequently (often).
3) They also have more energy, so more collisions have enough energy to make the reaction happen.

Increasing the Concentration or Pressure Increases the Rate

1) If a solution is more concentrated, it has more particles in the same volume.
2) And when the pressure of a gas is increased, it means the same number of particles are now in a smaller space.
3) So collisions between the reactant particles are more frequent.

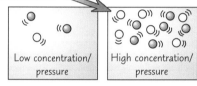

Low concentration/pressure   High concentration/pressure

Increasing the Surface Area Increases the Rate

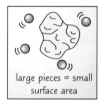

large pieces = small surface area

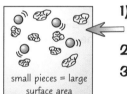

small pieces = large surface area

1) If one of the reactants is a solid, then breaking it up into smaller pieces will increase its surface area to volume ratio.
2) This means the same amount of solid has a bigger surface area.
3) So more of the solid's particles are available to particles of the other reactant. And collisions will be more frequent.

Using a Catalyst Increases the Rate

1) A catalyst is a substance that speeds up a reaction. None of it gets used up in the reaction.
2) This means it's not part of the reaction equation.
3) Different catalysts are needed for different reactions.
4) Catalysts work by providing a different pathway for a reaction. The new pathway has a lower activation energy, so less energy is needed for the reaction to happen.
5) Enzymes are biological catalysts — they catalyse reactions in living things.

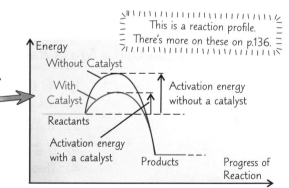

This is a reaction profile. There's more on these on p.136.

So, the more students in a room, the greater their concentration...?

Write down the 4 factors that affect rate. Check they're right. Write them down again. Check again. Repeat.

Q1   In an experiment, a 2 g strip of magnesium ribbon is reacted with hydrochloric acid. The experiment is then repeated using 2 g of powdered magnesium. Everything else is kept the same. Which experiment would have the fastest rate? Explain your answer.

[2 marks]

Topic C6 — The Rate and Extent of Chemical Change

PRACTICAL | Measuring Rates of Reaction

All this talk about reaction rate is fine and dandy, but it's no good if you can't measure it. You can investigate how concentration affects the rate of a reaction by measuring the volume of gas given off in a reaction.

Marble Chips and Hydrochloric Acid React to Produce Carbon Dioxide Gas

1) Measure out a set volume of dilute hydrochloric acid using a measuring cylinder.

2) Carefully pour it into a conical flask.

3) Measure out a set mass of marble chips.

4) Add the marble chips to the flask and quickly attach a delivery tube and gas syringe to the flask. You need to do this quickly before any gas escapes.

5) Start the stopwatch straight away.

6) Gas will start to collect in the gas syringe. Take readings of the volume of gas at regular intervals (e.g. every 10 seconds) and write them into a table.

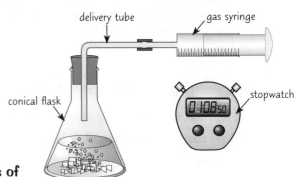

> Gas syringes usually give volumes to the nearest cm^3, so they're quite accurate.
>
> Be careful though — if the reaction is too vigorous, you could blow the plunger out of the syringe.

Repeat the Experiment Using Different Concentrations of Acid

1) To investigate the effect of concentration on the rate of reaction, you'll need to repeat the experiment using different concentrations of acid. For example, you might use three different concentrations.

2) To make your experiment a fair test, you should only change the concentration of acid.

3) All the other variables (that's everything else) need to be kept the same. For example, keep the volume of acid, the mass of marble chips and the temperature the same each time.

You Then Need to Interpret Your Results

1) The more gas given off in a set amount of time, the faster the reaction.

2) You can use the results in your table to draw a graph. This makes it easier to see how concentration has affected the rate. (See pages 142 and 143 for more on drawing graphs and calculating rates.)

You Could Also Use a Mass Balance to Measure Amount of Gas Produced

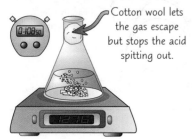

Cotton wool lets the gas escape but stops the acid spitting out.

1) As the gas forms and escapes from the container, the mass of the reaction mixture falls.

2) The quicker the reading on the balance drops, the faster the reaction.

3) If you take measurements at regular intervals, you can plot a graph.

4) This is a very accurate method because the mass balance is very accurate.

5) But it does release the gas into the room. That's not good if the gas is toxic (poisonous).

---

*OK, have you got your stopwatch ready... *BANG!* — oh...*

Ooh, chemistry in action, nothing beats it. That's why it's one of the best subjects out there. I think so, anyway.

Q1   Name one piece of equipment you could use to measure the volume of gas given off in a reaction. [1 mark]

Topic C6 — The Rate and Extent of Chemical Change

More on Measuring Rates

Here's another lovely page on another lovely <u>practical</u>. This practical also looks into what effect <u>concentration</u> has on the rate of a reaction. Get your safety goggles, grab your lab coat and let's go...

You Can Time How Long it Takes For a Solid Product to Form

1) Some reactions start with a <u>transparent</u> (see-through) <u>solution</u> and produce a <u>solid product</u>.

2) The solid product (called a <u>precipitate</u>) will make the solution go <u>cloudy</u>. Another way of saying this is to say that its <u>turbidity increases</u>.

3) You can look at a <u>mark</u> through the solution and measure how long it takes for it to <u>disappear</u>. The <u>faster</u> the mark disappears, the <u>quicker</u> the reaction.

4) The results are <u>subjective</u> (there isn't just one right answer). This is because <u>people</u> might not agree over the <u>exact</u> point when the mark 'disappears'.

Sodium Thiosulfate and Hydrochloric Acid Produce a Cloudy Precipitate

Sodium thiosulfate and hydrochloric acid are both <u>clear solutions</u>.
They react together to form a <u>yellow precipitate</u> of <u>sulfur</u>.

1) Start by adding a set volume of <u>dilute sodium thiosulfate</u> to a conical flask.

2) Place the flask on a piece of paper with a <u>black cross</u> drawn on it.

3) Add some <u>dilute hydrochloric acid</u> to the flask and start the stopwatch.

4) Watch the black cross <u>disappear</u> through the <u>cloudy sulfur</u> and <u>time</u> how long it takes to go.

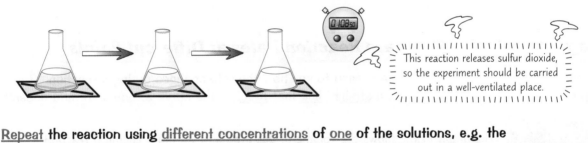

This reaction releases sulfur dioxide, so the experiment should be carried out in a well-ventilated place.

5) <u>Repeat</u> the reaction using <u>different concentrations</u> of <u>one</u> of the solutions, e.g. the hydrochloric acid. (Only change the concentration of <u>one reactant</u> at a time though.)

6) Make sure you <u>control</u> all the other <u>variables</u> (keep everything else the <u>same</u>). For example, the volumes of solutions, the temperature and the size of the flask all need to be kept the same.

7) You'll end up with a set of results that show <u>how long</u> it takes for the cross to disappear at <u>different concentrations</u> of acid. Like this:

Concentration of HCl (g/dm³)	18	36	54	72	90
Time taken for mark to disappear (s)	193	184	178	171	164

8) The <u>higher</u> the concentration, the <u>faster</u> the reaction, so the <u>less time</u> it takes for the mark to disappear.

Vanishing symbols, sulfurous clouds — real witchcraft this is...

You might come across slightly different experiments to measure rates. Or the same methods but different reactions. Either way — DON'T PANIC. If you understand the basics you'll be able to tackle them just fine.

Q1   A scientist carried out an experiment investigating the effect of changing the HCl concentration on the rate of reaction between HCl and Mg. State two factors that he should have kept constant.   [2 marks]

142

Graphs of Reaction Rate Experiments

Experiment time's over. Time to do some work with your <u>results</u>. Much more fun than actually doing the experiment. Maybe. Perhaps not. OK, almost certainly less fun. But it is important, and worth learning...

You Can Draw a Graph of Your Results

The <u>type</u> of graph you can draw depends on what <u>experiment</u> you did.
Here's how to draw a graph to show the <u>volume of gas</u> given off during a reaction.

EXAMPLE: Draw a graph of the results in the table.

Time (s)	0	10	20	30	40	50	60
Volume of gas (cm³)	0	9.5	15	18.5	20	20	20

1) Put <u>time</u> on the x-axis and <u>volume of gas</u> on the y-axis. (The x-axis goes along the page, the y-axis goes up it.)

2) Carefully draw a small cross to show how much gas had been produced at <u>each time interval</u>.

3) Draw a <u>line of best fit</u> through the points. You could do this by drawing a smooth <u>curve</u> of best fit.

4) Or, you could draw <u>two straight lines of best fit</u>, one for the <u>sloped</u> part of the graph and one for the <u>flat</u> part.

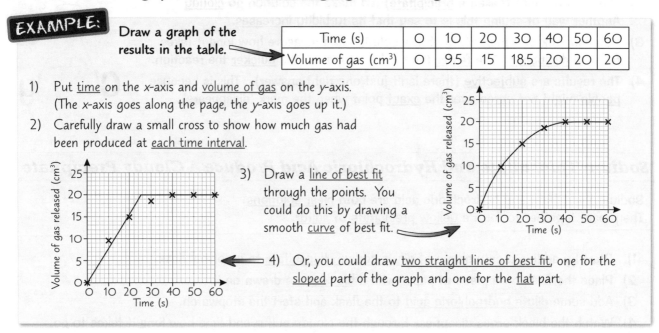

Tangents Help You Compare Reaction Rates at Different Points

If your graph is a <u>curve</u>, it's not always easy to see how the rate changes during a reaction. <u>Tangents</u> can help make this clearer. A tangent is a <u>straight line</u> that <u>touches</u> the curve at one point and doesn't cross it.

EXAMPLE: The graph below shows the volume of gas produced during a chemical reaction. Is the rate fastest at 20 seconds or 30 seconds?

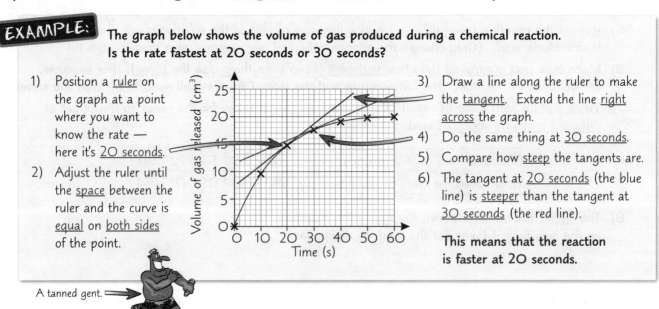

1) Position a <u>ruler</u> on the graph at a point where you want to know the rate — here it's <u>20 seconds</u>.

2) Adjust the ruler until the <u>space</u> between the ruler and the curve is <u>equal</u> on <u>both sides</u> of the point.

3) Draw a line along the ruler to make the <u>tangent</u>. Extend the line <u>right across</u> the graph.

4) Do the same thing at <u>30 seconds</u>.

5) Compare how <u>steep</u> the tangents are.

6) The tangent at <u>20 seconds</u> (the blue line) is <u>steeper</u> than the tangent at <u>30 seconds</u> (the red line).

This means that the reaction is faster at 20 seconds.

A tanned gent.

...and that's why I love cows — oh sorry, I went off on a tangent...

Graphs may look scary, but don't let them put you off. That's what they want. Don't let them win. Raaaarrrrr.

Q1 Draw a graph of the results in this table. Include a curved line of best fit. [3 marks]

Time (s)	0	10	20	30	40	50	60
Volume of CO₂ (cm³)	0	24	32	36	38	39	40

Topic C6 — The Rate and Extent of Chemical Change

Working Out Reaction Rates

As well as doing experiments and drawing graphs, you need to be able to do some <u>calculations</u> to work out <u>reaction rates</u>. Don't worry though, they're not too bad. Read on and all will be explained.

Here's How to Work Out the Rate of a Reaction

$$\text{Mean Rate of Reaction} = \frac{\text{Amount of reactant used or amount of product formed}}{\text{Time}}$$

This equation is for <u>mean</u> rate of reaction. So it lets you work out the <u>average rate</u> over an <u>amount of time</u>.

EXAMPLE:
A reaction takes 120 seconds. 3.0 g of product are made. Find the mean rate of reaction.

Mean Rate = amount of product formed ÷ time
= 3.0 g ÷ 120 s = 0.025 g/s ◄

Gases can be measured in <u>cm³</u>, so if the product you measured was a gas the rate could be measured in <u>cm³/s</u> rather than in <u>g/s</u>.

You Can Calculate the Mean Reaction Rate from a Graph

1) To find the <u>mean rate</u> for the <u>whole reaction</u>, start by working out when the reaction <u>finished</u>. This is when the line goes <u>flat</u>.

2) Then work out how much <u>product</u> was <u>formed</u> (or how much <u>reactant</u> was <u>used up</u>).

3) Then <u>divide this</u> by the <u>total time taken</u> for the reaction to finish.

EXAMPLE:
The graph shows the volume of gas released by a reaction, measured at regular intervals. Find the mean rate of the reaction.

1) Work out when the reaction <u>finished</u>.
2) Work out how much <u>product</u> was <u>formed</u>.
3) <u>Divide</u> this by the <u>time taken</u> for the reaction to finish.

The line goes flat at 50 s.
20 cm³ of gas was formed.
mean rate = 20 cm³ ÷ 50 s
= 0.40 cm³/s

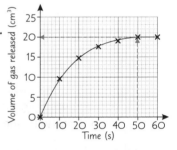

4) You can also use the graph to find the <u>mean rate</u> of reaction between <u>two points</u> in time:

EXAMPLE:
Find the mean rate of reaction between 20 s and 40 s.

1) Work out how much <u>gas</u> was produced <u>between</u> 20 s and 40 s.
2) Work out the <u>time difference</u> between 20 s and 40 s.
3) <u>Divide</u> the amount of gas produced by the time taken.

At 20 s, 15 cm³ had been produced.
At 40 s, 19 cm³ had been produced.
Volume released between 20 and 40 s was: 19 cm³ − 15 cm³ = 4.0 cm³
40 s − 20 s = 20 s
mean rate = 4.0 cm³ ÷ 20 s
= 0.20 cm³/s

Being asked to calculate reaction rates. That's just mean...

Whether you're calculating the mean rate from just numbers or using a graph, you always use the formula at the top of this page. Mean rate = amount of reactant used (or product formed) ÷ time. Learn it. It's important.

Q1   A reaction takes 200 s. 6.0 g of reactant are used up. What is the mean rate of the reaction?   [2 marks]

Reversible Reactions

Reversible reactions are what they sound like — <u>reactions</u> that can be <u>reversed</u>. So they can go <u>backwards</u>.

Reversible Reactions Go Both Ways

1) This equation shows a <u>reversible reaction</u>.  $A + B \rightleftharpoons C + D$

2) The <u>products</u> (C and D) react to form the <u>reactants</u> (A and B) again.

3) You can tell it's a reversible reaction because of the $\rightleftharpoons$ symbol.

4) The reaction of A and B is called the <u>forward reaction</u>. The reaction of C and D is the <u>backward reaction</u>.

Reversible Reactions Will Reach Equilibrium

1) As the <u>reactants</u> react, their concentrations <u>fall</u>. The <u>forward</u> reaction <u>slows down</u>.

2) As more and more <u>products</u> are made the <u>backward reaction</u> will <u>speed up</u>.

3) After a while the forward reaction and backward reaction will be going at <u>exactly the same rate</u>. The system is at <u>equilibrium</u>.

4) Equilibrium <u>doesn't</u> mean that there are the <u>same amounts</u> of products and reactants. It just means that the amounts of products and reactants <u>aren't changing</u> any more.

5) Equilibrium is only reached if the reaction takes place in a 'closed system'. A <u>closed system</u> just means that <u>none</u> of the reactants or products can <u>escape</u> and nothing else can get <u>in</u>.

Reversible Reactions Have an Overall Direction

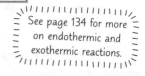

1) Once a reaction is at equilibrium, there could be <u>more</u> of the <u>products</u> than reactants. When this happens, we say the reaction is going in the <u>forwards direction</u>.

2) If there are <u>more reactants</u> than products then the reaction is going in the <u>backwards direction</u>.

3) You can <u>change</u> the <u>direction</u> by <u>changing</u> the <u>conditions</u> (the temperature, pressure or concentration).

> <u>Ammonium chloride</u> breaks down to form <u>ammonia</u> and <u>hydrogen chloride</u>. The hydrogen chloride can then react with the ammonia to make ammonium chloride again. The reaction equation is:
>
> $$\text{ammonium chloride} \underset{\text{cool}}{\overset{\text{heat}}{\rightleftharpoons}} \text{ammonia} + \text{hydrogen chloride}$$
>
> If you <u>heat</u> this reaction, it will go in the <u>forwards</u> direction. You'll get more ammonia and hydrogen chloride. If you <u>cool</u> it, it will go in the <u>backwards</u> direction. You'll get more ammonium chloride.

Reversible Reactions Can Be Endothermic and Exothermic

1) If the reaction is <u>endothermic</u> (takes in heat) in one direction, it will be <u>exothermic</u> (give out heat) in the other.

See page 134 for more on endothermic and exothermic reactions.

2) The amount of energy <u>taken in</u> by the endothermic reaction is the <u>same</u> as the amount <u>given out</u> during the exothermic reaction.

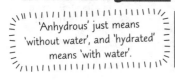
'Anhydrous' just means 'without water', and 'hydrated' means 'with water'.

$$\text{hydrated copper sulfate} \underset{\text{exothermic}}{\overset{\text{endothermic}}{\rightleftharpoons}} \text{anhydrous copper sulfate} + \text{water}$$
(which is blue)   (which is white)

Keep going in the forward direction. Onwards my friend...

Reversible reactions seem tricky but they're OK really. Read the page again until it's all sunk in.

Q1   What does it mean if a reaction is at equilibrium?   [1 mark]

Topic C6 — The Rate and Extent of Chemical Change

Revision Questions for Topic C6

We'll you've almost made it — you're just one more page away from a lovely cup of tea and a biscuit...

*   Try these questions and <u>tick off each one</u> when you <u>get it right</u>.
*   When you've done <u>all the questions</u> under a heading and are <u>completely happy</u> with it, tick it off.

Rates of Reaction (p.138-139) ☐

1) What is meant by the rate of a chemical reaction?
2) On a rate of reaction graph, what does the line getting steeper show?
3) What does a flat line on a graph of amount of products against time show?
4) According to collision theory, what needs to happen for a reaction to take place?
5) What are the four factors that affect the rate of a chemical reaction?
6) Why does increasing the temperature of a reaction mixture increase the rate of a reaction?
7) If a solid is broken up into smaller pieces, what will happen to its surface area to volume ratio?
8) What is a catalyst?
9) How does a catalyst increase the rate of a reaction?

Rate of Reaction Experiments (p.140-143) ☐

10) Describe how you could investigate the effect of increasing hydrochloric acid concentration on the rate of reaction between hydrochloric acid and magnesium.
11) Explain why measuring a mass change during a reaction is an accurate method of measuring rate.
12) Two clear solutions react together and form a precipitate.
    How could you investigate the rate of this reaction?
13) If you're drawing a graph to show the volume of gas produced over time, what axis should time go on?
14) What is a tangent?
15) How can you use tangents to compare the rates of reaction at two different times in the reaction?
16) Give two possible units for the rate of a chemical reaction.

Reversible Reactions (p.144) ☐

17) What symbol shows that a reaction is reversible?
18) Is this sentence true or false?
    'In a reaction at equilibrium, there is the same amount of products as reactants.'
19) What is a closed system?
20) How can you change the direction of a reversible reaction?
21) A reversible reaction is endothermic in the forwards direction.
    What does this tell you about the reaction in the backwards direction?

Topic C6 — The Rate and Extent of Chemical Change

Hydrocarbons

Organic chemistry is about compounds that contain <u>carbon</u>. <u>Hydrocarbons</u> are the simplest organic compounds.

Alkanes Only Have C–C and C–H Single Bonds

1) <u>Hydrocarbons</u> are compounds formed from carbon and hydrogen atoms <u>only</u>.
2) <u>Alkanes</u> are the simplest type of hydrocarbon. They have the general formula C_nH_{2n+2}.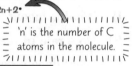

'n' is the number of C atoms in the molecule.

3) In alkanes, each carbon atom forms four <u>single covalent bonds</u>.
4) The first four alkanes are <u>methane</u>, <u>ethane</u>, <u>propane</u> and <u>butane</u>.

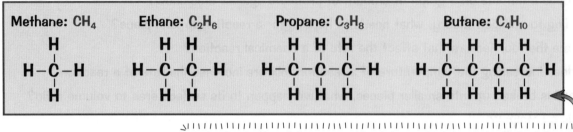

Methane: CH_4 Ethane: C_2H_6 Propane: C_3H_8 Butane: C_4H_{10}

A drawing showing all the atoms and bonds in a molecule is called a displayed formula.

Complete Combustion Occurs When There's Plenty of Oxygen

1) The <u>complete combustion</u> of a hydrocarbon in oxygen releases lots of energy. This makes them useful as <u>fuels</u>.

2) The only waste products are <u>carbon dioxide</u> and <u>water</u> vapour.

> hydrocarbon + oxygen → carbon dioxide + water   (+ energy)

3) During combustion, both carbon and hydrogen from the hydrocarbon are <u>oxidised</u>. <u>Oxidation</u> is the <u>gain of oxygen</u>.

4) You need to be able to give a <u>balanced symbol equation</u> for the <u>complete combustion</u> of a simple hydrocarbon when you're given its <u>molecular formula</u>. Here's an example:

See p.99 for more on balancing equations.

EXAMPLE: Write a balanced equation for the complete combustion of methane (CH_4).

1) On the <u>left hand side</u>, there's <u>one</u> carbon atom, so only <u>one</u> molecule of CO_2 is needed to balance this. $CH_4 + ?O_2 \rightarrow CO_2 + ?H_2O$

2) On the <u>left hand side</u>, there are <u>four</u> hydrogen atoms, so <u>two</u> water molecules are needed to balance them. $CH_4 + ?O_2 \rightarrow CO_2 + 2H_2O$

3) There are <u>four</u> oxygen atoms on the <u>right hand side</u> of the equation. <u>Two</u> oxygen molecules are needed on the left to balance them. $CH_4 + 2O_2 \rightarrow CO_2 + 2H_2O$

The name's bond — single covalent bond...

So hydrocarbons only contain two ingredients — carbon and hydrogen. Jamie Oliver would not be happy.

Q1   Write a balanced symbol equation for the complete combustion of propane, C_3H_8.   [2 marks]

Crude Oil

Crude oil has fuelled <u>modern life</u> — it would be a very different world if we hadn't discovered oil.

Crude Oil is Made Over a Long Period of Time

1) <u>Crude oil</u> is a <u>fossil fuel</u> found in <u>rocks</u>.
2) Fossil fuels are <u>natural</u> substances. They can be used as a source of <u>energy</u>.
3) Crude oil formed mainly from the remains of plankton, as well as other plants and animals. These died millions of years ago and were buried in mud.

> Plankton are tiny living plants and animals which float around in oceans and other large bodies of water.

 1) Fossil fuels like coal, oil and gas are called <u>non-renewable fuels</u>.
 2) This is because they take so long to make that they're being <u>used up</u> much faster than they're being formed.
 3) They're <u>finite</u> resources (see p.159) — one day they'll run out.

Crude Oil has Various Important Uses in Modern Life

1) <u>Oil</u> provides the <u>fuel</u> for most modern <u>transport</u> — cars, trains, planes, the lot.
2) Diesel oil, kerosene, heavy fuel oil and LPG (liquified petroleum gas) all come from crude oil.
3) <u>Petrochemicals</u> are compounds that come from crude oil. The <u>petrochemical industry</u> uses some of the compounds from crude oil as a <u>feedstock</u> to make <u>new compounds</u> for use in things like...

   • <u>polymers</u> (e.g. plastics)   • <u>lubricants</u>
   • <u>solvents</u>   • <u>detergents</u>

> A feedstock is a raw material used for a chemical process.

4) All the products you get from crude oil are examples of <u>organic compounds</u>. Organic compounds are compounds containing carbon atoms.
5) Most of the organic compounds in crude oil are <u>hydrocarbons</u> (see previous page).
6) You can get a large <u>variety</u> of products from crude oil. This is because carbon atoms can bond together to form different groups called <u>homologous series</u>.
7) These groups contain <u>similar compounds</u> which have many <u>properties</u> in common. <u>Alkanes</u> and <u>alkenes</u> are both examples of different homologous series.

Hydrocarbon Properties Change as the Chain Gets Longer

1) The hydrocarbons in crude oil are a range of <u>different sizes</u>.
2) As the <u>length</u> of the carbon chain changes, the <u>properties</u> of the hydrocarbons change.
3) The <u>shorter</u> the hydrocarbon <u>chain</u>...

   • ...the <u>more runny</u> a hydrocarbon is — that is, the <u>less viscous</u> (gloopy) it is.
   • ...the <u>lower</u> its <u>boiling points</u> will be.
   • ...the more <u>flammable</u> (easier to ignite) the hydrocarbon is.

4) The <u>properties</u> of hydrocarbons affect how they're used for fuels.

I know a good oil joke but it's a bit crude for this page...

Crude oil is dead important. We need it to make lots of important things, like plastics. If we didn't have it, you could have been completing your science exam with a quill and ink instead of a good old plastic pen.

Q1   What is crude oil formed from?   [1 mark]

Q2   Crude oil is finite. What does this mean?   [1 mark]

Fractional Distillation

Crude oil can be used to make loads of useful things, such as fuels. But you can't just put crude oil in your car. First, the different hydrocarbons have to be separated. That's where fractional distillation comes in.

Fractional Distillation can be Used to Separate Hydrocarbon Fractions

Crude oil is a mixture of lots of different hydrocarbons, most of which are alkanes. The different compounds in crude oil are separated by fractional distillation. Here's how it works:

Hydrocarbons are molecules containing only hydrogen and carbon.

1) The oil is heated until most of it has evaporated (turned into gas). The gases enter a fractionating column (and the liquid bit is drained off).

2) In the column it's hot at the bottom and gets cooler as you go up.

- The shorter hydrocarbons have low boiling points.
- This means that they're still gases at low temperatures. So they don't condense and turn back into liquids until they move up near the top of the column, where they cool down a lot.

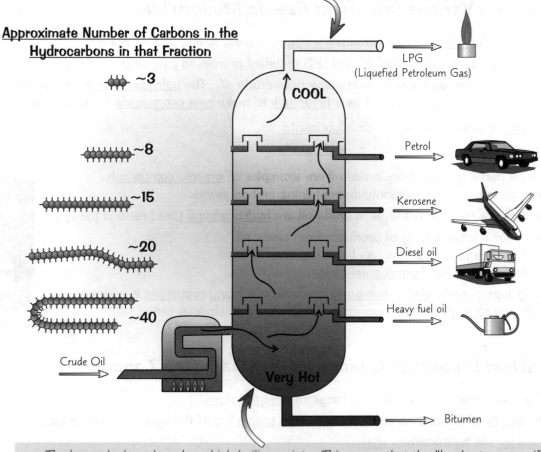

Approximate Number of Carbons in the Hydrocarbons in that Fraction

~3
~8
~15
~20
~40

Crude Oil

Very Hot

COOL

LPG (Liquefied Petroleum Gas)

Petrol

Kerosene

Diesel oil

Heavy fuel oil

Bitumen

- The longer hydrocarbons have high boiling points. This means that they'll only stay a gas if it's very hot.
- As they move up the fractionating column, it gets cooler. So they condense back into liquids and drain out of the column early on, when they're near the bottom.

3) You end up with the crude oil mixture separated into different fractions (parts), e.g. petrol and diesel oil.

4) Each fraction contains a mixture of hydrocarbons. All of the hydrocarbons in one fraction contain a similar number of carbon atoms. This means they'll have similar boiling points.

How much petrol is there in crude oil? Just a fraction...

Make sure you understand how fractional distillation works — it might just save your life... OK, maybe not.

Q1   Petrol drains further up a fractionating column than diesel.
      Compare the boiling points of the hydrocarbons in petrol with the hydrocarbons in diesel.   [1 mark]

Cracking

Crude oil fractions from fractional distillation can be split into smaller molecules. This is called cracking.
It's super important, otherwise we might not have enough fuel for cars and planes and things.

Cracking Means Splitting Up Long–Chain Hydrocarbons

1) There is a high demand for fuels with small molecules.

2) This is because short-chain hydrocarbons tend to be more useful than long-chain hydrocarbons.

3) So, lots of longer alkane molecules are turned into smaller, more useful ones.
This is done by a process called cracking.

Alkenes are a type of hydrocarbon.

4) Some of the products of cracking are useful as fuels, e.g. petrol for cars.

5) Cracking also makes alkenes. Alkenes are a lot more reactive than alkanes. They're used as a starting material when making lots of other compounds and can be used to make polymers (see p.118).

Bromine water can be used to test for alkenes:

1) When orange bromine water is added to an alkane, no reaction will happen and it'll stay bright orange.

2) If it's added to an alkene, the bromine reacts with the alkene to make a colourless compound. So the bromine water turns colourless.

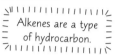

bromine water + an alkene   solution goes colourless

There are Different Methods of Cracking

1) Cracking is a thermal decomposition reaction. This means the molecules are broken down by heating them.

2) This can by done by catalytic cracking or by steam cracking.

Catalysts speed up reactions without getting used up (see p.139).

Steam cracking:

1) Long-chain hydrocarbons are heated to turn them into a gas (vapour).

2) The hydrocarbon vapour is mixed with steam.

3) They are then heated to a very high temperature which splits them into smaller molecules.

Catalytic cracking:

1) Long-chain hydrocarbons are heated to turn them into a gas.

2) Then the vapour is passed over a hot powdered aluminium oxide catalyst.

3) The long-chain molecules split apart on the surface of the specks of catalyst.

3) You might be asked to work out the formula of the products or reactants involved in a cracking reaction.
You can do this by balancing the number of carbons and hydrogens on each side of the reaction.

EXAMPLE: Decane can be cracked to form octane and one other product. The equation for the cracking of decane, $C_{10}H_{22}$, is shown in the equation below. Complete the equation.

$$C_{10}H_{22} \rightarrow C_8H_{18} + \text{.................}$$

1) There needs to be the same number of carbon and hydrogen atoms on each side of the equation.

2) The number of carbon atoms in the missing product equals the number of carbons in $C_{10}H_{22}$ minus the number of carbons in C_8H_{18}.

number of C atoms = 10 − 8 = 2

3) The number of hydrogen atoms in the missing product equals the number of hydrogens in $C_{10}H_{22}$ minus the number of hydrogens in C_8H_{18}.

number of H atoms = 22 − 18 = 4

4) Put these numbers into the formula of the missing product.

$$C_{10}H_{22} \rightarrow C_8H_{18} + C_2H_4$$

This page is tough — better get cracking...

Cracking's great because it means we make use of all the long chain hydrocarbons that we otherwise wouldn't need.

Q1   Pentane, C_5H_{12}, can be cracked into ethene, C_2H_4, and one other hydrocarbon.
Give the formula of the other hydrocarbon.

[1 mark]

Purity and Formulations

In a perfect world, every compound a chemist made would be <u>pure</u>. Unfortunately, in the real world it <u>doesn't</u> always work out like that. Luckily, there are ways to find out <u>how pure</u> a substance is.

Purity Has a Different Meaning in Chemistry to Everyday

1) <u>Usually</u> when you say that a <u>substance</u> is <u>pure</u> you mean that <u>nothing</u> has been <u>added</u> to it. So it's in its <u>natural state</u>. For example: pure milk or beeswax.

2) In <u>chemistry</u>, a pure substance is something that only contains <u>one compound</u> or <u>element</u> all the way through. It's <u>not mixed</u> with anything else.

The Boiling or Melting Point Tells You How Pure a Substance Is

1) A chemically pure substance will <u>melt</u> or <u>boil</u> at a <u>specific</u> temperature.

2) You can test how pure a known substance is by measuring its <u>melting</u> or <u>boiling point</u>. You then compare this value with the melting or boiling point of the <u>pure substance</u>. You can find this in a <u>data book</u>.

3) The <u>closer</u> your measured value is to the actual melting or boiling point, the <u>purer</u> your sample is.

4) Impurities in your sample will <u>lower</u> the <u>melting point</u>. They may also cause the sample to melt across a wider <u>range</u> of temperatures.

5) Impurities in your sample will <u>increase</u> the <u>boiling point</u>. They may also cause the sample to boil across a <u>range</u> of temperatures.

Formulations are Mixtures with Exact Amounts of its Parts

1) <u>Formulations</u> are useful mixtures that have been designed for a <u>particular use</u>.

2) They are made by following a '<u>formula</u>' (a recipe).

Take a look at p.100 for more on mixtures.

3) Each part of a formulation is <u>measured carefully</u> so that it's there in the <u>right amount</u>. This makes sure the formulation has right <u>properties</u> for it to work as it's supposed to.

> For example, <u>paints</u> are formulations.
> They are made up of:
> - <u>Pigment</u> — gives the paint colour.
> - <u>Solvent</u> — used to dissolve the other parts and change how runny the paint is.
> - <u>Binder</u> — holds the pigment in place after it's been painted on.
> - <u>Additives</u> — added to change the properties of the paint.
>
> The <u>chemicals</u> used and their <u>amounts</u> can be changed so the paint made is right for the job.

I think this musical formulation needs more funk.

4) In <u>everyday life</u>, formulations can be found in cleaning products, fuels, medicines, cosmetics, fertilisers, metal alloys and even food and drink.

Cake and tea are key to the revision success formula...

Knowing if a product is pure is really important for making things such as medicines or food. Luckily for us, chemists have lots of different ways to make sure they're making exactly what they want.

Q1   A student makes a sample of aspirin. The melting point of the sample is measured as being between 128-132 °C. The melting point of pure aspirin is 136 °C. Give two reasons why the melting point measured suggests that the sample is not pure.   [2 marks]

Paper Chromatography

You met chromatography on page 101. Now it's time to see how it works. Careful — things might get crazy...

Chromatography uses Two Phases

1) Chromatography is a method used to separate the substances in a mixture.

2) It can then be used to identify the substances.

3) The type of chromatography you need to know about is paper chromatography. Like all types of chromatography, it has two 'phases'.

- A mobile phase — where the molecules can move. In paper chromatography, this is a solvent (e.g. water or ethanol).
- A stationary phase — where the molecules can't move. In paper chromatography, this is the paper.

4) During paper chromatography the solvent moves up the paper. As the solvent moves, it carries the substances in the mixture with it.

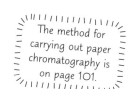
The method for carrying out paper chromatography is on page 101.

5) In a chromatography experiment, the amount of time a chemical spends dissolved in the solvent or stuck on the paper is called its 'distribution'.

6) The more soluble a chemical is, the more time it spends dissolved in the solvent. This means that the chemical will move further up the paper.

7) Different chemicals may be dissolved in the solvent for different amounts of time. So the different chemicals will move different distances up the paper.

8) This means they separate into different spots.

The Result of Chromatography is Shown on a Chromatogram | PRACTICAL

1) Chromatograms show the result of chromatography experiments.

2) The solvent front is the furthest point reached by the solvent during a chromatography experiment.

3) Chemicals move different distances up the paper. So different spots show different chemicals.

4) The number of spots on a chromatogram is the smallest possible number of chemicals in the mixture.

5) Sometimes more than one chemical may travel the same distance up the paper. This means that these chemicals will only form one spot between them.

6) If you repeat the experiment with a different solvent, you'll get a different chromatogram. The spots may have travelled different distances compared to the solvent front. There might also be a different number of spots on the chromatogram.

7) If you only get one spot in lots of different solvents, there's only one chemical in the substance. This means the substance is pure.

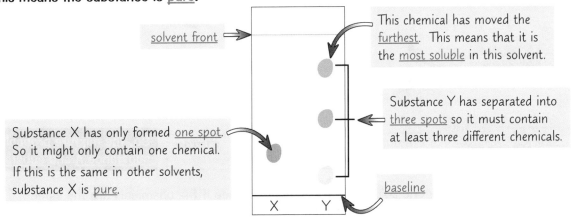

solvent front →

This chemical has moved the furthest. This means that it is the most soluble in this solvent.

Substance Y has separated into three spots so it must contain at least three different chemicals.

Substance X has only formed one spot. So it might only contain one chemical. If this is the same in other solvents, substance X is pure.

baseline

X   Y

Chromatography revision — it's a phase you have to get through...

You can't see the chemicals moving between the two phases, but it does happen. You'll just have to trust me.

Q1   What is the purpose of chromatography?   [1 mark]

Using Chromatograms

If you were sad the last page on chromatography was finished — fear not. There's more to come on this page.

You can Calculate the R_f Value for Each Chemical

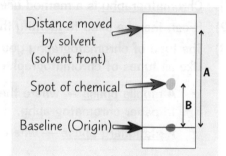

1) An R_f value is the ratio between the distance travelled by the dissolved substance and the distance travelled by the solvent.

2) The further a substance moves through the stationary phase, the larger the R_f value.

3) You can calculate R_f values using the formula:

$$R_f = \frac{\text{distance moved by substance (B)}}{\text{distance moved by solvent (A)}}$$

EXAMPLE:

A chromatography experiment looking at the colours in a dye produces the chromatogram shown on the right. Calculate the R_f value for the red spot.

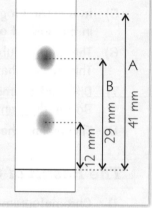

1) Measure the distance moved by the red spot (B). This is the distance from the baseline to the centre of the spot.   **29 mm**

2) Measure the distance moved by the solvent (A).   **41 mm**

3) Calculate the R_f value.

$$R_f = \frac{\text{distance moved by substance (B)}}{\text{distance moved by solvent (A)}} = \frac{29}{41} = 0.70731... = 0.71$$

Give your answer to the smallest number of significant figures in the calculation.

4) The R_f value of a chemical will change if you change the solvent.

You Can Identify Substances in Mixtures Using Chromatography

1) You can use chromatography to see if a mixture contains a certain substance.

2) To do this, you run a pure sample of that substance (a reference) next to the mixture.

3) If the R_f value of the reference compound matches one of the spots in the mixture, the substance could be in the mixture. For example:

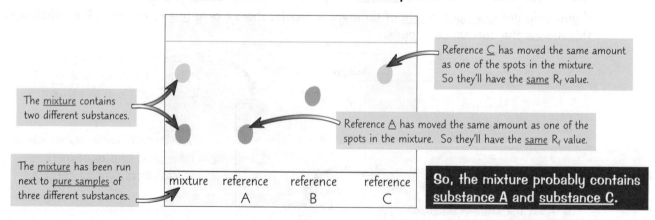

The mixture contains two different substances.

Reference C has moved the same amount as one of the spots in the mixture. So they'll have the same R_f value.

Reference A has moved the same amount as one of the spots in the mixture. So they'll have the same R_f value.

The mixture has been run next to pure samples of three different substances.

mixture   reference A   reference B   reference C

So, the mixture probably contains substance A and substance C.

4) If the R_f values match in one solvent, you can check to see if the chemicals are the same by repeating with a different solvent. If they match again, it's likely that they're the same.

Chromatogram — where chemists post photos of their brunch...

R_f values will always be between 0 and 1, so if your answer's outside this range, check through your working again.

Q1   For the chromatogram in the example above, calculate the R_f value of the blue spot.   [2 marks]

Tests for Gases

Yep, that's right, you need to revise tests for your test. There are a few ways to test for gases, but you only need to know these four. And two of them use fire. Pretty cool.

There are Tests for 4 Common Gases

1) Chlorine

Chlorine bleaches damp litmus paper, turning it white.

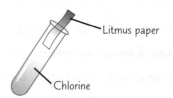

2) Oxygen

If you put a glowing splint inside a test tube containing oxygen, the oxygen will relight the glowing splint.

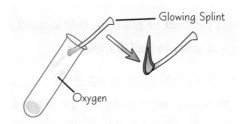

3) Carbon Dioxide

You can test for carbon dioxide by bubbling it through a solution of calcium hydroxide.
If the gas is carbon dioxide, the solution will turn cloudy.
You can also do this test by shaking the gas with the solution.

Calcium hydroxide solution is also called limewater.

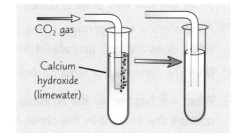

4) Hydrogen

If you hold a lit splint at the open end of a test tube containing hydrogen, you'll get a "squeaky pop".

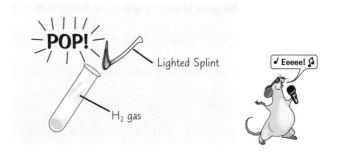

Hopefully this page won't be too testing for you...

Tests for gases are brilliant. You might think it's because you get to do a nice experiment in class, but I like them because you get to write 'squeaky pop' as a real result.

Q1   A student collects the gas given off during a reaction and bubbles it through limewater.
The limewater goes cloudy. Name the gas produced.

[1 mark]

Revision Questions for Topics C7 & C8

Well, that's it for Topics C7 & C8 — I think they were my favourite so far. Or maybe it was C1... or C2...
- Try these questions and tick off each one when you get it right.
- When you've done all the questions under a heading and are completely happy with it, tick it off.

Hydrocarbons (p.146) ☑

1) What two elements do hydrocarbons contain? ☑
2) What is the general formula for alkanes? ☑
3) Draw the displayed formula of butane. ☑
4) What two waste products form from the complete combustion of hydrocarbons? ☑

Crude Oil (p.147-149) ☑

5) Give three products that can be made from crude oil. ☑
6) Where do the shortest carbon chains condense in a fractional distillation column? ☑
7) Why is cracking used? ☑
8) Give a product of cracking that is used for making polymers. ☑
9) What is used to test for alkenes? ☑

Purity, Formulations and Paper Chromatography (p.150-152) ☐

10) In chemistry, what does it mean if a substance is pure? ☑
11) Describe how you could use the boiling point of a substance to test whether it is pure. ☑
12) What is a formulation? ☑
13) Why do the different parts of formulation need to be measured exactly? ☑
14) What are the two phases called in chromatography? ☑
15) A substance only produces one spot on a chromatogram in different solvents. What does this tell you about the purity of the substance? ☑
16) Give the formula for working out the R_f value of a substance. ☑
17) What will happen to the R_f value of a chemical if you change the solvent in the chromatography experiment? ☑

Tests for Gases (p.153) ☐

18) What colour does litmus paper turn in the presence of chlorine gas? ☑
19) How can you test if a gas in a test tube is oxygen? ☑

The Evolution of the Atmosphere

Theories for how the Earth's atmosphere evolved have changed a lot over the years. It's hard to gather evidence from such a long time period and from so long ago (4.6 billion years). Here's one idea we've got:

Phase 1 — Volcanoes Gave Out Gases

1) In the first billion years of the Earth's lifetime, its surface was covered in volcanoes.

2) These erupted and released lots of gases. Scientists think these gases formed the early atmosphere.

3) The early atmosphere was probably mostly carbon dioxide. There was little or no oxygen.

4) This is quite like the atmospheres of Mars and Venus today.

5) Volcanoes also released nitrogen (this built up in the atmosphere over time), water vapour and small amounts of methane and ammonia.

6) The oceans formed when the water vapour in the early atmosphere condensed (turned to liquid).

Phase 2 — Oceans, Algae and Green Plants Absorbed Carbon Dioxide

1) Over time, much of the carbon dioxide was removed from the atmosphere.

2) Lots of the carbon dioxide dissolved in the oceans.

3) The dissolved carbon dioxide formed carbonates that precipitated as small, solid particles (sediments).

> Precipitation is the formation of an insoluble solid from a solution.

4) When green plants and algae evolved, they took in some carbon dioxide during photosynthesis (see below).

- When sea organisms die, they fall to the seabed and get buried. Over millions of years, they're squashed down. This forms sedimentary rocks (e.g. coal and limestone), oil and gas. The carbon gets trapped within them.

- Things like coal, crude oil and natural gas that are made this way are called 'fossil fuels'.

- Crude oil and natural gas are formed from the remains of plankton that settled on the seabed.

- Coal is made from thick layers of plants that died and then settled on the seabed.

- Limestone is mostly made of calcium carbonate from the shells and skeletons of marine organisms.

Phase 3 — Green Plants and Algae Produced Oxygen

1) Algae evolved about 2.7 billion years ago. Then green plants evolved over the next billion years or so.

2) Green plants and algae produce oxygen in a reaction called photosynthesis:

$$\text{carbon dioxide} + \text{water} \xrightarrow{\text{light}} \text{glucose} + \text{oxygen}$$
$$6CO_2 + 6H_2O \xrightarrow{\text{light}} C_6H_{12}O_6 + 6O_2$$

3) Over time, oxygen levels built up in the atmosphere. This meant that animals could evolve.

4) The proportions of gases in the atmosphere have been similar for about the last 200 million years. It is made up of about 80% ($4/5$) nitrogen, 20% ($1/5$) oxygen. There are also small amounts (less than 1%) of other gases (mainly carbon dioxide, noble gases and water vapour).

The atmosphere's evolving — shut the window will you...

We can breathe easy knowing that our atmosphere has developed into a lovely oxygen rich one. Aaaahh.

Q1   Describe how sedimentary rocks are formed.   [2 marks]

Greenhouse Gases and Climate Change

Greenhouse gases are important but can also cause <u>problems</u> — it's all about keeping a delicate <u>balance</u>.

Carbon Dioxide is a Greenhouse Gas

1) Greenhouse gases include <u>carbon dioxide</u>, <u>methane</u> and <u>water vapour</u>.

2) Greenhouse gases keep the Earth <u>warm</u> enough to support <u>life</u>. Here's how they work:

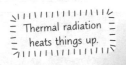
Thermal radiation heats things up.

Greenhouse gases

② This radiation is <u>reflected</u> back by the Earth as <u>long wavelength</u> radiation. This is <u>thermal</u> (heat) radiation. It's then <u>absorbed</u> by <u>greenhouse gases</u>.

③ Greenhouse gases then give out this radiation in <u>all directions</u>.

④ Some radiation heads back towards the <u>Earth</u> and <u>warms up</u> the surface. This is the <u>greenhouse effect</u>.

① The <u>sun</u> gives out <u>short wavelength</u> radiation.

3) Some forms of <u>human activity</u> increase the amount of greenhouse gases in the atmosphere. For example:

- <u>Deforestation</u>: fewer trees means that less carbon dioxide is taken in for <u>photosynthesis</u>.
- Burning <u>fossil fuels</u>: <u>releases</u> carbon dioxide.
- <u>Agriculture</u>: more <u>farm animals</u> produce more <u>methane</u> when they digest their food.
- <u>Creating waste</u>: more <u>landfill sites</u> and more waste from <u>farming</u> means more carbon dioxide and methane is released when the waste breaks down.

Increasing Carbon Dioxide is Linked to Climate Change

See page 2 for more on science in the media.

1) Recently, the average temperature of the Earth's surface has been <u>going up</u>.

2) Most scientists think this has been caused by the extra carbon dioxide from <u>human activity</u>.

3) They believe this will lead to <u>climate change</u>.

4) Evidence for this has been <u>peer-reviewed</u> (see page 1). This means that the information is <u>reliable</u>.

5) However, the Earth's climate is very <u>complex</u>. So, it's very hard to make a <u>model</u> that isn't <u>oversimplified</u>.

6) This has led to people forming their own <u>theories</u> and <u>opinions</u>, particularly in the <u>media</u>. These stories aren't based on good evidence — they may be <u>biased</u> or only give <u>some</u> of the information.

If something's biased, it favours one point of view in a way that's not backed up by facts.

Climate Change Could Have Dangerous Consequences

1) Higher global temperature could cause <u>ice</u> in the Arctic and Antarctic to <u>melt</u> — causing <u>sea levels</u> to <u>rise</u>. This could lead to <u>more flooding</u>.

2) Changes in <u>rainfall</u> may cause some regions to get <u>too much</u> or <u>too little</u> water.

3) <u>Storms</u> may become more <u>frequent</u> and <u>severe</u>.

4) Changes in <u>temperature</u> and <u>rainfall</u> may affect the <u>production of food</u> in certain places.

Give the climate some privacy — it's changing...

Everyone's talking about climate change these days — it's pretty scary stuff, so make sure you get it.

Q1   Give two potential consequences of climate change.   [2 marks]

Carbon Footprints

Many scientists believe that greenhouse gas emissions from <u>human activities</u> are causing <u>climate change</u>. Knowing what things release lots of carbon dioxide could be useful for <u>stopping</u> climate change from happening.

Carbon Footprints are Tricky to Measure

1) Carbon footprints are a <u>measure</u> of the amount of <u>carbon dioxide</u> and other <u>greenhouse gases</u> released over the <u>full life cycle</u> of something. That can be almost <u>anything</u>:
   - a service (e.g. the school bus).
   - an event (e.g. the Olympics).
   - a product (e.g. a toastie maker).

2) <u>Measuring</u> the total carbon footprint of something can be <u>really hard</u> or even <u>impossible</u>.

3) But a <u>rough calculation</u> can give a good idea of what things release the <u>most</u> greenhouse gases. So, people can then <u>avoid using them</u> in the future.

There are Ways of Reducing Carbon Footprints

1) You can reduce a carbon footprint by <u>reducing</u> the amount of <u>greenhouse gases</u> given out by a process.

2) Here are some things that can be done:

   - Using <u>renewable energy sources</u> (sources that won't run out) or <u>nuclear energy</u> instead of <u>fossil fuels</u>.
   - Using <u>processes</u> that use <u>less energy</u> or produces less <u>waste</u> (decomposing waste releases methane).
   - Governments could <u>tax</u> companies or individuals based on the amount of greenhouse gases they <u>emit</u>. This could encourage people to use processes which use less fuel and are <u>less polluting</u>.
   - Governments can also put a <u>limit</u> on emissions of <u>all</u> greenhouse gases that companies make. They can then <u>sell licences</u> for emissions <u>up to</u> that cap.
   - There's also technology that <u>captures</u> carbon dioxide <u>before</u> it's released into the atmosphere. This carbon dioxide is then <u>stored deep underground</u>.

But Making Reductions is Still Difficult

1) Reducing greenhouse gas emissions <u>isn't</u> simple.

2) <u>Alternative technologies</u> that release <u>less</u> carbon dioxide still need a lot of work.

3) Many <u>governments</u> are worried that making these changes will affect the <u>economies</u> of communities. This could be <u>bad</u> for people's <u>well-being</u> — especially those in <u>developing</u> countries.

4) This makes it hard for countries to <u>agree</u> to reduce emissions.

5) <u>Individuals</u> in developed countries also need to make changes to their <u>lifestyles</u>. But this is tricky when some <u>don't want to</u> and others don't understand <u>why</u> the changes are important or <u>how</u> to make them.

Who has the biggest carbon footprint then? Clowns of course...

Carbon footprints are a game of 'fortunately/unfortunately'. Unfortunately, carbon emissions can lead to global warming. Fortunately, there are steps we can take to cut our carbon dioxide emissions. Unfortunately, not everyone's on board. Fortunately, as time goes on, people are doing more to reduce their emissions. And so on...

Q1   State two things governments can do to try to reduce the greenhouse gas emissions of businesses. [2 marks]

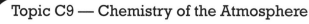

Air Pollution

Increasing carbon dioxide is causing climate change. But carbon dioxide isn't the only gas released when fossil fuels burn — you can also get other nasties like <u>oxides of nitrogen</u>, <u>sulfur dioxide</u> and <u>carbon monoxide</u>.

Combustion of Fossil Fuels Releases Gases and Particles

1) <u>Fossil fuels</u>, such as crude oil and coal, contain <u>hydrocarbons</u> (see page 146).

2) Hydrocarbons can <u>combust</u> (burn in oxygen). There are two types of combustion:

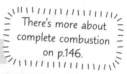

There's more about complete combustion on p.146.

<u>Complete combustion</u> — when there's <u>plenty</u> of oxygen around <u>all</u> of the fuel burns.

<u>Incomplete combustion</u> — when there's <u>not</u> enough oxygen around some of the fuel <u>does not</u> burn.

3) Both types of combustion release carbon dioxide and water vapour into the <u>atmosphere</u>.

4) During incomplete combustion, <u>solid particles</u> (called <u>particulates</u>) of soot (carbon) and <u>unburnt fuel</u> are also released. <u>Carbon monoxide</u> gas is also produced.

5) Particulates in the air and carbon monoxide can cause all sorts of <u>problems</u>:

<u>Particulates</u>
- If particulates are <u>breathed in</u>, they can get stuck in the <u>lungs</u> and cause <u>damage</u>. This can lead to <u>respiratory</u> (breathing) <u>problems</u>.
- They're also bad for the <u>environment</u> — they <u>reflect</u> sunlight back into space. This means that <u>less light</u> reaches the Earth — causing <u>global dimming</u>.

<u>Carbon monoxide</u>
- Carbon monoxide (CO) is really <u>dangerous</u> because it can stop your <u>blood</u> from <u>carrying enough oxygen</u> around the body.
- A <u>lack</u> of oxygen in the blood can lead to <u>fainting</u>, a <u>coma</u> or <u>even death</u>.
- Carbon monoxide doesn't have any <u>colour</u> or <u>smell</u>, so it's <u>very hard to detect</u>. This makes it even more <u>dangerous</u>.

Sulfur Dioxide and Oxides of Nitrogen Can be Released

1) Other pollutants are also released from <u>burning fossil fuels</u>.

2) <u>Sulfur dioxide</u> (SO_2) is released during the <u>combustion</u> of fossil fuels that contain <u>sulfur impurities</u>.

3) <u>Nitrogen oxides</u> form in a reaction between <u>nitrogen</u> and <u>oxygen</u> in the <u>air</u>. This reaction is caused by the <u>heat</u> of the burning fossil fuels.

4) These gases mix with <u>clouds</u> and cause <u>acid rain</u>.

5) Acid rain kills <u>plants</u>. It also <u>damages</u> buildings, statues and metals.

6) Sulfur dioxide and nitrogen oxides also cause <u>respiratory problems</u> if they're breathed in.

You can test for sulfur impurities in a fuel by bubbling the gases from combustion through a solution containing Universal indicator. If the fuel contains sulfur, the Universal indicator will turn red.

Revision and pollution — the biggest annoyances of modern life...

Burning fossil fuels is definitely useful but it sure does cause a lot of problems. At least this topic is kind of interesting and relevant to everyday life. Just think... you could see this kind of stuff on TV.

Q1   Name two pollutants that could be released during the combustion of hydrocarbons when there is not enough oxygen present.   [2 marks]

Finite and Renewable Resources

There are lots of different resources that humans use for things like electricity, heating, travelling, building materials and food. Some of these resources can be replaced, some can't.

Natural Resources Come From the Earth, Sea and Air

1) Natural resources form by themselves — they're not made by humans.
   They include anything that comes from the earth, sea or air, e.g. cotton and oil.

2) Some natural products can be replaced or improved by man-made products or processes.

> For example, rubber is a natural product that comes from the sap of a tree.
> But we can now make polymers (see p.118) to replace some natural rubber to make things like tyres.
> Wool is a natural product that comes from animals such as sheep. But scientists have developed synthetic (man-made) fibres that we can use instead of wool to make things like jumpers and blankets.

3) Agriculture (farming) helps to increase our supply of natural resources to provide food, timber, clothing and fuel. It also provides conditions which can make natural resources better for our needs.

> E.g. the development of fertilisers means we can increase the amount of crops grown in a given area.

Some Natural Resources will Run Out

1) Renewable resources can be remade at least as fast as we use them.

2) This means that they can be replaced fairly quickly.

> For example, timber is a renewable resource. Trees can be planted following a harvest and only take a few years to regrow. Other examples of renewable resources include fresh water and food.

3) Finite (non-renewable) resources are remade very slowly (or not at all).
   So we use them up quicker than we can replace them. This means that they'll eventually run out.

4) Finite resources include fossil fuels and nuclear fuels, as well as minerals and metals found in the ground.

5) We can process many finite resources to provide fuels and materials necessary for modern life.

> For example, fractional distillation (see p.148) is used to produce usable products such as petrol from crude oil. Metal ores are reduced to produce pure metals (see p.130).

Tables, Charts and Graphs can Tell You About Different Resources

You can interpret information about resources from information that's given to you.

EXAMPLE:

The table below shows how long it takes for three resources to form.
The resources are coal, wood and cotton. Work out which resource is coal.

	Time it takes to form
Resource 1	10 years
Resource 2	120-180 days
Resource 3	10^6 years

Wood and cotton are both renewable resources.
Coal is a finite resource.
Finite resources take a very long time to form.
Resource 3 takes a much longer amount of time to form compared to Resources 1 and 2.
Coal is Resource 3.

10^6 is a quick way of showing 1 000 000. This is because $10^6 = 10 \times 10 \times 10 \times 10 \times 10 \times 10 = 1 000 000$.

This book is a renewable resource — a gift that keeps on giving...

Unfortunately we can't just run around using every resource we get our hands on — we have to consider the effects of our actions. If you ever start a major mining project think... what would David Attenborough do?

Q1   State the difference between a finite and renewable resource.   [2 marks]

Reuse and Recycling

Supplies of many materials used in the modern world are <u>limited</u>. Once they're finished with, it's usually far better to <u>recycle</u> them than to use new finite resources, which will run out.

We Need to Consider the Future When Choosing Resources

1) <u>Sustainable development</u> means thinking about the needs of <u>people today</u> without damaging the lives of <u>people in the future</u>.

2) Using, extracting and processing resources can be unsustainable. This could be because:
   - Some resources are <u>non-renewable</u> — they'll run out one day. For example, the <u>raw materials</u> used to make metals, building materials, many plastics and things made from clay and glass are <u>limited</u>.
   - Extraction processes can use lots of <u>energy</u> and produce lots of <u>waste</u>.
   - Turning resources into useful materials, like <u>glass</u> or <u>bricks</u>, often uses <u>energy</u> made from <u>finite resources</u>.

Extraction processes separate the materials you want from the other things that they're mixed with.

3) One way to be more sustainable is to use <u>less</u> finite resources. This reduces both the use of that resource and anything needed to produce it.

4) We can do this by <u>reusing</u> and <u>recycling</u> materials when we're finished with them. During recycling, <u>waste</u> is <u>processed</u> so that it can be used to make <u>new products</u>.

5) We can't stop using finite resources completely. But scientists can <u>develop</u> processes that use <u>less</u> and <u>reduce</u> damage to the environment.

Recycling Metals is Important

1) <u>Mining</u> and <u>extracting</u> metals takes lots of <u>energy</u>. Most of this energy comes from burning <u>fossil fuels</u>.

2) It's usually <u>better</u> to <u>recycle</u> metals instead of making new metals.

<u>Benefits of recycling</u>:
- It often uses much <u>less energy</u> than the amount needed to make a new metal.
- It helps <u>save</u> some of the finite amount of each metal in the earth.
- It cuts down on the amount of <u>waste</u> getting sent to <u>landfill</u>.

3) Metals can be recycled by <u>melting</u> them and then moulding (<u>recasting</u>) them into the shape of a new product.

4) Sometimes, different metals won't need to be completely <u>separated</u> before recycling. The amount of <u>separation</u> depends on what the final product will be.

For example, waste steel and iron can be kept together. This is because they can both be added to iron in a <u>blast furnace</u>. This means that <u>less iron ore</u> will be needed.

A blast furnace is used to extract iron from its ore at a high temperature using carbon.

Glass can be Reused or Recycled

1) <u>Reusing</u> or <u>recycling</u> glass can help <u>sustainability</u>.

2) This <u>reduces</u> the amount of <u>energy</u> used for making new glass.

3) It also means that <u>less</u> glass is thrown away, so less <u>waste</u> is produced.

- <u>Glass bottles</u> can often be <u>reused</u> without reshaping.
- Some glass products can't be reused so they're <u>recycled</u> for a different use instead.
- The glass is <u>crushed</u> and <u>melted</u>. It's then reshaped to make other glass products like jars.

Stop trying to recycle your brother, Mark.

CGP Jokes — 85% recycled since 1996...

Recycling is really handy — as well as saving limited finite materials it also saves energy.

Q1   Give two positive effects of recycling metals.   [2 marks]

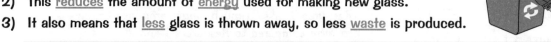

Life Cycle Assessments

If a company wants to manufacture a new product, they carry out a life cycle assessment (LCA).

Life Cycle Assessments Show Total Environmental Costs

A life cycle assessment (LCA) looks at every stage of a product's life to
assess the impact (effect) it would have on the environment.

1 Getting the Raw Materials:

1) Lots of raw materials need to be extracted (separated from other materials)
before we can use them for a product.

2) Extracting raw materials can damage the local environment, e.g. mining metals.

3) Extraction uses lots of energy. This can result in pollution.

4) Raw materials often need to be processed (e.g. by changing their shape and properties)
to turn them into useful materials.

5) This often needs large amounts of energy. E.g. extracting metals from ores
(see p.130 and 132) or fractional distillation of crude oil (see p.148).

2 Manufacture and Packaging:

1) Making products and their packaging can use a lot of energy and other resources.

2) It can cause lots of pollution too.

3) Chemical reactions are sometimes used to make products.
These reactions also produce waste products which need to be got rid of.

4) Some of this waste can be turned into other useful chemicals.
This reduces the amount that ends up polluting the environment.

3 Using the Product:

See page 156 for more
on greenhouse gases.

1) The use of a product can also damage the environment.

2) For example, burning fuels releases greenhouse gases and other harmful substances.
Fertilisers can drain into streams and rivers, causing harm to plants and animals.

3) It's also important to think about how long a product is used for or how many uses it gets.
Products that need lots of energy to produce but are used for ages mean less waste in the long run.

4 Product Disposal:

1) Products are often thrown away in landfill sites.

2) This takes up space and pollutes land and water.
For example, paint can wash off a product and get into rivers.

3) Energy is used to transport waste to landfill. This can release pollutants into
the atmosphere, such as carbon monoxide (see p.158) and carbon dioxide.

4) Products might be incinerated (burnt), which causes air pollution.

Need exercise? Go life-cycling then...

LCAs are great for showing how to improve products, so we can make them less damaging to the environment.

Q1   What are the four stages that need to be looked at when conducting a life cycle assessment?   [2 marks]

Using Life Cycle Assessments

You can compare the life cycle assessments of <u>similar products</u> to see which has the <u>smallest effect</u> on the environment. You might want to do this to see which material will affect the environment the <u>least</u>.

You Can Compare Life Cycle Assessments for Plastic and Paper Bags

1) You may be asked to <u>compare</u> life cycle assessment (LCA) information about <u>paper</u> and <u>plastic bags</u>.

2) You can then decide which type of bag is the <u>least harmful</u> to the environment.

Life Cycle Assessment Stage	Plastic Bag	Paper Bag
Raw Materials	Crude oil	Wood
Manufacturing and Packaging	Plastics are made from compounds extracted from crude oil by fractional distillation and processed by cracking and polymerisation. Waste is reduced as the other fractions of crude oil have other uses.	Pulped wood is processed using lots of energy. Lots of waste is made.
Using the Product	Can be reused several times. Can be used for other things as well as shopping. For example, as bin liners.	Usually only used once.
Product Disposal	Recyclable but many types aren't biodegradable. Take up space in landfill and pollute land.	Can be recycled. Biodegradable and non-toxic.

3) LCAs have shown that even though plastic bags <u>aren't</u> usually <u>biodegradable</u>, they may be <u>less harmful</u> to the environment.

4) This is because they take less energy to make and have a longer <u>lifespan</u> than paper bags.

If something's biodegradable, it can be broken down naturally by microorganisms (tiny living things like bacteria).

Do you ever feel like a plastic bag?

Do you ever feel so paper thin?

There are Problems with Life Cycle Assessments

1) It's quite easy to measure things like the use of <u>energy</u> or <u>resources</u>, and the <u>production</u> of some types of <u>waste</u>. So we can give all of these measurements a <u>number</u> in an LCA.

2) But measuring some effects is much <u>harder</u>.

For example, plastic bags that litter the environment <u>don't</u> look very nice. But measuring how unattractive something looks isn't easy. The person measuring it has to use their own <u>judgement</u>.

3) So, producing an LCA can involve the feelings of the person carrying out the <u>assessment</u> as well as facts. So the results could change depending on who does the assessment. This means LCAs can be <u>biased</u>.

4) <u>Selective LCAs</u> only show <u>some</u> of the impacts that a product has on the environment. So these can also be <u>biased</u> because they can be written to purposely support the claims of a company. This would give the company <u>positive advertising</u>.

If something is biased, that means it favours one point of view in a way that isn't backed up by facts.

A bag for life — my Uncle has such a sweet pet name for my Aunt...

You might have to compare different LCAs for paper and plastic bags. Each bag has good and bad points. So you'll need to pick the bag that affects the environment the least overall.

Q1   Give two reasons why a life cycle assessment may be biased.   [2 marks]

Potable Water

We all need safe drinking water. The <u>way</u> that water's made safe depends on <u>local conditions</u>.

Potable Water is Water You Can Drink

1) <u>Potable water</u> is water that's <u>safe</u> for <u>humans to drink</u>. We need it to <u>live</u>.

2) Some water is <u>naturally</u> potable, but most water needs to be <u>treated</u> before it's safe to drink.

3) Potable water isn't <u>pure</u>. Pure water <u>only</u> contains H_2O molecules but <u>potable water</u> can contain lots of other <u>dissolved substances</u>.

See p.150 for more on purity.

4) For water to be safe to drink, it must:
   - not have high <u>levels</u> of <u>dissolved salts</u>,
   - have a <u>pH</u> between <u>6.5</u> and <u>8.5</u>,
   - not have any bad things in it (like <u>bacteria</u> or other <u>microbes</u>).

The Way that Potable Water is Produced Depends on Where You Are

1) Fresh water is water that <u>doesn't</u> have much dissolved in it. Rainwater is a type of <u>fresh water</u>.

2) When it rains, water can either collect as <u>surface water</u> or as <u>ground water</u>.

   <u>SURFACE WATER</u>: collects in <u>lakes</u>, <u>rivers</u> and <u>reservoirs</u> (places for storing liquids).
   <u>GROUND WATER</u>: collects in rocks that trap water underground.

3) When producing potable water, companies need to choose a <u>suitable</u> source of freshwater. In the UK, the <u>source</u> of fresh water used depends on <u>location</u>.

4) Surface water tends to <u>dry up</u> first. So in <u>warm areas</u>, such as the south-east, <u>most</u> of the water supply comes from <u>ground water</u>. This is because it is underground so <u>doesn't</u> dry up.

Most Fresh Water Needs to be Treated to Make it Safe

1) Fresh water contains <u>low levels</u> of dissolved substances.

2) It still needs to be <u>treated</u> to make it <u>safe</u> before we use it.

3) This process includes:

Filter beds are made from grains of sand and gravel. Tiny bits of solid in the water are captured by the grains.

<u>Filtration</u> — the water is passed through a <u>wire mesh</u>. This stops large things like twigs from passing through. Next, <u>filter beds</u> are used to filter out any other <u>solid bits</u>.

<u>Sterilisation</u> — the water is <u>sterilised</u>. This means that any harmful <u>bacteria</u> or <u>microbes</u> in the water are killed. This can be done by bubbling <u>chlorine gas</u> through it or by using <u>ozone</u> or <u>ultraviolet light</u>.

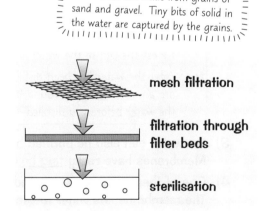

mesh filtration

filtration through filter beds

sterilisation

Ozone is a gas.

Potable water — nothing to do with gardening...

So a lot of the water that we drink comes from rain. Thankfully in the UK, we seem to have an endless supply...

Q1 Describe the steps used to treat fresh water to make it potable. [2 marks]

Desalination

Some countries have limited supplies of fresh water. They need to use other water sources, like the sea.

Potable Water Can Be Made From Seawater

1) In some very dry countries there's not enough surface or ground water. So instead they use seawater to provide potable water.

2) Seawater contains salts which need to be removed before we can drink it.

3) These salts are removed by a process called desalination.

Distillation Can Be Used to Purify Seawater

1) Distillation can be used to remove the salt from seawater (desalination).

2) You can test and purify a sample of water in the lab using distillation:

- Use a pH meter to test the pH of a sample of water. If the pH is too high or too low, you'll need to neutralise it (make it neutral). You do this by adding some acid (if the sample's alkaline) or some alkali (if the sample's acidic) until the pH is 7.

PRACTICAL

- Set up the equipment as shown in the diagram below.

Neutral solutions are neither acidic or alkaline. They have a pH of 7. E.g. pure water is neutral.

condenser   water out

round bottomed flask

salty water

fresh water   cold water in

Bunsen burner

- Heat the water in the flask using a Bunsen burner.

- As the water heats up, it becomes a gas (it evaporates). The gas then enters the condenser as steam. Cold water is pumped around the condenser to cool the steam inside of it. This drop in temperature makes the steam condense back into liquid water.

- Collect the water running out of the condenser in a beaker.

- Retest the pH of the water with a pH meter to check it's neutral.

- After the water has been distilled (all of the water has evaporated from the flask), see whether there are any crystals in the round bottomed flask. If there are crystals it means that there were salts in the water before you distilled it.

---

3) Seawater can also be purified by processes that use thin layers of material called membranes. Membranes have really tiny holes that only let certain things pass through them.

4) One of these processes is called reverse osmosis. The salty water is passed through a membrane. The membrane lets water molecules pass through but traps the salts. This separates them from the water.

5) Both distillation and reverse osmosis need loads of energy to work which makes them really expensive. This is why they're not used when there are other sources of fresh water available.

Revision and distillation — processes that require lots of energy...

...but revision is a practical solution for producing large amounts of success. So make sure you know this page.

Q1   Describe one way that membranes are used to purify seawater.   [1 mark]

Waste Water Treatment

Dealing with our waste is really important to make sure that we don't <u>pollute</u> the natural environment. It also means that we can access <u>nice clean water</u>. Super.

Waste Water Comes from Lots of Different Sources

1) We use water for lots of things at home — like <u>having a bath</u>, going to the <u>toilet</u> and doing the <u>washing-up</u>. When you flush this water and other waste matter down the drain, it goes into the <u>sewers</u> forming <u>sewage</u>. The sewage is then carried by the sewers to <u>sewage treatment plants</u>.

2) <u>Agricultural</u> (farming) <u>systems</u> also produce a lot of waste water.

3) Waste water has to be <u>treated</u> before it can be put <u>back</u> into freshwater sources like <u>rivers</u> or <u>lakes</u>. This is to remove any pollutants such as <u>organic matter</u> and <u>harmful microbes</u> (e.g. bacteria and viruses) so that the water doesn't cause <u>health problems</u>.

4) Waste water from <u>industrial processes</u> also has to be <u>collected</u> and <u>treated</u>.

5) Industrial waste water can contain organic matter and <u>harmful chemicals</u>. So it needs further treatment before it's safe to put back into the environment.

> Organic matter contains carbon compounds that come from the remains and waste of organisms.

Sewage Treatment Happens in Several Stages

1) Some of the <u>processes</u> involved in treating waste water at sewage treatment plants are shown below.

① The sewage is <u>screened</u> to remove any <u>large bits</u> of material (like twigs or plastic bags) and any <u>grit</u> (small bits of stone and sand).

② Then it goes through <u>sedimentation</u>. The <u>heavier</u> solids sink to the bottom to produce <u>sludge</u>. The lighter <u>effluent</u> (liquid waste) floats on the top.

③ The <u>effluent</u> is <u>removed</u> and treated by <u>biological aerobic digestion</u>. This is where <u>bacteria</u> break down any <u>organic matter</u> — including <u>other microbes</u> in the water.

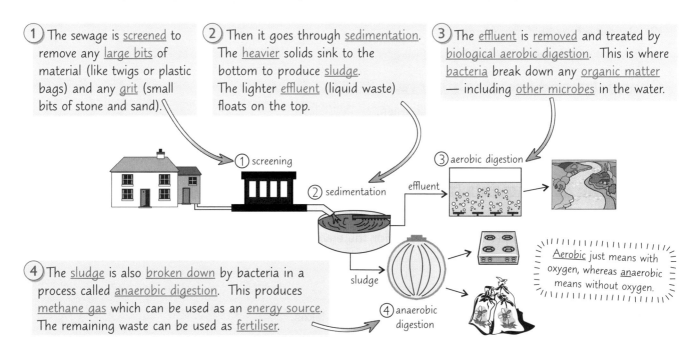

④ The <u>sludge</u> is also <u>broken down</u> by bacteria in a process called <u>anaerobic digestion</u>. This produces <u>methane gas</u> which can be used as an <u>energy source</u>. The remaining waste can be used as <u>fertiliser</u>.

> <u>Aerobic</u> just means with oxygen, whereas <u>anaerobic</u> means without oxygen.

2) Waste water containing <u>toxic substances</u> needs extra stages of treatment. This may include adding <u>chemicals</u>, <u>UV radiation</u> or using <u>membranes</u>.

3) Sewage treatment has <u>more stages</u> than treating <u>fresh water</u> but uses <u>less energy</u> than the <u>desalination</u> of <u>salt water</u>. So it could be used as an option in areas where there's not much fresh water. However, people don't like the idea of drinking water that used to be sewage.

Is it just me, or does this page stink? Phew...

Modern sewage systems have done wonders to make life much less... well... smelly.

Q1   List three stages of treatment that domestic sewage goes through at a sewage treatment plant.   [3 marks]

Revision Questions for Topics C9 & C10

That's all for Topics C9 and C10, but before you breathe a sigh of relief there are some questions to try.

- Try these questions and tick off each one when you get it right.
- When you've done all the questions under a heading and are completely happy with it, tick it off.

The Evolution of the Atmosphere (p.155) ☑

1) How did volcanoes help to form the early atmosphere?
2) Name three of the gases that scientists think were present in the early atmosphere.
3) Give one way that the levels of carbon dioxide in the early atmosphere were reduced.
4) Name the gas produced during photosynthesis.
5) What percentage of the Earth's atmosphere today is made up of nitrogen?

Pollution and Climate Change (p.156-158) ☑

6) Name two greenhouse gases.
7) Give two things that humans are doing that are causing a rise in carbon dioxide in the atmosphere.
8) What is a carbon footprint?
9) Give one reason why reducing carbon dioxide emissions can be difficult.
10) Why is carbon monoxide dangerous?
11) Describe how the following air pollutants are produced:
    a) sulfur dioxide   b) nitrogen oxides.
12) Describe how acid rain forms.
13) State two problems caused by acid rain.

Chemistry and Sustainability (p.159-160) ☑

14) Give two examples of renewable resources.
15) What is sustainable development?
16) What happens to glass when it's recycled into a new product?

Life Cycle Assessments (p.161-162) ☑

17) What do life cycle assessments (LCAs) do?
18) Give one way that paper bags are better for the environment than plastic bags.

Potable Water (p.163-164) ☑

19) What is potable water?
20) True or False? Ground water collects in rivers and lakes.
21) Name two processes you could use to purify sea water.

Waste Water Treatment (p.165) ☑

22) Name two different sources of waste water.
23) Why is it important to treat waste water before releasing it into the environment?
24) What happens during the screening step of sewage treatment?
25) Name a gas produced by the anaerobic digestion of sewage sludge.

Energy Stores and Systems

Energy is <u>never used up</u>. It's just the way that it's <u>stored</u> that <u>changes</u>.

Energy is Transferred Between Energy Stores

Energy is <u>stored</u> in the different <u>energy stores</u> of an object.
You need to know the following energy stores:

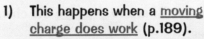
You may also see thermal energy stores called internal energy stores.

1) <u>KINETIC</u> — anything <u>moving</u> has energy in its <u>kinetic energy store</u>.

2) <u>THERMAL</u> — <u>all objects</u> have energy in this store. The <u>hotter</u> the object, the <u>more</u> energy in the store.

3) <u>CHEMICAL</u> — anything that can release energy by a <u>chemical reaction</u> has energy in this store, e.g. <u>food</u>.

4) <u>GRAVITATIONAL POTENTIAL</u> — any object <u>raised above ground level</u> has energy in this store.

5) <u>ELASTIC POTENTIAL</u> — anything stretched has energy in this store, like <u>springs</u> and <u>rubber bands</u>.

6) <u>ELECTROSTATIC</u> — e.g. two <u>charges</u> that attract or repel each other have energy in this store.

7) <u>MAGNETIC</u> — e.g. two <u>magnets</u> that attract or repel each other have energy in this store.

8) <u>NUCLEAR</u> — the <u>nucleus of an atom</u> releases energy from this store in <u>nuclear reactions</u> (p.199).

Energy can be Transferred in Four Ways

MECHANICALLY

1) This happens when a <u>force does work</u> (p.205) on an object.

2) For example, a force <u>pushing</u> an object along the floor.

ELECTRICALLY

1) This happens when a <u>moving charge does work</u> (p.189).

2) For example, when a <u>current flows</u> through a <u>light bulb</u>.

BY HEATING

1) When energy is transferred from a <u>hotter</u> object to a <u>colder</u> object.

2) For example, when a pan of water is <u>heated</u> on a hob.

BY RADIATION

1) This happens when energy is transferred by e.g. <u>sound</u> or <u>light</u>.

2) For example, when energy from the <u>Sun</u> travels to <u>Earth</u> by <u>light</u>.

When a System Changes, Energy is Transferred

1) A <u>system</u> is just the <u>single</u> object or a <u>group</u> of <u>objects</u> that you're interested in.

2) When a system <u>changes</u>, the way energy is <u>stored</u> changes in one of the ways above.

3) <u>Closed systems</u> are systems where <u>no matter</u> (stuff) or <u>energy</u> can <u>enter or leave</u>.

4) When a closed system changes, there is no <u>net (overall) change</u> in the <u>total energy</u> of the system.

> **For example...**
> - A <u>cold spoon</u> sealed in a flask of <u>hot soup</u> is a closed system.
> - Energy is <u>transferred</u> from the thermal energy store of the <u>soup</u> to the thermal energy store of the <u>spoon</u> by heating.
> - But <u>no energy</u> leaves the system. The total energy <u>stays the same</u>.

Transfer this information to your exam knowledge stores...

Energy stores pop up everywhere in physics. Make sure you understand them before you read the next page.

Q1 Name the four ways that energy can be transferred between stores. [4 marks]

Conservation of Energy and Energy Transfers

Repeat after me: <u>energy</u> is <u>NEVER</u> destroyed. Make sure you learn that fact, it's really important.
And then it's time to look at <u>mechanical energy transfers</u> a bit more. They happen when a <u>force does work</u>.

You Need to Know the Conservation of Energy Principle

Energy can be <u>transferred</u> usefully, stored or dissipated, but can <u>never</u> be <u>created</u> or <u>destroyed</u>.

1) This means that whenever a system <u>changes</u>,
   all the energy is simply <u>moved between stores</u>.
2) It <u>never</u> disappears.
3) This is true for <u>every</u> energy transfer.
4) Even when energy is <u>dissipated</u> (or wasted), it <u>isn't</u> gone.
5) It's just been transferred to an energy store that <u>we didn't want</u>.
6) There's <u>more</u> about wasted energy on p.173.

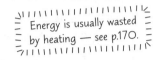
Energy is usually wasted
by heating — see p.170.

Forces Cause Mechanical Energy Transfers

1) If a <u>force</u> moves an object, then <u>work is done</u>.
2) Work done is <u>the same</u> as energy transferred.
3) So energy is transferred <u>mechanically</u> when a force moves an object.
4) For any given situation, you'll have to <u>describe</u> the changes in how energy is <u>stored</u>.
5) Here are a few <u>examples</u>:

There's more on work done on p.205.

Example 1 — A ball <u>thrown into the air</u>

1) A boy throws a ball <u>upwards</u>. The boy <u>exerts a force</u> on the ball.
2) Energy is transferred <u>mechanically</u> from the <u>chemical</u> energy store
   of the boy's <u>arm</u> to the <u>kinetic</u> energy stores of the <u>ball and arm</u>.

Example 2 — A ball <u>dropped from a height</u>

1) The ball is <u>accelerated</u> by the <u>constant force</u> of <u>gravity</u>.
2) Energy is <u>transferred mechanically</u> from the ball's
   <u>gravitational potential energy</u> store to its <u>kinetic</u> energy store.

Example 3 — A car <u>slowing down</u>

1) <u>Friction</u> acts between the car's <u>brakes</u> and its <u>wheels</u>.
2) Energy is transferred <u>mechanically</u> from the <u>wheels' kinetic</u>
   <u>energy</u> stores to the <u>thermal</u> energy store of the <u>surroundings</u>.

frictional forces
cause a transfer
of energy F

Example 4 — A car <u>hitting a wall</u>

1) When the <u>car</u> and the <u>wall touch</u>, there is a <u>normal contact force</u> (p.203) on both of them.
2) Energy is transferred <u>mechanically</u> from the car's <u>kinetic</u>
   energy store to <u>lots</u> of other energy stores.
3) Some energy is transferred to the <u>elastic potential</u> and
   <u>thermal</u> energy stores of the <u>wall</u> and the <u>car</u>.
4) Some energy might also be <u>transferred away</u> by <u>sound</u> waves.

All this work, I can feel my energy stores being drained...

The four examples above aren't the only ones you can be asked about. Test yourself by answering this question.

Q1   Describe the change in how energy is stored when the wind causes a windmill to spin.   [3 marks]

Kinetic and Potential Energy Stores

Now you've got your head around energy stores, it's time to work out how much energy is in them.

Movement Means Energy in an Object's Kinetic Energy Store

1) Energy is transferred to the kinetic energy store when an object speeds up.
2) Energy is transferred away from this store when an object slows down.
3) There's a slightly tricky formula for finding the energy in an object's kinetic energy store:

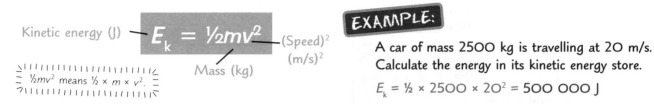

Kinetic energy (J)

$$E_k = \tfrac{1}{2}mv^2$$

(Speed)² (m/s)²

Mass (kg)

½mv² means ½ × m × v².

EXAMPLE:

A car of mass 2500 kg is travelling at 20 m/s. Calculate the energy in its kinetic energy store.

$E_k = \tfrac{1}{2} \times 2500 \times 20^2 = 500\,000$ J

Raised Objects Store Energy in Gravitational Potential Energy Stores

1) All objects raised above the ground gain energy in their gravitational potential energy (g.p.e.) store.
2) You can find the energy in an object's g.p.e. store using:

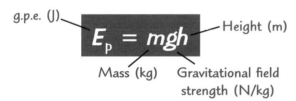

g.p.e. (J)

$$E_p = mgh$$

Height (m)

Mass (kg)   Gravitational field strength (N/kg)

Gravitational field strength on Earth is equal to 9.8 N/kg.

You Can Calculate Energy Transfers Using Conservation of Energy

You can also make calculations when energy is transferred between two stores. For example:

1) You saw on p.168 that a falling object transfers energy from its g.p.e. store to its kinetic energy store.
2) The conservation of energy principle (p.168) says that energy can't be destroyed.
3) So for a falling object when there's no air resistance:

> Energy lost from the g.p.e. store = Energy gained in the kinetic energy store

Stretching can Transfer Energy to Elastic Potential Energy Stores

1) Stretching or squashing an object can transfer energy to its elastic potential energy store.
2) The energy in the elastic potential energy store of a stretched spring can be found using:

$$E_e = \tfrac{1}{2}ke^2$$

(Extension)² (m)²

Elastic potential energy (J)   Spring constant (N/m)

3) This equation only works if the limit of proportionality has not been passed (p.206).

Make the most of your potential — jump on your bed...

That's a lot of energy equations. Make sure you're really happy using them before moving on.

Q1   A 2.0 kg object is raised by a height of 5.0 m.
       Calculate the energy gained in its gravitational potential energy store. $g = 9.8$ N/kg.   [2 marks]

Energy Transfers by Heating

Heating is just one way of <u>transferring energy</u>, as you saw back on p.167. Also coming up on this page — <u>specific heat capacity</u>. Which is really just a sciencey way of saying <u>how hard</u> it is to <u>heat</u> something up...

Energy can be Transferred by Heating

1) As a material is <u>heated</u>, energy is <u>transferred</u> to its <u>thermal</u> energy store.

2) This causes its <u>temperature to increase</u>.

3) You need to be able to <u>describe</u> the changes in how energy is stored when an object is <u>heated</u>.

4) For example, if you <u>boil water in an electric kettle</u>:

> 1) Energy is transferred <u>electrically</u> to the <u>thermal</u> energy store of the kettle's heating element.
>
> 2) Energy is then transferred <u>by heating</u> to the water's <u>thermal</u> energy store.
>
> 3) So the <u>temperature</u> of the water <u>increases</u>.

Different Materials Have Different Specific Heat Capacities

1) Some materials need <u>more energy</u> to <u>increase their temperature</u> than others.

2) These materials also <u>transfer</u> more energy when they <u>cool down</u> again.

3) They can '<u>store</u>' a lot of energy.

4) The <u>amount of energy</u> stored or released as a material <u>changes temperature</u> depends on the <u>specific heat capacity</u> of the material.

5) This energy can be found using:

Change in thermal energy (J)

$$\Delta E = mc\Delta \theta$$

Temperature change (°C)

Mass (kg)

Specific heat capacity (J/kg°C)

'Δ' just means change in.

6) <u>Specific heat capacity</u> is the amount of <u>energy</u> needed to raise the temperature of <u>1 kg</u> of a material by <u>1 °C</u>.

> **EXAMPLE:** A hot block of metal cools from 55 °C to 25 °C. The block has a mass of 0.50 kg and is made from a material that has a specific heat capacity of 320 J/kg°C. Calculate the energy transferred from the block as it cooled.
>
> 1) First, <u>calculate</u> the <u>change</u> in the block's <u>temperature</u>.   55 °C − 25 °C = 30 °C
> 2) The numbers are in the <u>correct units</u>. $\Delta E = mc\Delta \theta$
>   So put them into the <u>equation</u>.   = 0.50 × 320 × 30
> 3) The <u>unit</u> for energy is <u>joules</u> (J).   = 4800 J

All those symbols are leaving me a bit hot and bothered...

That equation is pretty nasty looking — make sure you can use it, as it's coming up again on the next page.

Q1   5.0 kg of water has an initial temperature of 5.0 °C. 50 000 J of energy is then transferred to the water. Find the final temperature of the water. The specific heat capacity of water is 4200 J/kg°C.   [3 marks]

Investigating Specific Heat Capacity

Time for a <u>practical</u>. Woohoo I hear you shout! Maybe not, but you do have to know it I'm afraid.

Investigate the Specific Heat Capacity of a Solid Block | PRACTICAL

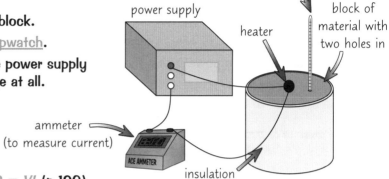

1) Measure the <u>mass</u> of the <u>block</u>.
2) Wrap it in an insulating layer (e.g. thick newspaper) to reduce <u>energy losses</u>.
3) Set up the <u>apparatus</u> as shown.
4) Measure the <u>starting temperature</u> of the block.
5) <u>Turn on</u> the power supply and <u>start</u> a <u>stopwatch</u>.
6) Record the <u>potential difference</u>, *V*, of the power supply and the <u>current</u>, *I*. They shouldn't change at all.
7) After <u>10 minutes</u>, take a reading of the block's <u>temperature</u>.
8) Turn off the heater and work out the <u>temperature change</u>.
9) Calculate the power of the heater using <u>*P = VI*</u> (p.190).

To calculate the <u>specific heat capacity</u>, you need ideas about <u>work done</u> and <u>energy transferred</u>:

1) When you turn on the power, the <u>current</u> in the circuit <u>does work</u> on the heater.
2) Energy is transferred <u>electrically</u> from the power supply to the heater's <u>thermal energy store</u>.
3) The energy transferred to the heater is given by <u>*E = Pt*</u> (p.172).
   (*P* is the <u>power</u> of the <u>heater</u> and *t* is <u>how long</u> the heater is on for.)
4) This energy is then transferred to the material's <u>thermal</u> energy store <u>by heating</u>.
5) So the value of *E* you calculated in step 3 is equal to the change in thermal energy of the block, ΔE, and you can use it to find the <u>specific heat capacity</u> of the block, *c*.
6) <u>Rearrange the equation</u> from page 170 to give you $c = \Delta E \div (m \times \Delta\theta)$, and put in your results.
7) The <u>temperature change</u>, $\Delta\theta$, and <u>mass</u>, *m*, were <u>measured</u> in the experiment. Use your value of *E* from step 3 as ΔE.
8) This <u>example</u> shows how to do the <u>calculation</u>:

EXAMPLE: A 1.0 kg block of material is heated using a 10 V power supply.
The starting temperature of the block is 20 °C.
The current through the heater is recorded as 10 A.
After 60 seconds, the final temperature of the block is 26 °C.
Calculate the specific heat capacity of the material of the block.

1) Calculate the <u>power</u> of the heater. $P = V \times I = 10 \times 10 = 100$ W
2) Calculate the <u>energy transferred</u>. $E = P \times t = 100 \times 60 = 6000$ J
3) Find the <u>change in temperature</u>. $\Delta\theta = 26 - 20 = 6$ °C
4) Calculate the <u>specific heat capacity</u>. $c = \Delta E \div (m \times \Delta\theta) = 6000 \div (1.0 \times 6) = 1000$ J/kg °C

10) You can <u>repeat</u> this experiment with <u>different materials</u> to see how their specific heat capacities <u>compare</u>.
11) For a <u>liquid</u>, place the <u>heater</u> and <u>thermometer</u> into an <u>insulated beaker</u> with a <u>known mass</u> of the liquid.
12) Then carry out the rest of the experiment in <u>exactly the same way</u> as above.

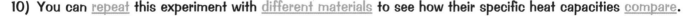

I've eaten five sausages — I have a high specific meat capacity...

This is quite a tricky experiment, with lots of steps. Go back and re-read this whole page to get it in your head.

Q1 A copper block is heated by an electric heater in order to calculate the specific heat capacity of copper. What values do you need to measure to find the specific heat capacity of copper? [4 marks]

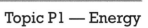

Power

Punch your fist in the air and repeat after me — 'I HAVE THE POWER'.

Power is the 'Rate of Doing Work' — i.e. How Much Work is Done per Second

1) Power is the rate of energy transfer.
2) You can also say it's the rate of doing work.
3) This just means that power is how fast energy is transferred or how fast work is done.
4) Power is measured in watts.
5) One watt = 1 joule of energy transferred per second.
6) You can calculate power using these equations:

Power (W) — $P = \dfrac{E}{t}$ — Energy transferred (J), Time (s)

Power (W) — $P = \dfrac{W}{t}$ — Work done (J), Time (s)

EXAMPLE:

a) It takes 8000 J of work to lift a stuntman to the top of a building.
A motor takes 50 s to make the lift.
Calculate the power of the motor.

1) The numbers are in the correct units.
2) Put the numbers into the equation for power in terms of work.

a) $P = W \div t$
= 8000 ÷ 50
= 160 W

b) A second motor has a power of 200 W.
It lifts the stuntman for 30 s.
Calculate the energy transferred by the motor.

1) Rearrange the power equation for energy transferred.
2) Put the numbers in.
3) Remember energy is in joules.

b) $P = E \div t$ so $E = P \times t$
= 200 × 30
= 6000 J

A Powerful Machine Transfers a Lot of Energy in a Short Space of Time

1) Take two cars that are the same in every way apart from the power of their engines.
2) Both cars race the same distance along a straight race track to a finish line.
3) The car with the more powerful engine will reach the finish line faster than the other car.
4) This is because it will transfer the same amount of energy but over a shorter time.

Watt's power? Power's watts...

You might be tired of hearing this, but energy transferred and work done are the same thing. That's why power can be described using energy or work done. It's also why those two equations at the top of the page look so similar.

Q1   A motor transfers 4800 J of energy in 2 minutes. Calculate its power.   [3 marks]

Reducing Unwanted Energy Transfers

There are a few ways you can <u>reduce</u> the amount of energy running off to a <u>completely useless</u> store.

Energy is Always Wasted in any Energy Transfer

1) When energy is <u>transferred</u> between stores, some energy is transferred to the store you <u>want</u> it in.
2) This energy is <u>usefully</u> transferred.
3) But in <u>any</u> energy transfer, some energy is <u>always dissipated</u>.
4) This means the energy is transferred to <u>useless stores</u>.
5) These useless energy stores are usually <u>thermal energy stores</u>.
6) This energy is often described as '<u>wasted</u>' energy.

> - When you use a mobile phone, energy is transferred from the <u>chemical</u> energy store of the <u>battery</u>.
> - Some energy is <u>usefully</u> transferred.
> - But some is <u>dissipated</u> to the <u>thermal</u> energy store of the <u>phone</u>.

7) There are a few ways you can <u>reduce</u> the amount of energy <u>wasted</u>.

Lubrication Reduces Frictional Forces

1) <u>Friction</u> acts between all objects that <u>rub together</u>.
2) This causes some energy in the system to be <u>dissipated</u>.
3) <u>Lubricants</u> can be used to <u>reduce the friction</u> between the objects.
4) For example, <u>oil</u> in <u>car engines</u> reduces friction between all of the moving parts.
5) This <u>reduces</u> the amount of <u>dissipated energy</u>.

Insulation Has a Low Thermal Conductivity

1) When part of a material is <u>heated</u>, that part of the material gains <u>energy</u>.
2) This energy is <u>transferred</u> across the material so that the rest of the material gets <u>warmer</u>.
3) For example, if you heated <u>one end</u> of a <u>metal rod</u>, the <u>other end</u> would <u>eventually</u> get warmer. This is known as <u>conduction</u>.
4) <u>Thermal conductivity</u> is a measure of how <u>quickly</u> energy is transferred by conduction through a material.
5) Materials with a <u>high thermal conductivity</u> transfer <u>lots</u> of energy in a <u>short time</u>.
6) Materials with a <u>low thermal conductivity</u> are called <u>thermal insulators</u>.
7) Thermal insulators can reduce unwanted transfers <u>by heating</u>, e.g. in the <u>home</u>.

Insulation is Important for Keeping Buildings Warm

You can keep your home cosy and <u>warm</u> by <u>reducing</u> the <u>rate of cooling</u>. How <u>quickly</u> a building cools depends on:

1) How <u>thick</u> its <u>walls</u> are. The <u>thicker</u> the walls are, the <u>slower</u> a building will <u>cool</u>.
2) The <u>thermal conductivity</u> of its walls. Building walls from a material with a <u>low thermal conductivity</u> reduces the rate of cooling.
3) How much <u>thermal insulation</u> there is, e.g. <u>loft insulation</u> reduces energy losses through the roof.

Energy can't be created or destroyed — only talked about a lot...

Remember, when energy is wasted it's <u>not destroyed</u> — it still exists, it just isn't stored usefully anymore.

Q1   A builder is designing a house.
       Give one way the builder could reduce the rate of cooling of the house.   [1 mark]

Efficiency

More! More! Tell me more about <u>energy transfers</u> please! Oh go on then, since you insist...

Energy Transfers Involve Some Wasted Energy

1) You saw on page 173 that some energy is always wasted when energy is transferred.

2) The <u>less energy</u> that is <u>wasted</u>, the <u>more efficient</u> the energy transfer is.

3) The <u>efficiency</u> of an energy transfer is a measure of the amount of energy that ends up in <u>useful</u> energy stores.

4) But as <u>some</u> energy is <u>always</u> wasted, <u>nothing is 100% efficient</u>.

There Are Two Efficiency Equations

1) The efficiency for any energy transfer can be <u>worked out</u> using this equation:

$$\text{Efficiency} = \frac{\text{Useful output energy transfer}}{\text{Total input energy transfer}}$$

This gives efficiency as a decimal, but you can turn it into a percentage — see below.

EXAMPLE: 36 000 J of energy is transferred to a television. It transfers 28 800 J of this energy usefully. Calculate the efficiency of the television. Give your answer as a percentage.

1) Put the numbers you're given <u>into the equation</u>.

2) To change a <u>decimal</u> to a <u>percentage</u>, <u>multiply</u> your answer <u>by 100</u>.

efficiency = useful output energy transfer
÷ total input energy transfer
= 28 800 ÷ 36 000
= 0.8
0.8 × 100 = 80, so efficiency = **80%**

2) You might not know the <u>energy</u> input and output of a device.

3) But you can use its <u>power input</u> and <u>output</u> to calculate its <u>efficiency</u>:

$$\text{Efficiency} = \frac{\text{Useful power output}}{\text{Total power input}}$$

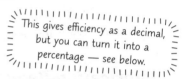

EXAMPLE: A blender is 70% efficient. It has a total input power of 600 W. Calculate the useful power output.

1) Change the <u>efficiency</u> from a <u>percentage</u> to a <u>decimal</u>. To do this, <u>divide</u> the percentage <u>by 100</u>.

2) <u>Rearrange</u> the equation for <u>useful power output</u>.

3) <u>Stick in</u> the numbers and find the useful power output.

efficiency = 70% ÷ 100 = 0.7

useful power output = efficiency × total power input

useful power output = 0.7 × 600 = **420 W**

Don't waste your energy — turn the TV off while you revise...

Make sure you can use and rearrange the equations for efficiency, then have a go at these questions.

Q1 A motor in a remote-controlled car transfers 300 J of energy into the car's energy stores. 225 J are transferred to the car's kinetic energy stores. Calculate the efficiency of the motor. [2 marks]

Q2 A machine has a useful power output of 900 W and an efficiency of 0.75. Calculate the total power input to the machine. [3 marks]

Energy Resources and Their Uses

Energy resources are mostly used to <u>generate electricity</u> or for <u>transport</u> and <u>heating</u>.

Non-Renewable Energy Resources Will Run Out One Day

1) Non-renewable energy resources are <u>fossil fuels</u> and <u>nuclear fuel</u>.
2) The <u>three main</u> fossil fuels are <u>coal</u>, <u>oil</u> and <u>(natural) gas</u>.
3) We <u>can't</u> replace non-renewable energy resources <u>as quickly as</u> we're using them.

Renewable Energy Resources Will Never Run Out

1) Renewable energy resources can be <u>replenished</u> (replaced) <u>as quickly as</u> they are being used.
2) The <u>renewable energy resources</u> you need to know are:

1) The Sun (Solar) 3) Water waves 5) Bio-fuels 7) Geothermal
2) Wind 4) Hydro-electricity 6) Tides

Energy Resources can be Used for Transport...

1) <u>Transport</u> uses both <u>renewable</u> and <u>non-renewable</u> energy resources. For example:

NON-RENEWABLE ENERGY RESOURCES
- <u>Petrol</u> or <u>diesel</u> is used in most vehicles. They're both created from <u>oil</u>.
- <u>Coal</u> is used in <u>steam trains</u> to boil water to produce steam.

RENEWABLE ENERGY RESOURCES
Vehicles can run on pure <u>bio-fuels</u> (p.178) or a <u>mix</u> of a bio-fuel and petrol or diesel.

2) <u>Electricity</u> can also be used for transport — e.g. <u>electric cars</u> and some <u>trains</u>.
3) The electricity can be <u>generated</u> using <u>renewable</u> or <u>non-renewable</u> energy resources (p.174-176).

...And for Heating

<u>Energy resources</u> are also needed for <u>heating</u> things, like your home.

NON-RENEWABLE ENERGY RESOURCES
- <u>Natural gas</u> is burnt to heat <u>water</u> in a boiler. This hot water is then pumped into <u>radiators</u>.
- <u>Gas fires</u> burn natural gas to heat rooms.
  - <u>Coal</u> is burnt in open <u>fireplaces</u>.
  - <u>Electric heaters</u> use electricity which can be generated from <u>non-renewable</u> energy resources.

RENEWABLE ENERGY RESOURCES
- <u>Bio-fuel</u> boilers work in the same way as gas boilers.
- A <u>geothermal heat pump</u> uses geothermal energy resources (p.176) to heat buildings.
- <u>Solar water heaters</u> use the Sun to heat <u>water</u> which is then pumped into radiators in the building.
- Electric heaters can use <u>electricity</u> generated from renewable resources.

I'm pretty sure natural gas is renewable — I make enough of it...

You need to know the difference between the two different types of energy resource, so get cracking.

Q1 Write down whether each of the following is a renewable or non-renewable energy resource.
a) Tidal power b) Natural gas c) Nuclear power d) Bio-fuel [4 marks]

Wind, Solar and Geothermal

Time for the first page on <u>renewable energy resources</u>. You've probably heard about a few of these already.

You Need to Be Able to Compare Resources

1) You're about to learn all about the <u>main energy resources</u>.
2) You need to be able to:
   - describe their effects on the <u>environment</u> (e.g. pollution).
   - compare their <u>reliability</u> (whether they can be <u>trusted</u> to provide energy when we need it).
3) So make sure you're <u>paying attention</u>.

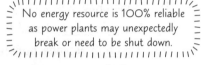

No energy resource is 100% reliable as power plants may unexpectedly break or need to be shut down.

Wind Power — Lots of Wind Turbines

1) <u>Wind turbines</u> are usually put up in <u>open spaces</u>.
2) When the wind <u>turns the blades</u>, electricity is produced.
3) They produce <u>no pollution</u> once they're built.
4) And they do <u>no permanent</u> (lasting) <u>damage</u> to the landscape. If you <u>remove</u> the turbines, the area goes <u>back to normal</u>.
5) However, they're <u>not as reliable</u> as other energy resources.
6) They don't produce electricity <u>when the wind stops</u>.
7) Turbines are also stopped if the wind is <u>too strong</u>. This stops them getting <u>damaged</u>.
8) It's also <u>impossible</u> to <u>increase supply</u> when there's <u>extra demand</u> (p.191) for electricity.

Solar Cells — Expensive but No Environmental Damage

1) <u>Solar cells</u> generate electricity directly from sunlight.
2) They create <u>no pollution</u> once they're built.
3) But quite a lot of energy is used to <u>build them</u>.
4) Solar power <u>only</u> generates electricity <u>during the day</u>.
5) In <u>sunny</u> countries solar power is a <u>very reliable source</u> of energy.
6) It's still <u>fairly reliable</u> in <u>cloudy countries</u> like Britain.
7) Like wind, you <u>can't increase the power output</u> when there is <u>extra demand</u>.

Time to recharge.

Geothermal Power — Energy in Underground Thermal Energy Stores

1) <u>Geothermal power</u> uses energy from the <u>thermal</u> energy stores of <u>hot rocks</u> below the Earth's surface.
2) It can be used to <u>generate electricity</u> or to <u>heat buildings</u>.
3) Geothermal power is very <u>reliable</u> because the hot rocks are <u>always</u> hot.
4) Most geothermal power stations only have a <u>small</u> impact on the <u>environment</u>.

People love the idea of wind power — just not in their back yard...

There are pros and cons to all energy resources. Make sure you know them for solar, wind and geothermal.

Q1   Explain why geothermal power is more reliable than wind power.   [2 marks]

Hydro-electricity, Waves and Tides

Good old <u>water</u>. Not only can we drink it, we can also use it to <u>generate electricity</u>.

Hydro-electric Power Uses Falling Water

1) <u>Hydro-electric power</u> usually involves building a big <u>dam</u> across a <u>valley</u>.
2) The valley is usually <u>flooded</u>.
3) Water is allowed to flow out <u>through turbines</u>, which generates electricity.
4) There is <u>no pollution</u> when it's running.
5) But there is a <u>big impact</u> on the <u>environment</u> due to the flooding of the valley.
6) Plants rot and release <u>greenhouse gases</u> which lead to global warming (see p.178).
7) Animals and plants also lose <u>their habitats</u> (where they live).
8) There's no problem with <u>reliability</u> in countries that get rain regularly.
9) And it can respond <u>straight away</u> when there's <u>extra demand</u> (p.191) for electricity.

Wave Power — Lots of Little Wave-Powered Turbines

1) <u>Turbines</u> around the coast are turned by water waves and electricity is generated.
2) There is <u>no pollution</u>.
3) But they <u>disturb the seabed</u> and the <u>habitats</u> of animals.
4) They are <u>fairly unreliable</u>, as waves tend to die down when the <u>wind drops</u>.

Tidal Barrages Use the Tides of the Sea

1) <u>Tidal barrages</u> are <u>big dams</u> (with turbines in them) built across <u>rivers</u>.
2) <u>Water</u> passing through the turbines <u>generates electricity</u>.
3) The amount of energy generated <u>changes</u> with the tides.
4) But tidal barrages are <u>very reliable</u>, as we can <u>predict</u> the tides (we know what they're going to do).
5) There is <u>no pollution</u>.
6) But they do <u>change the habitat</u> of the wildlife, e.g. birds and sea creatures.
7) And often <u>fish are killed</u> as they swim through the turbines.

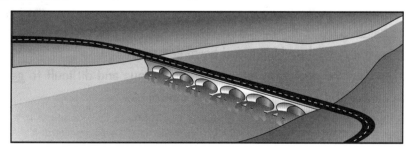

The hydro-electric power you're supplying — it's electrifying...

Learn the differences between all of these water-based resources before having a go at this question.

Q1   Give one negative environmental impact of wave power.   [1 mark]

Bio-fuels and Non-renewables

And the energy resources just keep on coming. It's over soon, I promise. Just a few more to go.

Bio-fuels are Made from Plants and Waste

1) Bio-fuels are fuels created from plant products or animal dung.
2) They can be burnt to produce electricity or used to run cars in the same way as fossil fuels.
3) They produce carbon dioxide when they're burnt.
4) But the plants used to make biofuels will have absorbed a lot of carbon dioxide while they were growing.
5) In some places, large areas of forest have been cleared to make room to grow bio-fuels.
6) This leads to lots of animals losing their natural habitats.
7) Crops can be grown throughout the year.
8) Extra bio-fuels can be constantly produced and stored for when they are needed.
9) So bio-fuels are fairly reliable.

Non-Renewables are Reliable...

1) Fossil fuels and nuclear energy are reliable.
2) There's enough fossil and nuclear fuels to meet current demand.
3) We always have some in stock so power plants can respond quickly to changes in demand.
4) However, these fuels are slowly running out. Some fossil fuels may run out within a hundred years.

...But Create Environmental Problems

1) Coal, oil and gas release CO_2 into the atmosphere when they're burned. All this CO_2 leads to global warming.
2) Burning coal and oil also releases sulfur dioxide, which causes acid rain.
3) Acid rain makes lakes and rivers acidic, which can kill animals and plants. It can also damage trees and soils.
4) Coal mining makes a mess of the landscape.
5) And it destroys the habitats of local animals and plants.
6) Oil spills cause big environmental problems and harm sea creatures.
7) Nuclear power is clean but the nuclear waste is very dangerous and difficult to get rid of.
8) Nuclear power also carries the risk of a big accident that could release a lot of radiation, like the Fukushima disaster in Japan.

Global warming is where greenhouse gases cause the Earth to warm up.

Radiation can be very dangerous to humans — see p.201 for more.

Bio-fuels are great — but don't burn your biology notes just yet...

Make sure you can talk about how bio-fuels and non-renewables affect the environment.

Q1 Give two benefits of using fossil fuels to generate electricity. [2 marks]

Q2 Give three environmental impacts of using oil as an energy resource. [3 marks]

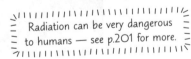

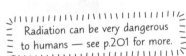

Trends in Energy Resource Use

Over time, the types of energy resources we use change. Read on to find out why.

Currently we Still Need Non-Renewables

1) Our use of electricity increased a lot in the 1900s.
2) This was because the population and the number of things that used electricity increased.
3) But electricity use in the UK has been falling slowly since around the year 2000.
4) This is because we're trying harder to be energy efficient and save energy.
5) At the moment, we use non-renewables for most of our electricity, transport and heating.

But People Want to use More Renewable Energy Resources

1) We now know that non-renewables are very bad for the environment and will run out one day (p.178).
2) This makes many people want to use renewable energy resources as they are better for the environment.
3) Many people also think it's better to move to renewables before non-renewables run out.
4) Pressure from other countries and the public has meant that governments have begun to introduce targets for using renewable energy resources.
5) This puts pressure on energy providers to build new renewable power plants. If they don't, they may lose business and money in the future.
6) Car companies have also had to change to become more environmentally-friendly.
7) Cars that can run on electricity are already on the market. The electricity can be generated using renewable energy resources.

The Use of Renewables is Limited by Lots of Factors

1) There's a lot of scientific evidence supporting renewables.
2) But scientists can only give advice. They don't have the power to make people, companies or governments change their ways (see p.2).
3) Moving to renewables can be limited by money.

   - Building new renewable power plants costs money.
   - Some renewable resources are less reliable than other resources, so a mixture of different resources would need to be used.
   - This costs even more money.
   - Cars that run on electricity are more expensive than petrol cars.

4) Moving to renewables can also be affected by politics, people and ethics (if something is right or wrong).

   - The cost of switching to renewable power will have to be paid through energy bills or taxes.
   - Governments often don't want to suggest raising taxes as this may make them unpopular.
   - Some people don't want to or can't afford to pay. There are arguments about whether it's ethical (right or wrong) to make them pay.
   - Many people also don't want to live near to a power plant (like a wind farm or hydro-electric dam).
   - And some think it's not ethical to make people put up with new power plants built near to them.

Going green is on-trend this season...

More people want to help the environment, so the energy resources we use are changing. But for lots of reasons, it's not happening very quickly. Make sure you learn the reasons listed on this page.

Q1   Give two reasons why we currently do not use more renewable energy resources in the UK.   [2 marks]

Current and Circuit Symbols

If the word <u>current</u> makes you think of delicious cakes instead of physics, that's all about to change.
Learn what it means, as well as some handy <u>symbols</u> to show things like <u>batteries</u> and <u>switches</u> in a circuit.

Learn these Circuit Diagram Symbols

1) You need to be able to <u>understand circuit diagrams</u>
   and <u>draw them</u> using the <u>correct symbols</u>.

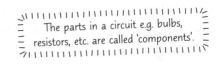
The parts in a circuit e.g. bulbs, resistors, etc. are called 'components'.

2) These are the <u>symbols</u> you need to know:

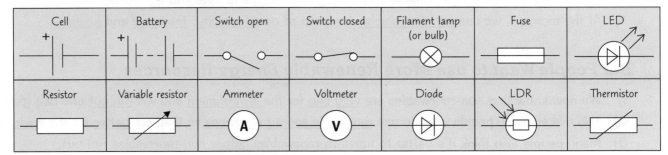

Cell	Battery	Switch open	Switch closed	Filament lamp (or bulb)	Fuse	LED
Resistor	Variable resistor	Ammeter	Voltmeter	Diode	LDR	Thermistor

3) Follow these <u>rules</u> to draw a circuit diagram:

- Make sure all the <u>wires</u> in your circuit are <u>straight lines</u>.
- Make sure that the circuit is <u>closed</u>. This means you can follow a wire from one end of the <u>cell</u> or <u>battery</u>, through any <u>components</u>, to the other end of the cell or battery.

Total Charge Through a Circuit Depends on Current and Time

1) <u>Electric current</u> is a flow of <u>electrical charge</u>.
2) Current is measured in <u>amperes</u>, **A**.
3) Charge is measured in <u>coulombs</u>, **C**.
4) Electrical charge will <u>only flow</u> round a complete (closed) circuit if something is providing a <u>potential difference</u>, e.g. a battery.
5) The <u>potential difference</u> is the '<u>driving force</u>' that pushes charge around the circuit.
6) <u>Resistance</u> is anything that <u>slows down</u> the flow of charge.
7) In a <u>single</u>, closed <u>loop</u> the current is the same <u>everywhere</u> in the circuit (see p.185).
8) The <u>size</u> of the <u>current</u> tells you <u>how fast</u> the charge is <u>flowing</u>. This is known as the <u>rate of flow of charge</u>.
9) <u>Charge flow</u>, <u>current</u> and <u>time</u> are related by this handy <u>equation</u>:

'Potential difference' is sometimes called 'voltage'. Exam questions will use 'potential difference', but you can use either.

Charge flow (C) = Current (A) × Time (s)	$Q = It$

EXAMPLE: A battery charger passes a current of 2 A through a cell over a period of 300 seconds. How much charge is transferred to the cell?

Just <u>substitute</u> the values into the equation above and <u>calculate</u> the <u>charge</u>.

$Q = It = 2 \times 300$
$= 600$ C

Remember charge is measured in coulombs.

I think it's about time you took charge...

Learn those symbols. It's no good if you're asked to draw a circuit diagram and you can't tell a resistor from a fuse.

Q1   A student creates a simple circuit containing a battery, a switch and a bulb.
        He connects them all in a single, closed loop. Draw the circuit diagram for this circuit.   [3 marks]

Resistance and V = IR

Potential difference, current and resistance are linked by a very important formula. Make sure you learn it.

There's a Formula Linking Potential Difference and Current

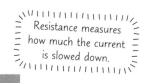
Resistance measures how much the current is slowed down.

1) The current flowing through a component depends on the potential difference across it and the resistance of the component.

> The greater the resistance across a component, the smaller the current that flows (for a given potential difference across the component).

2) The formula linking potential difference (pd) and current is:

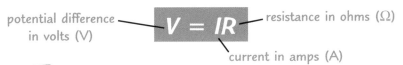

potential difference in volts (V)

$$V = IR$$

resistance in ohms (Ω)

current in amps (A)

EXAMPLE: A 4.0 Ω resistor in a circuit has a potential difference of 6.0 V across it. What is the current through the resistor?

1)	Cover the *I* in the formula triangle to find that $I = V \div R$.	$I = V \div R$
2)	Substitute in the values you have, and work out the current.	$I = 6.0 \div 4.0 = 1.5$ A

Ohmic Conductors Have a Constant Resistance

1) $V = IR$ works for components with a fixed resistance. This means the resistance of the component doesn't change with current.

2) These components are called ohmic conductors.

3) Ohmic conductors only have a fixed resistance if their temperature doesn't change.

4) Wires and resistors are examples of ohmic conductors.

5) For an ohmic conductor at a fixed temperature:

> The current flowing through it is directly proportional to the potential difference across it.

6) This means that if you multiply the potential difference by a certain amount, the current will be multiplied by the same amount. For example, if the potential difference doubles, the current doubles too.

Some Components Have a Changing Resistance

1) The resistance of some components DOES change with current. For example, a filament lamp or a diode.

2) Filament lamps contain a wire (the filament), which is designed to heat up and 'glow' as the current increases.

A higher current makes a filament glow brighter. So a higher pd means a brighter lamp.

3) So as the current increases, the temperature of the filament increases.

4) Resistance increases with temperature, so the resistance increases with current.

5) For diodes, the resistance depends on the direction of the current.

6) A diode will let current flow in one direction. It has a very high resistance in the opposite direction, which makes it hard for a current to flow that way.

Ohm sweet ohm...

There's loads more coming up on resistance, so make sure you're happy with this page before moving on.

Q1 An appliance is connected to a 230 V source. A current of 5.0 A is flowing through it. Calculate the resistance of the appliance.

[3 marks]

PRACTICAL Investigating Resistance

Woo, experiments. Here's a <u>simple experiment</u> for investigating resistance.

You Can Investigate the Factors Affecting Resistance

The <u>resistance</u> of a circuit can depend on a number of things, including:

- If components are in <u>series</u> or <u>parallel</u>. See p.185 for more on this.
- The <u>length of wire</u> used in the circuit.

Learn How to Investigate the Effect of Wire Length

You can investigate the effect of <u>wire length</u> using this circuit:

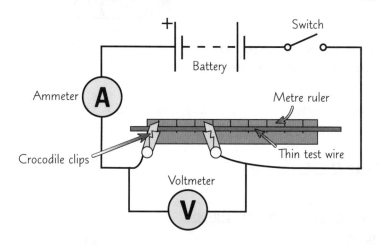

Measure Potential Difference and Current for Different Lengths

1) Attach a <u>crocodile clip</u> to the wire level with <u>0 cm</u> on the ruler.
2) Attach the <u>second crocodile clip</u> to the wire a short distance from the first clip.
3) Write down the <u>length</u> of the wire between the clips.
4) <u>Close the switch</u>, then record the <u>current</u> through the wire and the <u>pd</u> across it.
5) Use **R = V ÷ I** (from the equation **V = IR** on p.181) to <u>calculate</u> the <u>resistance</u> of the wire.
6) <u>Open the switch</u> and <u>move</u> the second crocodile clip along the wire.
7) Repeat steps 3 to 6 for a range of wire lengths.

Plot a Graph of your Results

1) Plot a <u>graph</u> of <u>resistance</u> against <u>wire length</u>.
2) Draw a <u>line of best fit</u> through your points.
3) Your graph should be a <u>straight line</u> through the <u>origin</u> (where length and resistance are both zero).
4) This means resistance is <u>directly proportional</u> to length — the <u>longer</u> the wire, the <u>greater</u> the resistance.

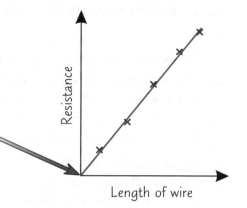

Measure gymnastics — use a vaultmeter...

Opening the switch between readings lets the circuit cool down. This reduces the error in your measurements.

Q1   A student performs an investigation into the effect of wire length on resistance.
Draw a circuit diagram of a circuit the student could use to carry out this investigation.
Use the symbol for a variable resistor to represent the test wire.   [3 marks]

I-V Characteristics

There are three different graphs to learn on this page — you have to know how you get them too.

I-V Characteristics Show How Current Changes With Pd

1) An 'I-V characteristic' is a graph showing how the current (I) flowing through a component changes as the potential difference (V) across it changes.

2) Components with straight line I-V characteristics are called linear components (e.g. a fixed resistor).

3) Components with curved I-V characteristics are non-linear components (e.g. a filament lamp or a diode).

4) To find the resistance at any point on the I-V characteristic, first read off the values of I and V at that point. Then use $R = V \div I$ (from $V = IR$ on page 181).

You Can Investigate I-V Characteristics   PRACTICAL

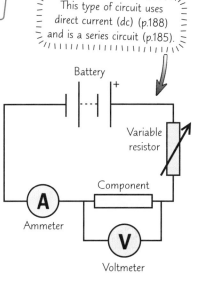

This type of circuit uses direct current (dc) (p.188) and is a series circuit (p.185).

You should do this experiment for different components, including a filament lamp, a diode and a resistor at a fixed temperature.

1) Set up the test circuit shown on the right.

2) The variable resistor is used to change the current in the circuit. This changes the potential difference across the component.

3) Now you need to get sets of current and potential difference readings:

   • Set the resistance of the variable resistor.

   • Measure the current through and potential difference across the component.

   • Take measurements at a number of different resistances.

4) Swap over the wires connected to the cell to reverse the direction of the current. The ammeter should now display negative readings.

5) Repeat step 3 to get results for negative values of current.

6) Plot a graph with current on the y-axis and potential difference on the x-axis.

7) Here are the graphs or 'I-V characteristics' you should get for different components:

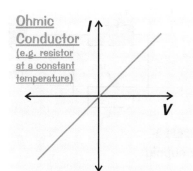

Ohmic Conductor (e.g. resistor at a constant temperature)

1) Current is directly proportional to potential difference.

2) So you get a straight line.

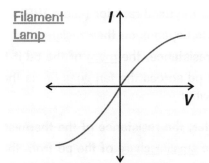

Filament Lamp

1) Temperature increases as current increases.

2) So resistance increases.

3) This makes it harder for current to flow.

4) So the graph gets less steep.

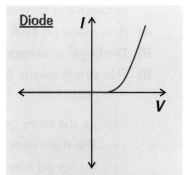

Diode

1) Current only flows in one direction.

2) The diode has very high resistance in the reverse direction.

In the end you'll have to learn this — resistance is futile...

Draw out those graphs until you're sketching them in your sleep.

Q1   Draw the I-V characteristic for: a) an ohmic conductor   b) a filament lamp   [4 marks]

Circuit Devices

For some components <u>resistance</u> can depend on things like <u>light</u> and <u>temperature</u>, and this can be really handy.

LDR is Short for Light Dependent Resistor

1) The <u>resistance</u> of an LDR changes as the <u>intensity</u> of <u>light</u> changes.
2) In <u>bright light</u>, the resistance is <u>low</u>.
3) In <u>darkness</u>, the resistance is <u>high</u>.
4) LDRs have lots of <u>uses</u> including turning on lights when it gets <u>dark</u>.
5) This can be used in <u>automatic night lights</u>, or outdoor lighting.
6) They're also used in <u>burglar detectors</u>.

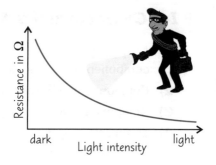

The Resistance of a Thermistor Depends on Temperature

1) A <u>thermistor</u> is a <u>temperature dependent</u> resistor.
2) In <u>hot</u> conditions, the resistance <u>drops</u>.
3) In <u>cool</u> conditions, the resistance goes <u>up</u>.
4) Thermistors are used in <u>car engines</u> and central heating <u>thermostats</u>.
5) <u>Thermostats</u> turn the heating <u>on</u> when it's <u>cool</u> and <u>off</u> when it's <u>warm</u>.

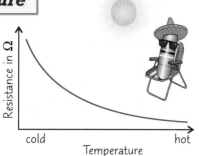

You Can Use LDRs and Thermistors in Sensing Circuits

1) <u>Sensing circuits</u> can be used to automatically <u>change the pd</u> across components depending on changes in the <u>environment</u>.
2) This circuit is a <u>sensing circuit</u> used to <u>control</u> a fan in a room.
3) The <u>potential difference</u> of the power supply is <u>shared out</u> between the thermistor and the fixed resistor (see p.185).
4) How much pd each one gets depends on their <u>resistances</u>.
5) The <u>larger</u> a component's resistance, the <u>more</u> of the pd it takes.
6) This circuit means that the pd across the fan <u>goes up</u> as the room <u>gets hotter</u>. Here's why:

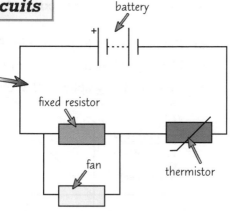

- As the room gets hotter, the resistance of the thermistor <u>decreases</u>.
- The thermistor takes a <u>smaller share</u> of the pd from the power supply.
- So the pd across the fixed resistor <u>rises</u>.
- The pd across the fixed resistor is <u>equal to</u> the pd across the <u>fan</u> (you'll see why on p.186).
- So the pd across the <u>fan</u> rises too, making the fan go <u>faster</u>.

7) If you connected the fan across the thermistor <u>instead</u>, the circuit would do the <u>opposite</u>.
8) The fan would <u>slow down</u> as the room got <u>hotter</u>.

LDRs — Light Dependent Rabbits...

The next time your heating turns on by itself, you can show off and tell everyone how thermistors made it happen.

Q1 Give one everyday use for the following components: a) an LDR   b) a thermistor   [2 marks]

Series Circuits

There's a difference between connecting components in <u>series</u> and <u>parallel</u> — first up, series.

Series Circuits — All or Nothing

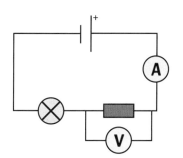

1) In <u>series circuits</u>, the components are all connected <u>in a line</u> between the ends of the power supply.

2) Only <u>voltmeters</u> break this rule. They're <u>always</u> in <u>parallel</u> (see p.186).

3) If you remove <u>one</u> component, the circuit is <u>broken</u>. So <u>all</u> the components <u>stop working</u>.

4) You can use the rules on this page to <u>design</u> series circuits to <u>measure</u> and <u>test</u> all sorts of things.

5) For example the <u>test circuit</u> on p.183 and the <u>sensing circuits</u> on p.184.

Potential Difference is Shared, Current is the Same Everywhere

1) In series circuits the <u>total pd</u> of the <u>supply</u> is <u>shared</u> between all of the <u>components</u>.

2) If you <u>add up</u> the pd across <u>each component</u>, you get the <u>pd of the power supply</u>.

3) The <u>bigger</u> a component's <u>resistance</u>, the bigger its <u>share</u> of the <u>total pd</u>.

4) If you connect <u>cells</u> in <u>series</u>, their pds <u>add together</u> to make the <u>total pd</u> across the circuit.

5) In series circuits the <u>same current</u> flows through <u>all components</u>.

Resistance Adds Up

1) In series circuits, the <u>total resistance</u> of two components is found by <u>adding up</u> their resistances.

2) R_{total} is the <u>total resistance</u> of the circuit. R_1 and R_2 are resistances of the <u>components</u>: ➜ $$R_{total} = R_1 + R_2$$

EXAMPLE: For the circuit diagram below, calculate the current passing through the circuit.

2 Ω   3 Ω

20 V

1) First find the <u>total resistance</u> by <u>adding together</u> the resistance of the two resistors. $R_{total} = 2 + 3 = 5\ \Omega$

2) Then <u>rearrange</u> $V = IR$ for I. $I = V \div R$

3) <u>Substitute</u> in the values you have and calculate the current. $= 20 \div 5$ $= 4\ A$

3) You need to be able to <u>explain</u> why adding resistors <u>in series</u> increases the total resistance of the circuit:

- Adding a resistor in <u>series</u> means the resistors have to <u>share</u> the total pd.
- This means the pd across each resistor is <u>lower</u>, so the <u>current</u> through each resistor is lower ($V = IR$).
- The current is the <u>same everywhere</u>.
- So the <u>total current</u> in the circuit is <u>reduced</u> when a resistor is added.
- This means the total <u>resistance</u> of the circuit has <u>gone up</u>.

Series circuits — they're no laughing matter...

Get those rules straightened out in your head, then have a quick go at this question to test what you can remember.

Q1   Calculate the total resistance of a 3 Ω resistor and a 7 Ω resistor connected in series.   [2 marks]

Parallel Circuits

Parallel circuits are much more sensible than series circuits, so they're much more common in real life.

Parallel Circuits — Every Component Connected Separately

1) In parallel circuits, each component is separately connected to the ends of the power supply.

2) Only ammeters break this rule, they're always in series (see p.185).

3) If you take out one of the loops in a parallel circuit, the things in the other loops won't be affected.

4) This means things in parallel can be switched on and off without affecting each other.

5) Everyday circuits often include a mixture of series and parallel parts.

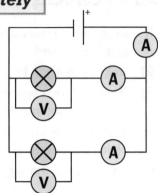

Current is Shared, Potential Difference is the Same Everywhere

1) In parallel circuits all components get the full source pd.

2) So the potential difference is the same across all components.

3) This means that identical bulbs connected in parallel will all be at the same brightness.

4) In parallel circuits the total current in a circuit is equal to the sum of all the currents through the separate components.

5) At junctions, the current either splits or rejoins.

6) The total current going into a junction must equal the total current leaving it. So in this circuit, $A_1 = A_2 + A_3$.

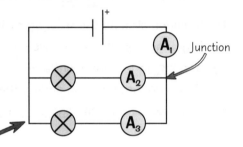

Junction

EXAMPLE:

Find the pd measured by V_1 and the current measured by A_1. The resistors are identical.

1) The resistors are in parallel, so the pd across each resistor is the same as the cell pd.

2) The current into the first junction is the same as the current out of it.

Cell pd = 6 V

$V_1 = 6$ V

In: 2 A   Out: 1 A + A_1

So $A_1 = 2 - 1 = 1$ A

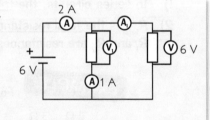

Adding a Resistor in Parallel Reduces the Total Resistance

1) The total resistance of two resistors connected in parallel, is less than the resistance of the smallest of the two resistors.

2) Here's why:

- If you add a resistor in parallel, both resistors still have the same potential difference across them as the power supply.
- This means the 'pushing force' making the current flow is still the same.
- But by adding another loop, the current has more than one direction to go in.
- More current can flow around the circuit, so the total current increases.
- This means the total resistance of the circuit is lower (as $R = V \div I$).

A current shared (between identical components) — is a current halved...

Parallel circuits are a bit more complicated but they crop up a lot, so get learning them.

Q1   Draw a circuit diagram for two filament lamps connected in parallel to a battery.   [2 marks]

Investigating Circuits

You saw on page 182 how the length of the wire affects its resistance. Now it's time to do an experiment to see how adding resistors in series or in parallel can affect the resistance of the whole circuit.

First Set Up the Basic Circuit

1) Find at least four identical resistors.
2) Build the circuit shown on the right.
3) Write down the pd of the battery. This is the pd of the circuit (V).
4) Read the current in the circuit (I) from the ammeter.
5) Calculate the resistance of the circuit using $R = V \div I$.

Investigate Adding Resistors in Series...

1) Add another resistor, in series with the first.
2) Measure the current again and calculate resistance again. The pd is the same as the pd of the battery.
3) Repeat steps 1 and 2 until you've added all of your resistors.

... and in Parallel

1) Build the basic circuit again. You already know its resistance.
2) Use the same equipment so it's a fair test.
3) Add another resistor, in parallel with the first.
4) Measure the total current through the circuit and calculate the overall resistance of the circuit. The pd is still the same as before.
5) Repeat steps 3 and 4 until you've added all of your resistors.

Draw Graphs so you can Compare your Results

1) Plot a graph of the number of resistors in the circuit against the total resistance.
2) You should get graphs that look like this:

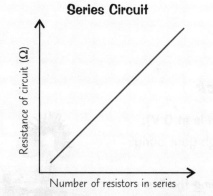

Series Circuit

Adding resistors in series increases the total resistance of the circuit.

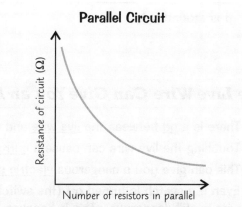

Parallel Circuit

The more resistors you add, the smaller the overall resistance becomes.

I can't resist a good practical...

Make sure you're completely happy building circuits from diagrams — this experiment is good practice.

Q1   A student is investigating how the resistance of a circuit changes as identical resistors are added in parallel. She plans to plot a graph of the total resistance of the circuit against the number of resistors in the circuit. Sketch the graph that you expect her to get.

[2 marks]

Electricity in the Home

There are two types of electricity supply — <u>alternating</u> and <u>direct currents</u>. Read on for more about both...

Mains Supply is ac, Battery Supply is dc

1) An <u>alternating potential difference</u> is a potential difference that is <u>constantly changing direction</u>. It produces an <u>alternating current</u> (<u>ac</u>).

2) In an <u>alternating current</u>, the <u>current</u> (flow of charge) is also <u>constantly changing direction</u>.

3) The <u>UK mains supply</u> (the electricity in your home) is an ac supply at around <u>230 V</u>.

4) The <u>frequency</u> (p.219) of the ac mains supply is <u>50 Hz</u> (hertz).

5) <u>Direct current</u> (<u>dc</u>) is a current that is always flowing in the <u>same direction</u>.

6) It's created by a <u>direct potential difference</u>. The <u>direction</u> of a direct potential difference is always the <u>same</u>.

Cells and batteries supply dc.

Most Cables Have Three Separate Wires

1) Most electrical appliances are connected to the mains supply by <u>three-core</u> cables.

2) They have <u>three wires</u> covered with <u>plastic insulation</u> inside them.

3) They are <u>coloured</u> so that it is easy to tell the different wires <u>apart</u>.

<u>LIVE WIRE</u> — <u>brown</u>.
1) The live wire provides the <u>alternating potential difference</u> from the mains supply.
2) It is at about <u>230 V</u>.

<u>NEUTRAL WIRE</u> — <u>blue</u>.
1) It <u>completes</u> the circuit.
2) Usually, current flows <u>in</u> through the <u>live</u> wire and <u>out</u> through the <u>neutral</u> wire.
3) It is around <u>0 V</u>.

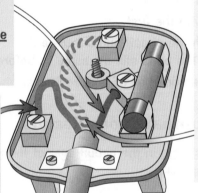

<u>EARTH WIRE</u> — <u>green</u> and <u>yellow</u>.
1) The earth wire is a <u>safety wire</u>.
2) It <u>stops</u> the appliance <u>becoming live</u>:
- It is connected to the <u>metal casing</u> of an appliance.
- If a <u>fault</u> causes the <u>live wire</u> to touch the casing, the <u>current</u> flows <u>away</u> through the <u>earth wire</u>.
3) It's <u>also</u> at 0 V.

The Live Wire Can Give You an Electric Shock

1) There is a <u>pd</u> between the <u>live wire</u> and your <u>body</u> (which is at 0 V).

2) Touching the live wire can cause a <u>current</u> to flow through your body.

3) This can give you a dangerous <u>electric shock</u>.

4) Even if a switch is turned <u>off</u> (the switch is <u>open</u>), touching the live wire is still <u>dangerous</u>. This is because it still has a pd of <u>230 V</u>.

5) <u>Any</u> connection between <u>live</u> and <u>earth</u> can be <u>dangerous</u>.

6) The pd could cause a <u>huge current</u> to flow, which could result in a <u>fire</u>.

Why are earth wires green and yellow — when mud is brown..?

Electricity is very useful, but it can also be very dangerous. Make sure you know the risks.

Q1   State the potential difference of: a) the live wire   b) the neutral wire   c) the earth wire.   [3 marks]

Power of Electrical Appliances

Energy is transferred between stores electrically (like you saw on page 167) by electrical appliances.

Energy is Transferred from Cells and Other Sources

1) When a charge moves around a circuit, work is done against the resistance of the circuit.
2) Whenever work is done, energy is transferred.
3) When the work is done by a charge, the energy is transferred electrically.
4) Electrical appliances transfer energy to components in the circuit when a current flows.

Kettles transfer energy electrically from the mains supply to the thermal energy store of the heating element inside the kettle.

Energy is transferred electrically from the battery of a handheld fan to the kinetic energy store of the fan's motor.

Energy Transferred Depends on the Power

1) The total energy transferred by an appliance depends on how long the appliance is on for and its power.
2) The power of an appliance is the energy that it transfers per second.
3) So the more energy it transfers in a given time, the higher its power.
4) The amount of energy transferred by electrical work is given by:

This equation should be familiar from page 172.

$$\text{Energy transferred (J)} = \text{Power (W)} \times \text{Time (s)} \qquad E = Pt$$

EXAMPLE: A 600 W microwave is used for 5 minutes. How much energy does it transfer?

1) Convert the time into seconds.
2) Substitute the numbers into $E = Pt$ to find the energy transferred.

$t = 5 \times 60 = 300 \text{ s}$
$E = Pt = 600 \times 300$
$\quad = 180\ 000 \text{ J}$

5) Appliances are often given a power rating. This is the power that they work at.
6) The power rating tells you how much energy is transferred between stores when the appliance is used.
7) An appliance with a higher power will cost more to run for a given time, as it uses more energy.

A 850 W microwave will transfer more energy between stores during 5 minutes than the 600 W microwave in the example above. This means it will cost more to use it for 5 minutes.

Have a break from all this work — or you'll have no energy left...

Get that equation for power stuck into your brain. Then become a powerful physicist by practising it.

Q1   An appliance transfers 6000 J of energy in 30 seconds. Calculate its power.   [3 marks]

Q2   Calculate the difference in the amount of energy transferred by a 250 W TV and a 375 W TV
         when they are both used for 60 seconds.   [4 marks]

More on Power

And we're not done yet. There are even more <u>power equations</u> for you to get your head around. How fun.

Potential Difference is Energy Transferred per Charge Passed

1) As a charge moves around a circuit, <u>energy</u> is transferred <u>to</u> or <u>from</u> it.

2) The <u>energy transferred</u> by a component depends on the <u>potential difference</u> across it and the <u>charge flowing</u> through it.

3) The <u>formula</u> is real simple:

Energy transferred (J) — $E = QV$ — Potential difference (V)

Charge flow (C)

EXAMPLE:

An electric toothbrush contains a 3.0 V battery.
140 C of charge passes through the toothbrush as it is used.
Calculate the energy transferred.

Just put the <u>charge</u> and <u>pd</u> values in to the equation: $E = QV = 140 × 3.0 = 420$ J

Power Also Depends on Current and Potential Difference

1) You saw on the previous page that power is <u>energy transferred</u> in a given <u>time</u>.

2) The <u>power</u> of an appliance can also be found using:

| Power (W) = Potential difference (V) × Current (A) | $P = VI$ |

3) You can also find the power if you <u>don't know</u> the <u>potential difference</u>, using:

Power (W) — $P = I^2R$ — Resistance (Ω)

(Current)^2
(A)^2

EXAMPLE:

A motor with a power of 1250 W has a resistance of 50 Ω. Calculate the current flowing through the motor.

Your calculator should have a '√' (square root) button to help with these calculations.

1) First <u>rearrange</u> the formula $P = I^2R$ to make I the subject.

   • <u>Divide</u> both sides by R.

   • Find the <u>square root</u> of both sides.

2) Now just <u>plug in</u> the numbers.

$P ÷ R = I^2$ so $I^2 = P ÷ R$

$I = \sqrt{P ÷ R}$

$I = \sqrt{1250 ÷ 50} = \sqrt{25}$
$= 5$ A

You have the power — now use your potential...

I'm afraid the best way to learn all of this is to just practise using those equations again and again. Sorry.

Q1 Calculate the energy transferred in a circuit with a pd of 200 V when 10 000 C of charge flows. [2 marks]

Q2 An appliance is connected to a 12 V source. A current of 4.0 A flows through it.
Calculate the power of the appliance. [2 marks]

The National Grid

Whoever you pay for your electricity, it's the national grid that gets it to you.

Electricity is Distributed via the National Grid

1) The national grid is a giant system of cables and transformers that covers the UK.

2) It transfers electrical power from power stations to consumers (anyone who is using electricity) across the UK.

3) Power stations have to produce enough electricity for everyone to have it when they need it.

4) More electricity is used when people get up in the morning, come home from school or work and when it starts to get dark or cold outside.

5) Power stations often run at well below their maximum power output, so that they can increase their power if needed.

6) This means that the national grid can cope with a high demand, even if another station shuts down without warning.

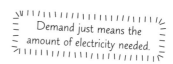
Demand just means the amount of electricity needed.

The National Grid Uses a High Pd and a Low Current

1) The national grid transfers loads of energy, so the power has to be very high.

2) To transmit this huge amount of power you need either a high potential difference or a high current.

3) This is because $P = VI$ (from the previous page).

4) A high current means loads of energy is lost to thermal energy stores as the wires heat up.

5) So the national grid transmits electricity at a very high pd. For a given power, the higher the pd the lower the current.

6) This reduces the energy lost, making the national grid an efficient way of transferring energy.

7) Step-up transformers are used to increase the pd from power stations to electric cables.

8) Step-down transformers bring the pd back down to safe levels before the electricity gets to homes.

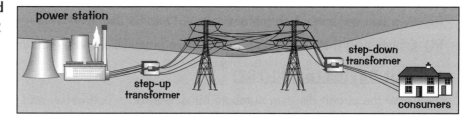

9) Transformers all have two coils, a primary coil and a secondary coil, joined with an iron core.

10) The potential difference across each coil and the currents through the coils are given by:

pd across primary coil (V)	×	current in primary coil (A)	=	pd across secondary coil (V)	×	current in secondary coil (A)

$$V_p I_p = V_s I_s$$

EXAMPLE:

A transformer has a pd of 6 V across its primary coil and a pd of 3 V across its secondary coil. The current through the secondary coil is 2 A. What is the current through the primary coil?

1) First rearrange the formula $V_p I_p = V_s I_s$ to make I_p the subject. Divide both sides by V_p.

$V_p I_p = V_s I_s$ so $I_p = (V_s I_s) \div V_p$

2) Now just plug in the numbers. Remember to do the multiplication in brackets first.

$I_p = (V_s I_s) \div V_p$
$= (3 × 2) \div 6 = 6 \div 6$
$= 1\,A$

Transformers — NOT robots in disguise...

Transformers can be a little tricky, but it's important that you can explain why they're used in the national grid.

Q1   What is the national grid?   [1 mark]

Revision Questions for Topics P1 & P2

And that's the end of Topic P2 — here's some revision questions to see how much has stuck in your head.

- Try these questions and tick off each one when you get it right.
- When you've done all the questions under a heading and are completely happy with it, tick it off.

Energy Stores and Transfers (p.167-169) ☑

1) Write down four energy stores. ☑
2) State the conservation of energy principle. ☑
3) Describe the energy transfers that occur as a ball is dropped. ☑
   but transferred that it's
4) If energy is transferred to an object's kinetic energy store, what happens to its speed? ☑

Specific Heat Capacity (p.170-171) ☑

5) What is the definition of the specific heat capacity of a material? ☑
6) Describe an experiment to find the specific heat capacity of a material. ☑

Power and Efficiency (p.172-174) ☑

7) Define power. Give two equations you could use to calculate power. ☑
8) How can you reduce unwanted energy transfers in a machine with moving parts? ☑
9) True or false? A high thermal conductivity means there is a high rate of energy transfer. ☑
10) What is the efficiency of an energy transfer? Give the equation that relates efficiency to power. ☑

Energy Resources and Trends in their Use (p.175-179) ☑

11) Name four renewable energy resources and four non-renewable energy resources. ☑
12) Give an example of how a renewable energy resource is used in everyday life. ☑
13) Give two ways in which the environment can be damaged when using fossil fuels. ☑
14) Explain why the UK is trying to use more renewable energy resources in the future. ☑

Circuit Basics (p.180-187) ☑

15) Draw the circuit diagram symbols for a resistor, a voltmeter, an LED and a diode. ☑
16) State an equation that links current, charge flow and time. Write down the units of each. ☑
17) What is the equation that links potential difference, current and resistance? ☑
18) Describe how you would investigate how the length of a wire affects its resistance. ☑
19) What is an *I-V* characteristic? ☑
20) What happens to the resistance of a thermistor as it gets hotter? ☑
21) True or false? Potential difference is shared between components in a series circuit. ☑
22) How does the overall resistance of a circuit change when a resistor is added in parallel? ☑
23) Describe an experiment to investigate how adding resistors in series and parallel affects the total resistance of the circuit. ☑

Electricity in the Home (p.188) ☑

24) What is the potential difference and the frequency of the UK mains supply? ☑
25) Name and give the colours of the three wires in a three-core cable. ☑

Power and the National Grid (p.189-191) ☑

26) Describe the useful energy transfer that occurs for a battery-powered fan. ☑
27) State three equations that can be used to calculate electrical power. ☑
28) How are step-up and step-down transformers used in the national grid? ☑

The Particle Model and Motion in Gases

Everything is made up of small particles. The particle model describes how these particles behave.

There are Three States of Matter

1) The three states of matter are solid (e.g. ice), liquid (e.g. water) and gas (e.g. water vapour).
2) The particle model explains the differences between the states of matter:
   - The particles of a certain material are always the same, no matter what state it is in.
   - But the particles have different amounts of energy in different states.
   - And the forces between particles are different in each state.
   - This means that the particles are arranged (laid out) differently in different states.

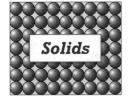
Solids

1) Particles are held close together by strong forces in a regular, fixed pattern.
2) The particles don't have much energy.
3) So they can only vibrate (jiggle about) around a fixed position.

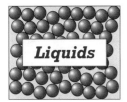
Liquids

1) The particles are held close together in an irregular pattern.
2) The particles have more energy than the particles in a solid.
3) They can move past each other in random directions at low speeds.

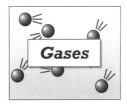
Gases

1) The particles aren't held close together. There are no forces between them.
2) The particles have more energy than in liquids and solids.
3) The particles constantly move around in random directions at a range of speeds.

Gas Particles Bump into Things and Create Pressure

1) Particles in a gas are free to move around.
2) They collide with (bump into) each other and the sides of the container they're in.
3) When they hit something, they apply a force to it. Pressure is the force applied over a given area.

Increasing the Temperature of a Gas Increases its Pressure

1) The temperature of a gas depends on the average energy in the kinetic energy stores of the gas particles.
2) The hotter the gas, the higher the average energy.
3) If particles have more energy in their kinetic stores, they move faster.
4) So the hotter the gas, the faster the particles move on average.
5) Faster particles hit the sides of the container more often. This increases the force on the container.
6) So increasing the temperature of a gas increases its pressure.
7) This only works if the space the gas takes up (the volume) doesn't change.

Don't let the pressure of exams get to you...

Get your head around the particle model before moving on to the rest of the topic.

Q1   Explain why decreasing the temperature of a gas in a fixed container decreases its pressure.   [3 marks]

Density of Materials

The <u>density</u> of an object tells you how many of its <u>particles</u> are squished into a <u>given space</u>.

The Particle Model can also Explain Density

1) <u>Density</u> is a measure of <u>how much mass</u> there is in a <u>certain space</u>.

2) You can work out density using:

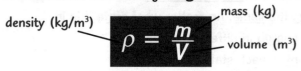

density (kg/m³)

mass (kg)

$$\rho = \frac{m}{V}$$

volume (m³)

3) The density of an object depends on <u>what it's made of</u> and how its <u>particles</u> are <u>arranged</u>.

4) A <u>dense</u> material has its particles <u>packed tightly</u> together.

5) So, <u>solids</u> are generally <u>denser</u> than <u>liquids</u>.

6) And <u>liquids</u> are generally <u>denser</u> than <u>gases</u>.

EXAMPLE:

A 0.0020 m³ block of aluminium has a mass of 5.4 kg.
Calculate the density of aluminium.

density = mass ÷ volume
= 5.4 ÷ 0.0020
= 2700 kg/m³

You Need to be Able to Measure Density in Different Ways

PRACTICAL

To find the density of a regularly shaped object (e.g. a cuboid)

1) Use a <u>balance</u> to measure its <u>mass</u> (see p.232).

2) Measure its <u>length</u>, <u>width</u> and <u>height</u> with a <u>ruler</u>.

3) Then calculate its <u>volume</u> using the <u>formula</u> for that shape.

4) Use <u>density = mass ÷ volume</u> to find the density.

The volume of a cuboid is equal to length × width × height.

To find the density of an irregularly shaped object (e.g. an awards statue)

1) Use a <u>balance</u> to measure its <u>mass</u>.

2) <u>Fill</u> a <u>eureka can</u> (a can with a spout in its side) with water.

3) Place a <u>measuring cylinder</u> (p.232) under the spout.

4) Place your object <u>into the water</u>.
This will <u>push</u> some of the water <u>out</u> through the spout.

5) <u>Measure the volume</u> of water that has collected in the measuring cylinder.

6) This is <u>equal to</u> the <u>volume</u> of the <u>object</u>.

7) Use the <u>formula</u> above to find the object's <u>density</u>.

There's more about eureka cans on page 233.

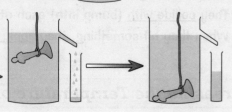

To find the density of a liquid

1) Place a <u>measuring cylinder</u> on a balance and <u>zero</u> the balance (p.232).

2) Pour <u>50 ml</u> of the liquid into the measuring cylinder.

3) Record the liquid's <u>mass</u> shown on the mass balance.

4) Use the <u>formula</u> above to find the <u>density</u>. The <u>volume</u> is <u>50 cm³</u>, or <u>0.00005 m³</u>.

For both of these experiments, you'll need to know that 1 ml = 1 cm³ and that 1 cm³ = 0.000001 m³.

Who can measure volume — the eureka can can, oh the eureka can can...

Remember — density is all about how close together the particles in a substance are. Nice and simple really.

Q1   A cube has a volume of 0.05 m³. It has a density of 40 kg/m³. Calculate its mass.   [3 marks]

Internal Energy and Changes of State

This page is all about heating things. Take a look at your <u>specific heat capacity</u> notes (p.170) before you start. You need to understand it and be able to use $\Delta E = mc\Delta\theta$ for this topic too I'm afraid.

Internal Energy is the Total Energy Stored by Particles in a System

1) The <u>energy stored</u> in a <u>system</u> (p.167) is stored by its <u>particles</u> (atoms and molecules).
2) The particles have energy in their <u>kinetic energy stores</u>.
3) They also have energy in their <u>potential energy stores</u> because of their <u>positions</u>.
4) The <u>internal energy</u> of a system is the <u>total energy</u> that all its particles have in their <u>kinetic</u> and <u>potential</u> energy stores.

Heating Increases Internal Energy

1) <u>Heating</u> a system <u>transfers</u> energy to its particles.
2) This increases the system's <u>internal energy</u>.
3) This leads to a <u>change in temperature</u> or a <u>change of state</u> (e.g. melting or boiling).
4) How much the temperature changes depends on the <u>mass</u> of the system, its <u>specific heat capacity</u> (p.170) and how much <u>energy</u> is transferred to it.
5) You can see this from the <u>equation</u> $\Delta E = mc\Delta\theta$.
6) A <u>change of state</u> happens when the particles have enough energy in their <u>kinetic energy stores</u> to <u>break the bonds</u> holding them together.

Mass Doesn't Change in a Change of State

1) A <u>change of state</u> can happen because of <u>cooling</u>, as well as heating.
2) The <u>changes of state</u> are:

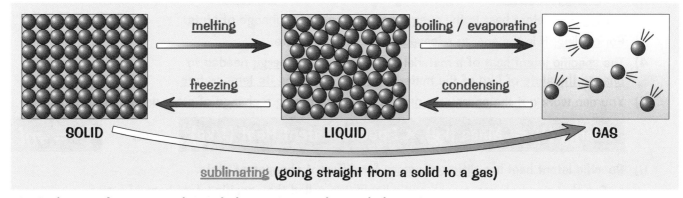

sublimating (going straight from a solid to a gas)

3) A <u>change of state</u> is a <u>physical</u> change (not a chemical change).
4) This means you <u>don't</u> end up with a <u>new material</u>.
5) The particles are just arranged in a <u>different way</u> (p.193).
6) The <u>number of particles</u> stays the same when the state changes.
7) This means the <u>mass is conserved</u> (it <u>doesn't change</u>).
8) If you <u>reverse</u> a change of state, the material will <u>get back</u> all the properties it had <u>before</u> the change.

Breaking Bonds — Blofeld never quite manages it...

I'll say it one more time — have a look back over your specific heat capacity notes. You'll need them, I promise.

Q1   Name the following changes of state:
   a) solid to liquid   b) liquid to gas   c) gas to liquid   [3 marks]

Specific Latent Heat

Specific latent heat sounds like specific heat capacity but it's very different. It's all to do with changing state.

A Change of State means Internal Energy Changes but Not Temperature

1) Heating a material transfers energy to the material.
2) This either increases the temperature of the material or changes its state (p.193).
3) During a change of state, the temperature doesn't change. But the internal energy does.
4) The energy transferred is used to break bonds between particles. It is not used to raise the temperature.
5) When a material cools, energy is transferred away from it.
6) As a material condenses or freezes, bonds form between particles. This causes energy to be released.
7) So its internal energy decreases, but its temperature stays the same during the change of state.
8) The flat spots on these graphs show that the temperature doesn't change during a change of state.

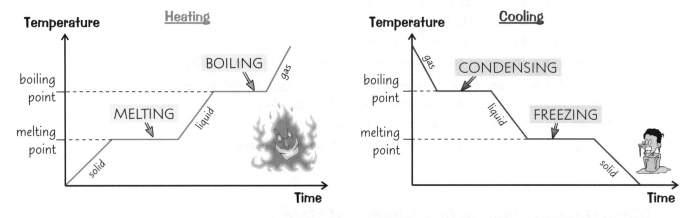

Specific Latent Heat is the Energy Needed to Change the State of a 1 kg Mass

1) The energy transferred during a change of state is called latent heat.
2) For heating, latent heat is the energy gained to cause a change of state.
3) For cooling, it is the energy released by a change in state.
4) The specific latent heat of a material is the amount of energy needed to change the state of 1 kg of the material without changing its temperature.

> Don't get this confused with specific heat capacity (p.170) which is to do with changes in temperature, not changes of state.

5) You can work out the energy needed (or released) during a change of state using this formula:

Energy (J) = Mass (kg) × Specific Latent Heat (J/kg)	or:	$E = mL$

6) Specific latent heat has different names for different changes of state:
   - For changing between a solid and a liquid it is called the specific latent heat of fusion.
   - For changing between a liquid and a gas it is called the specific latent heat of vaporisation.

EXAMPLE: The specific latent heat of vaporisation for water is 2 260 000 J/kg. How much energy is needed to completely boil 1.50 kg of water once it has reached its boiling point?

1) The mass and specific latent heat are in the right units, so just put them into the formula.

$$E = mL$$
$$= 1.50 × 2 260 000$$

2) The units for the answer are joules because it's energy.

$$= 3 390 000 \text{ J}$$

My specific latent heat of revision* is 500 J/kg...

There's a lot on this page. Re-read it and then have a go at this question to practise what you've learnt.

Q1   The specific latent heat of fusion for a solid is 120 000 J/kg. How much energy is needed to melt 0.250 kg of the solid when it is already at its melting temperature?   [2 marks]

*the amount of energy required to turn 1 kg of revision notes into exam success

The Current Model of the Atom

You need to know everything on page 104 for both your <u>chemistry</u> and <u>physics</u> exams.

Models of the Atom have Changed Over Time

1) <u>Scientific models</u> (p.1) change over <u>time</u>. This happens when <u>new evidence</u> is found that <u>can't</u> be explained by the <u>current model</u>.

2) This is what happened with the <u>model of the atom</u>.

3) You need to **LEARN** the <u>history of the atom</u> that's on page 104 for your physics exam. Make sure you can explain the <u>experiments</u> that led to <u>changes</u> in the model of the atom.

4) Based on current evidence scientists believe the <u>nuclear model of the atom</u> (see below) is the best description we have.

You Need to Know the Current Model of the Atom

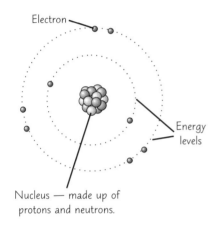

Electron

Nucleus — made up of protons and neutrons.

Energy levels

1) The current model of the atom is a <u>nuclear model</u>.

2) This means there is a <u>nucleus</u> in the <u>centre</u> surrounded by electrons.

3) Atoms are <u>very small</u>. The <u>radius</u> of an atom is about 1×10^{-10} m (see p.12 for more on standard form).

4) The <u>nucleus</u> is <u>tiny</u>, but it makes up most of the <u>mass</u> of the atom.

5) The radius of the nucleus is about <u>10 000</u> times smaller than the <u>radius</u> of the <u>atom</u>.

6) The <u>nucleus</u> is made up of <u>protons</u> and <u>neutrons</u>.

7) <u>Protons</u> are <u>positively charged</u> and <u>neutrons</u> have <u>no charge</u>. So the <u>nucleus</u> is <u>positively charged</u>.

8) Electrons have a <u>negative charge</u>. They move <u>around</u> (orbit) the nucleus at different distances.

9) These distances are known as <u>energy levels</u>.

10) <u>Atoms</u> have <u>no overall charge</u>. The <u>number of protons = the number of electrons</u>.

Electrons can Move Between Energy Levels

1) The <u>further</u> an <u>energy level</u> is from the <u>nucleus</u>, the <u>more energy</u> an electron in that energy level has.

2) <u>Electrons</u> can <u>move between energy levels</u> by <u>absorbing</u> (taking in) or <u>releasing electromagnetic radiation</u> (p.223).

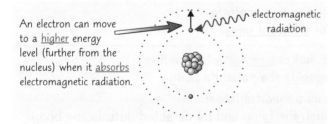

An electron can move to a <u>higher</u> energy level (further from the nucleus) when it <u>absorbs</u> electromagnetic radiation.

electromagnetic radiation

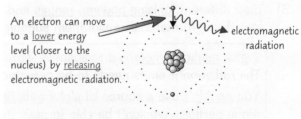

An electron can move to a <u>lower</u> energy level (closer to the nucleus) by <u>releasing</u> electromagnetic radiation.

electromagnetic radiation

3) If an electron in an <u>outer</u> energy level <u>absorbs</u> electromagnetic radiation, it can <u>leave the atom</u>.

4) If an atom <u>loses one or more electrons</u> it turns into a <u>positively charged ion</u>.

These models don't have anything on my toy trains...

This is science in action folks — as new evidence came along, the model of the atom was changed and updated.

Q1 a) What particles make up the nucleus?   [2 marks]
    b) State the radius of an atom and describe how this compares to the size of its nucleus.   [2 marks]

Isotopes and Nuclear Radiation

Isotopes and ionisation. They sound similar, but they're not, so read this page carefully.

Isotopes are Different Forms of the Same Element

1) The number of protons in an atom is called its atomic number.
2) The protons in a nucleus give the nucleus its positive charge.
   So the atomic number of an atom tells you the charge on the nucleus.
3) The mass number of an atom is the sum of the number of protons and the number of neutrons.
4) An element is a substance only containing atoms with the same number of protons.
5) You can show information about an atom of an element like this.
6) Atoms of an element with the same number of protons but a different number of neutrons are called isotopes.
7) Isotopes of an element have the same atomic number, but a different mass number.

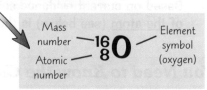

Mass number → $^{16}_{8}\text{O}$ ← Element symbol (oxygen)
Atomic number

Some Isotopes are Unstable

1) Some isotopes are unstable.
   They emit (give out) radiation from their nuclei to try and become more stable.
2) This process is called radioactive decay.
3) The radiation emitted is called nuclear radiation. There are four different types of nuclear radiation:
4) Isotopes that give out nuclear radiation are called radioactive isotopes.

Types of Nuclear Radiation

- An alpha particle (α) is two neutrons and two protons.
- A beta particle (β) is a fast-moving electron.
- Gamma rays (γ) are waves of electromagnetic radiation (p.223).
- Neutrons (n).

You Need to Know the Properties of Ionising Nuclear Radiation

1) Ionising radiation is radiation that can knock electrons off atoms and turn them into ions.
2) The ionising power of radiation is how easily it can do this.
3) Alpha particles, beta particles and gamma rays are all types of ionising radiation.
4) They all have different properties:

'Range in air' is the distance the radiation can travel through air.

Type of radiation	Ionising power	Range in air	Stopped by
alpha particles	strong	a few centimetres	a sheet of paper
beta particles	moderate	a few metres	a sheet of aluminium
gamma rays	weak	a long distance	thick sheets of lead or metres of concrete

5) Their different ionising powers, ranges and abilities to penetrate (get through) materials make them suitable for different uses.

> E.g. A medical tracer is a radioactive isotope that is injected into a patient.
> The radiation it emits needs to be detected outside the patient's body.
>
> You couldn't use a source of alpha radiation as a medical tracer.
> Alpha particles wouldn't be able to pass through the body and be detected outside the body.
> They are also very ionising and so could do a lot of damage (see p.201).
>
> Medical tracers usually emit gamma rays. Gamma rays are only weakly ionising and easily pass through the body. This means they can be easily detected and do less harm than alpha particles.

Isotopes of an outfit — same dress, different accessories...

Knowing the different kinds of radiation and what can stop them usually bags you a few marks in an exam.

Q1   Radiation is directed at medical equipment sealed in packaging. The radiation needs to reach the equipment to sterilise it. Explain whether alpha particles would be suitable for this use.   [2 marks]

Nuclear Equations

Nuclear equations show radioactive decay. They look quite scary but this should help you get the hang of them.

Mass and Atomic Numbers Have to Balance

1) Nuclear equations are a way of showing radioactive decay (p.198).

2) They're normally written like this:

> nucleus before decay → nucleus after decay + radiation emitted

3) There is one golden rule to remember:

> The total mass and atomic numbers must be equal on both sides of the arrow.

Alpha Decay Decreases the Charge and Mass of the Nucleus

1) Alpha decay is when an alpha particle is emitted from a radioactive nucleus.

2) An alpha particle is made up of two protons and two neutrons. It is the same as a helium nucleus.

3) When a nucleus emits an alpha particle, its atomic number goes down by 2 and its mass number goes down by 4.

4) The charge of the nucleus decreases when it gives out an alpha particle.

5) An alpha particle is usually written as a helium nucleus in a nuclear equation: ^4_2He.

The nuclear equation for the decay of uranium (U) to thorium (Th) is:

Mass number → $^{238}_{92}U \rightarrow ^{234}_{90}Th + ^4_2He$ ← Atomic number

The mass numbers on each side are equal: $238 = 234 + 4$

The atomic numbers on each side are equal: $92 = 90 + 2$

Beta Decay Increases the Charge of the Nucleus

1) Beta decay is when a beta particle is emitted from a radioactive nucleus.

2) During beta decay, a neutron in the nucleus turns into a proton.

3) This means the nucleus has one more proton, so its atomic number goes up by 1.

4) It also means the positive charge of the nucleus increases.

5) A beta particle has an atomic number of −1 so the atomic numbers balance on each side of the equation.

6) Protons and neutrons have the same mass, so the mass of the nucleus doesn't change.

7) A beta particle is an electron. It is written as $^0_{-1}e$ in nuclear equations.

The nuclear equation for the decay of carbon (C) to nitrogen (N) is:

$^{14}_6C \rightarrow ^{14}_7N + ^0_{-1}e$

The mass numbers on each side are equal: $14 = 14 + 0$

The atomic numbers on each side are equal: $6 = 7 - 1$

Gamma Rays Don't Change the Charge or Mass of the Nucleus

1) Gamma rays are a way of getting rid of extra energy from a nucleus.

2) When they are emitted, they don't change the mass or charge of the atom and nucleus.

Did someone say something about gammon?

Nuclear equations need practice to really get your head around. Why not try this question on for size?

Q1 What type of radiation is given off in this decay? $^8_3Li \rightarrow ^8_4Be + radiation$. [1 mark]

Half-life

How quickly unstable isotopes decay is measured using <u>activity</u> and <u>half-life</u> — two very <u>important</u> terms.

The Activity of a Source is the Number of Decays per Second

1) The <u>radiation</u> given out by a <u>radioactive decay</u> can be measured with a <u>Geiger-Muller</u> tube and <u>counter</u> detector.

2) The <u>number of decays</u> the counter measures <u>every second</u> is called the <u>count-rate</u>.

3) The <u>activity</u> of a radioactive source is the <u>rate</u> at which it decays. This means how many <u>unstable nuclei</u> decay <u>every second</u>.

4) Activity is measured in <u>becquerels</u>, <u>Bq</u>. 1 Bq is <u>1 decay per second</u>.

Radioactivity is a Totally Random Process

1) Radioactive decay is entirely <u>random</u>. So you <u>can't predict</u> exactly <u>which</u> nucleus in a sample will decay <u>next</u>, or <u>when</u> any one of them will decay.

2) But you <u>can</u> predict <u>how long</u> it will take for half of the <u>nuclei</u> to decay. This is known as a <u>half-life</u>.

Nuclei means more than one nucleus.

> The <u>half-life</u> is the time taken for the <u>number of nuclei</u> of a radioactive isotope in a sample to <u>halve</u>.

3) Half-life is also the <u>time</u> taken for the <u>count-rate</u> or <u>activity</u> of a sample to fall to <u>half</u> of its <u>initial (starting) value</u>.

4) The half-life of a radioactive sample will <u>always be the same</u>. This means it doesn't matter what activity you <u>start</u> with when doing half-life calculations (see below).

You Need to be able to Calculate Half-Lives

1) You may be asked to calculate the <u>half-life</u> of a source.

2) You just need to find out <u>how long</u> it takes for the <u>activity</u> or <u>count-rate</u> of the source to <u>halve</u>.

EXAMPLE: The activity of a radioactive source over time is shown on the graph on the right. Using the graph find the half-life of the source.

1) The <u>initial activity</u> when time = 0 s is 800 Bq.

2) Use the graph to find the time when the activity has halved to <u>400 Bq</u>. This was at $t = $ <u>2 s</u>.

3) So, the time for the activity to halve was <u>2 s</u>.

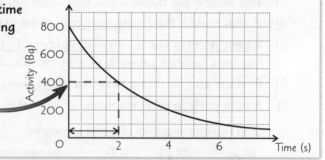

EXAMPLE: The activity of a radioactive isotope was measured. Initially it was 64 Bq. 12 seconds later it had fallen to 16 Bq. Calculate the half-life of the sample.

1) First, find how many half-lives it takes for the activity to fall to from <u>64 Bq</u> to <u>16 Bq</u>.

After one half life, the activity will be 64 ÷ 2 = 32 Bq. After two half lives, the activity will be 32 ÷ 2 = 16 Bq

2) So you know 12 s is equal to <u>two</u> half lives. <u>Divide 12</u> by <u>2</u> to find the time for <u>one half life</u>.

Time for one half life = 12 ÷ 2 = **6 s**

The half-life of a box of chocolates is about five minutes...

Half-life is really important in radioactivity. Make sure you know what it is and how to calculate it.

Q1   What is meant by the activity of a radioactive substance?   [1 mark]

Irradiation and Contamination

There are <u>risks</u> when working with radiation. Make sure you know how to <u>reduce them</u>.

Ionising Radiation can Damage Cells

1) There are <u>hazards</u> (dangers) you need to <u>protect yourself</u> from when working with <u>radioactive sources</u>.

2) <u>Ionising radiation</u> can enter <u>living cells</u> and <u>ionise</u> (p.197) atoms in them.

3) This can <u>damage</u> the cells. This may cause <u>cancer</u> or <u>kill</u> cells off completely.

We need to know how radiation affects the human body, so we can protect ourselves from harm. So it's really important for research into the effects of radiation to be published and checked by peer review — see page 1.

Exposure to Radiation is called Irradiation

1) Objects <u>near</u> a radioactive source can be <u>irradiated</u> by it. This means <u>radiation</u> from the radioactive <u>source</u> will reach the object.

2) Irradiated objects <u>don't become radioactive</u> themselves.

3) The <u>further</u> you are from a particular source, the <u>less radiation</u> will <u>reach</u> you.

4) To help <u>stop irradiation</u> happening, you should:

- <u>Store</u> radioactive sources in <u>lead-lined boxes</u> when they're not being used.
- Stand behind <u>barriers</u> that will absorb radiation when using sources.
- Keep the source as <u>far away</u> from you as possible, e.g. hold it at arm's length.

Warning: You won't become a superhero from being irradiated.

Contamination is Radioactive Particles Getting Onto Objects

1) If <u>unwanted radioactive atoms</u> get onto or into an object, the object is <u>contaminated</u>.

2) These <u>contaminating atoms</u> might then decay and release <u>radiation</u> which could <u>harm</u> you.

3) Being contaminated by a source may cause <u>more damage</u> than if you are irradiated by the same source, as you may <u>carry</u> it for a <u>long time</u>.

4) To help <u>stop contamination</u>, you should wear <u>gloves</u> and use <u>tongs</u> when handling radioactive sources.

People whose jobs involve radioactive materials often wear protective suits and face masks to help stop them being contaminated.

How Dangerous Irradiation and Contamination are Depends on the Source

1) <u>Beta</u> and <u>gamma</u> sources are the <u>most dangerous</u> to be <u>IRRADIATED</u> by. These types of radiation have <u>long ranges</u> (p.198). That means <u>more radiation</u> will <u>reach you</u> from a beta or gamma source than from an alpha source at the same distance.

2) They can also <u>penetrate</u> (travel through) your body and may damage your <u>organs</u>. Alpha is <u>less dangerous</u> because it <u>can't get through the skin</u> and is easily blocked, e.g. by a <u>small air gap</u> (p.198).

1) <u>INSIDE the body</u>, alpha sources are the <u>most dangerous</u> to be <u>CONTAMINATED</u> by. This is because <u>alpha particles</u> are the <u>most ionising</u> type of radiation.

2) <u>Beta</u> particles and <u>gamma rays</u> are <u>less damaging</u> because they are <u>less ionising</u>.

3) <u>Gamma</u> sources are the <u>least dangerous</u> inside the body. This is because <u>gamma rays</u> are the <u>least ionising</u> type of radiation and they mostly <u>pass straight</u> out without doing any damage.

4) <u>OUTSIDE</u> of the body, an <u>alpha</u> source is the <u>least dangerous</u> to be <u>contaminated</u> by. This is because alpha particles <u>can't</u> get through the <u>skin</u> and <u>damage your organs</u>.

Top tip number 364 — if something is radioactive, don't lick it...

Make sure you can describe how to prevent irradiation and contamination, and why it's so important that you do.

Q1 Explain why a gamma source is more dangerous to be irradiated by than an alpha source. [2 marks]

Revision Questions for Topics P3 & P4

Well, that's the end of Topic P4 — hopefully it wasn't too painful. Time to see how much you've absorbed.
- Try these questions and tick off each one when you get it right.
- When you've done all the questions under a heading and are completely happy with it, tick it off.

The Particle Model and Motion in Gases (p.193) ☑

1) What are the three states of matter? ☑
2) Describe how particles are arranged in each state of matter. ☑
3) True or false? The colder a gas, the higher the average energy in the kinetic energy stores of its particles. ☑

Density of Materials (p.194) ☑

4) What is the formula for density? ☑
5) True or false? Solids are usually denser than gases. ☑
6) Describe how you could find the volume of an irregularly shaped object. ☑

Internal Energy and Changes of State (p.195-196) ☑

7) What is internal energy? ☑
8) What happens to the particles in a substance when that substance is heated? ☑
9) Name the five changes of state. ☑
10) True or false? Mass stays the same when a substance changes state. ☑
11) Sketch a graph of temperature against time for a gas being cooled. Your graph should show the point that the gas turns into a liquid and the point that the liquid turns into a solid. ☑
12) What is specific latent heat? ☑

The Atomic Model (p.197) ☑

13) What is the overall charge of an atom? ☑
14) What happens when an electron in an atom gives out electromagnetic radiation? ☑
15) What happens to an atom if it loses one or more of its electrons? ☑

Nuclear Decay and Half-life (p.198-200) ☑

16) What is the atomic number of an atom? What is the mass number of an atom? ☑
17) Which number is the same for all atoms of an element: the atomic number or the mass number? ☑
18) What is an isotope? ☑
19) For the three types of ionising nuclear radiation, give: a) their ionising power, b) their range in air. ☑
20) How does the emission of an alpha particle change the atomic number of an atom? ☑
21) Draw the symbols for both alpha and beta radiation in nuclear equations. ☑
22) What is the activity of a substance measured in? ☑
23) Define half-life in terms of the number of nuclei of a radioactive isotope. ☑
24) Describe how to find a radioactive source's half-life, given a graph of its activity over time. ☑

Irradiation and Contamination (p.201) ☑

25) What is irradiation? ☑
26) Give two examples of how to stop: a) contamination,   b) irradiation. ☑
27) Compare the hazards of being irradiated and contaminated by:
     a) an alpha source,   b) a gamma source. ☑

Contact and Non-Contact Forces

When you're talking about the <u>forces</u> acting on an object, it's not enough to just talk about the <u>size</u> of each force. You need to know their <u>direction</u> too — force is a <u>vector</u>, with a size and a direction.

Force is a Vector Quantity

1) Vector quantities have a <u>magnitude (size)</u> and a <u>direction</u>. For example:

   <u>Vector quantities</u>: force, velocity, displacement, acceleration, momentum

2) Some quantities have a magnitude but <u>no direction</u>. These are called <u>scalar quantities</u>. Here are some examples of scalar quantities:

   <u>Scalar quantities</u>: speed, distance, mass, temperature, time

3) Vectors are usually represented by an <u>arrow</u>.
4) The <u>length</u> of the arrow shows the <u>magnitude</u>.
5) The <u>direction</u> of the arrow shows the <u>direction of the quantity</u>.

Forces Can be Contact or Non-Contact

I should have chosen a non-contact sport...

1) A <u>force</u> is a <u>push</u> or a <u>pull</u> that acts on an object.
2) Forces are caused by objects <u>interacting</u> with each other.
3) All forces are either <u>contact</u> or <u>non-contact</u> forces.
4) When <u>two objects</u> have to be <u>touching</u> for a force to act, the force is a <u>contact force</u>.

   <u>Contact force examples</u>: friction, air resistance, tension, normal contact force

5) If the objects <u>do not need to be touching</u> for the force to act, the force is a <u>non-contact force</u>.

   When an object exerts a force on a second object, the second object pushes back. This is the normal contact force.

   <u>Non-contact force examples</u>: magnetic force, gravitational force, electrostatic force

6) When two objects <u>interact</u>, a <u>force</u> is produced on <u>both</u> objects. The forces on the two objects are <u>equal in size</u> but act in <u>opposite directions</u>.
7) These two forces are called an <u>interaction pair</u>.

> • The <u>gravitational attraction</u> between the Earth and the Sun is an example of an <u>interaction pair</u>.
> • A gravitational force acts on the Earth <u>attracting</u> it to the Sun.
> • At the same time a force acts on the Sun <u>attracting</u> it towards the Earth.
> • These forces are the <u>same size</u> but act in <u>opposite directions</u>.

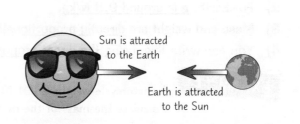

Sun is attracted to the Earth

Earth is attracted to the Sun

My life's feeling pretty scalar — I've no idea where I'm headed...

This stuff is vital to understand if you want to make it through the rest of this topic. Better get your head down.

Q1   Name two examples of: a) a scalar quantity   b) a vector quantity   [4 marks]

Q2   A tennis ball is dropped from a height. Name one contact force and one non-contact force that act on the ball as it falls.   [2 marks]

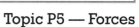

Weight, Mass and Gravity

Mass and weight are <u>NOT</u> the same... Read on to find out <u>why</u>. You know you want to.

Mass is Measured in kg

1) <u>Mass</u> is just the amount of <u>matter (stuff)</u> in an object.
2) It's measured in <u>kilograms</u>, kg.
3) Scientists sometimes think of all the mass in an object as being at <u>one single point</u> in the object.
4) This point is called the <u>centre of mass</u>.

Weight is Measured in Newtons

1) <u>Weight</u> is the <u>force</u> acting on an object due to <u>gravity</u>.
2) You can think of this force as acting from an object's <u>centre of mass</u>.
3) Close to Earth, this force is caused by the <u>gravitational field</u> around the Earth.
4) The <u>weight</u> of an object depends on its <u>mass</u> and the <u>strength of the gravitational field</u> it's in.
5) The <u>gravitational field strength of Earth</u> changes slightly depending on <u>where you are</u>.
6) So the weight of an object depends on its <u>location</u>.
7) Unlike the <u>mass</u> of an object which is <u>always the same</u>.
8) Weight is measured in <u>newtons</u>, <u>N</u>.
9) It can be measured with a calibrated <u>spring</u> balance (or <u>newtonmeter</u>).

centre of mass

weight

Mass and Weight are Directly Proportional

1) You can calculate the <u>weight</u> of an object if you know its <u>mass</u> (*m*) and the <u>strength</u> of the <u>gravitational field</u> that it is in (*g*):

> Weight (N) = Mass (kg) × Gravitational Field Strength (N/kg)

2) For Earth, <u>*g* is around 9.8 N/kg</u>.
3) Mass and weight are <u>directly proportional</u>.
4) You can write this, using the <u>direct proportionality symbol</u>, as $W \propto m$.

EXAMPLE: A motorcycle weighs 2401 N on Earth.
Calculate the mass of the motorcycle. (*g* = 9.8 N/kg)

1) First, <u>rearrange</u> $W = mg$ to find <u>mass</u>.   mass = weight ÷ gravitational field strength
2) Then, put in the numbers to <u>calculate</u> the mass.   mass = 2401 ÷ 9.8 = 245 kg

Diet tip — move to the moon*...

Remember that weight is a force due to gravity and mass is just how much stuff there is.

Q1   Calculate the weight in newtons of a 5 kg mass:
   a) on Earth (*g* = 9.8 N/kg)   b) on the Moon (*g* = 1.6 N/kg)   [4 marks]

*If you don't get it, have a go at Q1

Resultant Forces and Work Done

I'm sure you're no stranger to <u>doing work</u>, but in physics it's all to do with <u>transferring energy</u>.

A Resultant Force is the Overall Force on a Point or Object

1) If a <u>number of forces</u> act at a single point, you can replace them with a <u>single force</u>.

2) This single force is called the <u>resultant force</u>.

3) It has the <u>same effect</u> as all the original forces added together.

4) You can find the resultant force when forces are acting in a <u>straight line</u>.
   <u>Add together</u> forces acting in the <u>same</u> direction and <u>take away</u> any going in the <u>opposite</u> direction.

A <u>trolley</u> is pulled by two children. One child pulls the trolley with a force of 5 N to the <u>left</u>. The other pulls the trolley with a force of 10 N to the <u>right</u>.

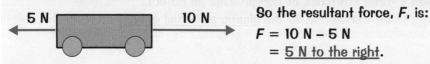

So the resultant force, *F*, is:

F = 10 N – 5 N

= <u>5 N to the right</u>.

If a Force Moves an Object, Work is Done

When a <u>force</u> moves an object through a <u>distance</u>, <u>ENERGY IS TRANSFERRED</u> and <u>WORK IS DONE</u> on the object.

1) To make an object move, a force <u>must</u> act on it.

2) The force does '<u>work</u>' to move the object.

3) This causes <u>energy</u> to be <u>transferred to</u> the object.

4) The force usually <u>does work</u> against frictional forces too.

5) Doing work against frictional forces causes energy to be transferred to the <u>thermal energy store</u> of the object.

6) This causes the <u>temperature</u> of the object to <u>increase</u>.

'Work done' and 'energy transferred' are the same thing. You need to be able to <u>describe</u> how energy is transferred when work is done. Look back at p.168 for more on this.

- When you <u>push</u> something along a <u>rough surface</u> (like a <u>carpet</u>) you are doing work <u>against frictional forces</u>.
- Some energy is <u>transferred</u> to the <u>kinetic energy store</u> of the <u>object</u> because it starts <u>moving</u>.
- Some is also transferred to <u>thermal energy stores</u> due to the work done against friction.
- This causes the overall <u>temperature</u> of the object to <u>increase</u>.

7) You can find out <u>how much work</u> has been done using:

The line of action of the force is the direction of the force.

Work done (J) ——— $$W = Fs$$ ——— Force (N)

Distance (moved along the line of action of the force) (m)

8) <u>One joule of work</u> is done when a <u>force of one newton</u> causes an object to move a <u>distance of one metre</u> in the direction of the force.

9) You need to be able to <u>convert</u> joules to newton metres: <u>1 J = 1 Nm</u>.

Force yourself to do some work and learn this page...

Remember, when you move an object, you do work. And if you do work, energy is transferred.

Q1 A force of 20 N pushes an object 20 cm in the direction of the force.
Calculate the work done on the object.

[3 marks]

Forces and Elasticity

You can use forces to stretch things too. The fun never ends...

Stretching, Compressing or Bending Transfers Energy

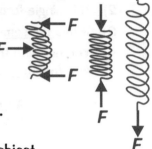

1) When you apply a force to an object you may cause it to <u>deform</u> (<u>stretch</u>, <u>compress</u> or <u>bend</u>).

2) To do this, you need <u>more than one</u> force acting on the object. <u>One</u> force would just make the object <u>move</u>, not change its shape.

3) An object has been <u>elastically deformed</u> if it can <u>go back</u> to its <u>original shape</u> and <u>length</u> after the force has been removed.

4) If the object <u>doesn't</u> go back to how it was, it has been <u>inelastically deformed</u>.

5) Objects that can be elastically deformed are called <u>elastic objects</u> (e.g. a spring).

6) <u>Work is done</u> when a force stretches or compresses an object. This causes energy to be transferred to the <u>elastic potential energy</u> store of the object.

Extension is Directly Proportional to Force...

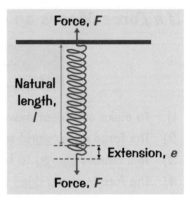

1) When a force <u>stretches</u> a spring, it causes it to <u>extend</u>.

2) This <u>extension</u> is the <u>difference in length</u> between the stretched and unstretched spring.

3) Up to a <u>given force</u>, the extension is <u>directly proportional</u> to force.

4) So long as a spring hasn't been stretched <u>past</u> its <u>limit of proportionality</u> (see below), you can use:

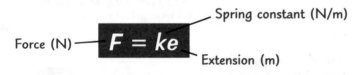

Spring constant (N/m)

Force (N) — $F = ke$

Extension (m)

5) The <u>spring constant</u> depends on the <u>object</u> that you are stretching.

6) The equation also works for <u>compression</u> (where e is the <u>difference</u> between the <u>natural</u> and <u>compressed</u> lengths — the <u>compression</u>).

The length of the unstretched spring is sometimes called the spring's natural length.

...but this Stops Working when the Force is Great Enough

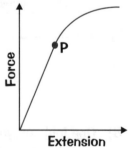

1) You can plot a <u>graph</u> of the force applied to a spring and the extension caused.

2) When the graph is a <u>straight line</u>, there is a <u>linear relationship</u> between force and extension.

3) This shows force and extension are <u>directly proportional</u>.

4) The <u>gradient</u> of the <u>straight line</u> is equal to k, the <u>spring constant</u>.

5) When the line begins to <u>bend</u>, the relationship is now <u>non-linear</u>. Force and extension are <u>no longer</u> directly proportional.

6) Point P on the graph (when the line starts to bend) is the <u>limit of proportionality</u>. <u>Past</u> this point, the equation $F = ke$ is <u>no longer</u> true.

I could make a joke, but I don't want to stretch myself...

Make sure you don't skip over any bits of this page — it's all rather important. Have a go at the question below.

Q1   A force of 1 N extends a spring by 2 cm. Calculate the spring constant of the spring.   [4 marks]

Investigating Springs

You can do an easy <u>experiment</u> to see exactly how adding <u>masses</u> to a spring causes it to <u>stretch</u>.

You Can Investigate the Link Between Force and Extension

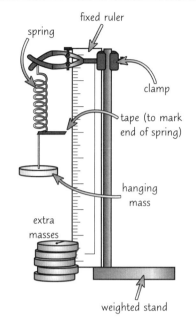

1) Set up the apparatus as shown in the diagram.
2) Measure the <u>mass</u> of each mass.
3) Calculate its <u>weight</u> (the <u>force</u> applied) using $W = mg$ (p.204).
4) Measure the original (natural) <u>length</u> of the spring.
5) Add a mass to the spring and allow it to come to <u>rest</u>.
6) Record the force and measure the new <u>length</u> of the spring.
7) Find the <u>extension</u>.

> extension = new length − original length

8) <u>Repeat</u> steps 5 to 7 until you've added all the masses.
9) <u>Plot</u> a <u>force-extension graph</u> of your results.
10) You should make sure you have <u>at least</u> 5 measurements before the <u>limit of proportionality</u> (where the line starts to curve).

You Can Work Out Energy Stored for Linear Relationships

1) If a spring is not stretched <u>past</u> its <u>limit of proportionality</u>, the <u>work done</u> in stretching the spring can be found using:
2) For an <u>elastic deformation</u>, this formula can be used to calculate the energy stored in a spring's <u>elastic potential energy store</u>.
3) It's also the energy <u>transferred to</u> the spring as it's <u>deformed</u>, or <u>transferred by</u> the spring as it returns to its <u>original shape</u>.

Spring constant (N/m)

$$E_e = \tfrac{1}{2}ke^2$$

Elastic potential energy (J) (Extension)² (m)²

You can also use this equation to calculate the energy stored when a spring is compressed.

EXAMPLE:

A spring with a spring constant of 500 N/m extends elastically by 10 cm.
It doesn't pass its limit of proportionality.
Calculate the amount of energy stored in its elastic potential energy store.

1) First, you need to <u>convert</u> the extension of the spring into <u>metres</u>.   10 cm ÷ 100 = 0.1 m
2) Then put in the <u>numbers</u> you've been given. $E_e = \tfrac{1}{2}ke^2 = 0.5 \times 500 \times 0.1^2$
   = 2.5 J

Time to spring into action and learn all this...

Make sure you know how to carry out the experiment on this page — you might be asked about it in your exam.

Q1   A spring with a spring constant of 40 N/m extends elastically by 2.5 cm.
Calculate the amount of energy stored in its elastic potential energy store.   [3 marks]

Distance, Displacement, Speed and Velocity

Time for a quick recap on <u>distance</u> and <u>speed</u>. You should race through this page. On your marks...

Distance is Scalar, Displacement is a Vector

I'm like a boy band — I only ever move in one direction.

1) <u>Distance</u> is just <u>how far</u> an object has moved.
2) Distance is a <u>scalar</u> quantity (p.203), so it doesn't involve <u>direction</u>.
3) <u>Displacement</u> is a <u>vector</u> quantity.
4) It measures the distance and direction in a <u>straight line</u> from an object's <u>starting point</u> to its <u>finishing point</u>.
5) The direction could be <u>in relation to a point</u>, e.g. <u>towards the school</u>.
6) If you walk 5 m <u>north</u>, then 5 m <u>south</u>, your <u>displacement</u> is <u>0 m</u> but the <u>distance</u> travelled is <u>10 m</u>.

Speed and Velocity are Both How Fast You're Going

1) <u>Speed</u> is a <u>scalar</u> and <u>velocity</u> is a <u>vector</u>:

> <u>Speed</u> is just <u>how fast</u> you're going (e.g. 30 mph or 20 m/s) with no regard to the direction.
> <u>Velocity</u> is speed in a given <u>direction</u>, e.g. 30 mph north or 20 m/s to the right.

2) To <u>measure</u> the <u>speed</u> of an object that's moving with a <u>constant speed</u>, <u>time</u> how long it takes the object to travel a certain <u>distance</u>. Make sure you use the correct equipment (see p.233).

3) You can then <u>calculate</u> the object's <u>speed</u> using this <u>formula</u>:

$$s = vt$$ 　　distance travelled (m) = speed (m/s) × time (s)

4) Objects <u>rarely</u> travel at a <u>constant speed</u>.
5) When you <u>walk</u>, <u>run</u> or travel in a <u>car</u>, your speed is <u>always changing</u>.
6) In these cases, the formula above gives the <u>average</u> (<u>mean</u>) speed during that time.

You Need to Know Some Typical Everyday Speeds

1) You need to know the <u>typical</u> (usual) <u>speeds</u> of objects:

A person <u>walking</u> — <u>1.5 m/s</u>	A person <u>cycling</u> — <u>6 m/s</u>	A <u>train</u> — <u>30 m/s</u>
A person <u>running</u> — <u>3 m/s</u>	A <u>car</u> — <u>25 m/s</u>	A <u>passenger plane</u> — <u>250 m/s</u>

2) Lots of different things can <u>affect</u> the speed something travels at.
3) The speed at which a person can <u>walk</u>, <u>run</u> or <u>cycle</u> depends on, among other things:
   - their <u>fitness</u>
   - the <u>distance they've travelled</u>
   - their <u>age</u>
   - the <u>terrain</u> (what type of ground they are on)
4) The speeds of <u>sound</u> and <u>wind</u> also vary. A typical speed for sound in air is <u>330 m/s</u>.

Ah, speed equals distance over time — that old chestnut...

Remember those typical speeds of objects — you might need to use them to make estimates.

Q1　A sprinter runs 200 m in 25 s. Calculate his average speed.　　　　　　　[3 marks]

Acceleration

Uniform acceleration sounds fancy, but it's just speeding up (or slowing down) at a constant rate.

Acceleration is How Quickly You're Speeding Up

1) Acceleration is the change in velocity in a certain amount of time.
2) You can find the average acceleration of an object using:

$$a = \frac{\Delta v}{t}$$

Acceleration (m/s^2) —
Change in velocity (m/s)
Time taken (s)

3) Deceleration (when something slows down) is just negative acceleration.

You Need to be Able to Estimate Accelerations

You might have to estimate the acceleration of an object. To do this, you need the typical speeds from the previous page:

An estimate is just a guess using rough numbers for things.

 **EXAMPLE:** A man gets onto a bike and accelerates to a typical speed from stationary in 10 seconds. Estimate the acceleration of the bicycle.

1) First, give a sensible speed for the bicycle to be travelling at.
2) Put these numbers into the acceleration equation.
3) The ~ symbol just means it's an approximate answer.

The typical speed of a bike is about 6 m/s.
The bicycle accelerates in 10 s.
$a = \Delta v \div t$
$= 6 \div 10 = 0.6 \ m/s^2$
So the acceleration is ~0.6 m/s^2

Uniform Acceleration Means a Constant Acceleration

1) Constant acceleration is sometimes called uniform acceleration.
2) Acceleration due to gravity (g) is uniform for objects falling freely.
3) It's roughly equal to 9.8 m/s^2 near the Earth's surface.
4) You can use this equation for uniform acceleration:

$$v^2 - u^2 = 2as$$

(Final velocity)^2 $(m/s)^2$
Acceleration (m/s^2)
Distance (m)
(Initial velocity)^2 $(m/s)^2$

Initial velocity is just the starting velocity of the object.

 **EXAMPLE:** A van travelling at 23 m/s starts decelerating uniformly at 2.0 m/s^2 as it heads towards a built-up area 112 m away. What will its speed be when it reaches the built-up area?

1) First, rearrange the equation so v^2 is on one side.
2) Now put the numbers in — remember a is negative because it's a deceleration.
3) Finally, square root the whole thing.

$v^2 = u^2 + 2as$
$v^2 = 23^2 + (2 \times -2.0 \times 112)$
$= 81$
$v = \sqrt{81} = 9$ m/s

Uniform problems — get a clip-on tie or use the equation above...

You might not be told what equation to use in the exam, so make sure you can spot when to use the one for uniform acceleration. Make a list of the information you're given to help you see what to do.

Q1 A car accelerates from 23 m/s to 30 m/s in 2.5 s. Calculate the acceleration of the car. [3 marks]

Distance-Time Graphs

You need to be able to <u>draw</u> and <u>understand distance-time graphs</u>.

You Can Show Journeys on Distance-Time Graphs

1) If an object moves in a <u>straight line</u>, the <u>distance</u> it travels can be plotted on a <u>distance-time</u> graph.

2) You may be asked to <u>draw</u> a distance-time graph for a journey.

3) Or you might have to <u>describe</u> a journey if you're shown a distance-time graph.

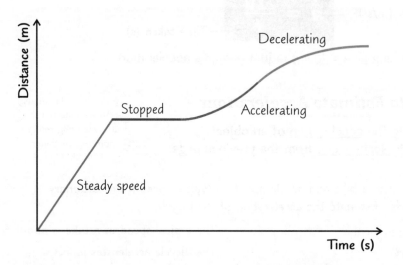

- <u>Gradient = speed</u>. The <u>steeper</u> the graph, the <u>faster</u> it's going.
- <u>Flat</u> sections are where it's <u>stationary</u> — it's <u>stopped</u>.
- <u>Straight</u> uphill (/) sections mean it is travelling at a <u>steady speed</u>.
- <u>Curves</u> represent <u>acceleration</u> or <u>deceleration</u> (p.209).
- A curve that is <u>getting steeper</u> means it's <u>speeding up</u> (accelerating).
- A <u>levelling off</u> curve means it's <u>slowing down</u> (decelerating).

4) You might also have to <u>calculate</u> an object's <u>speed</u> from the graph:

EXAMPLE:

Using the distance-time graph on the right, calculate the speed of the car.

1) The <u>gradient</u> of the graph is the <u>speed</u> of the car.

2) Gradient = $\dfrac{\text{change in vertical axis}}{\text{change in horizontal axis}}$.

3) Draw a <u>large triangle</u>, that takes up most of the straight line.

4) Use the <u>horizontal</u> side of the triangle to find the change in time.

5) Use the <u>vertical side</u> of the triangle to find the change in distance.

6) Put the values for vertical and horizontal into the <u>equation</u>.

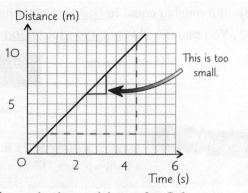

Change in time = 4.4 − 0.8 = 3.6 s

Change in distance = 11 − 2 = 9 m

Gradient = 9 ÷ 3.6 = 2.5

So speed = 2.5 m/s

Understanding motion graphs — it can be a real uphill struggle...

Make sure you know how to use distance-time graphs to find the speed of an object travelling at a constant speed.

Q1 Sketch the distance-time graph for an object that accelerates before travelling at a steady speed. [2 marks]

Velocity-Time Graphs and Terminal Velocity

This page is on velocity-time graphs and terminal velocity. Just when you thought it couldn't get more exciting.

Journeys Can be Shown on a Velocity-Time Graph

1) How an object's velocity changes as it travels can be plotted on a velocity-time graph.
2) You might have to draw a velocity-time graph for a journey.
3) Or you might have to describe a journey from a velocity-time graph.

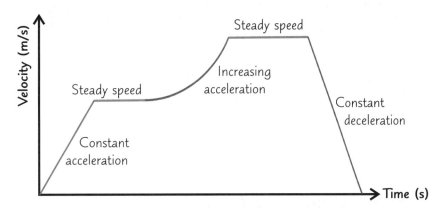

- Gradient = acceleration. You can calculate this with a similar method to the example on the last page.
- Flat sections represent travelling at a steady speed.
- The steeper the graph, the greater the acceleration or deceleration.
- Uphill sections (/) are acceleration.
- Downhill sections (\) are deceleration.
- A curve means changing acceleration.

Friction is Always There to Slow Things Down

1) Gases and liquids are both fluids.
2) Objects moving through fluids experience drag.
3) Drag is the resistance you get in a fluid. Air resistance is a type of drag.
4) Drag acts in the opposite direction to the movement of the object.
5) Drag increases as the speed of the object increases.

Falling Objects Reach a Terminal Velocity

1) When an object first starts falling, the force of gravity is much larger than the drag slowing it down.
2) This means the object accelerates (the object speeds up).
3) As the speed increases, so does the drag.
4) This reduces the acceleration until the drag is equal to the gravitational force. The resultant force (p.205) on the object is then zero.
5) The object will fall at a constant speed. This speed is called its terminal velocity.

Falling with style

Don't let air resistance drag you down...

Make sure you know what a velocity-time graph is telling you about the acceleration of an object.

Q1   Sketch a velocity-time graph for an object that accelerates at a constant rate, then travels at a constant speed and then decelerates at a constant rate.
[3 marks]

Newton's First and Second Laws

In the 1660s, a chap called <u>Isaac Newton</u> worked out his dead useful <u>Laws of Motion</u>. Here are the first <u>two</u>.

A Force is Needed to Change Motion

1) <u>Newton's First Law</u> says that a resultant force (p.205) is needed to make something <u>start moving</u>, <u>speed up</u> or <u>slow down</u>:

> If the resultant force on a <u>stationary</u> object is <u>zero</u>, the object will <u>remain stationary</u>. If the resultant force on a <u>moving object</u> is <u>zero</u>, it'll just carry on moving at the <u>same velocity</u> (the same speed <u>and</u> direction).

2) So, when a train or car or bus or anything else is <u>moving</u> at a <u>constant velocity</u>, the <u>driving</u> and <u>resistive</u> forces on it must be <u>balanced</u>.

3) Its velocity will <u>only</u> change if there's a <u>non-zero</u> resultant force acting on it.

4) A non-zero <u>resultant</u> force will always produce <u>acceleration</u> (or deceleration) in the <u>direction of the force</u>.

Acceleration is Proportional to the Resultant Force

1) The <u>larger</u> the <u>resultant force</u> acting on an object, the <u>more</u> the object accelerates.

2) <u>Newton's Second Law</u> says that the force acting on an object and the acceleration of the object are <u>directly proportional</u>. This can be shown as $F \propto a$.

3) Newton's Second Law also says that acceleration is <u>inversely proportional</u> to the mass of the object.

4) So an object with a <u>larger</u> mass will accelerate <u>less</u> than one with a smaller mass, for a <u>given force</u>.

5) There's a <u>formula</u> that describes <u>Newton's Second Law</u>:

$$\text{Resultant force (N)} \longrightarrow \boxed{F = ma} \begin{array}{l} \nearrow \text{Acceleration (m/s}^2\text{)} \\ \searrow \text{Mass (kg)} \end{array}$$

6) You can use <u>Newton's Second Law</u> to get an idea of the forces involved in <u>large accelerations</u> of everyday transport.

7) You may need some typical vehicle masses first though:
    <u>Car</u> — 1000 kg, <u>Bus</u> — 10 000 kg, <u>Loaded Lorry</u> — 30 000 kg

EXAMPLE: Estimate the resultant force on an average car as it accelerates from rest to a typical speed.

1) <u>Estimate</u> the <u>speed</u> of the car and the <u>time</u> taken to reach that speed.

    A typical speed of a car is ~25 m/s. It takes ~10 s to reach this.

2) Use the <u>speed</u> and <u>time</u> taken to estimate the <u>acceleration</u> of the car.

    So $a = \Delta v \div t$
    $= 25 \div 10 = 2.5$ m/s^2

    Remember, the ~ sign means approximately.

3) Put these numbers and the mass of the car into $F = ma$.

    Mass of a car is ~1000 kg.
    $F = ma = 1000 \times 2.5 = 2500$ N
    So the resultant force is ~2500 N.

Accelerate your learning — force yourself to revise...

Make sure you've got your head around both of those laws, before moving on to Newton's third and final law.

Q1   Find the force needed for an 80 kg man on a 10 kg bike to accelerate at 0.25 m/s^2.   [2 marks]

Newton's Third Law

This page is on Newton's Third Law. Make sure you really understand what's going on with it.

Newton's Third Law: Equal and Opposite Forces Act on Interacting Objects

Newton's Third Law says:

> When <u>two objects interact</u>, the forces they exert on each other are <u>equal and opposite</u>.

1) This means if you <u>push</u> something, it will <u>push back</u> against you, <u>just as hard</u>.
2) And as soon as you <u>stop</u> pushing, <u>so does the object</u>.
3) You may be thinking "if the forces are always equal, <u>how does anything ever go anywhere</u>?".
4) The important thing to remember is that the two forces are acting on <u>different objects</u>.

Push — Normal contact force

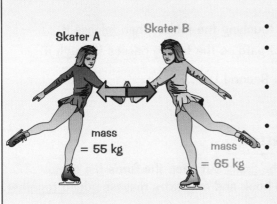

Skater A   Skater B

mass = 55 kg   mass = 65 kg

- Skater A pushes on skater B.
- When she does, she feels an <u>equal</u> and <u>opposite</u> force from skater B's hand.
- Both skaters feel the <u>same sized force</u>, in <u>opposite directions</u>.
- This causes them to accelerate away from each other.
- Skater A will be <u>accelerated more than</u> skater B, because she has a smaller mass.
- Remember $a = F \div m$.

It's More Complicated for an Object in Equilibrium

Imagine a <u>book</u> sat on a <u>table</u> in <u>equilibrium</u> (the <u>resultant force</u> on the book is <u>zero</u>):

1) The <u>weight</u> of the book <u>pulls</u> it <u>down</u>, and the <u>normal contact force</u> from the table <u>pushes</u> it <u>up</u>.
2) This is <u>NOT</u> Newton's Third Law.
3) These forces are <u>different types</u> and they're both <u>acting on</u> the <u>book</u>.

The <u>pairs of forces</u> due to Newton's Third Law in this case are:

- The book being <u>pulled down</u> by <u>gravity</u> towards the Earth (W_B) and the Earth being <u>pulled up</u> by the <u>book</u> (W_E).
- The <u>normal contact force</u> from the <u>table</u> pushing <u>up</u> on the book (R_B) and the <u>normal contact force</u> from the book <u>pushing down</u> on the table (R_T).

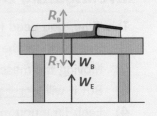

R_B↑

R_T↓↓ W_B

↑ W_E

Newton's fourth law — revision must be done with tea...

Thankfully, Newton only came up with three laws that you have to learn. His third law can be quite tricky, but just take your time. Look at each object one at a time and work out all the forces acting on it before you move on.

Q1   State Newton's Third Law.   [1 mark]

PRACTICAL | Investigating Motion

Now you've learnt the different <u>laws of motion</u> why not test them with a practical...

You can Investigate how Mass and Force Affect Acceleration

It's time for an experiment that tests <u>Newton's Second Law</u>, **F** = ma (p.212).

1) Set up the <u>apparatus</u> as shown on the right.

2) The <u>mass</u>, m, that you'll be accelerating is the <u>total mass</u> of the <u>trolley</u>, <u>hook</u> and the <u>added masses</u>.

3) You can measure m using a <u>mass balance</u>.

4) The <u>force</u>, **F**, causing the acceleration is the <u>weight</u> of the <u>hook and the masses on the hook</u>.

5) To find **F**, first measure the <u>mass</u> of the <u>hook</u> and any masses <u>on the hook</u>. Then <u>multiply this by g</u> (as W = mg, see page 204).

6) The <u>acceleration</u>, a, is found by following this method:

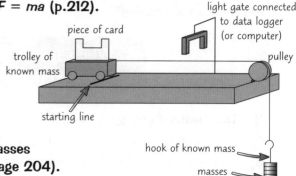

light gate connected to data logger (or computer)

piece of card

trolley of known mass

pulley

starting line

hook of known mass

masses

> 1) Mark a <u>starting line</u> on the table the trolley is on. This is so that the trolley always travels the <u>same distance</u> to the light gate.
>
> 2) Place the trolley on the <u>starting line</u>.
>
> 3) Hold the trolley so the string is <u>tight</u> and not touching the table. Then <u>release</u> it.
>
> 4) Record the <u>acceleration</u> measured by the light gate as the trolley passes through it.

> For more on how light gates work have a look at page 239.

Now you can <u>investigate</u> the things that affect Newton's Second Law...

Investigating How Mass Affects Acceleration

To investigate the effect of mass, you need to <u>change the mass</u> but keep the force <u>the same</u>. Remember, the <u>mass</u> (m) is the mass of the trolley, the hook and any extra masses <u>added together</u>.

1) The force is the <u>weight</u> of the <u>hook and any masses on the hook</u>.

2) So, keep the mass <u>on the hook</u> the <u>same</u>.

3) <u>Add masses</u> to the <u>trolley</u> one at a time to increase the <u>total mass</u> being accelerated.

4) Record the <u>acceleration</u>, a, for <u>each total mass</u>, m.

5) You should find that as the mass <u>goes up</u>, the acceleration <u>goes down</u>.

6) This <u>agrees</u> with Newton's Second Law — mass and acceleration are <u>inversely proportional</u>.

Investigating How Force Affects Acceleration

This time, you need to <u>change</u> the force <u>without changing</u> the <u>total mass</u> of the trolley, hook and masses.

1) Start with <u>all</u> the extra masses loaded onto the <u>trolley</u>.

2) Moving the masses <u>from</u> the trolley to the hook will keep the <u>total mass</u>, m, the same.

3) But it will <u>increase</u> the force, **F** (the <u>weight</u> of the <u>hook and the masses on the hook</u>).

4) <u>Each time</u> you <u>move</u> a mass, record the <u>new force</u>, and measure the <u>acceleration</u>.

5) You should find that as the force <u>goes up</u>, the acceleration <u>goes up</u>.

6) This <u>agrees</u> with Newton's Second Law — force and acceleration are <u>directly proportional</u>.

My acceleration increases with nearby cake...

Know the ins and outs of that experiment — you could be asked about any part of it, or to describe the whole thing.

Q1   In the experiment above, what force is accelerating the trolley?   [1 mark]

Stopping Distance and Thinking Distance

This page is all about cars, but unfortunately it's not as fun as it sounds... It's even better — it's about safety...

Stopping Distance = Thinking Distance + Braking Distance

1) In an emergency, a driver may perform an emergency stop.
2) During an emergency stop, the maximum force is applied by the brakes. This is so the vehicle stops in the shortest possible distance.
3) The distance it takes to stop a vehicle in an emergency is its stopping distance. It is found by:

> Stopping Distance = Thinking Distance + Braking Distance

4) THINKING DISTANCE is how far the vehicle travels during the driver's reaction time.
5) The reaction time is the time between the driver seeing a hazard and applying the brakes.
6) BRAKING DISTANCE is the distance taken to stop under the braking force (once the brakes are applied).

Stopping Distances for Different Speeds can be Estimated

1) You need to be able to estimate the stopping distance of vehicles.
2) The heavier a vehicle is, or the faster it's travelling, the longer its stopping distance will be.
3) As a guide, typical car stopping distances are: 23 m at 30 mph, 73 m at 60 mph, 96 m at 70 mph.

Stopping Distances Affect Safety

1) The longer it takes to perform an emergency stop, the higher the risk of crashing into whatever's in front.
2) So the shorter a vehicle's stopping distance, the safer it is.
3) You need to be able to describe how different factors can affect the safety of a journey.
4) For example, how driving if you're tired is unsafe. There's more on this below.

Thinking Distance is Determined by the Driver's Reactions

1) Thinking distance is affected by:
   • Your SPEED — the faster you're going, the further you'll travel during the time you take to react.
   • Your REACTION TIME — the longer your reaction time (see p.217), the longer your thinking distance.
2) A driver's reaction times can be affected by tiredness, drugs or alcohol.
3) Distractions can also affect your ability to react.

   • Driving while tired is unsafe as it makes you slower to react.
   • This increases your reaction time, which increases your thinking distance.
   • This means your stopping distance is longer, so you're more likely to crash.

   • Driving above the speed limit is unsafe.
   • You travel further in your reaction time than you would at a lower speed.
   • This increases your thinking (and so stopping) distance.

Stop right there — and learn this page...

Before moving on, make sure you can explain the factors that affect a person's thinking distance.

Q1 Give one factor that affects thinking distance. [1 mark]

Braking Distance

You need to know what energy changes occur when a car stops. Don't worry — it'll all make sense soon enough.

Braking Distance Depends on a Few Different Factors Affecting the Car

Braking distance is affected by:

1) Your SPEED: for a given braking force, the faster a vehicle travels, the longer it takes to stop.
2) WEATHER or ROAD SURFACE:
   • If there is less grip between a vehicle's tyres and the road, it can cause the vehicle to skid.
   • Skidding increases the braking distance of a car.
   • Water, ice, oil or leaves on the road all reduce grip.

   > Icy conditions increase the chance of skidding. This increases the braking distance, which increases the stopping distance. So more room should be left between cars to be safe.

3) The CONDITION of your TYRES:
   • Bald tyres (ones that don't have any tread left) cannot get rid of water in wet conditions.
   • This leads to them skidding on top of the water.

4) How good your BRAKES are:
   • If brakes are worn, they won't be able to apply as much force.
   • So it takes longer to stop a vehicle travelling at a given speed (see below).

Braking Relies on Friction Between the Brakes and Wheels

1) When the brake pedal is pushed, brake pads are pressed onto the wheels.
2) The brake pads cause friction, which causes work to be done (p.205).
3) Remember, when work is done, energy is transferred (p.168).
4) Energy is transferred from the kinetic energy store of the vehicle to the thermal energy stores of the brakes.
5) The brakes increase in temperature.
6) To stop a vehicle, the brakes must transfer all of the energy from the kinetic store, so:

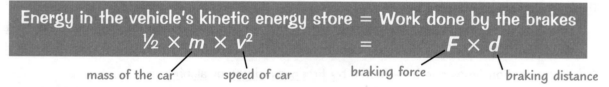

Energy in the vehicle's kinetic energy store = Work done by the brakes

$$\tfrac{1}{2} \times m \times v^2 \qquad = \qquad F \times d$$

mass of the car   speed of car   braking force   braking distance

7) The faster a vehicle is going, the more energy it has in its kinetic energy store.
8) So more work needs to be done to stop it.
9) This means that as the speed of a vehicle increases, the force needed to make it stop within a certain distance also increases.
10) A larger braking force means a larger deceleration.
11) Very large decelerations can be dangerous because they may cause brakes to overheat. This means the brakes won't work as well.
12) Very large decelerations may also cause the vehicle to skid.

To claim your free brakes test, stop here...

If you ever find yourself in charge of a motor vehicle, hopefully you'll remember this page and it'll help you to be safer on the roads. Even if you don't ever plan on driving, this page is still very important for your exams.

Q1   Explain why large decelerations in vehicles can lead to accidents.   [2 marks]

Reaction Times

Go long! You need fast <u>reaction times</u> to avoid getting hit in the face when playing catch.

A Typical Reaction Time is 0.2 s – 0.9 s

1) <u>Everyone's</u> reaction time is <u>different</u>.

2) A <u>typical</u> reaction time is between <u>0.2</u> and <u>0.9 s</u>.

3) You can do <u>simple experiments</u> to investigate your reaction time — more on these below.

You can Measure Reaction Times with the Ruler Drop Test

1) As reaction times are <u>so short</u>, you haven't got a chance of measuring one with a <u>stopwatch</u>.

2) One way of measuring reaction times is to use a <u>computer-based test</u>. For example, <u>clicking a mouse</u> when the screen changes colour.

Another method to measure reaction times is the <u>ruler drop test</u>:

1) Sit with your arm resting on the edge of a table.

2) Get someone else to hold a ruler so it <u>hangs between</u> your thumb and forefinger, lined up with <u>zero</u>.

3) You may need a <u>third person</u> to be at <u>eye level with the ruler</u> to check it's lined up.

4) Without giving any warning, the person holding the ruler should <u>drop it</u>.

5) Close your thumb and finger to try to <u>catch the ruler as quickly as possible</u>.

ruler hanging between thumb and forefinger

finger in line with zero

ruler is dropped without warning

ruler caught between thumb and finger

distance fallen

6) The measurement on the ruler at the point where it is caught is <u>how far</u> the ruler dropped in the time it took you to react.

7) The <u>longer</u> the <u>distance</u>, the <u>longer</u> the <u>reaction time</u>.

8) You can calculate <u>how long</u> the ruler falls for (the <u>reaction time</u>) because <u>acceleration due to gravity is constant</u>.

9) To find the <u>reaction time</u>, you'll need to use the equation:

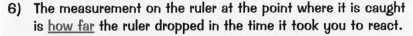

$$t = \frac{\sqrt{2as}}{a}$$

You <u>DON'T</u> need to learn this equation. It comes from squishing $v^2 - u^2 = 2as$ and $a = \Delta v \div t$ from p.209 together.

- t is the <u>reaction time</u> in seconds, s.
- a is the <u>acceleration due to gravity</u>. $a = 9.8$ m/s^2.
- s is <u>how far</u> the ruler fell before it was caught, in metres, m.

10) It's <u>hard</u> to do this experiment <u>accurately</u>, but you can do a few things to <u>improve</u> your <u>results</u>.

- Do a lot of <u>repeats</u> and calculate an <u>average</u> reaction time.
- Add a <u>blob of modelling clay</u> to the bottom to help the ruler to fall straight down.
- Make it a <u>fair test</u> — use the <u>same ruler</u> for each repeat, and have the <u>same person</u> dropping it.

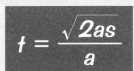

Test a friend's reaction time by throwing this book at them...

Not really. Instead re-read this page and make sure you can describe the experiment. Much more fun.

Q1   What is a typical reaction time for a human? [1 mark]

Q2   Mark wants to measure his reaction time, state one way of doing this. [1 mark]

Revision Questions for Topic P5

Well, that's <u>Topic P5</u> over and done with — have a quick break, then see how you've done with this summary.

- Try these questions and <u>tick off each one</u> when you <u>get it right</u>.
- When you've done <u>all the questions</u> under a heading and are <u>completely happy</u> with it, tick it off.

<u>Forces and Work Done (p.203-205)</u> ☑

1) Explain the difference between scalar and vector quantities. ☑
2) True or false? Time is a vector quantity. ☑
3) What is the difference between contact and non-contact forces? ☑
4) True or false? Mass is a force measured in newtons. ☑
5) What is the formula for calculating the weight of an object? ☑
6) What is a resultant force? ☑
7) Give the formula for calculating the work done by a force. Explain what each symbol means. ☑
8) How many joules of work does 1 Nm equal? ☑

<u>Stretching, Compressing and Bending (p.206-207)</u> ☑

9) What is the difference between an elastic and an inelastic deformation? ☑
10) What is the limit of proportionality? ☑
11) Give the equation that links force, extension and the spring constant of an object. ☑
12) Describe an experiment you could do to investigate the relationship between force and extension. ☑

<u>Motion (p.208-214)</u> ☑

13) What is the difference between displacement and distance? ☑
14) Estimate the speed of a person walking. ☑
15) Write down the equation that links acceleration, velocity and time. ☑
16) For what type of acceleration can you use the equation $v^2 - u^2 = 2as$? ☑
17) What does the gradient represent for: a) a distance-time graph? b) a velocity-time graph? ☑
18) State Newton's three laws of motion. ☑
19) Describe an experiment that you could do to investigate Newton's Second Law. ☑

<u>Car Safety (p.215-217)</u> ☑

20) What is the stopping distance of a vehicle? How can it be calculated? ☑
21) Give two things that affect a person's reaction time. ☑
22) State four things that can affect the braking distance of a vehicle. ☑
23) Explain why the temperature of a car's brakes increase during braking. ☑
24) What is a typical reaction time? ☑
25) Briefly describe an experiment you could do to compare people's reaction times. ☑

Transverse and Longitudinal Waves

Waves <u>transfer energy</u> from one place to another <u>without</u> transferring any <u>matter</u> (stuff).

Waves Transfer Energy but not Matter

1) When a wave <u>travels through</u> a medium, the particles of the <u>medium</u> vibrate.

2) A <u>medium</u> is just a fancy word for whatever the wave is <u>travelling through</u> (e.g. water, air).

3) The particles <u>transfer energy</u> between each other as they vibrate (see p.167).

4) <u>BUT</u> overall, the particles stay in the <u>same place</u> — <u>only energy</u> is transferred.

- For example, if you drop a twig into calm water, <u>ripples</u> spread out. The ripples <u>don't</u> carry the <u>water</u> (or the twig) away with them though.
- And if you strum a <u>guitar string</u>, the sound waves don't carry the <u>air</u> away from the guitar. If they did, you'd feel a <u>wind</u> whenever there was a sound.

All Waves are Either Transverse or Longitudinal

1) In <u>transverse waves</u>, the vibrations are <u>perpendicular</u> (at right angles) to the <u>direction</u> of energy transfer.

2) <u>Examples</u> of transverse waves are <u>light</u> (p.223), <u>ripples</u> on water (see p.221) and waves on a <u>string</u>.

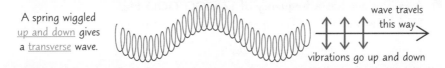

A spring wiggled <u>up and down</u> gives a <u>transverse</u> wave.

wave travels this way

vibrations go up and down

3) In <u>longitudinal waves</u>, the vibrations are in the <u>same direction</u> as the energy transfer.

4) They have <u>compressions</u> (where the particles squish together), and <u>rarefactions</u> (where they spread out).

5) A <u>sound wave</u> is an <u>example</u> of a longitudinal wave.

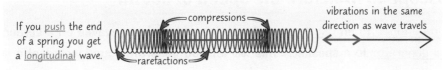

If you <u>push</u> the end of a spring you get a <u>longitudinal</u> wave.

compressions

rarefactions

vibrations in the same direction as wave travels

You Need to Know these Words to Describe Waves

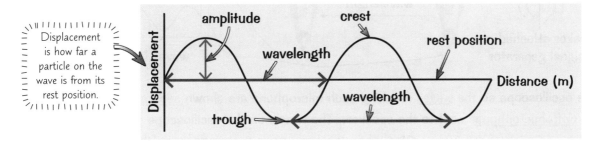

Displacement is how far a particle on the wave is from its rest position.

amplitude

crest

wavelength

rest position

Displacement

Distance (m)

wavelength

trough

1) The <u>amplitude</u> is the <u>maximum displacement</u> of a point on the wave from its <u>undisturbed (rest) position</u>.

2) The <u>wavelength</u> is the distance between <u>one point</u> on a wave and the <u>same point</u> on the <u>next wave</u>. For example, the distance between the <u>trough</u> of one wave and the <u>trough</u> of the wave <u>next to it</u>.

3) <u>Frequency</u> is the <u>number of complete waves</u> passing a certain point <u>each second</u>.

4) Frequency is measured in <u>hertz</u> (Hz). 1 Hz is <u>1 wave per second</u>.

5) <u>Period</u> is the amount of <u>time</u> it takes for <u>one</u> complete wave to <u>pass</u> a certain point.

So, that's the wave basics...

Make sure you've got all this clear in your head, otherwise the rest of the topic will just be a blur of nonsense.

Q1   Give two examples of transverse waves.   [2 marks]

Frequency, Period and Wave Speed

You need to know how to __calculate__ and __measure__ the speed of a wave.

Frequency and Period are Linked

You can find the __period__ of a wave from its __frequency__:

Period (s) — $T = \dfrac{1}{f}$ — Frequency (Hz)

Calculate the period of a wave with a frequency of 2 Hz.
$T = 1 \div f = 1 \div 2 = 0.5 \text{ s}$

Wave Speed = Frequency × Wavelength

1) The __wave speed__ is how fast the __wave__ is moving.
2) It is the speed at which __energy is being transferred__ through the __medium__.
3) The __wave equation__ applies to __all waves__:

$$\text{Wave speed (m/s)} = \text{frequency (Hz)} \times \text{wavelength (m)} \qquad v = f\lambda$$

EXAMPLE:
A radio wave has a frequency of 12 000 000 Hz.
Find its wavelength. (The speed of radio waves in air is 3×10^8 m/s.)

1) __Rearrange__ the wave speed equation for __wavelength__. $\lambda = v \div f$
2) Put in the __values__ you've been __given__. $= (3 \times 10^8) \div (12\ 000\ 000)$
   Watch out — the speed is in __standard form__ (p.12). $= 25 \text{ m}$

Use an Oscilloscope to Measure the Speed of Sound

1) Connect __two microphones__ to an __oscilloscope__ (a device which shows waves on a screen).
2) Connect a __signal generator__ to a speaker. This will let you generate __sound waves__ at a __set frequency__.

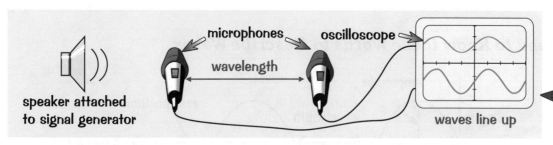

speaker attached to signal generator   microphones   wavelength   oscilloscope   waves line up

3) Set up the oscilloscope so the __waves__ reaching each microphone are shown __separately__.
4) Start with __both microphones__ next to the speaker. The waves on the oscilloscope __should line up__.
5) Slowly __move one microphone__ away. Stop when the two waves __line up__ again on the display.
6) This means the microphones are now __exactly one wavelength apart__.
7) Measure the __distance between the microphones__ to find the __wavelength__ (λ).
8) Use the formula $v = f\lambda$ to find the __speed__ (v) of the __sound waves__ passing through the __air__.
9) The __frequency__ (f) is whatever you set the __signal generator__ to.
10) The speed of sound in air is around __330 m/s__, so check your results __roughly agree__ with this.

Looks like the perfect setup for a karaoke duet...

Make sure you understand each step of that method above — you could be tested on it in the exams.

Q1   A wave has a speed of 0.15 m/s and a wavelength of 0.75 m. Calculate its frequency.   [3 marks]

Investigating Waves

Choosing <u>suitable equipment</u> means making sure it's <u>right</u> for the job. It's important here.

Measure the Speed of Water Ripples Using a Ripple Tank

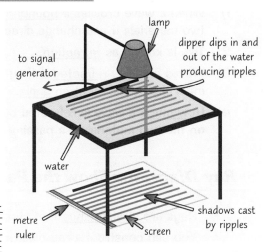

lamp

dipper dips in and out of the water producing ripples

to signal generator

water

metre ruler

screen

shadows cast by ripples

1) Attach a <u>signal generator</u> to the <u>ripple tank dipper</u>.

2) Turn on the signal generator to create <u>waves</u>.

3) Find the <u>frequency</u> of the waves by <u>counting</u> the number of <u>ripples</u> that pass a point in 10 seconds and <u>dividing by 10</u>.

4) Use a <u>lamp</u> to create <u>shadows</u> of the ripples on a screen below the tank. Place a <u>metre ruler</u> beside the shadows.

5) The distance between each shadow line is equal to <u>one wavelength</u>.

6) Measure the wavelength <u>accurately</u> like this:

- Measure the <u>distance</u> across <u>10 gaps</u> between the shadow lines.

- <u>Divide</u> this distance <u>by 10</u> to find the <u>average wavelength</u>.

This is a good method for measuring the wavelength of moving waves or small wavelengths.

Make sure you do this experiment in a darkened room.

7) If you're struggling to measure the distance, you could take a <u>photo</u> of the <u>shadows and ruler</u>, and find the wavelength from the photo instead.

8) Use $v = f\lambda$ to calculate the wave <u>speed</u> of the waves.

9) This set-up is <u>suitable</u> for investigating waves, because it allows you to <u>measure</u> the wavelength without <u>disturbing</u> the waves.

You can Use the Wave Equation for Waves on Strings

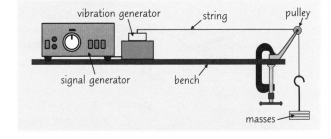

vibration generator

string

pulley

signal generator

bench

masses

1) Set up the equipment shown on the right.

2) The <u>vibration generator vibrates</u> at a <u>fixed frequency</u>, set by the signal generator.

3) <u>Turn on</u> the signal generator and the string will start to <u>vibrate</u>.

4) Adjust the <u>frequency</u> of the signal generator until there's a <u>clear wave</u> on the string.

To measure the <u>wavelength</u> of these waves accurately:

- Count <u>how many</u> wavelengths are on the string. Each <u>vibrating loop</u> is <u>half a wavelength</u>.

- Measure the <u>length</u> of the <u>whole</u> vibrating string.

- <u>Divide</u> by the number of <u>wavelengths</u> to give the length of <u>one wavelength</u>.

measure this distance

there are 2 wavelengths on the string, so divide the distance by 2

5) The <u>frequency</u> of the wave is whatever the <u>signal generator</u> is set to.

6) You can find the <u>speed</u> of the wave using $v = f\lambda$.

7) This set-up is <u>suitable</u> for investigating waves on a string because it's easy to <u>see</u> and <u>measure</u> the wavelength (and frequency).

It's ok if you don't have a whole number of wavelengths on the string. If there are 3 loops, there are one-and-a-half wavelengths on the string. Divide the length of the string by 1.5.

Surf's up, it's time to, like, totally measure some waves...

We use sound waves, ripples and waves on strings as they're easy to make and there are ways of 'seeing' them.

Q1   Describe a suitable experiment to measure the wavelength of a water wave.   [3 marks]

Refraction

Grab a glass of water and put a straw in it. The straw looks like it's <u>bending</u>. But it's not magic, it's refraction.

Refraction — Waves Changing Direction

1) When a wave crosses a <u>boundary</u> between two materials it can change direction.

2) This is known as <u>refraction</u>.

3) Waves are <u>only refracted</u> if they meet the boundary <u>at an angle</u>.

4) <u>How much</u> a wave is refracted by depends on the two materials it's passing between.

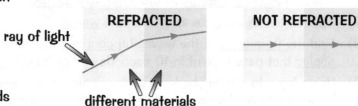

ray of light

REFRACTED   NOT REFRACTED

different materials

Ray Diagrams Show the Path of a Wave

- Rays are <u>straight lines</u> that show the <u>direction</u> a wave is <u>travelling</u> in.
- You can construct a <u>ray diagram</u> for a <u>refracted light ray</u>.

1) Start by drawing the <u>boundary</u> between your two materials.

2) Then draw a dotted line <u>at right angles</u> to the boundary.

3) This line is known as the '<u>normal</u>' to the boundary. Normal just means 'at right angles'.

4) Next draw the <u>incident ray</u>. This is the ray that <u>meets</u> the <u>boundary</u> at the <u>normal</u>.

5) The angle <u>between</u> the incident <u>ray</u> and the <u>normal</u> is called the <u>angle of incidence</u>.

6) You need to use a <u>protractor</u> to draw or measure it.

7) So to draw an incident ray with an <u>angle of incidence</u> of <u>50°</u>:

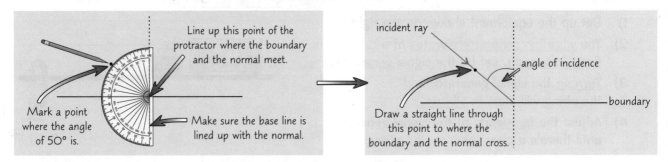

Line up this point of the protractor where the boundary and the normal meet.

Mark a point where the angle of 50° is.

Make sure the base line is lined up with the normal.

incident ray

angle of incidence

boundary

Draw a straight line through this point to where the boundary and the normal cross.

8) Now draw the <u>refracted</u> ray on the <u>other side</u> of the boundary.

9) <u>The angle of refraction</u> is the angle between the <u>refracted ray</u> and the normal.

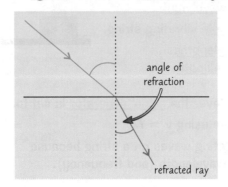

angle of refraction

refracted ray

Lights, camera, refraction...

Refraction is a common behaviour of waves, so make sure you really understand it before moving on.

Q1   Draw a ray of light meeting a boundary at an angle of incidence of 32°.   [2 marks]

Topic P6 — Waves

Electromagnetic Waves

The light waves that we see are just one small part of a big group of electromagnetic waves...

Electromagnetic Waves Transfer Energy

1) Electromagnetic (EM) waves are transverse waves (p.219).
2) They transfer energy from a source to an absorber.

> 1) A camp fire is a source.
> 2) It transfers energy to its surroundings by giving out infrared radiation.
> 3) Infrared radiation is a type of EM wave.
> 4) These infrared waves are absorbed by objects.
> 5) Energy is transferred to the objects' thermal energy stores.
> 6) This causes the objects to warm up.

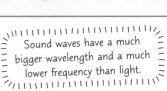

3) All EM waves travel at the same speed through air or a vacuum (space).
4) This speed is much faster than the speed of sound in air.

Sound waves have a much bigger wavelength and a much lower frequency than light.

There's a Continuous Spectrum of EM Waves

1) EM waves vary in wavelength and frequency.
2) There are EM waves of every wavelength within a certain range.
3) This is known as a continuous spectrum.
4) The spectrum is split up into seven groups based on wavelength and frequency.

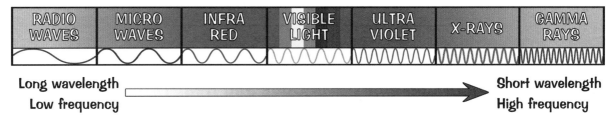

| RADIO WAVES | MICRO WAVES | INFRA RED | VISIBLE LIGHT | ULTRA VIOLET | X-RAYS | GAMMA RAYS |

Long wavelength
Low frequency ➞ Short wavelength
High frequency

5) Our eyes can only detect a small part of this spectrum — visible light.

Changes In Atoms Produce the Spectrum of EM Waves

1) EM radiation can be absorbed or produced by changes in atoms and their nuclei.
2) There are lots of different changes that can happen in atoms. For example:
   - Electrons can move between energy levels in atoms (see p.197).
   - Changes in the nucleus of an atom can create gamma rays (see p.199).
3) Each different change produces or absorbs a different frequency of EM wave.
4) This is why atoms can generate (create) EM waves over a large range of frequencies.
5) It is also why atoms can absorb a range of frequencies.

Learn about the EM spectrum and wave goodbye to exam stress...

Nothing too difficult here, just a lot of facts to remember. Here's a handy way to remember the order of EM waves: 'Rock Music Is Very Useful for eXperiments with Goats'.

Q1   State the type of electromagnetic wave that has the lowest frequency.   [1 mark]

Q2   Name the section of the electromagnetic spectrum that humans can see.   [1 mark]

Uses of EM Waves

EM waves are used for all sorts of stuff — and radio waves are definitely the most fun.
They make your car radio and your TV work. Life would be pretty quiet without them.

Radio Waves are Used Mainly for Communication

1) Radio and TV signals can be sent by radio waves.
2) Very short wavelength signals are used for FM radio and TV.
3) They have to be in direct sight of the receiver when they're sent, with nothing in the way, so they can't travel very far.
4) Longer wavelength radio waves can travel further.
5) They can be used to send radio signals around the world.

Microwaves are Used for Satellites and Cooking

1) Communication with satellites uses microwaves, e.g. for satellite TV and satellite phones.
2) A signal is sent into space to a satellite dish high above the Earth.
3) The satellite sends the signal back to Earth in a different direction.
4) A satellite dish on the ground receives the signal.

1) Microwave ovens use microwaves to cook food.
2) The oven gives out microwaves, which are absorbed by water in the food.
3) Energy carried by the microwaves is transferred to the water molecules, causing them to heat up.
4) This causes the rest of the food to heat up and quickly cooks it.

Infrared Radiation Can be Used to Cook and Heat Things

1) Infrared (IR) radiation is given out by all objects.
2) The hotter the object, the more infrared radiation it gives out.
3) When an object absorbs infrared radiation, energy is transferred to the object's thermal energy store. This makes it warm up.
4) Infrared radiation can be used in many ways:

1) Infrared cameras detect IR radiation and create a picture.
2) This is useful for seeing where a house is losing energy.
3) It can also allow you to see hot objects in the dark.

1) Infrared radiation can also be used to warm things.
2) Electric heaters release lots of IR radiation to warm a room.
3) And food can be cooked using infrared radiation.

The different colours mean different amounts of IR radiation are being detected from those areas. Here, the redder the colour, the more infrared radiation is being detected.

Surfers hate microwaves...

Who knew we used microwaves for more than cooking chips in less than 3 minutes? Turns out, they're dead handy.

Q1   State one use of radio waves.   [1 mark]

More Uses of EM Waves

Haven't had enough uses of EM waves? Good, because here's a few more. Get learning.

Fibre Optic Cables Use Visible Light to Send Data

1) Optical fibres are thin glass or plastic tubes that can carry data over long distances.
2) They're often used to send information to telephones or computers.
3) Information is sent as light rays that bounce back and forth along the fibre.

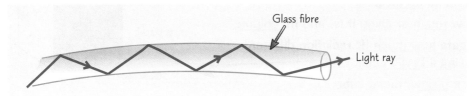

Glass fibre

Light ray

Ultraviolet Radiation Gives You a Suntan

1) When some materials absorb UV light, they give off visible light.
2) This can be pretty useful:

   1) Energy-efficient lights use UV radiation to produce visible light.
   2) Security pens can be used to mark property with your name (e.g. laptops).
   3) Under UV light the ink will glow, but it's invisible otherwise.
   4) This can help the police find out who stolen property belongs to.

3) Ultraviolet radiation (UV) is also produced by the Sun. It's what gives you a suntan.
4) UV lamps can be used to give people a suntan without the Sun (but this can be dangerous).

X-rays and Gamma Rays are Used in Medicine

1) X-rays pass easily through flesh but not through bones or metal.
2) This can be used to create an X-ray image to check for broken bones.
3) X-rays can also treat people with cancer.
4) This is because they can kill cells. They are aimed at the cancer cells to kill them.

1) Gamma rays (p.198) can also kill cells.
2) They can be used to treat cancer in the same way as X-rays.
3) They can also be used to sterilise (remove germs from) medical equipment.
   The equipment is blasted with gamma rays which kills any living things on it.
4) Gamma rays are also really good at passing through your body.
5) This is why small amounts of them are used in 'medical tracers'.
   How they move around the body can be tracked.
   This can tell doctors if organs are working as they should.

Don't lie to an X-ray — they can see right through you...

I hate to say it, but go back to page 224 and read all of the uses for EM waves again to really learn them.

Q1 State two uses of X-rays. [2 marks]

PRACTICAL | Investigating IR Radiation

Now it's time to see how the <u>surface</u> of an object affects <u>how much</u> infrared radiation it gives out.
I know, you can hardly contain your excitement. Neither can I.

Different Surfaces Emit Different Amounts of IR Radiation

1) The amount of <u>infrared radiation</u> an object gives out depends on its <u>temperature</u> — see p.224.

2) It also depends on its <u>surface</u>.

3) This includes how <u>rough</u> or <u>shiny</u> it is, and its <u>colour</u>.

4) You can investigate <u>how much</u> IR radiation different surfaces emit using a <u>Leslie cube</u>.

5) A <u>Leslie cube</u> is a <u>hollow</u>, metal cube.

6) The <u>four side faces</u> have <u>different surfaces</u>.

7) For example, <u>matt</u> (dull) <u>black paint</u>, matt <u>white paint</u>, <u>shiny</u> metal and <u>dull</u> metal.

You Can Investigate Emission With a Leslie Cube

1) Place an <u>empty Leslie cube</u> on a <u>heat-proof</u> mat.

2) <u>Draw</u> a square around the cube that is 10 cm from <u>all faces</u> of the cube.

3) <u>Fill</u> the <u>Leslie cube</u> with boiling water and wait for the cube to <u>warm up</u>.

4) Use the square you've drawn to hold an <u>infrared detector</u> 10 cm away from one of the cube's vertical faces.

5) Record the <u>amount of IR radiation</u> it detects.

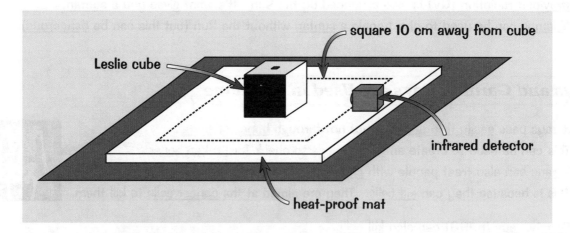

6) <u>Repeat</u> steps 4) and 5) for <u>each</u> of the <u>four faces</u>.

7) The face that had the <u>highest reading</u> is giving off the most IR radiation.

8) You should find that the <u>black</u> surface is radiating more IR radiation than the <u>white</u> one.

9) <u>Matt</u> surfaces should give off more than <u>shiny</u> ones.

10) As always, you should <u>repeat</u> the experiment to check your <u>results</u>.

Feelin' hot hot hot...

When doing this experiment, you could also place your hand <u>near</u> each surface of the cube (but not touching, it'll be super hot). You'll be able to feel which surface is giving off more infrared radiation.

Q1   What surface is the best emitter of infrared radiation out of:
    a) a black surface and a white surface?   b) a shiny surface and a matt surface?   [2 marks]

Topic P6 — Waves

Investigating IR Absorption   PRACTICAL

Have you ever noticed that wearing <u>black clothes</u> on a <u>hot day</u> makes you feel really warm?
   Turns out there's some <u>science</u> behind it...

You Can Investigate Absorption with the Melting Wax Trick

1) The amount of infrared radiation <u>absorbed</u> by different materials also depends on the <u>surface</u>.
2) You can do an experiment to show this.
3) You'll need a <u>Bunsen burner</u>, <u>candle wax</u>, <u>metal plates</u> and <u>metal balls</u>.
4) The metal plates should be identical except their <u>back surface</u>.
5) E.g. one plate will have a <u>black back</u>, and the other will have a <u>white back</u>.
6) Set up the equipment as shown:

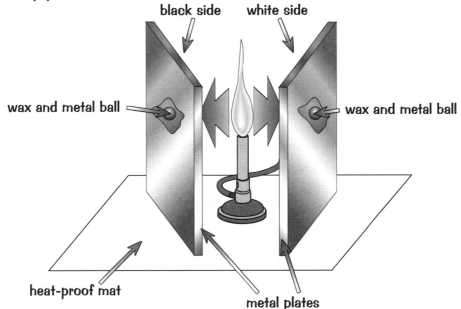

Here's how to do it:
1) Place a Bunsen burner on a <u>heat-proof mat</u>.
2) Stick a <u>metal ball</u> to each <u>identical side</u> of the metal plates with hot <u>candle wax</u>.
3) Leave the candle wax to <u>cool</u>. The wax will <u>harden</u> and hold the ball in place.
4) Then face the <u>back</u> of these plates towards the <u>flame</u>.
5) They should both be the <u>same distance</u> away from the flame.
6) Record which <u>ball falls</u> first.

Explaining the Results

1) The plates absorb <u>infrared radiation</u> given out by the <u>Bunsen burner</u>.
2) <u>Energy is transferred</u> to the <u>thermal energy stores</u> of the candle wax.
3) The candle wax starts to <u>melt</u>, causing the <u>balls to fall</u>.
4) The <u>ball</u> will fall <u>quicker</u> from the plate that is <u>better</u> at absorbing <u>infrared radiation</u>.
5) You should find that the ball on the plate with the <u>black back</u> falls first.
6) This means the black surface was <u>better</u> at <u>absorbing infrared radiation</u> than the white surface.

Wear a black hat to help your brain absorb this information...

...probably best not to rely on that for the exam, though. There's nothing for it — get learning.

Q1   Give two ways in which the experiment above is made a fair test.   [2 marks]

Dangers of Electromagnetic Waves

Okay, so you know how <u>useful</u> electromagnetic radiation can be — well, it can also be pretty <u>dangerous</u>.

Some EM Radiation Can be Harmful to People

1) When EM radiation enters <u>living tissue</u> — like <u>you</u> — it can be <u>dangerous</u>.
2) <u>High frequency</u> waves like <u>UV</u>, <u>X-rays</u> and <u>gamma rays</u> can all cause <u>lots of damage</u>.
3) <u>UV radiation</u> damages surface cells.
4) This can lead to <u>sunburn</u> and can cause <u>skin</u> to <u>age faster</u> than it should.
5) Some more serious effects are <u>blindness</u> and a <u>higher risk of skin cancer</u>.
6) <u>X-rays</u> and <u>gamma rays</u> are types of <u>ionising radiation</u>.
   This means they can <u>knock electrons off atoms</u>, p.197.
7) This can <u>destroy</u> cells or <u>mutate</u> (change) genes. This can cause <u>cancer</u>.

You Can Measure Risk Using the Radiation Dose in Sieverts

1) UV radiation, X-rays and gamma rays can all be <u>useful</u> as well as <u>harmful</u> (see page 225).
2) <u>Radiation dose</u> (measured in <u>sieverts</u>) is a measure of the <u>risk</u> of harm from the body being exposed to radiation.
3) The risk depends on the <u>total amount of radiation</u> absorbed <u>and</u> how <u>harmful</u> the <u>type</u> of radiation is.
4) A sievert is pretty big, so <u>millisieverts</u> (mSv) are often used.
   <u>1000 mSv = 1 Sv</u>.

Risk can be Different for Different Parts of the Body

1) A CT scan uses <u>X-rays</u> to create a detailed picture of inside a patient's body.
2) The table shows the <u>radiation dose</u> received by two <u>different parts</u> of a patient's body when having CT scans.

	Radiation dose (mSv)
Head	2.0
Chest	8.0

3) You can see that the radiation dose from a <u>chest scan</u> is <u>4 times larger</u> than from a <u>head scan</u> — (<u>2.0 mSv × 4 = 8.0 mSv</u>).
4) Remember, radiation dose measures the <u>risk</u> of harm.
5) This means that if a patient has a CT scan on their <u>chest</u>, they are <u>four times more likely</u> to be harmed than if they have a <u>head</u> scan.

This is not an excuse to stay in bed all day...

A small dose of radiation every now and then is very low risk — so X-rays are nothing to worry about.

Q1   Give two effects of a person being exposed to too much UV radiation.   [2 marks]

Q2   What property of gamma rays and X-rays makes them dangerous to humans?   [1 mark]

Permanent and Induced Magnets

I think magnetism is an <u>attractive</u> subject, but don't get <u>repelled</u> by the exam — <u>revise</u>.

Magnets Exert Forces on Each Other

1) All magnets have a <u>north (or north seeking) pole</u> and a <u>south (or south seeking) pole</u>.
2) When two magnets are close, they exert a <u>non-contact force</u> on each other.
3) Two poles that are the <u>same</u> (<u>like poles</u>) <u>repel</u> each other.
4) Two <u>different</u> (<u>unlike</u>) poles <u>attract</u> each other.
5) There are also forces between magnets and <u>magnetic materials</u>. These forces are <u>always attractive</u>.
6) <u>Iron</u>, <u>steel</u>, <u>nickel</u> and <u>cobalt</u> are all magnetic materials.

Objects don't need to be touching for a non-contact force to act between them — see p.203.

1) The area <u>around a magnet</u> where it can exert a <u>force</u> is its <u>magnetic field</u>.
2) Magnetic fields can be shown with <u>magnetic field lines</u>.
3) The lines go from <u>north to south</u>. They show <u>which way</u> the force would push a <u>north pole</u> at that point.
4) Lines <u>closer together</u> mean a <u>stronger</u> magnetic field.
5) The <u>closer</u> to a magnet you are, the <u>stronger</u> the field is.
6) The magnetic field is <u>strongest</u> at the <u>poles</u>.
7) This means the magnetic <u>force</u> is strongest here too.

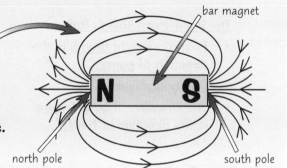
bar magnet
north pole
south pole

A Compass Shows the Direction of a Magnetic Field

1) The <u>needle</u> of a <u>compass</u> is a tiny <u>bar magnet</u>. It <u>points</u> in the <u>direction</u> of any <u>magnetic field</u> that it's in.
2) So you can use a <u>compass</u> to plot magnetic field patterns:

- <u>Draw around</u> a magnet on a <u>piece of paper</u>.
- Put a <u>compass</u> by the magnet.
- <u>Mark</u> the <u>direction</u> the compass needle points in by drawing <u>a dot at each end</u> of the needle.
- <u>Move</u> the compass so that the <u>tail end</u> of the needle is where the <u>tip</u> of the needle was before.
- Repeat this lots of times. <u>Join up</u> all the marks. You will end up with a <u>drawing</u> of one <u>field line</u>.

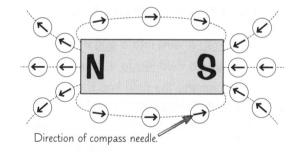
Direction of compass needle.

3) When they're not <u>near</u> a magnet, compasses <u>always point north</u>.
4) This is because they point in the direction of the <u>Earth's magnetic field</u>.
5) So the <u>inside</u> (<u>core</u>) of the Earth must be <u>magnetic</u>.

Magnets Can be Permanent or Induced

1) <u>Permanent</u> magnets create their <u>own</u> magnetic field.
2) An <u>induced</u> magnet <u>turns into</u> a magnet when it's put into another magnetic field.
3) When you <u>take away</u> the magnetic field, induced magnets quickly <u>stop being magnets</u>. A fancy way to say this is to say that they <u>lose their magnetism</u> (or most of it).
4) Permanent magnets and induced magnets <u>always attract</u> each other.

Magnets are like farmers — surrounded by fields...

Magnetism is tricky and takes a while to make sense. Learn these basics — you'll need them.

Q1   What will happen when the north poles of two magnets are brought close together?   [1 mark]

Electromagnetism

A <u>magnetic field</u> is also found around a <u>wire</u> that has a <u>current</u> passing through it.

A Current Creates a Magnetic Field

1) A <u>current</u> flowing through a <u>wire</u> creates a <u>magnetic field</u>.

2) You can see this by placing a <u>compass</u> near to the wire.
The compass will <u>move</u> to point in the <u>direction of the field</u>.

3) You can use this to <u>draw the field</u>, just like on the previous page.

4) The field is made up of <u>circles</u> around the wire (see below).

5) You can also use the <u>right-hand thumb rule</u> to quickly work out which way the field goes:

<u>The Right-Hand Thumb Rule</u>
- Point your <u>right thumb</u> in the direction of <u>current</u>.
- <u>Curl</u> your fingers.
- The direction of your <u>fingers</u> is the direction of the <u>field</u>.

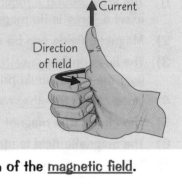

6) Reversing (swapping) the <u>direction</u> of the <u>current</u> reverses the direction of the <u>magnetic field</u>.

7) The <u>closer</u> to the wire you are, the <u>stronger</u> the magnetic field gets.

8) And the <u>larger</u> the <u>current</u> through the wire is, the <u>stronger</u> the field is.

A Solenoid is a Coil of Wire

1) If you <u>wrap</u> a wire into a <u>coil</u> it's called a <u>solenoid</u>.

2) The magnetic field <u>inside</u> a solenoid is <u>strong</u> and <u>uniform</u>.

3) <u>Uniform</u> means the field has the <u>same</u> <u>strength</u> and <u>direction</u> everywhere.

4) The magnetic field <u>outside</u> a coil, is just like the one around a <u>bar magnet</u>.

5) Wrapping a wire into a solenoid <u>increases the strength</u> of the magnetic field produced by the current in the wire.

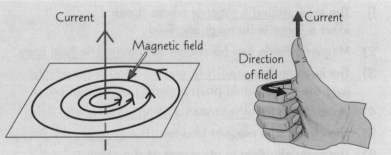

- This is because the <u>field lines</u> around <u>each loop</u> of wire <u>line up</u> with each other.
- So <u>lots</u> of <u>field lines</u> end up <u>close</u> to each other and pointing in the <u>same direction</u>.
- The <u>closer together</u> field lines are, the <u>stronger the field</u> is.

6) You can <u>increase</u> the field strength <u>even more</u> by putting a block of <u>iron</u> in the coil.

7) A <u>solenoid with an iron core</u> is called an **ELECTROMAGNET**.

Strong, in uniform and a magnetic personality — I'm a catch...

Short, but not very sweet. Electromagnetism is tricky to get your head around, so have another read of this page.

Q1   Draw the magnetic field for a current-carrying wire.
Show the directions of the current and the magnetic field.

[2 marks]

Revision Questions for Topics P6 & P7

Whew, the end of Topic P7 — time to see how much you can remember about the last two topics.
- Try these questions and tick off each one when you get it right.
- When you've done all the questions under a heading and are completely happy with it, tick it off.

Wave Properties (p.219-222) ☐

1) What is the difference between transverse and longitudinal waves? ☐
2) What is the amplitude of a wave? ☐
3) What is the wavelength of a wave? ☐
4) How are the frequency and period of a wave linked? ☐
5) Write down the equation that links wave speed, frequency and wavelength. ☐
6) Describe an experiment you could do to measure:
   a) the speed of sound in air.   b) the speed of waves on a string. ☐
7) Sketch a ray diagram showing the refraction of a light ray between two materials. ☐

Uses and Dangers of Electromagnetic Waves (p.223-228) ☐

8) True or false? All electromagnetic waves are transverse. ☐
9) Give an example of electromagnetic waves transferring energy from a source to an absorber. ☐
10) True or false? Gamma rays have the longest wavelength of EM waves. ☐
11) Give an everyday use of infrared radiation. ☐
12) What type of radiation is used to transmit a signal through an optical fibre? ☐
13) How could you use a Leslie cube to investigate infrared emission by different surfaces? ☐
14) True or false? The amount of infrared radiation absorbed
    by an object depends on the surface of the object. ☐
15) What does the term 'ionising radiation' mean? ☐
16) What does radiation dose in sieverts measure? ☐

Magnets (p.229) ☐

17) True or false? The force between a north pole and a south pole is attractive. ☐
18) True or false? A magnet always repels a magnetic material. ☐
19) In what direction do magnetic field lines point? ☐
20) How can you draw a magnetic field pattern of a bar magnet using a compass? ☐
21) Describe the behaviour of a compass that is far away from any magnets. ☐

Electromagnetism (p.230) ☐

22) Explain how to use the right-hand thumb rule to find the direction of a magnetic field around a wire. ☐
23) What is a solenoid? ☐
24) Sketch the shape of the magnetic field around a solenoid. ☐
25) How can you increase the strength of a solenoid's magnetic field? ☐

Measuring Techniques

Safety specs out and lab coats on, it's time to find out about the skills you'll need in <u>experiments</u>...

Mass Should Be Measured Using a Balance

1) To measure mass, put the <u>container</u> you're measuring the substance <u>into</u> on the <u>balance</u>.

2) Set the balance to exactly <u>zero</u>. Then <u>add</u> your substance and <u>read off</u> the <u>mass</u>.

3) If you want to transfer the substance to a new container, you need to make sure that the mass you <u>transfer</u> is the <u>same</u> as the mass you <u>measured</u>. There are different ways you can do this. For example:

> • If you're <u>dissolving</u> a mass of a solid in a solvent to make a <u>solution</u>, you could <u>wash</u> any remaining solid into the new container using the <u>solvent</u>.
>
> • You could set the balance <u>to zero</u> before you put your <u>weighing container</u> on the balance. Then <u>reweigh</u> the weighing container <u>after</u> you've transferred the substance. Use the <u>difference</u> in mass to work out <u>exactly</u> how much substance you've transferred.

Different Ways to Measure Liquids

1) There are a few methods you might use to transfer a volume of liquid:

> <u>Dropping pipette</u> — Use this if you only want a <u>couple of drops</u> of liquid. It's also used if you <u>don't</u> need an <u>accurate volume</u> of liquid.

> <u>Pipette</u> — Use this if you want an <u>accurate</u> volume of liquid. The <u>pipette filler</u> lets you <u>safely</u> <u>control</u> the amount of liquid you're drawing up.

> <u>Measuring cylinders</u> — These come in many different <u>sizes</u>. You need to use one that's the <u>right size</u> for the measurement you want to make (you don't want one that's <u>too big</u>).

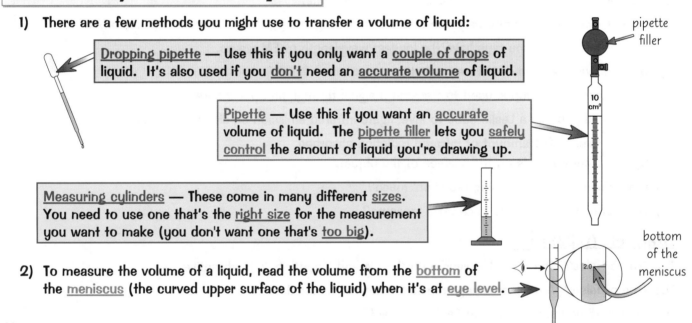

pipette filler

10 cm³

bottom of the meniscus

2) To measure the volume of a liquid, read the volume from the <u>bottom</u> of the <u>meniscus</u> (the curved upper surface of the liquid) when it's at <u>eye level</u>.

You Can Measure Gas Volumes

There are a few ways you can measure the volume of a gas:

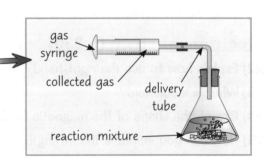

gas syringe

collected gas

delivery tube

reaction mixture

1) <u>Gas syringe</u> — this is the <u>most accurate</u> way to measure gas volume.

> • Make sure the gas syringe is the <u>right size</u> for your measurements.
> • Make sure the plunger moves <u>smoothly</u>.
> • Read the volume from the <u>scale</u> on the syringe.

2) <u>Upturned measuring cylinder</u> filled with <u>water</u> — read more about this on page 237.

3) <u>Counting the bubbles</u> produced or measuring the <u>length</u> of a <u>gas bubble</u> drawn along a tube (see p.52).

> • These methods are <u>less accurate</u>.
> • But they will give you <u>results</u> that you can <u>compare</u>.

Always make sure your equipment is <u>sealed</u> so no gas can escape. This will make your results more <u>accurate</u>.

Measuring Techniques

Eureka Cans Measure the Volumes of Solids

1) A <u>eureka can</u> is a <u>beaker with a spout</u>.

2) It's used with a <u>measuring cylinder</u> to find the <u>volume</u> of an <u>irregularly shaped solid object</u> (p.194).

3) Here are a few things you need to do when you <u>use</u> one:

- Fill it with water so the water level is <u>above the spout</u>.
- Let the water <u>drain</u> from the spout, leaving the water level <u>just below</u> the start of the spout. (This means <u>all</u> the water moved by an object goes into the measuring cylinder.)
- After adding the object, wait until the spout has <u>stopped dripping</u> before measuring the volume. This will give you a more <u>accurate</u> result.

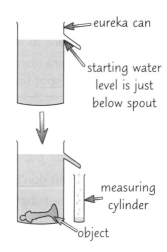

Measure Most Lengths with a Ruler

1) Make sure you <u>choose</u> the <u>right ruler</u> to measure length:
- In most cases a <u>centimetre ruler</u> can be used.
- <u>Metre rulers</u> are handy for <u>large</u> distances.
- <u>Micrometers</u> are used for measuring <u>tiny</u> things (e.g. the <u>diameter of a wire</u>).

2) The ruler should always be <u>alongside</u> what you want to measure.

3) It may be <u>tricky</u> to measure just <u>one</u> of something (e.g. water ripples, p.221). Instead, you can measure the length of <u>ten</u> of them together. Then <u>divide by ten</u> to find the <u>length of one</u>.

4) You might need to take <u>lots of measurements</u> of the <u>same</u> object (e.g. a spring). If so, make sure you always measure from the <u>same point</u> on the object. Draw or stick small <u>markers</u> onto the object to line your ruler up against.

5) Make sure the ruler and the object are always at <u>eye level</u> when you take a reading.

Use a Protractor to Find Angles

1) Place the <u>middle</u> of the protractor on the <u>pointy bit</u> of the angle.

2) <u>Line up</u> the <u>base line</u> of the protractor with one line of the angle.

3) Use the <u>scale</u> on the protractor to measure the angle of the other line.

4) Use a <u>sharp pencil</u> to draw lines at an angle (e.g. in ray diagrams). This helps to <u>reduce errors</u> when measuring the angles.

Measure Temperature Using a Thermometer

1) Make sure the <u>bulb</u> of your thermometer is <u>completely under the surface</u> of the substance.

2) If you're taking a <u>starting temperature</u>, you should wait for the temperature to <u>stop changing</u>.

3) Read your measurement off the <u>scale</u> at <u>eye level</u>.

You May Have to Measure the Time Taken for a Change

1) You should use a <u>stopwatch</u> to <u>time</u> experiments. These measure to the nearest <u>0.1 s</u>.

2) Always make sure you <u>start</u> and <u>stop</u> the stopwatch at exactly the right time.

3) You can set an <u>alarm</u> on the stopwatch so you know exactly when to stop an experiment or take a reading.

Practical Skills

Measuring Techniques

There are Different Methods for Measuring pH

1) <u>Indicator solutions</u> can be used to estimate pH. Add a <u>couple of drops</u> of the indicator to the solution you want to test. It will <u>change colour</u> depending on if it's in an <u>acid</u> or an <u>alkali</u> (see p.128).

2) There are also <u>paper indicators</u>. These are <u>strips of paper</u> that contain indicator.
If you <u>spot</u> some solution onto indicator paper, the paper will <u>change colour</u> to show the pH.

   - <u>Litmus paper</u> turns <u>red</u> in acidic conditions and <u>blue</u> in alkaline conditions.
   - <u>Universal indicator paper</u> can be used to <u>estimate</u> the pH based on its colour.

litmus paper

3) Indicator paper is <u>useful</u> when:

   - You <u>don't</u> want to change the colour of <u>all</u> of the substance.
   - The substance is <u>already</u> coloured (so it might <u>hide</u> the colour of the indicator).
   - You want to find the pH of a <u>gas</u> — hold a piece of <u>damp indicator paper</u> in a <u>gas sample</u>.

4) <u>pH probes</u> measure pH <u>electronically</u> (see page 128). They are more <u>accurate</u> than indicators.

You Can Measure the Size of a Single Cell

When viewing <u>cells</u> under a <u>microscope</u>, you might need to work out their <u>size</u>.

To work out the size of a <u>single cell</u>:

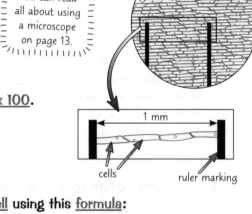

You can read all about using a microscope on page 13.

1) Place a <u>clear, plastic ruler</u> on <u>top</u> of your microscope <u>slide</u>.

2) <u>Clip</u> the <u>ruler</u> and <u>slide</u> onto the <u>stage</u>.

3) Select the <u>objective lens</u> that gives an overall magnification of <u>x 100</u>.

4) Use the <u>coarse adjustment knob</u> and the <u>fine adjustment knob</u> to see a <u>clear image</u> of the cells.

5) <u>Move</u> the ruler so that the cells are <u>lined up</u> along <u>1 mm</u>.

1 mm

cells   ruler marking

6) <u>Count</u> the <u>number of cells</u> along this <u>1 mm sample</u>.

7) 1 mm = 1000 μm. So you can <u>calculate</u> the <u>size</u> of a <u>single cell</u> using this <u>formula</u>:

$$\text{length of cell } (\mu m) = \frac{1000\ \mu m}{\text{number of cells counted in sample}}$$

EXAMPLE:

Under a microscope, 4 cells were counted in 1 mm.
Calculate the size of one cell. Give your answer in μm.

1 mm is the <u>same</u> as 1000 μm, so you just need to put the <u>number of cells</u> into the formula.

$$\text{length of cell } (\mu m) = \frac{1000\ \mu m}{4} = 250\ \mu m$$

Experimentus apparatus...

It's too bad, but being a wizard won't help you here. Make sure you get your head down and learn these techniques inside out. They need to be second nature when it comes to any practicals.

Safety and Ethics

Before you start any experiment, you need to know what safety measures you should be taking. They depend on your method, your equipment and the chemicals you're using.

To Make Sure You're Working Safely in the Lab You Need to...

1) Wear sensible clothing (e.g. shoes that will protect your feet from spillages). Also:
   - Wear a lab coat to protect your skin and clothing.
   - Wear safety goggles to protect your eyes, and gloves to protect your hands.
2) Be aware of general safety in the lab. E.g. don't touch any hot equipment.
3) Follow any instructions that your teacher gives you carefully.
4) Chemicals and equipment can be hazardous (dangerous). E.g. some chemicals are flammable (they catch fire easily) — this means you must be careful not to use a Bunsen burner near them.
5) Here are some tips for working with chemicals and equipment safely...

Working with chemicals

1) Make sure you're working in an area that's well ventilated (has a good flow of air).
2) If you're doing an experiment that produces nasty gases (such as chlorine), carry out the experiment in a fume hood. This means the gas can't escape out into the room you're working in.
3) Never touch any chemicals (even if you're wearing gloves):
   - Use a spatula to transfer solids between containers.
   - Carefully pour liquids between containers using a funnel. This will help prevent spillages.
4) Be careful when you're mixing chemicals, as a reaction might occur. E.g. if you're diluting a liquid, always add the concentrated substance to the water. This stops it getting hot.

Working with equipment

1) Use clamp stands to stop masses and equipment falling.
2) Make sure masses are not too heavy (so they don't break the equipment they're used with).
3) Use pulleys that are not too long (so hanging masses don't hit the floor during the experiment).
4) Let hot materials cool before moving them. Or wear insulated gloves while handling them.
5) If you're using an immersion heater, you should always let it dry out in air. This is just in case any liquid has leaked inside the heater.
6) When working with electronics, make sure you use a low voltage and current. This prevents the wires overheating. It also stops damage to components.

You Need to Think About Ethical Issues

Any organisms that you use in your experiments need to be treated safely and ethically. This means:
1) Animals should be handled carefully.
2) Any captured wild animals should be returned to their habitat after the experiment.
3) Any animals kept in the lab should be well cared for. E.g. they should have plenty of space.
4) Other students that take part in any experiment should be happy to do so.

Safety first...

I know — lab safety isn't the most exciting topic. But it's very important. Not only will it stop you from blowing your eyebrows off, it'll help you pick up more marks in the exam. And that IS worth getting excited about...

Setting Up Experiments

Setting up the equipment for an experiment in the right way is <u>important</u>. Learn these set-ups...

You Can Identify the Products of Electrolysis

There's more about electrolysis on p.132-133.

1) When you <u>electrolyse</u> a <u>salt solution</u>:

- At the <u>cathode</u>, you'll get a <u>pure metal</u> coating the electrode OR bubbles of <u>hydrogen gas</u>.
- At the <u>anode</u>, you'll get bubbles of <u>oxygen gas</u> OR a <u>halogen</u>.

2) You may have to <u>do some tests</u> to find out what's been <u>made</u>.

3) To do this, you need to <u>set up the equipment</u> correctly to <u>collect</u> any <u>gas</u> that's produced. The easiest way to collect the gas is in a <u>test tube</u>.

4) Here's how to set up the equipment...

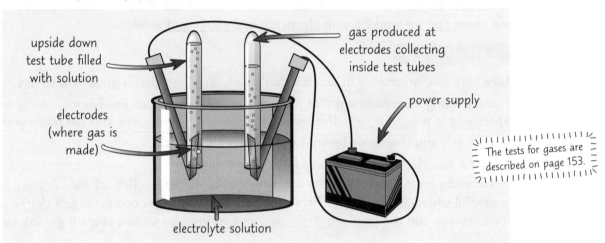

upside down test tube filled with solution

gas produced at electrodes collecting inside test tubes

power supply

electrodes (where gas is made)

The tests for gases are described on page 153.

electrolyte solution

Set Up a Potometer to Measure Transpiration Rate

1) A <u>potometer</u> is a special piece of equipment.

2) You set it up as shown in the diagram.

3) You can use a <u>potometer</u> to <u>estimate</u> <u>transpiration rate</u> (see page 40). Here's what you do:

- Record the <u>starting position</u> of the <u>air bubble</u>.
- Start a <u>stopwatch</u>.
- As the plant takes up water, the air bubble gets <u>sucked</u> along the tube.
- Record <u>how far</u> the air bubble moves in a <u>set time</u>.
- Then you can <u>estimate</u> the <u>transpiration rate</u>.

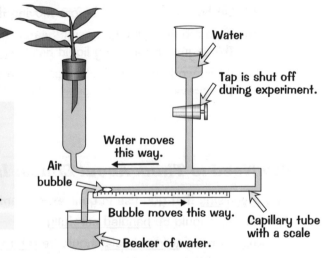

Water

Tap is shut off during experiment.

Water moves this way.

Air bubble

Bubble moves this way.

Capillary tube with a scale

Beaker of water.

EXAMPLE:
A potometer was used to estimate the transpiration rate of a plant cutting. The bubble moved 25 mm in 10 minutes. Estimate the transpiration rate.

To estimate the <u>transpiration rate</u>, divide the <u>distance</u> the bubble moved by the <u>time taken</u>.

$$\text{Transpiration rate} = \frac{\text{distance bubble moved}}{\text{time taken}} = \frac{25 \text{ mm}}{10 \text{ min}}$$
$$= 2.5 \text{ mm/min}$$

Practical Skills

Setting Up Experiments

You Can Collect a Gas in a Measuring Cylinder

1) You can use a <u>measuring cylinder</u> turned <u>upside down</u> and filled with <u>water</u> to <u>collect gas</u>.

2) Then you can <u>measure</u> the <u>gas volume</u>. Here's how you do it:

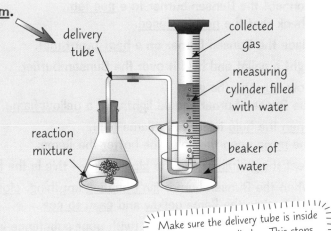

1) <u>Set up</u> the <u>equipment</u> like in the <u>diagram</u>.
2) Record the <u>starting level</u> of the water in the measuring cylinder.
3) Any gas from the reaction will pass <u>through</u> the delivery tube and <u>into</u> the <u>measuring cylinder</u>.
4) The gas will <u>push the water out</u> of the measuring cylinder.
5) Record the <u>end level</u> of water in the measuring cylinder.
6) Calculate the <u>volume</u> of gas produced — <u>subtract</u> the <u>end level</u> of water from the <u>starting level</u> of water.

delivery tube

collected gas

measuring cylinder filled with water

reaction mixture

beaker of water

Make sure the delivery tube is inside the measuring cylinder. This stops the gas escaping out into the air.

3) You can use the method above to collect a <u>gas sample</u> to <u>test</u>.
- Use a <u>test tube</u> instead of a measuring cylinder.
- When the test tube is full of gas, you can <u>put a bung in it</u>. This lets you <u>store</u> the gas for later.

Make Sure You Can Draw Diagrams of Your Equipment

1) Your <u>method</u> should include a <u>labelled diagram</u> of how your equipment will be <u>set up</u>.

2) Use <u>scientific drawings</u> — each piece of equipment is drawn as if you're looking at it <u>from the side</u>.

3) For example:

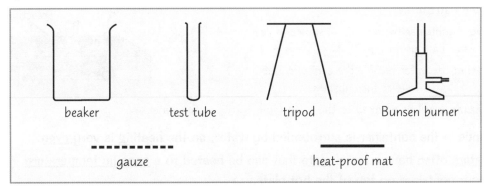

beaker　　　test tube　　　tripod　　　Bunsen burner

gauze　　　　　　　heat-proof mat

4) The <u>beaker</u> and <u>test tube</u> above <u>aren't sealed</u>. To show them <u>sealed</u>, draw a <u>bung</u> in the top.

Science exams — they're a set-up...

It looks like there's a lot of equipment to remember on these pages. Have a go at drawing diagrams of each set-up and labelling the equipment. Then look back at the page and see what you got right. It'll soon stick like superglue.

Practical Skills

Heating Substances

You need to be able to decide on the best and safest method for heating a substance...

Bunsen Burners Heat Things Quickly

Here's how to use a Bunsen burner...

1) Connect the Bunsen burner to a gas tap.
   Check that the hole is closed.

2) Place the Bunsen burner on a heat-proof mat.

3) Light a splint and hold it over the Bunsen burner.

4) Now, turn on the gas.
   The Bunsen burner should light with a yellow flame.

5) Open the hole to turn the flame blue.
   The more open the hole, the hotter the flame.

6) Heat things just above the blue cone — this is the hottest part of the flame.

7) When the Bunsen burner isn't heating anything, close the hole.
   This makes the flame yellow and easy to see.

8) If you're heating a container (with your substance in it) in the flame, hold it at the top with a pair of tongs.

9) If you're heating a container over the flame, put a tripod and gauze over the Bunsen burner before you light it. Then place the container on the gauze.

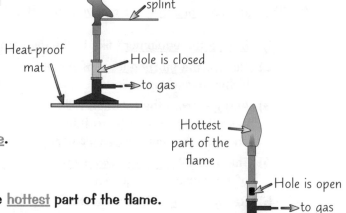

Water Baths & Electric Heaters Have Set Temperatures

1) A water bath is a container filled with water. It can be heated to a specific temperature.

2) A simple water bath can be made by heating a beaker of water over a Bunsen burner.
   • The temperature is checked with a thermometer.
   • However, it's hard to keep the temperature of the water constant.

3) An electric water bath will check and change the temperature for you. Here's how you use one:

   • Set the temperature on the water bath.
   • Allow the water to heat up.
   • Place your container (with your substance in it) in the water bath using tongs.
   • The level of the water outside the container should be just above the level of the substance inside it.
   • The substance will be warmed to the same temperature as the water.

   The substance in the container is surrounded by water, so the heating is very even.

4) Electric heaters often have a metal plate that can be heated to a specific temperature.
   • Place your container on top of the hot plate.
   • You can heat substances to higher temperatures than you can in a water bath.
     (You can't use a water bath to heat something higher than 100 °C.)
   • You have to stir the substance to make sure it's heated evenly.

A bath and an electric heater — how I spend my January nights...

My science teacher used to play power ballads when the Bunsens were alight. Then he'd sway like he was at a gig.

Working with Electronics

Electrical devices are used in loads of experiments. Make sure you know how to use them.

There Are a Few Ways to Measure Potential Difference and Current

Voltmeters Measure Potential Difference

1) Connect the voltmeter in parallel (p.186) across the component you want to test.
2) The wires that come with a voltmeter are usually red (positive) and black (negative). These go into the red and black coloured ports on the voltmeter.
3) Then read the potential difference from the scale (or from the screen if the voltmeter is digital).

Ammeters Measure Current

1) Connect the ammeter in series (p.185) with the component you want to test.
2) Ammeters usually have red and black ports to show you where to connect your wires.
3) Read off the current shown on the scale (or screen).

Turn your circuit off between readings. This stops wires overheating and affecting your results (page 181).

Multimeters Measure Both

1) Multimeters measure a range of things — usually potential difference, current and resistance.
2) To find potential difference, plug the red wire into the port that has a 'V' (for volts).
3) To find the current, use the port labelled 'A' (for amps).
4) The dial on the multimeter should then be turned to the relevant section — for example, to measure the current in amps, turn the dial to 'A'.
5) The screen will display the value you're measuring.

Light Gates Measure Time, Speed and Acceleration

1) A light gate sends a beam of light from one side of the gate to a detector on the other side.
2) When something passes through the gate, the light beam is interrupted.
3) The gate measures when the beam was interrupted and how long it was interrupted for.
4) Light gates can be connected to a computer.
5) To find the speed of an object, type the length of the object into the computer. The computer will calculate the speed of the object as it passes through the beam.
6) To measure acceleration, use an object that interrupts the signal twice, e.g. a piece of card with a gap cut into the middle.
7) The light gate measures the speed for each section of the object. It uses this to calculate the object's acceleration. This can then be read from the computer screen.
8) Light gates can be used instead of a stop watch. This will reduce the errors in your experiment.

Light gate

Beam of light

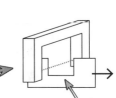

Piece of card

Have a look at page 214 for an example of a light gate being used.

That's not a gate — where are the hinges...

After finishing this page, you should be able to take on any electrical experiment that they throw at you... ouch.

Sampling

I love samples... especially when I'm a bit peckish in the supermarket and they're handing out free cheese. Unfortunately, this page isn't about those samples. It's a lot more useful than that...

Sampling Should be Random

1) When you're investigating a population, it's usually not possible to study every single organism in it.
2) This means that you need to take samples of the population.
3) The samples need to accurately represent the whole population.
   This is so you can use them to draw conclusions about the whole population.
4) To make sure a sample represents the population, it should be random.

Organisms Should Be Sampled At Random Sites in an Area

1) Quadrats can be used to take population samples of an organism in an area (see page 87).
2) If you're looking at plant species in a field...

- Divide the field into a grid.
- Label the grid along the bottom and up the side with numbers.
- Use a random number generator (e.g. on a computer or calculator) to select coordinates, e.g. (2,7).
- Place your quadrats at these coordinates to take your samples.

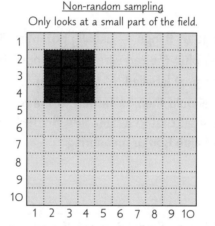

Non-random sampling
Only looks at a small part of the field.

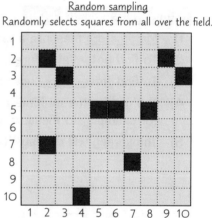

Random sampling
Randomly selects squares from all over the field.

Health Data Should be Taken from Randomly Selected People

You need to use random sampling to choose members of the population you're interested in.

E.g. a scientist is looking at health data in country X. She wants to know how many people in the country have both Type 2 diabetes and heart disease:

1) Hospital records show that 270 196 people in the country have Type 2 diabetes.
2) These people are given a number between 1 and 270 196.
3) A random number generator is used to choose the sample group
   — e.g. it selects individuals with the numbers #72 063, #11 822, #193 123, etc.
4) The records of the sample group are used to find the number of people with heart disease in it.
5) The proportion of people in the sample group who have heart disease is worked out.
6) This can be used to estimate the total number of people with Type 2 diabetes who also have heart disease.

'Eeny, meeny, miny, moe' just doesn't cut it any more...

Sampling is an important part of an investigation. It needs to be done randomly, or the data won't be worth much.

Comparing Results

Being able to <u>compare</u> your results is really important. Here is one way you might do it. I spoil you.

Percentage Change Allows you to Compare Results

1) When investigating the <u>change</u> in a variable, you may want to <u>compare</u> results that didn't have the <u>same starting value</u>.

> *   For example, you may want to compare the <u>change in mass</u> of <u>potato cylinders</u> left in different concentrations of <u>sugar solution</u> (see page 18).
> *   The cylinders probably all had <u>different masses</u> to <u>start with</u>.

2) To do this you can calculate the <u>percentage change</u>. You work it out like this:

$$\text{percentage (\%) change} = \frac{\text{final value} - \text{original value}}{\text{original value}} \times 100$$

3) A <u>positive</u> percentage change means that the value <u>increased</u>.
A <u>negative</u> percentage change means that the value <u>decreased</u>.

 **EXAMPLE:**

A student is investigating the effect of the concentration of sugar solution on potato cells.

She records the mass of potato cylinders before and after placing them in sugar solutions of different concentrations. The table below shows some of her results.

Potato cylinder	Concentration (mol/dm^3)	Mass at start (g)	Mass at end (g)
1	0.0	7.5	8.7
2	1.0	8.0	6.8

Which potato cylinder had the largest percentage change?

1) Stick each set of results into the <u>equation</u>: $\% \text{ change} = \dfrac{\text{final value} - \text{original value}}{\text{original value}} \times 100$

The mass at the <u>start</u> is the <u>original value</u>.

potato cylinder 1: $\dfrac{8.7 - 7.5}{7.5} \times 100 = 16\%$

The mass at the <u>end</u> is the <u>final value</u>.

potato cylinder 2: $\dfrac{6.8 - 8.0}{8.0} \times 100 = -15\%$ — Here, the mass has <u>decreased</u> so the percentage change is <u>negative</u>.

2) <u>Compare</u> the results.

16% is greater than 15%. So potato cylinder 1 (in the 0.0 mol/dm^3 sugar solution) had the largest percentage change.

Percentage change in how much I love maths after this page — 0%

Aaaand that's the end of Practical Skills, folks. Go forth, and science like you've never scienced before...

Answers

Topic B1 — Cell Biology

p.11 — Cells
Q1 Any two from: e.g. bacterial cells are smaller than animal cells *[1 mark]*. / Bacterial cells don't have mitochondria but animal cells do *[1 mark]*. / Bacterial cells don't have a true nucleus but animal cells do *[1 mark]*. / Bacterial cells have circular DNA but animal cells don't *[1 mark]* / Bacterial cells have a cell wall but animal cells don't *[1 mark]*. / Bacterial cells have plasmids but animal cells don't *[1 mark]*.

p.12 — Microscopy
Q1 magnification = image size ÷ real size
= 7.5 mm ÷ 0.075
= × 100 *[1 mark]*

p.13 — More on Microscopy
Q1 To make parts of the cell easier to see *[1 mark]*.

p.14 — Cell Differentiation and Specialisation
Q1 The cell has a hair-like shape, which gives it a large surface area *[1 mark]* to absorb water and minerals from the soil *[1 mark]*.

p.15 — Chromosomes and Mitosis
Q1 The cell has to increase the amount of its subcellular structures *[1 mark]* and copy its DNA *[1 mark]*.

p.16 — Stem Cells
Q1 Copies of the plant can be made by taking stem cells from the meristem of the plant *[1 mark]* and growing them into new, genetically identical plants (clones) *[1 mark]*.

p.17 — Diffusion
Q1 The larger the surface area of the membrane the faster the diffusion rate *[1 mark]*. This is because more particles can pass through at the same time *[1 mark]*.

p.18 — Osmosis
Q1 Water will move out of the piece of potato by osmosis *[1 mark]*, so its mass will decrease *[1 mark]*.

p.19 — Active Transport
Q1 Active transport allows nutrients such as glucose to move from a lower concentration in the gut to a higher concentration in the blood (against the concentration gradient) *[1 mark]*.

p.20 — Exchanging Substances
Q1 Surface area:
(2 × 2) × 2 = 8
(2 × 1) × 4 = 8
8 + 8 = 16 μm² *[1 mark]*
Volume:
2 × 2 × 1 = 4 μm³ *[1 mark]*
So the surface area to volume ratio is 16 : 4, or 4 : 1 *[1 mark]*.

p.22 — More on Exchanging Substances
Q1 Any two from: e.g. it's made up of lots of thin plates that give a large surface area. / The plates have lots of capillaries. / The plates have a thin layer of surface cells. *[2 marks — 1 mark for each correct answer]*

Topic B2 — Organisation

p.24 — Cell Organisation
Q1 That it is made up of different tissues *[1 mark]* that work together to perform a particular function *[1 mark]*.

p.25 — Enzymes
Q1 If the pH is too high it affects the bonds holding the active site together *[1 mark]*. This changes the shape of the active site and denatures the enzyme *[1 mark]*.

p.26 — Investigating Enzymatic Reactions
Q1 1000 ÷ 50 = 20 s⁻¹ *[1 mark]*

p.27 — Enzymes and Digestion
Q1 Bile neutralises the stomach acid and makes conditions in the small intestine alkaline *[1 mark]*. The enzymes of the small intestine work best in these alkaline conditions *[1 mark]*. It also emulsifies fats / breaks down fats into tiny droplets *[1 mark]*. This gives a bigger surface area of fat for the enzyme lipase to work on, which makes digestion faster *[1 mark]*.

p.28 — Food Tests
Q1 iodine solution *[1 mark]*

p.29 — The Lungs
Q1 492 ÷ 12 = 41 breaths per minute *[1 mark]*

p.30 — Circulatory System — The Heart
Q1 The right ventricle *[1 mark]*.

p.31 — Circulatory System — Blood Vessels
Q1 They have a big lumen to help the blood flow despite the low pressure *[1 mark]*. They have valves to keep the blood flowing in the right direction *[1 mark]*.

p.32 — Circulatory System — Blood
Q1 They help the blood to clot at a wound *[1 mark]*.
Q2 They have a large surface area for absorbing oxygen *[1 mark]*. They don't have a nucleus, which allows more room for carrying oxygen *[1 mark]*. They contain haemoglobin, which allows red blood cells to carry oxygen *[1 mark]*.

p.33 — Cardiovascular Disease
Q1 Any two from: e.g. there is a risk of a heart attack during the operation. / There's a risk of infection from surgery. / There's a risk of the patient developing a blood clot near the stent *[2 marks]*.

p.34 — More on Cardiovascular Disease
Q1 Any one from: e.g. surgery to fit an artificial heart can lead to bleeding and infection. / Artificial hearts don't work as well as healthy natural ones. / Blood doesn't flow through the heart as smoothly, which could cause clots and lead to strokes. / The patient has to take blood thinning drugs to prevent blood clots, which could cause problems with bleeding if they're hurt in an accident *[1 mark]*.

p.35 — Health and Disease
Q1 The state of physical and mental wellbeing *[1 mark]*.

p.36 — Risk Factors for Non-Communicable Diseases
Q1 Substances in a person's body. / Substances in a person's environment *[1 mark]*.

p.37 — Cancer
Q1 Uncontrolled growth and division of cells *[1 mark]*.
Q2 Any three from: e.g. smoking / obesity / UV exposure / viral infection *[3 marks]*.

p.38 — Plant Cell Organisation
Q1 Meristem tissue is found at the growing tips of roots and shoots *[1 mark]*.

p.39 — Transpiration and Translocation
Q1 Xylem is made up of dead cells joined together end to end *[1 mark]* with no end walls between them and a hole down the middle *[1 mark]*. It is strengthened by lignin *[1 mark]*.

p.40 — Transpiration and Stomata
Q1 As it gets darker, the stomata begin to close *[1 mark]*. This means that very little water can escape *[1 mark]*. So the rate of transpiration decreases *[1 mark]*.

Topic B3 — Infection and Response

p.42 — Communicable Disease
Q1 Any two from: e.g. bacteria / viruses / protists / fungi *[2 marks]*.
Q2 To prevent pathogens being spread onto food and then being eaten by someone else (infecting them) *[1 mark]*.

p.43 — Bacterial Diseases
Q1 Any two from: fever / stomach cramps / vomiting / diarrhoea *[2 marks]*.
Q2 New strains of the bacteria that are resistant to antibiotics/penicillin *[1 mark]*.

p.44 — Viral Diseases
Q1 By sexual contact / exchanging bodily fluids / sharing needles *[1 mark]*.

p.45 — Fungal and Protist Diseases
Q1 Using a fungicide *[1 mark]* and by stripping the affected leaves off the plant and destroying them *[1 mark]*.
Q2 a protist *[1 mark]*

p.46 — Fighting Disease
Q1 They release mucus *[1 mark]* to trap pathogens *[1 mark]*. / They have cilia *[1 mark]*, which move the mucus (containing pathogens) up to the back of the throat where it can be swallowed *[1 mark]*.

p.47 — Fighting Disease — Vaccination
Q1 antibodies *[1 mark]*

p.48 — Fighting Disease — Drugs
Q1 bacteria *[1 mark]*

p.49 — Developing Drugs
Q1 Whether the drug works and has the effect you're looking for *[1 mark]*.
Q2 To make sure that the drug doesn't have any harmful side effects when the body is working normally *[1 mark]*.

243

Topic B4 — Bioenergetics

p.50 — Photosynthesis
Q1 Glucose *[1 mark]* and oxygen *[1 mark]*.

p.52 — The Rate of Photosynthesis
Q1 Intensity of light *[1 mark]*, concentration of carbon dioxide *[1 mark]*, temperature *[1 mark]*, amount of chlorophyll *[1 mark]*.

p.53 — Respiration and Metabolism
Q1 Any two from: e.g. to build up larger molecules from smaller ones. / To move about. / In mammals and birds, to keep warm. *[2 marks — 1 mark for each correct answer]*
Q2 The sum of all of the reactions that happen in a cell or the body *[1 mark]*.

p.54 — Aerobic and Anaerobic Respiration
Q1 glucose + oxygen → carbon dioxide + water *[2 marks — 1 mark for correct reactants, 1 mark for correct products]*
Q2 fermentation *[1 mark]*

p.55 — Exercise
Q1 Long periods of exercise *[1 mark]*.

Topic B5 — Homeostasis and Response

p.57 — Homeostasis
Q1 To maintain the right conditions for cells to work properly and for enzymes to work properly *[1 mark]*.
Q2 receptor *[1 mark]*

p.58 — The Nervous System
Q1 Muscles *[1 mark]*, glands *[1 mark]*.

p.59 — Synapses and Reflexes
Q1 a) muscle *[1 mark]*
b) The stimulus is detected by receptors *[1 mark]*, which send impulses along a sensory neurone to the CNS *[1 mark]*. The impulse is sent along a relay neurone *[1 mark]*. It is then passed on to a motor neurone and travels along it to the effector *[1 mark]*.

p.60 — Investigating Reaction Time
Q1 242 + 256 + 253 + 249 + 235 = 1235 *[1 mark]*
1235 ÷ 5 = 247 ms *[1 mark]*

p.61 — The Endocrine System
Q1 They are carried in the blood *[1 mark]*.

p.62 — Controlling Blood Glucose
Q1 Insulin causes glucose to move from the blood into liver and muscle cells *[1 mark]*. In the cells, glucose is turned into glycogen for storage *[1 mark]*.

p.63 — Puberty and the Menstrual Cycle
Q1 FSH/follicle-stimulating hormone *[1 mark]*
Q2 testes *[1 mark]*

p.64 — Controlling Fertility
Q1 Any two from: e.g. oral contraceptives / contraceptive patch / contraceptive injection / contraceptive implant / some IUDs *[2 marks]*.

p.65 — More on Controlling Fertility
Q1 They stop the sperm from getting to the egg *[1 mark]*.

Topic B6 — Inheritance, Variation and Evolution

p.66 — DNA
Q1 A small section of DNA found on a chromosome *[1 mark]*.
Q2 All of the genetic material in the organism *[1 mark]*.

p.67 — Reproduction
Q1 mitosis *[1 mark]*
Q2 Because there are two parents, the offspring contain a mixture of their parents' genes *[1 mark]*. This mixture of genes produces variation *[1 mark]*.

p.68 — Meiosis
Q1 two *[1 mark]*

p.69 — X and Y Chromosomes
Q1 XX *[1 mark]*

p.70 — Genetic Diagrams
Q1 The mix of alleles you have *[1 mark]*.

p.71 — Inherited Disorders
Q1 two *[1 mark]*

p.72 — Family Trees and Embryo Screening
Q1 To test embryos for inherited disorders *[1 mark]*.

p.73 — Variation
Q1 Differences between members of the same species *[1 mark]* that have been caused by the environment/conditions something lives in *[1 mark]*.

p.74 — Evolution
Q1 Any three from: e.g. the environment changes too quickly. / A new predator kills all the individuals. / A new disease kills all the individuals. / They can't compete with another species for food. / A catastrophic event kills all the individuals. *[3 marks — 1 mark for each correct answer]*

p.75 — Antibiotic-Resistant Bacteria
Q1 E.g. there is no effective treatment for the infection / people are not immune to the new strain *[1 mark]*.

p.76 — More on Antibiotic-Resistant Bacteria
Q1 Taking the complete course makes sure that all the bacteria are destroyed *[1 mark]*. This means that there are none left to mutate and develop into antibiotic-resistant strains *[1 mark]*.

p.77 — Selective Breeding
Q1 E.g. to make animals that produce more meat/milk / to produce crops with disease resistance *[1 mark]*.

p.78 — Genetic Engineering
Q1 E.g. disease resistance / herbicide resistance / resistance to insect attack / bigger fruit / better fruit *[1 mark]*.

p.79 — Fossils
Q1 Fossils are the remains of organisms from many thousands of years ago *[1 mark]*, found in rocks *[1 mark]*.

p.81 — Classification
Q1 *Castor* *[1 mark]*

Topic B7 — Ecology

p.83 — Competition
Q1 The interaction of a community of organisms with the non-living parts of their environment *[1 mark]*.
Q2 Any three from: e.g. light / water / space / mineral ions *[3 marks]*.

p.84 — Abiotic and Biotic Factors
Q1 Any four from: moisture level / light intensity / temperature / carbon dioxide level / wind intensity / wind direction / soil pH / mineral content of soil *[4 marks]*.

p.85 — Adaptations
Q1 a) A behavioural adaptation *[1 mark]*
b) E.g. it has webbed feet/flippers to help it swim for food *[1 mark]*. / It has a thick layer of fat to help it keep in heat *[1 mark]*.

p.86 — Food Chains
Q1 a) grass *[1 mark]*
b) grasshopper *[1 mark]*

p.87 — Using Quadrats
Q1 1200 ÷ 0.25 = 4800
4800 × 0.75 = 3600 buttercups in total *[2 marks for correct answer, otherwise 1 mark for correct working]*

p.88 — Using Transects
Q1 They could mark out a line across the field *[1 mark]*. Then they could count all of the dandelions that touch the line / count the number of dandelions in quadrats placed along the line *[1 mark]*.

p.89 — The Water Cycle
Q1 a) By evaporation / transpiration *[1 mark]*.
b) By providing them with fresh water *[1 mark]*.

p.90 — The Carbon Cycle
Q1 Microorganisms break them down *[1 mark]*.
Q2 By plants in photosynthesis *[1 mark]*.

p.91 — Biodiversity and Waste Management
Q1 The variety of different species of organisms on Earth, or within an ecosystem *[1 mark]*.

p.92 — Global Warming
Q1 Global warming causes higher temperatures, which cause ice to melt and seawater to expand *[1 mark]*. This causes the sea level to rise *[1 mark]*, which could lead to flooding of low-lying land and therefore the loss of habitats *[1 mark]*.

p.93 — Deforestation and Land Use
Q1 To clear land for farming to provide more food *[1 mark]*. To grow crops to make biofuels *[1 mark]*.

p.94 — Maintaining Ecosystems and Biodiversity
Q1 Hedgerows and field margins can be reintroduced around single-crop fields *[1 mark]*. These provide a habitat for lots of types of organisms *[1 mark]*.
Q2 Breeding programmes breed endangered animals in captivity to make sure the species survives if they die out in the wild *[1 mark]*. Individuals can sometimes be released into the wild to boost or replace a population *[1 mark]*.

Answers

Topic C1 — Atomic Structure and the Periodic Table

p.96 — Atoms
Q1 protons = atomic number = 7 *[1 mark]*
electrons = protons = 7 *[1 mark]*
neutrons = mass number
– atomic number
= 14 – 7 = 7 *[1 mark]*

p.97 — Elements
Q1 E.g. isotopes are atoms with the same number of protons but a different number of neutrons / isotopes have the same atomic number but different mass numbers *[1 mark]*.

p.98 — Compounds
Q1 (2 × Na) + (1 × C) + (3 × O) = 6 *[1 mark]*
Q2 A substance that contains atoms of different elements *[1 mark]* bonded together *[1 mark]*. The elements are in fixed proportions *[1 mark]*.

p.99 — Chemical Equations
Q1 $2Fe + 3Cl_2 \rightarrow 2FeCl_3$ *[1 mark]*

p.100 — Mixtures
Q1 Any two from: e.g. filtration / crystallisation / simple distillation / fractional distillation /chromatography *[1 mark for each]*.

p.101 — Chromatography
Q1 The dye cannot dissolve in the solvent *[1 mark]*.

p.102 — More Separation Techniques
Q1 Pour the solution into an evaporating dish and slowly heat the solution until crystals start to form or some of the solvent has evaporated *[1 mark]*. Leave the dish to cool until crystals form *[1 mark]*. Filter *[1 mark]* and then dry the crystals *[1 mark]*.

p.103 — Distillation
Q1 Liquid B will be collected in the first fraction *[1 mark]* because it has the lowest boiling point so will evaporate first *[1 mark]*.

p.104 — The History of the Atom
Q1 In the plum pudding model, the atom is a ball of positive charge with electrons spread throughout it *[1 mark]*.

p.105 — Electronic Structure
Q1 2 *[1 mark]*
Q2 2,8,8 or

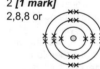

[1 mark]

p.106 — Development of the Periodic Table
Q1 By relative atomic mass *[1 mark]*.
Q2 He left gaps *[1 mark]*. He switched the order of some elements *[1 mark]*.

p.107 — The Modern Periodic Table
Q1 2 *[1 mark]*
Q2 Both chlorine and bromine are in Group 7 and so have the same number of electrons in their outer shell *[1 mark]*.

p.108 — Metals and Non-Metals
Q1 non-metal *[1 mark]*
Q2 Any two from: e.g. metals tend to be strong / good conductors of heat / good at conducting electricity / malleable / high melting/boiling temperatures *[1 mark for each]*.

p.109 — Group 1 Elements
Q1 All Group 1 metals have the same number of electrons in their outer shell *[1 mark]*.
Q2 potassium + water
→ potassium hydroxide + hydrogen *[1 mark]*

p.110 — Group 7 Elements
Q1 Bromine is more reactive than iodine *[1 mark]*.

p.111 — Group 0 Elements
Q1 Xenon has a higher boiling point than neon *[1 mark]*.

Topic C2 — Bonding, Structure and Properties of Matter

p.113 — Formation of Ions
Q1 A charged particle *[1 mark]*.
Q2 a) 1– *[1 mark]*
 b) 2+ *[1 mark]*
 c) 1+ *[1 mark]*

p.114 — Ionic Bonding
Q1 electrostatic forces/ionic bonds *[1 mark]*
Q2

[1 mark for arrow showing electrons transferred from potassium to oxygen, 1 mark for correct outer shell electron configurations (with or without inner shells), 1 mark for correct charges]

p.115 — Ionic Compounds
Q1 a) It will have a high melting point *[1 mark]* because a lot of energy is needed to break the strong attraction between the ions/the strong ionic bonds *[1 mark]*.
 b) When melted, the ions are free to move, so they can carry an electric current *[1 mark]*.

p.116 — Covalent Bonding
Q1

[1 mark for 3 shared pairs of electrons, 1 mark for correct number of electrons in outer shell of each atom (with or without inner shells on nitrogen)]

p.117 — Simple Molecular Substances
Q1 The intermolecular forces between molecules of O_2 are weak and don't need much energy to break *[1 mark]*.
Q2 N_2 molecules aren't charged/There aren't any free electrons or ions *[1 mark]*.

p.118 — Polymers and Giant Covalent Structures
Q1 $(C_2H_3Cl)_n$ *[1 mark]*
Q2 To melt diamond you have to break the covalent bonds between atoms which are very strong *[1 mark]* but to melt poly(ethene) you only have to break the weaker intermolecular forces which needs less energy *[1 mark]*. So diamond has a higher melting point *[1 mark]*.

p.119 — Structures of Carbon
Q1 E.g. graphite contains layers of carbon atoms *[1 mark]* arranged in hexagons *[1 mark]*. Each carbon atom forms three covalent bonds *[1 mark]*. There are no covalent bonds between the sheets *[1 mark]*.

p.120 — Metallic Bonding
Q1 The electrostatic attraction *[1 mark]* between the positive metal ions and the shared negative electrons *[1 mark]*.
Q2 Copper is a good electrical conductor *[1 mark]*.
Q3 E.g. alloys are harder than pure metals *[1 mark]*, so an alloy of copper would last longer as a door hinge than pure copper *[1 mark]*.

p.121 — States of Matter
Q1 The gaseous state *[1 mark]*.

p.122 — Changing State
Q1 a) solid *[1 mark]*
 b) liquid *[1 mark]*
 c) liquid *[1 mark]*
 d) gas *[1 mark]*

Topic C3 — Quantitative Chemistry

p.123 — Relative Formula Mass
Q1 a) A_r of H = 1 and A_r of O = 16
M_r of H_2O = (2 × 1) + 16 = 18 *[1 mark]*
 b) A_r of Li = 7, A_r of O = 16 and A_r of H = 1
So M_r of LiOH = 7 + 16 + 1 = 24 *[1 mark]*
 c) A_r of H = 1, A_r of S = 32 and A_r of O = 16
M_r of H_2SO_4 = (2 × 1) + 32 + (4 × 16) = 98 *[1 mark]*
Q2 A_r of K = 39, A_r of O = 16 and A_r of H = 1
M_r of KOH = 39 + 16 + 1 = 56 *[1 mark]*
$\frac{39 \times 1}{56} \times 100 = 70\%$ *[1 mark]*

p.124 — Conservation of Mass
Q1 Total mass of reactants = 6.00 g
Known mass of products = 3.36 g
Mass of CO_2 = 6.00 – 3.36 *[1 mark]*
= 2.64 g *[1 mark]*

p.125 — More on Conservation of Mass
Q1 One of the reactants is a gas *[1 mark]* and the products are solid, liquid or aqueous *[1 mark]*.
Q2 The mass will decrease *[1 mark]*.

p.126 — Concentrations of Solutions
Q1 mass = concentration × volume
= 32 × 0.25
= 8 g *[1 mark]*
Q2 concentration = mass ÷ volume
= 0.6 ÷ 0.015
= 40 g/dm³ *[1 mark]*

Topic C4 — Chemical Changes

p.128 — Acids and Bases
Q1 red/orange *[1 mark]*
Q2 alkaline *[1 mark]*

p.129 — Reactions of Acids
Q1 calcium carbonate + hydrochloric acid → calcium chloride + carbon dioxide + water *[1 mark for calcium chloride, 1 mark for carbon dioxide and water]*

p.130 — The Reactivity Series and Extracting Metals
Q1 Carbon is less reactive than calcium and therefore will not reduce calcium oxide / Calcium is more reactive than carbon, so calcium oxide won't be reduced by carbon *[1 mark]*.

p.131 — Reactions of Metals
Q1 sodium + water → sodium hydroxide + hydrogen *[1 mark for each correct product]*

p.132 — Electrolysis
Q1 a) chlorine gas/Cl_2 *[1 mark]*
b) sodium metal/Na *[1 mark]*

p.133 — Electrolysis of Aqueous Solutions
Q1 a) chlorine *[1 mark]*
b) copper *[1 mark]*

Topic C5 — Energy Changes

p.134 — Exothermic and Endothermic Reactions
Q1 exothermic *[1 mark]*

p.135 — Measuring Energy Changes
Q1 They help to stop energy being lost to the surroundings *[1 mark]*.

p.136 — Reaction Profiles
Q1

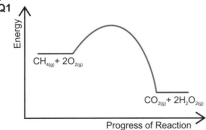

[1 mark for correct axes, 1 mark for correct energy levels of reactants and products, 1 mark for correct shape of curve linking the reactants to the products]

Topic C6 — The Rate and Extent of Chemical Change

p.138 — Rates of Reaction
Q1 The activation energy for a reaction is the minimum amount of energy that particles need to react *[1 mark]*.

p.139 — Factors Affecting Rates of Reaction
Q1 The experiment using the powdered magnesium *[1 mark]*, because the powder has a higher surface area to volume ratio than the solid strip *[1 mark]*.

p.140 — Measuring Rates of Reaction
Q1 E.g. a gas syringe *[1 mark]*.

p.141 — More on Measuring Rates
Q1 Any two from: e.g. volume of HCl added *[1 mark]*, mass of magnesium used *[1 mark]*, surface area of the magnesium *[1 mark]*.

p.142 — Graphs of Reaction Rate Experiments
Q1 E.g.

[1 mark for correctly marking on all 7 points, 1 mark for choosing a sensible scale for the axes, 1 mark for drawing a line of best fit]

p.143 — Working Out Reaction Rates
Q1 Mean rate = amount of reactant used ÷ time
= 6.0 g ÷ 200 s *[1 mark]*
= 0.03 g/s *[1 mark]*

p.144 — Reversible Reactions
Q1 A reaction is at equilibrium when both the forward and backward reactions are happening at the same rate *[1 mark]*.

Topic C7 — Organic Chemistry

p.146 — Hydrocarbons
Q1 $C_3H_8 + 5O_2 \rightarrow 3CO_2 + 4H_2O$ *[1 mark for correct reactants and products, 1 mark for correctly balancing]*

p.147 — Crude Oil
Q1 Crude oil is formed from the remains of plankton/plants and animals that died millions of years ago *[1 mark]*.
Q2 One day crude oil will run out *[1 mark]*.

p.148 — Fractional Distillation
Q1 The hydrocarbons in petrol have a lower boiling point than those in diesel / the hydrocarbons in diesel have a higher boiling point than those in petrol *[1 mark]*.

p.149 — Cracking
Q1 Number of C atoms = 5 − 2 = 3
Number of H atoms = 12 − 4 = 8
Formula = C_3H_8 *[1 mark]*

Topic C8 — Chemical Analysis

p.150 — Purity and Formulations
Q1 The sample melts over a range of temperatures *[1 mark]*. The melting point is lower than that of pure aspirin *[1 mark]*.

p.151 — Paper Chromatography
Q1 E.g. to identify substances in a mixture *[1 mark]*.

p.152 — Using Chromatograms
Q1 $R_f = \dfrac{\text{distance moved by substance}}{\text{distance moved by solvent}}$
$= \dfrac{12}{41}$ *[1 mark]* = 0.292682...
= 0.29 *[1 mark]*

p.153 — Tests for Gases
Q1 carbon dioxide *[1 mark]*

Topic C9 — Chemistry of the Atmosphere

p.155 — The Evolution of the Atmosphere
Q1 Sedimentary rocks are formed when sea organisms die and fall to the seabed *[1 mark]*. These become buried and squashed down over millions of years forming rocks *[1 mark]*.

p.156 — Greenhouse Gases and Climate Change
Q1 Any two from: e.g. ice melting in the Arctic and Antarctic / sea levels rising / changes in rainfall / some regions may have too much or too little water / it may be difficult to produce food / there may be an increase in the frequency and severity of storms *[1 mark for each, up to a maximum of 2 marks]*.

p.157 — Carbon Footprints
Q1 E.g. governments can put a limit on the amount of greenhouse gases that a business can make and sell licences for emissions up to this point *[1 mark]*. They can tax companies based on the amount of greenhouse gases that they emit to encourage them to cut down on emissions *[1 mark]*.

p.158 — Air Pollution
Q1 Any two from, e.g. particulates (soot) / unburnt fuels / carbon monoxide / carbon dioxide / water vapour *[1 mark for each, up to a maximum of 2 marks]*.

Topic C10 — Using Resources

p.159 — Finite and Renewable Resources
Q1 A finite resource will take a long time to be remade or will not be remade at all *[1 mark]*. A renewable resource can be replaced within a fairly short amount of time *[1 mark]*.

p.160 — Reuse and Recycling
Q1 Any two from: e.g. saves energy needed to make new metals / saves limited supplies of metals from the earth / cuts down on the amount of waste going to landfill *[2 marks]*.

p.161 — Life Cycle Assessments
Q1 Getting the raw materials / manufacture and packaging / using the product / product disposal *[2 marks for all four stages — otherwise 1 mark for two correct stages]*.

p.162 — Using Life Cycle Assessments
Q1 E.g. the measurements of some effects are based on the judgement and feelings of the person carrying out the assessment *[1 mark]*. Some life cycle assessments only show some of the impacts on the environment *[1 mark]*.

p.163 — Potable Water
Q1 E.g. filter the water first, using a wire mesh followed by filter beds *[1 mark]*. Then sterilise the filtered water using chlorine / ozone / ultraviolet light *[1 mark]*.

p.164 — Desalination
Q1 E.g. seawater is passed through a membrane. The membrane purifies the water by letting the water molecules through but trapping the salts *[1 mark]*.

p.165 — Waste Water Treatment
Q1 E.g. screening *[1 mark]*, sedimentation *[1 mark]*, digestion (aerobic / anaerobic) *[1 mark]*.

Topic P1 — Energy

p.167 — Energy Stores and Systems
Q1 Mechanically *[1 mark]*, electrically *[1 mark]*, by heating *[1 mark]* and by radiation *[1 mark]*.

p.168 — Conservation of Energy and Energy Transfers
Q1 Energy is transferred mechanically *[1 mark]* from the kinetic energy store of the wind *[1 mark]* to the kinetic energy store of the windmill *[1 mark]*.

p.169 — Kinetic and Potential Energy Stores
Q1 $E_p = mgh$
  $= 2.0 \times 9.8 \times 5.0$ *[1 mark]*
  $= 98$ J *[1 mark]*

p.170 — Energy Transfers by Heating
Q1 $\Delta E = mc\Delta\theta$ so
  $\Delta\theta = \Delta E \div (m \times c)$ *[1 mark]*
    $= 50\,000 \div (5.0 \times 4200)$
    $= 2.4\,°C$ *[1 mark]*
  So the new temperature
    $= 5.0 + 2.4 = 7.4\,°C$ *[1 mark]*

p.171 — Investigating Specific Heat Capacity
Q1 The starting temperature and the final temperature of the block *[1 mark]*. The current and potential difference / the power of the heater *[1 mark]*. The time that the block was heated for *[1 mark]*. The mass of the block *[1 mark]*.

p.172 — Power
Q1 $P = E \div t$
  $t = 2 \times 60 = 120$ s *[1 mark]*
  $P = 4800 \div 120$ *[1 mark]*
    $= 40$ W *[1 mark]*

p.173 — Reducing Unwanted Energy Transfers
Q1 Any one from: e.g. make the walls thicker / make the walls out of a material with a low thermal conductivity / put in thermal insulation (e.g. loft insulation) *[1 mark]*.

p.174 — Efficiency
Q1 efficiency = useful output energy transfer
      ÷ total input energy transfer
    $= 225 \div 300$ *[1 mark]*
    $= 0.75$ *[1 mark]*
Q2 efficiency = useful power output
        ÷ total power input
  total power input = useful power output
          ÷ efficiency *[1 mark]*
    $= 900 \div 0.75$ *[1 mark]*
    $= 1200$ W *[1 mark]*

p.175 — Energy Resources and Their Uses
Q1 a) renewable *[1 mark]*
  b) non-renewable *[1 mark]*
  c) non-renewable *[1 mark]*
  d) renewable *[1 mark]*

p.176 — Wind, Solar and Geothermal
Q1 E.g. wind power can be unreliable as they don't provide a constant supply of energy because sometimes there's no wind / the turbines have to be stopped because the wind is too strong *[1 mark]*. Geothermal power plants are reliable because the hot rocks are always hot *[1 mark]*.

p.177 — Hydro-electricity, Waves and Tides
Q1 E.g. it disturbs the seabed / it disturbs the habitats of animals *[1 mark]*

p.178 — Bio-fuels and Non-renewables
Q1 E.g. they're reliable / they can respond quickly to changes in demand *[2 marks — 1 mark for each correct answer]*
Q2 E.g. burning oil releases carbon dioxide, which contributes to global warming. / It produces sulfur dioxide which causes acid rain, which is harmful to trees and animals. / Oil spills can occur when transporting oil, which can harm/kill animals that live in and around the sea *[3 marks —1 mark for each correct answer]*.

p.179 — Trends in Energy Resource Use
Q1 Any two from: e.g. building new renewable power plants is expensive / people don't want to live near new power plants / renewable energy resources are less reliable than non-renewable energy resources / electric cars are more expensive than petrol cars. *[2 marks — 1 mark for each correct answer]*

Topic P2 — Electricity

p.180 — Current and Circuit Symbols
Q1 E.g.

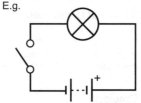

[3 marks for all symbols correctly drawn and connected in a single loop, otherwise 2 marks for all three symbols correct or 1 mark for one or two symbols correct]

p.181 — Resistance and V = IR
Q1 $V = IR$ so $R = V \div I$ *[1 mark]*
    $= 230 \div 5.0$ *[1 mark]*
    $= 46\,\Omega$ *[1 mark]*

p.182 — Investigating Resistance
Q1 E.g.

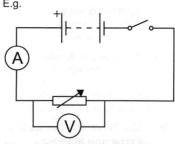

[1 mark for all circuit symbols correct, 1 mark for battery, variable resistor (test wire) and ammeter connected in series, 1 mark for voltmeter connected in parallel with the variable resistor (test wire)]

You'll still get the marks if you didn't include a switch in your circuit — but it's useful to help you control your experiment.

p.183 — I-V Characteristics
Q1 a)

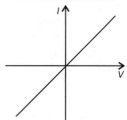

[1 mark for correct axes, 1 mark for an upwards sloping straight line through the origin]

  b)

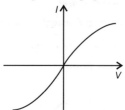

[1 mark for correct axes, 1 mark for correct shape]

p.184 — Circuit Devices
Q1 a) E.g. automatic night lights (a light automatically turns on when it gets dark) *[1 mark]*.
  b) E.g. thermostats (the heating automatically turns on/off at a certain temperature) *[1 mark]*.

p.185 — Series Circuits
Q1 $R_{total} = R_1 + R_2 = 3 + 7$ *[1 mark]*
      $= 10\,\Omega$ *[1 mark]*

p.186 — Parallel Circuits
Q1 E.g.

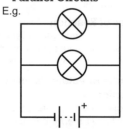

[1 mark for the correct circuit symbols, 1 mark for two bulbs connected in parallel]

p.187 — Investigating Circuits
Q1

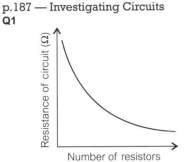

[1 mark for correct axes, 1 mark for correctly drawn curve]

p.188 — Electricity in the Home
Q1 a) 230 V *[1 mark]*
b) (around) 0 V *[1 mark]*
c) 0 V *[1 mark]*

p.189 — Power of Electrical Appliances
Q1 $E = P \times t$ so $P = E \div t$ *[1 mark]*
$= 6000 \div 30$ *[1 mark]*
$= 200$ W *[1 mark]*
Q2 For 250 W TV:
$E = P \times t$
$= 250 \times 60$ *[1 mark]*
$= 15\ 000$ J *[1 mark]*
For 375 W TV:
$E = P \times t$
$= 375 \times 60 = 22\ 500$ J *[1 mark]*
So difference in energy is
$22\ 500 - 15\ 000 = 7500$ J *[1 mark]*

p.190 — More on Power
Q1 $E = Q \times V$
$= 10\ 000 \times 200$ *[1 mark]*
$= 2\ 000\ 000$ J *[1 mark]*
Q2 $P = V \times I$
$= 12 \times 4.0$ *[1 mark]*
$= 48$ W *[1 mark]*

p.191 — The National Grid
Q1 The national grid is a system of cables and transformers *[1 mark]*.

Topic P3 — Particle Model of Matter

p.193 — The Particle Model and Motion in Gases
Q1 Decreasing the temperature of the gas means that the gas particles have less energy in their kinetic energy stores *[1 mark]*. They hit the container walls less often so the total force applied is lower *[1 mark]*. A lower force means a lower pressure *[1 mark]*.

p.194 — Density of Materials
Q1 $\rho = m \div V$
so $m = \rho \times V$ *[1 mark]*
$= 40 \times 0.05$ *[1 mark]*
$= 2$ kg *[1 mark]*

p.195 — Internal Energy and Changes of State
Q1 a) melting *[1 mark]*
b) boiling / evaporating *[1 mark]*
c) condensing *[1 mark]*

p.196 — Specific Latent Heat
Q1 $E = mL$
$= 0.250 \times 120\ 000$ *[1 mark]*
$= 30\ 000$ J *[1 mark]*

Topic P4 — Atomic Structure

p.197 — The Current Model of the Atom
Q1 a) neutrons *[1 mark]*, protons *[1 mark]*
b) The radius of an atom is around 1×10^{-10} m *[1 mark]*. The radius of a nucleus is less than 1/10 000 of this *[1 mark]*.

p.198 — Isotopes and Nuclear Radiation
Q1 E.g. alpha particles would not be suitable because they are stopped by a few cm of air or a sheet of paper *[1 mark]*. They would not be able to pass through the packaging to sterilise the equipment *[1 mark]*.

p.199 — Nuclear Equations
Q1 beta particle *[1 mark]*

p.200 — Half-life
Q1 The number of decays per second *[1 mark]*.

p.201 — Irradiation and Contamination
Q1 Gamma rays can penetrate through skin and can get to organs *[1 mark]* whereas alpha particles are stopped by skin and blocked by a small air gap *[1 mark]*.

Topic P5 — Forces

p.203 — Contact and Non-Contact Forces
Q1 a) Any two from: e.g. speed / distance / mass / temperature / time *[2 marks]*
b) Any two from: e.g. displacement / momentum / force / acceleration / velocity *[2 marks]*
Q2 Contact force: air resistance *[1 mark]*
Non-contact force: gravitational force *[1 mark]*

p.204 — Weight, Mass and Gravity
Q1 a) $W = mg = 5 \times 9.8$ *[1 mark]*
$= 49$ N *[1 mark]*
b) $W = 5 \times 1.6$ *[1 mark]* $= 8$ N *[1 mark]*

p.205 — Resultant Forces and Work Done
Q1 20 cm = 0.2 m *[1 mark]*
$W = Fs = 20 \times 0.2$ *[1 mark]*
$= 4$ J *[1 mark]*

p.206 — Forces and Elasticity
Q1 2 cm = 0.02 m *[1 mark]*
$F = ke$ so $k = F \div e$ *[1 mark]*
$= 1 \div 0.02$ *[1 mark]*
$= 50$ N/m *[1 mark]*

p.207 — Investigating Springs
Q1 2.5 cm = 0.025 m *[1 mark]*
$E_e = \frac{1}{2}ke^2 = \frac{1}{2} \times 40 \times (0.025)^2$ *[1 mark]*
$= 0.0125$ J *[1 mark]*

p.208 — Distance, Displacement, Speed and Velocity
Q1 $s = vt$ so $v = s \div t$ *[1 mark]*
$= 200 \div 25$ *[1 mark]*
$= 8$ m/s *[1 mark]*

p.209 — Acceleration
Q1 $\Delta v = 30 - 23 = 7$ m/s *[1 mark]*
$a = \Delta v \div t = 7 \div 2.5$ *[1 mark]*
$= 2.8$ m/s^2 *[1 mark]*

p.210 — Distance-Time Graphs
Q1 E.g.

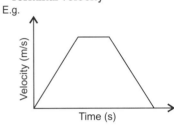

[1 mark for a curved line with an increasing positive gradient, 1 mark for the line becoming a straight line with a positive gradient]

p.211 — Velocity-Time Graphs and Terminal Velocity
Q1 E.g.

[1 mark for a straight line with a positive gradient initially, 1 mark for the line then becoming level, then 1 mark for a straight line with a negative gradient]

p.212 — Newton's First and Second Laws
Q1 $F = ma = (80 + 10) \times 0.25$ *[1 mark]*
$= 22.5$ N *[1 mark]*

p.213 — Newton's Third Law
Q1 When two objects interact, the forces they exert on each other are equal and opposite *[1 mark]*.

p.214 — Investigating Motion
Q1 The weight of the hook and the masses attached to it *[1 mark]*.

p.215 — Stopping Distance and Thinking Distance
Q1 E.g. speed / reaction time / tiredness / drugs / alcohol / distractions *[1 mark]*

p.216 — Braking Distance
Q1 E.g. they may cause the brakes to overheat and not work correctly *[1 mark]*. The vehicle could skid *[1 mark]*.

p.217 — Reaction Times
Q1 0.2 - 0.9 s *[1 mark]*
Q2 E.g. using the ruler drop test e.g. dropping a ruler and catching it as quickly as possible / using a computer-based test, e.g. clicking a mouse when the screen colour changes *[1 mark]*.

Topic P6 — Waves

p.219 — Transverse and Longitudinal Waves
Q1 Any two from: e.g. light / ripples on water / waves on a string *[2 marks]*

p.220 — Frequency, Period and Wave Speed
Q1 wave speed = frequency × wavelength, so frequency = wave speed ÷ wavelength *[1 mark]*
$= 0.15 \div 0.75$ *[1 mark]*
$= 0.2$ Hz *[1 mark]*

p.221 — Investigating Waves

Q1 E.g. attach a signal generator to a dipper and place it in a ripple tank filled with water to create some waves *[1 mark]*. Place a screen underneath the ripple tank, then turn on a lamp and dim the other lights in the room *[1 mark]*. Measure the distance between shadow lines that are 10 wavelengths apart on the screen beneath the tank, then divide this number by 10 — this is equal to the wavelength of the water waves *[1 mark]*.

p.222 — Refraction

Q1 E.g.

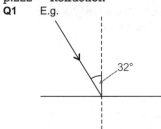

[1 mark for correctly drawing the boundary and the normal, 1 mark for drawing an incident ray at the correct angle]

p.223 — Electromagnetic Waves

Q1 Radio waves *[1 mark]*

Q2 Visible light *[1 mark]*

p.224 — Uses of EM Waves

Q1 E.g. TV / radio signals *[1 mark]*.

p.225 — More Uses of EM Waves

Q1 E.g. seeing broken bones *[1 mark]* treating cancer *[1 mark]*

p.226 — Investigating IR Radiation

Q1 a) black *[1 mark]*

   b) matt *[1 mark]*

p.227 — Investigating IR Absorption

Q1 Any two from: e.g. the plates are an equal distance from the bunsen burner / the same wax is used / the same amount of wax is used / identical metal balls are used / the plates are identical (except for their different coloured sides). *[2 marks — 1 mark for each correct answer]*

p.228 — Dangers of Electromagnetic Waves

Q1 Any two from: e.g. damage to surface cells / sunburn / faster ageing of the skin / blindness / increased risk of skin cancer. *[2 marks — 1 mark for each correct effect]*

Q2 E.g. They are both ionising (which means they can knock electrons off atoms) *[1 mark]*.

Topic P7 — Magnetism and Electromagnetism

p.229 — Permanent and Induced Magnets

Q1 They'll repel each other *[1 mark]*.

p.230 — Electromagnetism

Q1 E.g. for current out of the page:

[1 mark for correct shape, 1 mark for field direction matching current direction]

Index

Index

Index

Index